The Handbook for School Safety and Security

The Handbook for School Safety and Security
Best Practices and Procedures

Edited by

Lawrence J. Fennelly

Marianna A. Perry

ELSEVIER

AMSTERDAM • BOSTON • HEIDELBERG • LONDON
NEW YORK • OXFORD • PARIS • SAN DIEGO
SAN FRANCISCO • SINGAPORE • SYDNEY • TOKYO
Butterworth-Heinemann is an imprint of Elsevier

Acquiring Editor: *Brian Romer*
Editorial Project Manager: *Keira Bunn*
Project Manager: *Punithavathy Govindaradjane*
Designer: *Greg Harris*

Butterworth-Heinemann is an imprint of Elsevier
The Boulevard, Langford Lane, Kidlington, Oxford, OX5 1GB, UK
225 Wyman Street, Waltham, MA 02451, USA

Notices
Knowledge and best practice in this field are constantly changing. As new research and experience broaden our understanding, changes in research methods, professional practices, or medical treatment may become necessary.

Practitioners and researchers must always rely on their own experience and knowledge in evaluating and using any information, methods, compounds, or experiments described herein. In using such information or methods they should be mindful of their own safety and the safety of others, including parties for whom they have a professional responsibility.

To the fullest extent of the law, neither the Publisher nor the authors, contributors, or editors, assume any liability for any injury and/or damage to persons or property as a matter of products liability, negligence or otherwise, or from any use or operation of any methods, products, instructions, or ideas contained in the material herein.

Library of Congress Cataloging-in-Publication Data
Application submitted

British Library Cataloguing-in-Publication Data
A catalogue record for this book is available from the British Library.

ISBN: 978-0-12-800568-2

For information on all Butterworth-Heinemann publications
visit our website at store.elsevier.com

This book has been manufactured using Print On Demand technology. Each copy is produced to order and is limited to black ink. The online version of this book will show color figures where appropriate.

Working together
to grow libraries in
developing countries

www.elsevier.com • www.bookaid.org

To my husband, Tom . . . for your support and understanding while I was working on this book and your patience with my many other projects. I'm glad that the new chapter in my life includes you.

I Love You. Marianna

He once said no one ever dedicated a book to him. So here it is, Bill Fenn. This is dedicated to you, my son.

Love you. Dad

Security implies a stable, relatively predictable environment in which an individual or group may pursue its ends without disruption or harm and without fear of disturbance or injury.

Robert Fischer, Edward Halibozek, and David Walters,
Introduction to Security, 9th ed., 2012

Contents

FOREWORD

Over the years, school security has been forced to evolve to meet the ever-changing threats facing our schools today. It has moved from a soft approach to high tech, more hardened security solutions to keep students, faculty, and staff in our schools safe. There have been incidents on school campuses throughout history; however, the shootings at Columbine, Red Lake, Virginia Tech, and Sandy Hook, to name a few, have changed how we as security professionals analyze and approach school security. We are always learning and improving our security management after an incident in an effort to stay in front of the latest trends.

With this book, Larry Fennelly and Marianna Perry are delivering much needed, high-quality, safety and security advice that is feasible as well as practical, for K-12 schools. Both Larry and Marianna, along with their contributing authors, are among the most respected names in the security industry today, and they propose a holistic, all encompassing approach to security *to keep our schools safe*. We as security professionals must lead the way to help prevent more incidents from occurring in our schools. In order to do this, we are forced to change the way we think about school security and move away from traditional approaches that unfortunately, in most cases, are no longer effective.

School administrators and security professionals alike will benefit greatly from the information in this book. The book contains several international chapters, whose problems as well as solutions are the very same as ours. *From the first chapter to the last this is a must read.*

Chris Hertig, CPP, said about the announcement of this book on Linkedin, "A Comprehensive Foundation and Forward-Leaning book on this is needed," and I agree.

Linda Watson, CPP, CSC, CHS-V
Whirlaway Group, LLC
Independent Security Consultant
Chairperson, ASIS International School Safety and Security Council
Member, International Association of Professional Security Consultants

PREFACE

We completed this book in about 6 months. Normally, this undertaking would take 18-24 months. We know that it's hard to believe, but it's true. We both know that the faster we could complete this book, get it published and into the hands of those who are responsible for school security, then possibly we could help prevent another incident from happening at a school.

We found ourselves calling each other after incidents were reported on the news: Atlanta, a shopping mall shooting; schools closed down in New Hampshire and Kansas City; the list goes on and on. We recently addressed 80 school administrators and told them that a violent incident was going to happen again this year at a school, but we couldn't tell them when or where—and they knew it also. It is difficult to say these kinds of things, but we're sure it was even more difficult for them to hear.

Set security standards for your schools. Conduct a security assessment. Follow CPTED principles and security best practices. After you've done so, call your local media to promote your accomplishments. Let the bad guys know that you take crime prevention and effective security at *your* school serious!

Times have changed. You know that. We are concerned because we know that many of our schools do not have adequate security in place to protect our children. We are not advocating that you make your school a prison for children, and we do not want you to turn your school into a cold, uninviting fortress. Instead, we want schools to be safe environments where our children learn and grow, but also has effective security in place to address vulnerabilities. Our children should feel safe and secure at school and parents should have the peace of mind that they will see their children happy and healthy at the end of the school day. It's simply a matter of changing the way you think about schools. Be smart about securing your school by training your students, faculty and staff about keeping themselves safe—increase awareness, but not fear. Talk with other schools and find out what they are doing that is working. Establish partnerships and teams to implement security measures that are effective, but not overly intrusive. We are all playing by a different set of rules now, so let's play to win!

We wish to sincerely thank all of our contributors who made this book possible. We truly believe that compiling the knowledge of many security professionals is a more comprehensive approach to addressing the issue of school security. We thank you for your professionalism as well as your contributions. We will measure the success of this project by the number of incidents that do *not* occur in our schools because of the information in this book.

Marianna Perry
Lawrence J. Fennelly

ABOUT THE EDITORS AND CONTRIBUTORS

EDITORS

Lawrence J. Fennelly, Security Expert Witness and Consultant, Litigation Consultants Inc.

Lawrence J. Fennelly is an internationally recognized authority on crime prevention, security planning and analysis, and on the study of how environmental factors (CPTED), physical hardware, alarms, lighting, site design, management practices, litigation consultants, security policies and procedures, and guard management contribute to criminal victimization.

Mr. Fennelly was previously employed with Apollo Security and Computershare, Inc., as well as a sergeant at Harvard College, employed by the Harvard University Police Department in Cambridge, Massachusetts. He was trained as a crime prevention specialist and served in this capacity for over 21 years at Harvard. He was also the department's training officer and assistant court officer. As part of his role as an officer at Harvard, Larry also was a deputy sheriff in both Suffolk and Middlesex counties (Massachusetts).

Mr. Fennelly is a frequent speaker and lecturer on CPTED, physical security, school crime, and other issues. He serves as an expert witness who works closely with attorneys in defense as well as plaintiff cases, assisting in case preparation, offering knowledgeable questions to ask the opposing side, etc. He has also done a considerable amount of consultant work throughout the United States. His experience ranges from identifying vulnerabilities to conducting security and lighting surveys, working with architects to design and implement security, and developing long-range guard training programs and risk assessments of various facilities.

He is also a prolific author. His titles include such well-known security tomes as "Crime Prevention Through Environmental Design," "Effective Physical Security," and "Handbook of Loss Prevention and Crime Prevention."

Marianna A. Perry, Training and Development Manager for Securitas Security Services USA, Inc.

Marianna A. Perry is currently a training and development manager for Securitas Security Services USA, Inc. She also operates Loss Prevention and Safety Management, LLC and is adjunct faculty at Sullivan University (Kentucky). She is a former detective with the Kentucky State Police and was previously the director of the National Crime Prevention Institute (NCPI) at the University of Louisville. She is vice chair of the Crime Prevention and Loss Prevention Council and a member of the School Safety and Security Council.

Marianna has been a contributing author for several security publications, has written numerous articles on safety and security topics, and is a frequent speaker on crime prevention topics. Marianna also develops training programs and conducts physical security assessments for educational institutions and other organizations.

CONTRIBUTORS

Raymond V. Andersson, RSecP, ICPS, FSyI, AFAIM, International, National, and Corporate Security Professional

Raymond Andersson is an international, national, and corporate security professional, employed in the national government sector in Australia. He is a member of the Australasian Council of Security Professionals (ACSP), the peak representational body for the security profession in Australia and New Zealand, and chairs its Ethics and Behaviour Standards Committee.

Ray is a fellow of the Security Institute (FSyI), a United Kingdom-based professional body for security professionals. He is a member of ASIS International Queensland/Northern Territory Chapter and an active member and secretary of the ASIS International Crime and Loss Prevention Council. The Council establishes and sustains relationships for the common purpose of preventing crime, as well as encourages the exchange of effective security concepts and other information between law enforcement, private security, and ASIS.

Ray was awarded the designation of International Crime Prevention Specialist (ICPS) on mastery and testing of the International Society of Crime Prevention Practitioners (ISCPP), International Crime Prevention Specialist Curriculum. ISCPP is a network of crime prevention practitioners whose mission is to provide leadership, foster cooperation, encourage information exchange, and seek involvement from all segments of society in the expansion and improvement of crime prevention programs internationally.

Ray is an elected member and Northern Territory of Australia representative on the Australian Crime Prevention Council. The objectives for the Council are: to assist and promote the prevention of crime, to develop awareness and better understanding of the problems of crime and methods properly available to prevent it, to encourage participation by citizens in the prevention of crime and the alleviation of social injustices, and to provide a forum for the free discussion of crime prevention issues.

Ray is an elected member of the Worshipful Company of Security Professionals which is the 108th and newest Livery Company of the City of London, a charitable organization providing education and health services to members of the security profession.

Ray has been employed in private and public sector organizations providing advice on security and business risk, protective security, crime prevention, security and business policy and planning for over 28 years. He is also a registered security professional (RSecP) and associate fellow of the Australian Institute of Management (AFAIM).

Mark H. Beaudry, Ph.D., CPP, Instructor, Researcher, and Author in Security Studies at Various Universities in Massachusetts

Mark Beaudry is a retired intelligence chief and antiterrorism instructor from the United States Marine Corps. He is a security practitioner since 1976 and an educator since 1989 (adjunct for Northeastern University, UMass Lowell, Anna Maria College, and others). Dr. Beaudry received an Associate in Science degree in Criminal Justice from Mount Wachusett Community College, a Bachelor and Master of Science in Criminal Justice from Northeastern University, and a PhD in Criminal Justice at Capella University.

Dr. Beaudry has also been a member of ASIS International since 1982 and a Certified Protection Professional (CPP) since 1996. He is an active participant in many groups within ASIS, including the Academic Practitioner Symposium, Crime Prevention and Loss Prevention Council, Critical Infrastructure Working Group, the Research Council (vice chair), and the Leadership Management and Practices Council (chair).

Dr. Beaudry is a frequent contributor of articles and book reviews to security journals. He has authored the following publications and contributed chapters:

- Authored, *Contemporary Lodging Security*, Butterworth-Heinemann, Woburn, MA.
- Fennelly, Lawrence. *Handbook on Crime Prevention and Loss Prevention*. Butterworth-Heinemann, Woburn, MA. Contributed a chapter on lodging security.

- ASIS Standing Committee on Lodging Security Anthology: Tactics that Work; An Overview of Security Management.
- Workplace Violence Research Institute: Premises Security & Liability—Contributed a chapter on "Lodging Security."
- ASIS International Standard—Private Security Officer Selection and Training Guideline, committee member.
- International Real Estate Management. Contributed chapter on "Managing Computer Security Risks."
- ASIS Protection of Assets Manual. Contributed chapter on "Terrorism."
- Co-authored, Security in the Year 2020, ASIS International.
- PhD Dissertation: Faculty Perceptions of Factors to Develop a Paradigm for Security Studies.

Gregory Bernardo, CHS-IV, CDT, CVI, Vice President, Aella Consulting Group, Inc.

Gregory Bernardo, CHS-IV, CDT, CVI, is the vice president of Aella Consulting Group, Inc. In his career, Mr. Bernardo spent time with a major CCTV manufacturer (Vicon Industries) with responsibilities in design response and project engineering. Considerable time with this manufacturer was spent in engineering oversight of large-scale end-user projects in cooperation with the integrator and client. As a subject matter expert and strong application design and project management experience, Mr. Bernardo was with Ross & Baruzzini, a prestigious international architect and engineering firm, where he performed site surveys and security assessments, development of mitigation plans, systems design, bid project specification documentation, drafting, equipment and labor estimation, and grant writing.

As a parent of a school-aged children and as a security professional, the subject of security within schools continues to be an area he addresses and maintains involvement. His involvement has been in many areas including national councils working to develop standards and continuing to provide information and expertise whenever possible. Mr. Bernardo has written other published works and holds design patents within the physical security field.

Inge Sebyan Black, B.A., CPP, CFE, CPOI, Principal Consultant and Owner of Security Investigations Consulting

Inge Sebyan Black, B.A., CPP, CFE, CPOI, is the principal consultant and owner of Security Investigations Consulting, providing security, fraud, investigations and emergency management consulting. Inge has been in security management for 35 years, joining ASIS in 1983. Inge earned her bachelor's degree in Criminal Justice from Metropolitan State University, along with a degree in Police Science. Inge is a Certified Protection Professional (CPP), Certified Fraud Examiner (CFE), and Certified Protection Officer Instructor (CPOI), and is also certified as an Emergency Manager through FEMA and the State of Minnesota.

Inge has held her license as a Private Investigator in Minnesota, Ontario and Quebec. She is certified in Minnesota to train security personnel and taught security management at St. Paul Technical College in St. Paul, MN.

Although based in the United States, Inge spent 2 years in Canada conducting security risk assessments for both the government and private sector. She also conducts security audits and writes policies and procedures. She has trained security management in areas of contract security, emergency planning and physical security audits, interviews and investigations.

Inge is also an author and has written numerous publications, most recently wrote *The Art of Investigative Interviewing*, third edition, and has been a presenter for sessions and workshops at various ASIS International conferences. Inge currently serves as chair for the ASIS International Council for Crime Prevention and Loss Prevention and was on the Physical Security Council for 4 years previously.

Sjoerd Boersma, Senior Advisor and Partner, DSP-groep and Co-owner of IRIS

Sjoerd Boersma got his master's degree in International Land and Water Management at the University of Wageningen (Netherlands). During his studies, he specialized in the social side of technology development. The interface between technology and people is the common thread in his work.

After his graduation, Sjoerd joined the EYE film institute as head of the department of projection technology. His work involved the development and introduction of several new systems in the field of sound, image and subtitles. In 1997 he became involved in new media. As a project and account manager he developed many Web sites and CD-rom's for a variety of customers.

IRIS Safe & Secure schools started in 2004 following an investigation on the safety situation in schools in Amsterdam. Sjoerd was involved in the development and implementation of IRIS in many Dutch schools.

IRIS is a licensed software package for schools to register incidents, carry out surveys, assess the crime situation in schools, and to conduct audits (app). The results are presented on a simple dashboard and because the information is stored in a central database it is easy to make a comparison of the safety situation in all schools that use IRIS.

In 2012, Sjoerd co-founded LearningStone.com, a digital learning and communication platform. LearningStone is internationally used in formal education and by training professionals in agencies, companies, and institutions who need to support class based or blended learning. Sjoerd joined DSP in 2004 and is co-owner of IRIS.

Michael D. Brown, CPP, PCI, PSP, Founder and Director, MDB Consulting Agency

Michael D. Brown, CPP, PCI, PSP is the founder of MDB Consulting Agency and serves as its director of corporate security administration. Before founding MDB Consulting Agency, Michael completed a 20-year career with the Buffalo Police Department in Buffalo, New York, serving as a detective from 1999 to his retirement in 2008. He worked in the Robbery Squad, Special Frauds Unit, General Investigations Unit and the Narcotics Squad. Upon retiring, Michael joined Securitas Security Services, USA, first as an account manager for Toyota Motor Manufacturing of Alabama until he was promoted to branch manager for the Huntsville, Alabama branch, which encompasses Northern Alabama and Eastern Mississippi. Michael worked in this capacity for Securitas until October 2012, when the foundation was laid for the formation of MDB Consulting Agency.

Michael is one of approximately 80 people out of 40,000 security professionals to hold all three certifications issued by the ASIS International: Certified Protection Professional (CPP), Professional Certified Investigator (PCI), and Physical Security Professional (PSP).

Victor Cooper, MSM, CPP, Emergency Preparedness Program Manager, Aria Health System

Victor Cooper, MSM, CPP, is a former New Jersey State Trooper with over 25 years of experience in the law enforcement/security industry. He has expertly managed and directed all aspects of physical security for the Philadelphia Eagles football team. Victor assisted in coordinating security operations for two NFL championship football games, three Army/Navy football games (one with a presidential visit, George Bush), international soccer, concerts, and NCAA lacrosse tournaments. He also provided security for Super Bowls forty-one, forty-two, and forty-three and is a former committee member for the Pennsylvania Governor's Homeland Security Council on Terrorism. Victor is currently an adjunct professor of Criminal Justice at Penn State University, emergency preparedness program manager for the Aria Health System, and president of Victor L. Cooper Associates, LLC.

Frank J. Davies, CHS-IV, CIPS, CVI, President, Aella Consulting Group, Inc.

Frank J. Davies, CHS-IV, CIPS, CVI, is the president of Aella Consulting Group, Inc. He is a 30-year veteran in the physical and electronic security industry. Mr. Davies has designed and implemented many sophisticated integrated security systems for the US Federal Government, airports, Fortune 500 companies, and school and university clientele. As an expert in physical security, he has provided expert witness testimony and detailed reports regarding systems design, compliance, and functionality on high profile cases. Through his schooling, training, certifications, and years of practical application he provides security threat and risk assessments to his clients. As a parent of a school-aged child and security professional, the subject of security within schools continues to be an area he addresses and maintains involvement. His involvement has been in many areas including national councils working to develop standards and continuing to provide information and expertise whenever possible. Mr. Davies has written other published works and holds design patents within the physical security field.

Rick Draper, Principal Advisor and Managing Director, Amtac Professional Services Pty. Ltd.

Rick Draper is a security and crime prevention professional with over 30 years of experience in Australia, New Zealand, Canada, Papua New Guinea, and parts of Asia. He is the principal advisor and managing director of Amtac Professional Services Pty. Ltd. He is also an adjunct senior lecturer in security management and crime prevention in the School of Criminology and Criminal Justice at Griffith University in Queensland, Australia.

Rick's project experience spans a wide range of settings in both the public and private sectors, including undertaking numerous projects for schools, colleges, and universities. Over the past 20 years, he has also demonstrated significant expertise in developing Web-based tools to enhance security and gain efficiency, including solutions for incident reporting, access control management, plotting security observations, and loss prevention. He has written numerous papers, articles, and book chapters on a diverse range of security and crime prevention-related topics, as well as developing and facilitating training and professional development programs in areas of security management, crime prevention, fire safety, and security technology. In 1992, Rick was awarded the Security Australia Annual Achievement Award for the "Pursuit of Excellence and Services to the Security Industry."

Donald R. Green, CPP, CEMA, Director of Operations, Educational Safety Services

Donald R. Green, CPP, CEMA is the director of operations for Educational Safety Services, which provides consulting services and emergency response equipment to K-12 and higher education organizations. He is also the supervisor of security and emergency management for Newport News, Virginia Public Schools, an urban public school district serving over 30,000 students. Green has over 25 years of experience in security and law enforcement management and has worked in disasters and exercises including hurricanes, active shooters, and radiological emergencies.

He is board certified in security management as a Certified Protection Professional (CPP) through ASIS International and is a Certified Emergency Management Assistant (CEMA) through the Virginia Emergency Management Association. Green is also a Certified Gang Specialist and a U.S. Air Force Anti-Terrorism Officer, Level II. He uses his experience and expertise to prepare teachers, administrators, students, support staff, security officers and law enforcement officers for both routine and unique emergency situations in their schools.

Jim Harper, CRL, CIL, K-12 and University Specialist, ASSA ABLOY

Jim Harper has over 39 years of lock industry experience. Since 2006, he has served as K-12 and university end user specialist for ASSA ABLOY, covering 1300 school districts in the New England Region. Prior to this role, Jim has worked with such institutions as Best Locking Systems of New England, John Hancock Mutual Life Insurance Company in Boston, Clark Security Products, and Boston Children's Hospital.

Jim is a past president of the Institutional Locksmith's Association and remains a life member. He is also an instructor for the Associated Locksmiths of America. Jim also performs services as a legal expert witness in negligent security legation. He is recognized as an expert in masterkey system design and key control procedures.

Robert F. (Bob) Lang, CPP, CEM, Chief Security Officer at Kennesaw State University

Robert F. (Bob) Lang, CPP, CEM, is currently the chief security officer at Kennesaw State University. Prior to this position, Bob spent 19 years at Georgia Tech University and the Georgia Tech Research Institute as the director of homeland security and the director of research security directing classified operations security. He came to Georgia Tech from the Lockheed Corporation in Marietta, GA where he also directed the classified operations security as well as physical plant and guard units. Prior to Lockheed he was with the Federal Bureau of Investigation (FBI) in Fort Lauderdale, FL.

Bob has bachelor and master's degrees in criminal justice and is a graduate of the Lockheed Emory and Georgia Tech Management Institutes.

Bob is the author of many articles on security technology, emergency preparedness, business continuity, and risk management. He also has experience with the 1992 Olympics in Barcelona, Spain; the Goodwill Games in 1994 in St. Petersburg, Russia; the 1995 World University Games in Buffalo, NY; and the Atlanta Olympic Games in 1996, where he was the head security planner for the Olympic Village on Georgia Tech's campus.

Joseph C. Nelson, CPP, Vice President of Global Security, State Street Corporation

Joseph C. Nelson, CPP, is currently a vice president, global security with State Street Corporation. Joe is a contributing author to several security industry books, standards, and publications including the *Handbook of Loss Prevention and Crime Prevention*. Joe has over 30 years of diverse physical security leadership experience, maintaining the professional designation of Certified Protection Professional (CPP) since 1990.

Joe holds a Bachelor of Science degree from Northeastern University's College of Criminal Justice and a leadership certificate from Georgetown University. He has served as an emeritus faculty member with the Security Executive Council. Joe has also held global director positions within Iron Mountain, IBM, Lotus, Teradyne, and CMGI.

Jack Poole, PE, FSFPE, Principal, Poole Fire Protection, Inc.

Jack Poole graduated from the University of Maryland in 1986 with a Bachelor's of Science degree in Fire Protection Engineering. Mr. Poole is a principal at Poole Fire Protection located in Olathe, Kansas. Mr. Poole is a registered Professional Engineer (PE) in Fire Protection, licensed in 52 states and territories, and his expertise includes designing fire suppression and detection systems. He has designed hundreds of fire alarm and mass notification systems for public and private clients all around the world. Mr. Poole serves on several NFPA Technical Committees, including NFPA 72; is the chairman of NFPA 520 and serves on the Board of Directors for the Society of Fire Protection Engineers (SFPE); and is an SFPE Fellow.

Philip Purpura, CPP, Director of the Security and Justice Institute, Florence Darlington Technical College

Philip P. Purpura has been a criminal justice educator for more than 20 years. He has directed criminal justice, security, and paralegal programs, and has practical experience as a security consultant, expert witness, security manager, corporate investigator, and police officer. Mr. Purpura is the author of several other textbooks and numerous articles published in newsletters, magazines, and journals.

Rick Shaw, Founder, CEO, and CDO of Awareity

Rick Shaw is the founder, CEO, and CDO of Awareity, with 30 plus years of experience in risk mitigation and prevention processes. Rick's experiences in management, consulting and white-hat hacking across all types of organizations in multiple industries has provided Rick many lessons learned to share with business leaders.

Rick's leadership in creating innovative incident management and prevention services has been honored by leading risk management and insurance experts, including the Risk Innovator award from *Risk & Insurance* magazine, the Responsibility Leader award from Liberty Mutual, the Business Innovation award from Business Insurance, and the Readers' Choice Top 100 award from *District Administration* magazine.

Brad Spicer, Chief Executive Officer, SafePlans, LLC

Brad Spicer began his career as an intelligence analyst in the United States Army and is a veteran of Operations Desert Shield and Desert Storm. Following his enlistment, he spent 11 years with the Missouri State Highway Patrol, serving with the Patrol's Special Emergency Response Team (SERT) and in the Governor's Security Division.

During his time on the State's Governor's Security Detail, Mr. Spicer coordinated security operations during presidential visits and became a nationally recognized expert in the fields of dignitary protection and security. He has received advanced threat assessment training from the United States Secret Service and Gavin de Becker & Associates.

In 2001, Mr. Spicer developed the Emergency Response Information Portal (ERIP™), a comprehensive cloud-based emergency preparedness application, and founded SafePlans. He has grown SafePlans into a national firm with clients in over 25 states, including fortune 500 companies and two of the five largest schools systems in the United States. SafePlans is an Advanced Level IBM Business Partner and ERIP is designated by the U.S. Department of Homeland Security as a Qualified Anti-Terrorism Technology.

Paul Timm, PSP, President, RETA Security, Inc.

Paul Timm, PSP, is a board-certified Physical Security Professional (PSP), president of RETA Security, Inc., and a nationally acclaimed expert in school security. In addition to conducting numerous vulnerability assessments and his frequent keynote addresses, Paul is an experienced School Crisis Assistance Team volunteer through the National Organization for Victims Assistance (NOVA). He is certified in Vulnerability Assessment Methodology (VAM) through Sandia National Laboratories and ALPHA™ vulnerability assessment methodology.

He is also a member of ASIS International, where he serves as vice chairman of the School Safety and Security Council, and is a member of the Illinois Association of School Business Officials (IASBO). Paul is currently working on his MDiv at Moody Theological Seminary. He also holds a degree in Speech Communications and a Certificate in Business Administration from the University of Illinois.

Paul van Soomeren, CEO, DSP-groep (http://www.dsp-groep.eu/); Director of the Board, the International CPTED Association and the European Designing Out Crime Association

Paul van Soomeren is the CEO and one of the founders of DSP-groep (www.DSP-groep.eu) a research, consultancy, and management bureau with a staff of 50 based in Amsterdam, the Netherlands. Paul works as management consultant and policy researcher for national and local authorities, the European Union, and international organizations and institutions.

Paul is director of the board of the International CPTED Association (crime prevention through environmental design) and the European Designing Out Crime Association (http://www.e-doca.eu/). In that capacity he travels all over the world to lecture on these subjects.

Areas of expertise include urban planning and design, crime prevention, safety and security, schools, education and social management. Paul is a member of the international COST action Management Committee of the European Cooperation in Science and Technology (domain: Transport and Urban Development) which runs until 2017. He is also a visiting professor at the University of Salford (Greater Manchester, UK).

Paul studied Social Geography, and Urban and Regional Planning at the University of Amsterdam. He was a teacher at an Amsterdam high school and worked for the Ministries of Security and Justice and the ministry of Interior (National Crime Prevention Institute) for 3 years before he founded DSP-groep in 1984.

Linda Watson, M.A., CPP, CSC, CHS-V, Principal, Independent Security Consultant at Whirlaway Group LLC

Linda Watson, M.A., CPP, CSC, CHS-V is the principal consultant at Whirlaway Group LLC. She is Board Certified in Security Management by ASIS International, and a Certified Security Consultant by International Association of Professional Security Consultants. Linda has served as a police officer in Massachusetts for more than 20 years. As an independent security consultant specializing in threat assessment, security management, and preparedness planning for private educational institutions and houses of worship. The firm was founded in 2004 by Linda Watson.

APPROACHES AND BEST PRACTICES FOR SCHOOL CRIME PREVENTION

BEST PRACTICES—A SIXTEEN-POINT MASTER PLAN

Lawrence J. Fennelly, CPO, CSS, HLS-III
Security expert witness and consultant, Litigation Consultants Inc.
Marianna A. Perry, M.S., CPP
Training and development manager, Securitas Security Services USA, Inc.
Paul Timm, PSP
President, RETA Security, Inc.

INTRODUCTION

This chapter was reviewed by members of the ASIS International Crime Prevention and Loss Prevention Council, the School Safety and Security Council, and approximately 50 individuals who attended an educational session on school security at the 2013 ASIS Seminar and Exhibits in Chicago, IL.

Master planning is a catalyst for defining a vision for security that touches all aspects of service delivery, including technology, IT integration, command and control, and communication with stakeholders and employees. The plan should identify areas where security can be repositioned as a core function, contributing to the bottom line of the school. The master planning process enables schools to gain valuable exposure to tools and techniques that increase the value and integrity of their departments. Comprehensive, proactive protection solutions require collaboration among students, teachers, and administrators. You must explore ways to adapt successful emergency response procedures for your particular educational setting.

PART A. ADMINISTRATIVE PROCEDURES

1. Director of Safety and Security
   * The school district or campus should have a director of safety and security to oversee the program.
   * If utilizing a school resource officer (SRO) on your campus, he/she should be an on-duty, law enforcement officer who is highly visible and required to make random rounds of the property.
   * Be aware of the many anonymous tip lines for safety and security concerns on the campus, e.g., Crime Stoppers.
   * Implement an anti-bullying policy that is strictly enforced.
   * Develop threat assessment teams and have training conducted by a qualified individual.

* When managing your security program and today's software, anticipate the future needs of the school and campus. Install systems and programs with long-term expansion capabilities to accommodate future security needs and upgrades.

2. Vulnerability Assessment (See Chapter 3)
   * Our culture has changed and crimes on school property have changed as well. Needs and deficiencies must be determined in order to have a security program that is effective.
   * Vulnerability assessment is a critical on-site examination used to observe security that is currently in place, identify security deficiencies or excesses, determine what level of security is needed, and finally, to make recommendations for improvement to effectively control the identified risks.
   * After the vulnerability assessment, you and the assessor together will conduct a cost-benefit analysis to determine if the recommendations are affordable, feasible, and practical and if they can be budgeted for as short-term or long-term projects.
   * The assessor will gather statistical data from law enforcement, such as the Uniform Crime Reporting system (UCR), National Incident-Based Reporting System (NIBRS), National Crime Victimization Survey (NCVS), and the Department of Homeland Security (DHS) to examine the frequency of events in your area to determine what can be done to remove or reduce the threat to your campus.
   * A vulnerability assessment should be completed annually (or more often, if there are issues or significant changes to the building or campus) by a qualified individual. At this time, a review of all programs, policies, and training will be done to ensure that you are addressing current security issues.

3. Security Program Management (See Chapter 17)
   * Establish security policies and procedures that address identified risks and ensure that the security program has the approval and "buy in" of the school district and principal of the school. It is important that policies and procedures are documented and that they address violence prevention and intervention. Security policies and procedures must be supported by school faculty and staff and be consistently enforced.
   * The school district, as well as each individual campus, needs to effectively manage its security program using multilevels of communication, policies and procedures, physical security, and training, as well as response plans. There should be an effective implementation process for short-term and long-term projects.
   * Involve the parents (PTA and other volunteers) as well as students in the School Safety and Security Program. All parties will assist and help educate students about the policies and procedures.
   * Identify and manage your assets by ensuring all prevention, detection, and notification systems (alarms, lighting, video surveillance, intercoms, etc.) are working properly and that high-theft and high-risk areas have the proper coverage.
   * Integrate solutions with existing security systems and infrastructure for maximum return on your investment.
   * Lock classrooms during classes using properly installed hardware.

4. Background Checks
   * Conduct diligent criminal background investigations (preemployment, annual, as needed) and drug testing (preemployment, for cause, random, post accident or incident) for all faculty, staff, volunteers, contractors, and vendors who are on school property.
   * Implement fingerprinting for all school faculty, staff, volunteers, contractors, and vendors who are on school property.

PART B. PHYSICAL SECURITY (SEE PART II)

5. Lobby of the Administration Building
- Install an intercom with a door-release button, inside the lobby vestibule.
- Have video surveillance of the area.
- Issue and require all students (in grades 9-12), faculty, and staff to visibly display color-coded, identification badges (or smart cards).
- Implement a visitor management system, including sign-in, photo verification, visitor badge (that must be displayed), and escort, if required. Use a driver's license scanner for positive visitor identification. Consider a color-coded badge system for access to specific floors or areas.
- Utilize a computer database sign-in system either in the lobby or online when appointments are requested.
- Exterior doors should be locked at the start of school day (others are egress only and monitored) and only one entrance should be utilized, which should be equipped with intercom and a video surveillance system.
- Determine if walk-through metal detectors and/or handheld units are needed.
- Utilize a panic button or duress alarm in the lobby, which transmits a signal to a central station, who in turn will call the police.
- Have a written procedure for the use of panic buttons or duress alarms. Determine if this should include an automatic lockdown of the school.

6. Signage
- Install signage on campus to direct visitors, contractors, and vendors to the office area to be processed for access.
- Doors (interior and exterior) and windows need to be identified by placement of a number or letter (which is approved by police or fire responders) to identify various rooms in the building and on the campus. Obtain information from other schools and your local fire department to meet standards. Some schools currently have 10"- to 12"-high room numbers. Use the same size for numbers on the front door. (Consider using retro-reflective, 3M Scotchlite™-type material.)
- In a conspicuous location, post emergency escape route-of-travel maps on walls in all buildings and in all rooms.

7. Perimeter of the Campus (See Chapter 4)
- Clearly identify the perimeter of the campus and utilize the Crime Prevention Through Environmental Design (CPTED) concept of territorial reinforcement so that the school property is easily identifiable from public property. Install fencing and lighting, as necessary.
- In remote or high-risk areas of the campus, consider the ASIS International standard for fencing: 7′ in height (with three strands of barbed wire placed 6″ apart), if necessary.
- Follow the CPTED concept of maintaining bushes no higher than 3′ and tree branches trimmed to 8′ from the ground.

8. Perimeter of the Building (See Chapter 4)
- Improve, upgrade, and maintain the door hardware on all outside entry doors and install anti-prop alarms.
- Have full perimeter lockdown capability, either manually or automatic, but ensure that it meets local codes.

- Consider the use of bollards to prevent vehicular access to buildings.
- Enforce the policy of no-parking areas and designated drop-off areas. No-standing and no-loitering areas must be addressed and enforced.
- Before planting shrubs or bushes around buildings, consider the growth rate and the maintenance that will be required. Bushes should be no taller than 3′ and set back 1 yard from buildings or walkways, per CPTED concepts.

9. Access Control Systems (See Chapter 23)
   - A closed-campus proactive capability, with electronic access control, audit database, and anti-pass-back feature should be utilized.
   - Keep access points to a minimum. The general idea is to have one (or few) entrance(s) and many exits.
   - Monitor the school parking lot with video surveillance and issue color-coded parking permits with designated parking areas for students, faculty, staff, and visitors.
   - Before an incident occurs, ensure first responders will have access to buildings (issue all-access cards or master keys at training exercises).

10. Key Control (See Chapter 19)
    - If you don't have 100% control over your master and grand master keys, then you must rekey.
    - Establish a key/card management program and assign someone to manage it.
    - Rekey mechanical locks if keys are lost, stolen, not returned at a termination, or otherwise unaccounted for.
    - Consider the use of keyless access control systems so that access can immediately be terminated if a card or code is lost, stolen, or if someone is terminated.

11. Lighting (See Chapter 20)
    - Install adequate lighting on campus—especially by walkways, around doorways, and in parking areas. A properly illuminated area acts as a psychological and physical deterrent and can reduce criminal opportunity.
    - Refer to Occupational Safety and Health Administration (OSHA), Illuminating Engineering Society of North America (IESNA), and American National Standards Institute (ANSI) for lux and foot-candle lighting-level recommendations. Test illumination annually with a light meter and be cognizant that foliage on trees may obstruct lighting.
    - Be aware of light trespass on neighboring properties.
    - Consider installing cost-effective LED lighting.
    - Have a lighting maintenance plan in place to quickly identify burned-out bulbs or inoperable lights. Assign and display numbers on light poles and fixtures so that those requiring attention can be easily identified. Inoperable fixtures or burned-out bulbs must be repaired or replaced within 24 hours.
    - Lighting needs to be uniform and cost effective with correct foot-candles at various locations.

12. Video Surveillance (See Chapter 22)
    - Retain 30 days of video surveillance footage, unless otherwise required.
    - Consider utilizing digital recorders and cloud-based storage.
    - Ensure video surveillance coverage is adequate and utilize video analytics.
    - Install Internet protocol (IP) video cameras and determine if you need a fixed camera or a pan, tilt, zoom (PTZ) unit (PTZ cameras work well but are expensive—almost three times the cost of a fixed camera—and need on-site monitoring to be effective). Budget for this type

of investment. Determine the purpose of your video surveillance program: monitoring and response, forensic purposes only, or both.

- Exterior lighting should be adequate for video surveillance resolution and color rendition index (CRI).
- Integrate video surveillance with access control, especially visitor management.
- Install video surveillance around the perimeter of the building, with attention to doors and accessible windows.
- There are standard locations established for certain types of cameras and monitoring, for example, at the main entrance, exterior entry points, cafeteria, hallways, high-risk areas, high-theft areas, computer labs, and so forth. Cameras are never installed at any location where there is a reasonable expectation of privacy, such as in a restroom or a locker room. Cameras are also typically not installed in instructional areas such as classrooms. There may be other areas identified by school staff, faculty, or assessment that are identified as "hot spots" where video surveillance would be beneficial.
- Integrate video surveillance with alarm (intrusion detection) systems. For example, if a door is propped open, the camera zooms in to determine the cause and then sends notification that a response is required.
- Establish a partnership with local law enforcement to give them remote access to video surveillance for a critical incident or a crime in progress. If the school has an intrusion detection system and it is activated at night, law enforcement or security can respond remotely and disrupt a crime in progress. In this instance, video surveillance may also be used as evidence for prosecution.

13. Fire Alarm Systems (See Chapter 24)
    - Conduct regular fire drills and ensure faculty and staff can quickly determine if all students are accounted for. Your visitor management system will help you determine if all visitors have been evacuated in the event of a fire or other emergency.
    - Comply with all applicable state codes

14. Emergency Planning (See Chapter 15)
    - Develop an emergency response plan and provide training for the staff.
    - Establish emergency procedures with standardized actions and directives for inclement weather (tornado, earthquake, hurricane, flooding, etc.), medical issues, fire, building evacuations, shelter-in-place, lockdown, workplace violence, and active shooter as well as a business continuity plan for after the incident (OSHA, National Fire Protection Association [NFPA], FEMA, etc.)
    - Ensure your emergency procedures comply with Americans with Disabilities Act (ADA) standards (physically handicapped, sight-impaired, hearing-impaired, or special needs students, faculty, staff, visitors, etc.). Have designated individuals trained to assist.
    - Conduct training for emergency procedures with the local fire and police departments, EMS, and other local officials. Provide floor plans for each building on the campus to each of these departments. Consider supplying building plans and layout of the campus in a digital format for quicker access by more responders.
    - Establish a crisis management team, with documentation. Determine who will make the decision to lockdown the school, how notifications will be made, and who will make notifications to faculty, staff, and parents.

- The crisis management team will handle procedures during and after a crisis situation.
- Develop mass notification procedures (see below).
- Provide two-way radios (or another alternative method for communication) for faculty and staff, and establish a designated command center area or location.
- Ensure you are in compliance with all applicable OSHA regulations, life safety codes, and local and state fire codes.
- The NFPA 1600 document is needed for all-hazards planning.
  Provide FEMA training for administration and crisis team members. An introductory course on incident command systems (ICS) for schools is offered by FEMA: http://training.fema.gov/EMIWeb/IS/courseOverview.aspx?code=is-100.sca.
- Conduct fire, evacuation, lockdown, shelter-in-place, and other emergency drills.
- Consider using the Standard Response Protocol of the I Love U Guys Foundation (www.iloveuguys.org).
- Develop crisis kits with all necessary supplies for an emergency situation.
- Collaborate with local law enforcement and other emergency responders to determine if interior door windows are to be covered and/or if shades are to be left open or pulled down in a lockdown situation.
- Develop a mutual aid agreement with other schools and businesses.
- Have well-stocked first aid kits on site (e.g., tourniquets, quick-clot gauze, chest seals, pressure bandages).

15. Mass Notification Procedures (See Chapter 10)
    - Develop a mass notification program, which includes e-mails, text messages, social media, and public address system announcements, as well as audible and visual alarms.
    - Ensure your mass notification program complies with ADA standards (physically handicapped, visually impaired, hearing-impaired, or special needs students, faculty, staff and visitors, etc.). Have designated individuals trained to assist.
    - Ensure that your procedures meet NFPA Standards & Guidelines, which include a communication program, an incident management system, and individuals trained in ICS.

16. Training for Faculty and Staff (See Chapter 27)
    - When hired, conduct classroom training on school policies and procedures and repeat annually at in-service training, or as necessary.
    - Develop a policy for faculty and staff about when to use a fire extinguisher. Discuss when to fight a fire and when to flee a fire. Train faculty and staff on how to use a fire extinguisher.
    - Conduct first aid, CPR/AED, and blood-borne pathogens trainings (29 CFR 1910. 151) and repeat recertification as required.
    - Conduct training on how to respond to medical issues, fire, inclement weather, building evacuations, shelter-in-place, lockdown, workplace violence, active shooter, etc. Teachers and staff will train students.
    - Ask local, state, and federal agencies to participate in your classroom, tabletop, or incident training.
    - Educate students, faculty, and staff about bullying behavior.
    - Inform students, faculty, and staff that they should report and/or challenge anyone on the property who is not displaying an identification badge.

- Educate students, faculty, and staff about "If You See Something, Say Something," and empower them to report suspicious behavior or behaviors of concern.
- Train faculty and staff in all school security policies and procedures and repeat training as needed or when a change is made. Faculty and staff must consistently follow and fairly enforce all security procedures. There must be clear disciplinary action for anyone not following established rules or procedures.

THREATS AND HAZARDS AT EDUCATIONAL INSTITUTIONS*

Philip Purpura, CPP

Director of the Security and Justice Institute, Florence Darlington Technical College

EDUCATIONAL INSTITUTIONS

Two major types of educational systems are emphasized here: school districts and higher education. A key difference between school districts and college and university campuses is that, in the former, students normally go home at night and buildings often are empty. On campuses, students often live on the premises in dormitories. Exceptions are community and technical colleges whose students typically commute. School districts and campuses both schedule evening and weekend activities such as classes, sports events, and meetings. A major factor for those who plan and implement protection programs for these institutions is that the security and safety measures must cater to the needs and characteristics of the particular institution.

School districts and higher education are known as the education facilities subsector (EFS) of the government facilities sector under the National Infrastructure Protection Plan (NIPP). The U.S. Department of Education's (ED) Office of Safe and Drug-Free Schools (OSDFS) served as the sector-specific agency for the EFS. OSDFS promoted policy and recommendations on safety, health, security, emergency management, and resilience for the EFS. In 2011, the OSDFS became the Office of Safe and Healthy Students.[1] Under the Tenth Amendment ("…powers…reserved to the States…"), the general authority to administer the EFS is empowered to the states. The EFS is highly decentralized and protection is primarily a local responsibility.[2]

THREATS AND HAZARDS AT EDUCATIONAL INSTITUTIONS

Educational institutions are subject to a host of threats and hazards similar to other segments of society. Examples are crimes of violence, bomb threats, illegal drugs, property crimes, cybercrimes, and vandalism. Additional concerns are fire, accident, disaster, gangs, terrorism, infectious disease outbreaks, food recalls, suicide, date rape, bullying, hazing, crowd control for sports and other events, traffic, parking, student activism, graffiti, the discharge of toxic substances (e.g., the release of pepper spray

---

*This chapter is excerpted from Purpura P. Protecting Commercial and Institutional Critical Infrastructure. *Security and Loss Prevention*. Boston, MA: Butterworth-Heinemann; 2013. Updated by the author, 2014.

[1] U.S. Department of Education (2011). "Office of Safe and Drug-Free Schools." www.ed.gov, retrieved April 15, 2012.

[2] U.S. Departments of Homeland Security and Education (2010). *Education Facilities Sector-Specific Plan: An Annex to the Government Facilities Sector-Specific Plan*. www.dhs.gov, retrieved April 14, 2012, p. 55.

in a crowded hall), and the release of an animal in a school as a prank. Incidents may involve cross-sector protective efforts that assist in mitigation. For example, health-care and public health sector, transportation sector (e.g., school buses), commercial facilities sector (e.g., stadiums and arenas), and IT communications sector.

PROTECTION FOR EDUCATIONAL INSTITUTIONS

The following list describes measures for security and safety of school districts and institutions of higher education:

- Establish a security and safety committee and meet at least monthly.
- Ensure that all stakeholders and first responders are involved in security and safety planning and programs.
- Conduct risk analyses and prepare comprehensive, all-hazards protection.
- Offer counseling services and programs to assist students in crisis.
- Conduct substance abuse education and prevention programs.
- Typical security measures are access controls, emergency telephones, mass notification systems, intrusion and fire alarms, patrols, CPTED, lighting, and digital surveillance systems (closed-circuit TV, CCTV).
- Use vandal-resistant construction materials.
- If graffiti is an issue, photograph it before removing it and show the photos to police.
- Carefully consider the use of unarmed students to supplement police and security forces; provide good training.
- Research online resources on protection, training programs, and grants (see the Web site addresses at the end of this book).

SCHOOL DISTRICTS

More than 55 million students are enrolled in U.S. elementary through high schools.[3] From July 1, 2009 to June 30, 2010, there were 33 "school-associated violent deaths," defined as a homicide, suicide, or legal intervention (by police), in which death occurred at an elementary or secondary school in the USA. In 2010, for students aged between 12 and 18, 828,400 nonfatal victimizations occurred at school; this includes 358,600 victims of violence and 469,800 victims of theft. During this same year, for students aged between 12 and 18, 652,500 nonfatal victimizations occurred away from school; this includes 281,200 victims of violence and 371,300 victims of theft. It is difficult to draw conclusions about crime victimization and safety "at school" versus "away from school" because of reporting practices of victims and officials. Besides the physical and psychological effect of victimizations at schools, it can lead to increased dropout rates, decline in learning, early retirements, and increased fear.[4]

---

[3]U.S. Census (2011). "Back to School: 2011-2012." www.census.gov, retrieved April 14, 2012.
[4]National Center for Education Statistics (2012). *Indicators of School Crime and Safety: 2011*. http://nces.ed.gov, retrieved April 15, 2012.

LEGISLATION FOR SCHOOL DISTRICTS

The *Safe and Drug-Free Schools and Communities Act* supports programs that prevent violence in and around schools, mitigates the illegal drug problem, facilitates parent and community involvement in school challenges, and appropriates funds to local schools and higher education facilities victimized by violence or a traumatic incident. As a requirement for grant funding, the Act necessitates a crisis management plan. In 2011, Congress eliminated programs implemented under this Act. At the same time, the Office of Safe and Healthy Students continues to promote drug and violence prevention programs.[5]

In an attempt to reduce school violence, Congress enacted the *Gun-Free Schools Act*, which requires that each state receiving federal funds under the Elementary and Secondary Education Act must have a state law requiring local educational agencies to expel from school for a period of not less than 1 year a student who is determined to have brought a weapon to school. Each state's law also must allow the chief administering officer of the local educational agency to modify the expulsion requirement on a case-by-case basis.[6] This law resulted in many schools adopting a *zero-tolerance policy* for weapons being brought to school. In other words, any infraction results in full punishment. This same policy extends to alcohol and drugs. Meadows[7] writes that the intent of such a policy is both preventive and punitive. He notes the following: "Although zero-tolerance policies have a place in school security, there is the threat of over enforcement, which may undermine school-community relations and label students unfairly."

The *Family Educational Rights and Privacy Act* (FERPA) protects the privacy of students by limiting the types of information school officials can release. School records and personal information are protected. FERPA does not protect information disclosed during an emergency or obtained through observation or personal knowledge (e.g., a teacher hearing a threat from a student).

PROTECTION FOR SCHOOL DISTRICTS

A comprehensive school district loss prevention program must involve the community: students, teachers and administrators, parents, public safety agencies, civic groups, and businesses. The program can be divided into four components: special programs, personnel, physical security, and emergency management.[8]

Special programs include character education to help students distinguish right from wrong, conflict resolution, diversity, prevention of bullying, anonymous tip lines, and programs that involve parents. Since gangs are a problem in many schools and communities, and they are often linked to violence and drugs, school administrators should be proactive to reduce this problem by, for example, meeting police gang specialists on a regular basis to exchange information and antigang strategies. One popular

[5]U.S. Department of Education (2011). "Office of Safe and Drug-Free Schools." www.ed.gov, retrieved April 15, 2012. U.S. Departments of Homeland Security and Education (2010). *Education Facilities Sector-Specific Plan: An Annex to the Government Facilities Sector-Specific Plan*. www.dhs.gov, retrieved April 14, 2012, p. 55.

[6]Anderson, J. (2012). "Gun-Free Schools Act". Education Law (February 14). http://lawhighereducation.com, retrieved April 15, 2012.

[7]Meadows, R. (2007). *Understanding Violence and Victimization*, 4th ed. Upper Saddle River, NJ: Pearson Prentice Hall, p. 170.

[8]Decker, S. (2000). "Increasing School Safety through Juvenile Accountability Programs." Washington, DC: U.S. Department of Justice.

program is the *Gang Resistance Education and Training (GREAT)* program that provides students with tools to resist the lure and trap of gangs. Modeled after the Drug Abuse Resistance Education (DARE) program, the GREAT program seeks to prevent violence and introduces students to conflict resolution skills, cultural sensitivity, and negative aspects of gang life. This program has spread to all 50 states and several other countries.[9]

All employees at schools should be trained on early warning signs of inappropriate behavior or violence. These signs include feelings of isolation, rejection, and being persecuted, plus behaviors indicating anger or violence, such as threats. Intervention and counseling are vital in response to such signs.

A combined counseling and education approach might reduce student hostility and funnel student time into constructive activities. Traditional suspension from school often sends troublesome students to the streets, where more trouble is likely. On the other hand, if students remain at school in an appropriate program, improved results are probable.

Personnel consist of teachers, teacher aids, administrators, counselors, security officers, and school resource officers (SRO). SROs are police officers on duty at schools; they provide visibility, create rapport with students, and respond to incidents. Parents and volunteers play an important role in supplementing employees. All those who perform job duties at schools should undergo background screening, receive constant training, and clearly understand the policies and procedures for day-to-day events, such as student discipline problems and how to care for people during emergencies.

Physical security examples are handheld and walk-through metal detectors and duress alarms. Students must be safe without feeling as if they are in a prison. Students can swipe an ID card when they climb onto a bus and when they arrive and leave school; RFID tracks their movements. At the same time, CCTV cameras watch students on buses and on school premises. Visitors can be asked for their driver's license to check against a database of sex offenders. The strategies that are implemented should be subject to research and evaluation to produce the best possible solutions and utilization of resources.

Emergency management consists of plans to respond to violence, weapons, hostage situations, bombs/explosions, abused students, aggressive parents who are on the premises, and incidents involving parental rights. Many school districts distribute their crisis plans to public safety agencies that have a ready reference containing maps and building plans, utility shutoffs, staff and parent contact information, a yearbook to identify people, and a set of keys.

The National Center for Education Statistics[10] surveyed public schools and reports a host of safety and security measures at schools, including the following:

- Controlled access and locked doors. Nearly all public schools require visitors to sign in and obtain a visitors badge
- Restrictions on student access to certain Web sites on school computers
- Prohibiting certain electronic devices (e.g., cell phones)
- Anonymous threat reporting
- Drug testing of athletes and other students in extracurricular activities. Random dog sniffs to check for drugs
- Other measures include picture ID, searches, student uniforms, and mass notification systems

---

[9]Institute for Intergovernmental Research (2012). "Welcome to the G.R.E.A.T. Web Site." www.great-online.org, retrieved April 16, 2012.

[10]National Center for Education Statistics (2012). *Indicators of School Crime and Safety: 2011.* http://nces.ed.gov, retrieved April 15, 2012.

Research by Sobel[11] found that surveillance and searches at a high school were viewed in a positive light by male and female employees. Although students viewed surveillance positively, a majority of students viewed searches of lockers, backpacks, and self negatively.

The *Guide for Preventing and Responding to School Violence*, 2nd edition,[12] offers numerous suggestions, including the topics above and the following: establish a climate for reporting threats and violence, create an antibullying program, use a student court for noncriminal offenses, and educate students about drugs, alcohol, suicide prevention, gangs, and other important topics.

ARE EDUCATIONAL INSTITUTIONS "SOFT" TARGETS?

Terrorists search for "soft" targets containing limited security to increase the likelihood of a successful attack. Examples of *"soft" targets* are educational institutions, houses of worship, shopping malls, and theaters. *"Hard" targets* include military bases and fortified government buildings.

Emergency management became an important priority at many schools following the 1999 *Columbine High School massacre.* During this incident in Jefferson County, Colorado, two teenage students, armed with a variety of weapons and bombs, killed 12 students and a teacher, wounded 24, and then committed suicide. Prior to the attack, one of the killers showed warning signs of violence through a Web site, which contained violent threats, information on how to make bombs, and a log of mischief. The massacre fueled debate over gun violence, gun control, and the influence of the media on violence. In addition, the event reinforced attention to warning signs to prevent violence.

Another, more deadly massacre, tied to terrorism, was the *Beslan Elementary School massacre* in 2004. This attack was part of the Chechen war for independence against Russia. Russia has fought an insurgency in the breakaway republic of Chechnya since the 1990s, a time when the former Soviet Union collapsed. The 3-day hostage standoff at the elementary school in Beslan, where Chechen rebels rigged bombs around 1200 hostages, ended in gunfire, explosions, and 338 deaths, mostly children. Each side blamed the other for the battle at the school that caused more controversy over Chechen terrorism and Russian responses.

The carnage began when 32 attackers—armed with AK-47s, a machine gun, grenade launchers, explosives, and two dogs (to protect against chemical attack)—drove to the crowded school and herded children, teachers, and parents into the school gym, which was quickly wired with explosives. Male hostages were forced to build barricades at doors and windows, and when the work was complete, they were executed and their bodies were thrown out of the building. Two female suicide bombers were among the attackers, which illustrated the resolve of the attackers and the possible outcome. The attackers demanded the release of Chechen rebels, the withdrawal of Russian troops from Chechnya, and Chechen independence. The Russian government's options were very limited, and giving in to terrorist demands fueled new hostage events. By the second day, the terrorists continued to refuse water, food, and medicine for the hostages. In their desperation, the hostages began to drink their own urine. On the third day, the terrorists permitted a crew to collect the bodies of 20 male hostages that had been thrown out of the building. At this point, a bomb exploded within the gym, supposedly by accident, a fire began, the roof collapsed, and as hostages escaped, the terrorists shot them. The terrorists were killed, and two that escaped were caught by a mob and lynched. As the disaster unfolded, "finger-pointing" began to explain what went wrong. Explanations were that Special Forces were not ordered to rescue the hostages and assault the building, no one wanted to take responsibility to order the rescue and assault, and armed volunteers interfered with the hostage situation and were not kept back. The disaster shocked the world, and the Russian government promised reform of the police and military.[13]

---

[11]Sobel, R. (2012). "Perception of Violence on a High School Campus." *Journal of Applied Security Research*, 7 (January-March). pp. 11–21.

[12]International Association of Chiefs of Police and Bureau of Justice Assistance (n.d.). *Guide for Preventing and Responding to School Violence*, 2nd ed. www.theiacp.org, retrieved April 16, 2012.

[13]Abdullaev, N. (2004). "Beslan, Russia.. Terror! In The Schoolhouse!" Homeland Defense Journal, 2 (September), pp. 28–35.

ARE EDUCATIONAL INSTITUTIONS "SOFT" TARGETS?—Cont'd

On April 16, 2007, the *Virginia Tech massacre* became the worst school mass murder incident in U.S. history when a mentally disturbed student murdered 32 people and then committed suicide. Among the questions that followed the shootings were: Why did it take over 2 hours to release a notification that a killer was on the loose after two students were found shot earlier in another building? Was the police response quick enough to end the threat of an "active shooter"? Many factors must be considered when attempting to answer these questions. For instance, rushing into a building without a team and a plan is risky. Harwood[14] writes of strategies that require refinement: behavioral threat assessment teams to identify risky students, mass notification systems, and "active shooter" response. The federal government, including the U.S. Secret Service and the FBI, studied campus violence and concluded that although most (73%) violent acts on campus targeted a specific individual because of a triggering event (e.g., romantic breakup or academic failure), "understanding what leads an offender to exclusively target random individuals remains a complex and difficult challenge." The study also noted the importance of college and university threat assessment teams to evaluate "persons of concern."[15]

COLLEGES AND UNIVERSITIES
LEGISLATION FOR COLLEGES AND UNIVERSITIES

In response to increasing crime on college campuses and the need for more accurate statistics, Congress passed the *Student-Right-to-Know and Campus Security Act of 1990*. This Act is also known as the "Clery Act," named after Jeanne Clery, a college student who was raped and murdered in her dorm room. For institutions receiving federal student aid, this legislation requires crime awareness and prevention policies and an annual report of campus crime sent to the FBI Uniform Crime Reports program, while making these statistics available to students and the general public. Such data, available on the Web, enable comparisons among colleges and universities. Amendments to this Act include the requirement that a campus community must be notified immediately of an emergency or threat to safety, disclosure of emergency plans, reporting on hate crimes, and reporting of relationship of campus police with state and local police. For campuses with housing, the amendments require procedures for missing students and methods of fire protection reporting.[16]

Congress enacted the *Campus Sexual Assault Victims' Bill of Rights* in 1992, requiring schools receiving federal student aid to afford sexual assault victims basic rights and to develop policies to deal with sexual assault on campus.

There is conjecture that some schools omit reporting acts of violence to protect recruiting efforts and their reputations.[17] FBI crime data have been criticized over the years because they represent crimes *reported* to police, and many crimes are never reported or recorded, as shown by victimization studies.[18]

---

[14]Harwood, M. (2007). Preventing the next campus shooting. *Security Management*, 51, 55–65.

[15]Drysdale, D., et al. (2010). *Campus Attacks: Targeted Violence Affecting Institutions of Higher Education*. Washington, DC: U.S. Secret Service, FBI, DHS, and U.S. Department of Education.

[16] U.S. Department of Education (2011). *The Handbook for Campus Safety and Security Reporting*. www2.ed.gov/admins/lead/safety/handbook-2.pdf, retrieved March 10, 2011.

[17] Jaeger, S. (2001). "Crime Concerns on Campus." *Security Technology & Design*, 12 (March). p. 6.

[18] Purpura, P. (1997). *Criminal Justice: An Introduction*. Boston: Butterworth-Heinemann.

PROTECTION FOR COLLEGES AND UNIVERSITIES

Campus Security Guidelines were prepared by the Major Cities Chiefs Association and Bureau of Justice Assistance.[19] These guidelines focus on policies, coordination among local and campus police, interoperable communications, risk assessment, prevention, preparedness, emergency management, and external relations.

Numerous campuses have implemented the strategy of many public police agencies, namely, *community policing*. It aims to control crime through a partnership of police and citizens, and it strives to become a dominant philosophy throughout a police department. Community policing includes a proactive approach to problem solving, rather than responding repeatedly to the same problem. High priorities for protection on campuses are programs that focus on crime prevention, self-protection, and neighborhood watch.

In 2004, a National Summit on Campus Public Safety was held in Baltimore, Maryland. It was supported by the U.S. Department of Justice, Office of Community Oriented Policing Services[20]; the International Association of Campus Law Enforcement Administrators (IACLEA, see below); the International Association of Chiefs of Police; the U.S. Department of Homeland Security; and the FBI. Some of the main points from this summit are as follows:

- There is a need for a national center for campus safety to support information sharing, standards, model practices, and research.
- Many campuses house sensitive materials and information and serve as contractors for the Department of Defense, Department of Justice, National Security Agency, other government bodies, and corporations.
- Securing chemical, biological, and radiological materials in an accessible environment, 24 hours a day, 7 days a week, creates security challenges.
- Many campuses have a substantial number of international students who entered the country through student visas. In addition, many U.S. educational institutions maintain campuses overseas.
- Special events (e.g., sports, graduation, lectures) draw thousands of people to campuses and create vulnerabilities.
- U.S. educational institutions should be more closely linked to local and regional emergency management plans.

Research by Fisher and Sloan[21] produced the following points that should be considered when evaluating programs designed to reduce campus crime.

- A comprehensive approach includes security, faculty members, staff members, students, and public law enforcement personnel.
- Campus administrators should conduct surveys of the campus community to understand the nature and extent of crime and fear, perceptions of the effectiveness of security, and participation

---

[19] Major Cities Chiefs Association and Bureau of Justice Assistance (2009). *Campus Security Guidelines: Recommended Operational Policies for Local and Campus Law Enforcement Agencies.* www.majorcitieschiefs.com/pdf/MCC_CampusSecurity.pdf, retrieved April 19, 2012.

[20] U.S. Department of Justice, Office of Community Oriented Policing Services (2005). "National Summit on Campus Public Safety." Washington, DC: U.S. Department of Justice.

[21] Fisher, B., and Sloan, J. (1993). "University Response to the Campus Security Act of 1990: Evaluating Programs Designed to Reduce Campus Crime." *Journal of Security Administration*, 16, 67–77.

in crime prevention programs and whether participants adopted any of the preventive measures. Until evaluations become an integral part of responding to campus crime, administrators will continue to make poor decisions on security strategies.

- Research has confirmed that crime on campuses is influenced by poor lighting, excessive foliage, blocked views, and difficulty of escape by victims. (These issues relate to CPTED.)
- Location measures (e.g., proximity to urban areas with high unemployment) are predictors of high campus crime rates.

One particular group that has advanced the professionalism of campus safety and security is the IACLEA. This group began in 1958 with 11 schools, and today, it represents 1200 colleges and universities in 20 countries. The group maintains a Web site of resources; holds an annual conference; offers training, professional development, and standards and accreditation; and publishes the *Campus Law Enforcement*.[22]

SAFETY AND FIRE PROTECTION AT EDUCATIONAL INSTITUTIONS

The NFPA 101 Life Safety Code offers guidance to protect educational facilities from fire. Examples of fire hazards endangering life in places of public assembly are (1) overcrowding; (2) blocking, impairing, or locking exits; (3) storing combustibles in dangerous locations; and (4) using combustible decorations. Furthermore, hazards of educational buildings vary with construction characteristics and with the age group of students. Younger students, for example, require protection different from that for older students. The NFPA Life Safety Code specifies that kindergarten and first grade rooms should be on the floor of exit discharge so that stairs do not endanger these students. Because junior and senior high schools contain laboratories, shops, and home economics rooms, these facilities should have fire-resistant construction. School kitchens require similar protection. A fire alarm system is required for all educational buildings. Most schools conduct fire drills for pupils. The Life Safety Code and many good building codes provide numerous standards for increasing fire safety.

For colleges and universities, the Life Safety Code is applied depending on building characteristics and use. If buildings are windowless, the Life Safety Code requirements for special structures are applicable. This includes, for instance, venting systems for smoke. Because many campus buildings are multistory, specific safeguards are necessary. Fire drills and training are important for residence halls and academic buildings. If a campus contains "high-risk" chemicals, it may be subject to regulations of the Chemical Facilities Anti-Terrorism Standards (CFATS).[23]

---

[22] International Association of Campus Law Enforcement Administrators (2011). "About IACLEA." www.iaclea.org/, retrieved April 17, 2012.

[23] U.S. Departments of Homeland Security and Education (2010). *Education Facilities Sector-Specific Plan: An Annex to the Government Facilities Sector-Specific Plan*. www.dhs.gov, retrieved April 14, 2012, p. 24.

SECURITY ASSESSMENTS AND PREVENTION FOR K-12 SCHOOLS

Linda Watson, M.A., CPP, CSC, CHS-V

Principal, independent security consultant, Whirlaway Group LLC

INTRODUCTION

Our nation's children are welcomed into their schools every day by their teachers and staff. Our educators are focused on educating their students in a safe and secure environment which allows their students to excel. However, safety has become a very complex issue in our schools. Deadly shootings at Columbine, Virginia Tech, and Sandy Hook, to name only a few, have significantly impacted our schools. School shootings are still a rare event, but an event that must be prepared for nevertheless. The sheer number of people who are affected by school safety is compelling:

"As of fall 2010 approximately 75.9 million people were projected as enrolled in public and private schools at all levels including elementary, secondary, and postsecondary degree-granting. In addition, the number of professional, administrative, and support staff employed in educational institutions was projected at 5.4 million." (U.S. Department of Education 2010)[1]

CRIME PREVENTION THROUGH ENVIRONMENTAL DESIGN
SCHOOL CPTED SURVEY/ASSESSMENT[2]

Crime prevention through environmental design (CPTED) is a concept that was first introduced in the 1970s. Timothy Crowe and Lawrence Fennelly provide the following definition of CPTED in their 2013 book, *Crime Prevention Through Environmental Design*:

> A CPTED assessment attempts to evaluate the physical setting of facility and maintenance factors that affect the safety and crime quotient capability of a particular school. Environmental factors such as the types of neighborhoods, housing facilities, businesses, streets, and institutions surrounding the school affect the school's operation.

---

[1]Buildings and Infrastructure Protection Series Primer to Design Safe Schools Projects in case of Terrorist Attacks and School Shootings. FEMA −428/BIPS-07/ January 2012 Edition 2.

[2]Crime prevention through environmental design / Timothy D. Crowe; revised by Lawrence Fennelly—Third edition Appendix B.

Classrooms, security systems, lighting and color designs, accessibility, and quality of maintenance all evaluated to determine their effect on the school climate, natural supervision, defensible space, and differentiated space. The survey items are to be rated as satisfactory (S), unsatisfactory (U), or not applicable (NA).[3]

SCHOOL CPTED SURVEY OR ASSESSMENT[4]

A thorough CPTED survey should cover the following thirty points:

1. Poor visibility at entry to site
2. Easy vehicular access onto grounds
3. Off-site activity generator
4. Inadequate distance between school and neighbors
5. Easy-access hiding places
6. Area hidden by planting
7. School adjacent to traffic hazard
8. Portion of building inaccessible to emergency vehicles
9. Secluded hangout area
10. Vegetation hides part of the building
11. Site not visible from street
12. No barrier between parking and lawn
13. Gravel in parking area
14. Dangerous vehicular circulation
15. Enclosed courtyard conceals vandals
16. High parapet hides vandals
17. Trees located where visibility is required
18. Pedestrian-vehicle conflict
19. Structure provides hideout
20. Building walls subject to bouncing balls
21. Parts of bus shelter not visible
22. Mechanical equipment accessible
23. Stacked materials and downspouts provide roof access
24. Recessed entry obscures intruders
25. Portions of building not visible from vehicle areas
26. Walkway roof eases access to building roof
27. Recess hides vandals
28. Skylight proves easy access
29. Mechanical screen conceals vandals
30. Access through complex

---

[3]Crime prevention through environmental design / Timothy D. Crowe: revised by Lawrence Fennelly—Third edition.
[4]Crime prevention through environmental design / Timothy D. Crowe; revised by Lawrence Fennelly—Third edition Appendix B.

SECURITY CPTED ASSESSMENT

Conducting a security CPTED assessment or survey of a school starts with the physical security exterior areas described in the above security survey. Additionally, it is important to interview the stakeholders who work in the school. These stakeholders are the eyes and ears of the school and they can identify the problems which exist within their school.

Using an all-hazards approach will cover many of the natural events that are possible: fire, hurricane, tornado, earthquake, flood, or severe wind. Add in manmade events such as chemical, hazardous, and biological catastrophes, and you can see many of the threats to be considered. These events are more likely to occur than a school shooting or a terrorist attack. With the all-hazards approach, you prepare for all possible events versus "just" a school shooting or terrorist attack. An all-hazards approach is the approach that best serves every school, large or small, public or private.

A security assessment is a process of identifying the security risks that a school may be exposed to and how you will respond to them. When identifying risks you must decide if it is too costly to protect or replace an item(s). If that is the case, then you may choose to protect the existing item, but know if a loss occurs it will not be replaced. This is the basis of a security assessment: mitigation, preparedness, and response. Every school is unique and there is no one security assessment that fits every school. By speaking with the stakeholders you get to learn about the community and how the school fits into that community. As you identify the threats, you can then evaluate and rate the level of the threats to the school as a whole. Use a scale starting with very low (1) through very high (10). By rating the threats you are assessing the likelihood or credibility of a threat. These threats are evaluated on the type of loss or damage that would result from an event. This subject has been successfully covered in great detail in the book *Crime Prevention Through Environmental Design, 3e* by Timothy D. Crowe, revised by Lawrence Fennelly. We have attached two appendices to complement this chapter. Appendix A discusses ten key questions that should guide the assessment of a threat. The use of the Security Assessment/Survey in Appendix B will help you evaluate the interior and exterior of the school's facility.

Much has been written on the methodologies of how to conduct and evaluate security assessments for school systems. There are many useful tools located on the U.S. Department of Education and American Clearinghouse on Educational Facilities websites.

It is important to emphasize how essential the physical security assessment is as the basis of all other security work. An assessment encourages you to evaluate the potential for internal threats within a school, and when evaluating these internal threats it is wise to look at the vulnerabilities within the school and evaluate "how" the school would be attacked. When you look at the security assessments from this perspective, your individual stakeholders can contribute regarding where they think an attack might be launched from. The internal threats may be a jilted lover or a recently fired employee who feels "wronged." These potential threats are very dangerous because of the "actor's" (the person who acts) intimate knowledge of the campus and the unique culture within the educational institution. These actors know all the rules of getting into and out of the campus buildings and where there are vulnerabilities they can exploit because they are a known face at a dorm or classroom complex.

When you look back at past violent school events we can see many patterns emerging within the events themselves. Lessons learned from past school shootings at Columbine, Virginia Tech, and Sandy Hook teach us how to improve our communications with students, visitors, staff, and faculty during an emerging critical event on campus. Unfortunately, the active shooters can also study the past attacks and may have learned from the mistakes of the past as well.

Many times after a tragic event on a school campus, people who have taught the student or were acquainted with the faculty member responsible for the attack say they noticed odd things prior to the event but did not think to report it to authorities. Having an independent reporting system in place that is widely advertised gives concerned persons the ability to report their observations without the fear of reprisals.

In his book, *The Gift of Fear*, Gavin de Becker discusses in great detail the cues that are usually present before an incident (pre-incident cues) but are often ignored by coworkers or faculty and staff. Many times after an event when the media is interviewing persons who knew the actor, a pattern of odd or unusual behavior emerges. However, many of these persons only know the actor in the context of school or work. They do not have the opportunity to compare notes with other parties who also know the actor in a different venue.

TRAGEDIES

After the Columbine, Virginia Tech, and Sandy Hook tragedies we have learned that having a critical incident team (CIT) in place and ready to evaluate a potential at-risk student, faculty member or employee is very important. These teams focus on a holistic approach to evaluating the at-risk individual. The CIT can be composed of many different professionals: commonly there will be administrative, human resources, mental health, legal and law enforcement members. This diversity gives the team the opportunity to evaluate an at-risk person from their "specialty" and report back to their CIT peers with their findings.

In the past, communication was an issue if a student went before the student review board for a violation of some student infraction. Many times, the student review board did not pass their findings onto law enforcement or the mental health counselors. The advantage of a CIT is that they now have the ability to follow up on the student and make cross-department notes with other CIT peers. They are immediately getting involved and holistically evaluating the potential risks that are exhibited by an at-risk student.

In some past tragedies, family members have told the interviewing authorities that they were unaware of any issues involving their loved ones at school prior to the tragic event. With a CIT in place, they can get the family involved in evaluating and discussing their plans for how the student should proceed since the last known issue that has been brought to their attention.

Family members often say in hindsight that given the opportunity to get involved with their loved one they would have done whatever would have been helpful to defuse the situation and avoid the tragic event that occurred.

A review of many of the recent tragic events that have occurred at educational institutions reveals that many times there appears to have been a mental health issue that is only brought to the community's attention after the incident. Children that have been bullied or attacked on social media after school have nowhere to hide now. Prior to smartphones and current technology, when a child got off the bus at the end of the day, they had a break from school until the next day. Now a child can connect 24/7 with their peers, which can cause them to feel that there is no escape from the harassment or bullying. Despite established rules designed to protect at-risk students from cyber bullying, many times the student does not disengage from social media when school ends.

The impact of being bullied or picked on can become enormous, forcing a student to withdraw from the school environment. Some students become isolated and may not have adequate parental supervision or a trusted adult who can help them engage in a healthy dialog with their peers. Some students react to bullying by acting out with violence.

CONCLUSION

In conclusion, security assessments for K-12 schools should also include a CIT component to evaluate the threats and risks to a school from internal threats. The emphasis in the past was on the facility and threats to that facility. This emphasis remains very important, but we now must look at internal threats such as the risk from students, visitors, vendors, and faculty or staff members. By having an open dialog across departments, the likelihood of thwarting an internal threat is much greater. People are your greatest asset and your greatest vulnerability.

APPENDIX A: U.S. SECRET SERVICE THREAT ASSESSMENT SUGGESTIONS

This appendix is reprinted from "Guide for Preventing and Responding to School Violence," Bureau of Justice Assistance, 2007, page 18, Grant 2007-DD-BX-K112.

School and law enforcement officials are frequently placed in the difficult position of having to assess specific people (students, staff, teachers, and others) who may be likely to engage in targeted violence in which there is a known or knowable target or potential assailant. The following suggestions for threat assessment investigations are based on guidelines developed by the U.S. Secret Service's National Threat Assessment Center (NTAC). They were developed primarily for preventing the assassination of public officials, so they may not be applicable to all school situations. To identify threats, school officials are advised to take the following steps:

1. Focus on individuals' thinking and behavior as indicators of their progress on a pathway to violent actions. Avoid profiling or basing assumptions on sociopsychological characteristics. In reality, accurate profiles for those likely to commit acts of targeted violence do not exist. School shootings are infrequent and most people who happen to match a particular profile do not commit violent acts. In addition, many individuals who commit violent acts do not match profiles.
2. Focus on individuals who pose a threat, not only on those who explicitly communicate a threat. Many individuals who make direct threats do not pose an actual risk, while many people who ultimately commit acts of targeted violence never communicate threats to their targets. Before making an attack, potential aggressors may provide evidence they have engaged in thinking, planning, and logistical preparations. They may communicate their intentions to family, friends, or colleagues, or write about their plans in a diary or journal. They may have engaged in attack-related behaviors: deciding on a victim or set of victims, determining a time and approach to attack, and selecting a means of attack. They may have collected information about their intended targets and the setting of the attack as well as information about similar attacks that have previously occurred.

Once individuals who may pose a threat have been identified, 10 key questions should guide the assessment of the threat:

1. What motivated the individual to make the statement or take the action that caused him or her to come to attention?
2. What has the individual communicated to anyone concerning his or her intentions?
3. Has the individual shown an interest in targeted violence, perpetrators of targeted violence, weapons, extremist groups, or murder?

4. Has the individual engaged in attack-related behavior, including any menacing, harassing, or stalking-type behavior?
5. Does the individual have a history of mental illness involving command hallucinations, delusional ideas, feelings of persecution, and so on, with indications that the individual has acted on those beliefs?
6. How organized is the individual? Is he or she capable of developing and carrying out a plan?
7. Has the individual experienced a recent loss or loss of status, and has this led to feelings of desperation and despair?
8. Corroboration: What is the individual saying, and is it consistent with his or her actions?
9. Is there concern among those who know the individual that he or she might take action based on inappropriate ideas?
10. What factors in the individual's life and environment might increase or decrease the likelihood of the individual attempting to attack a target?

Source: R. Fein and B. Vossekuil, National Threat Assessment Center, U.S. Secret Service.

APPENDIX B: SCHOOL SAFETY AND SECURITY CHECKLIST

SCHOOL SAFETY AND SECURITY CHECKLIST			
School District:		**School:**	**Address:**
Team Members:			
Date:		*School Representative:*	

Instructions: This checklist is designed to help evaluate the safety and security of your school. The best way to use it is to form teams to conduct the survey at locations other than their own to keep observations neutral and objective. Each survey team should ensure that local law and fire personnel are invited to help with the evaluations and planning. Audit team members should review the following documents and materials, preferably in advance of the onsite visit:

1. Student / staff code of conduct

2. Data on student discipline referrals

3. Criminal data (reported by the school and by the surrounding community)

4. Blueprint of the school

5. Crisis management plan

6. Information and data protection (records, examinations, etc.)

The checklist does not take the place of crisis management plans or emergency plans but supports the testing and adequacy of these plans. School safety and security requires policies and procedures for management of disciplinary issues and dangerous students.

You can contact _____, if you have questions or need assistance at _____.

SAFETY AND SECURITY TEAM NOTES		
SCHOOL EXTERIOR AND PLAY AREAS	**YES**	**NO**
1. School grounds are fenced.		
2. What kind?		
3. If yes, approximate height (security fencing should meet zoning and code standards. Best height prevents unauthorized entry and is 6-8 ft tall with a turned top to restrict scaling) Are gates secured by locks?		
4. There is one clearly marked and designated entrance for visitors.		
5. Signs are posted for visitors to report to main office through a designated entrance.		
6. Restricted areas are clearly marked.		
7. Shrubs and foliage are trimmed to allow for good line of sight (3'-0"/8'-0" rule).		
8. Shrubs near building have been trimmed "up" to allow view of bottom of building.		
9. Bus loading and drop-off zones are clearly defined.		
10. Access to bus loading area is restricted to other vehicles during loading/unloading.		
11. Staff is assigned to bus loading/drop off areas.		
12. There is a schedule for maintenance of:		
a. Outside lights		
b. Locks/hardware		
c. Storage sheds		
d. Windows		
e. Other exterior buildings		
13. There is adequate lighting around the building.		
14. Lighting is provided at entrances and points of possible intrusion.		
15. Play areas are fenced. Visual surveillance of playground areas is possible from a single point.		
16. Playground equipment has tamper-proof fasteners.		
17. Visual surveillance of parking lots from main office is possible.		
18. Parking lot is lighted properly and all lights are functioning.		
19. All areas of school buildings and grounds are accessible to patrolling security vehicles.		
20. Students/staff are issued parking stickers for assigned parking areas.		
21. Student access to parking area is restricted to arrival and dismissal times.		
22. Staff and visitor parking has been designated.		

23. Outside hardware has been removed from all doors except at points of entry.		
24. Ground floor windows:		
a. Broken panes		
b. Locking hardware in working order		
25. Basement windows are protected with grill or well cover.		
26. Doors are locked when classrooms are vacant.		
27. High-risk areas are protected by high security locks and an alarm system		
a. Main office		
b. Cafeteria		
c. Computer labs, information and data protection (records, examinations, etc.)		
d. Industrial arts rooms		
e. Science labs		
f. Nurse's office		
g. Boiler room		
h. Electrical rooms		
i. Phone line access closet		
28. Unused areas of the school can be closed off during after school activities.		
29. There is two-way communication between the main office and:		
a. Classroom (each classroom has a phone or direct intercom connection)		
b. Duty stations		
c. Re-locatable classrooms		
d. Staff and faculty outside building (all locations have communications)		
e. Buses		
30. Students are restricted from loitering in corridors, hallways, and restrooms.		
31. Restricted areas are properly identified.		
32. There are written policies restricting student access to school grounds and buildings.		
SCHOOL INTERIOR AREAS	**YES**	**NO**
33. There is a central alarm system in the school. If yes, briefly describe:		
34. The main entrance is visible from the main office.		
35. There is only one clearly marked and designated entrance for visitors.		
36. Multiple entries to the building are controlled and supervised.		
37. Administrative staff maintain a highly visible profile.		
38. Signage directing visitors to the main office is clearly posted.		

39. Visitors are required to sign in.		
40. Visitors are issued ID cards or badges.		
41. Proper identification is required of vendors, repairmen.		

42. The following areas are properly lighted:
    a. Hallways
    b. Bathrooms
    c. Stairwells		

43. Hallways and bathrooms are supervised by staff.		
44. Doors accessing internal courtyards are securely locked from the inside.		
45. Exit signs are clearly visible and pointing in the correct direction.		
46. Switches and controls are properly located and protected.		
47. Access to electrical panels is restricted.		
48. Faculty members are required to lock classrooms upon leaving.		

49. One person is designated to perform the following security checks at the end of day:
    a. All classrooms and offices are empty and locked
    b. All restrooms are empty
    c. All locker rooms are empty
    d. All exterior entrances are locked
    e. All night lights are working
    f. Check the alarm system		

50. The telephone numbers of the principal or other designated contact person are provided to the police department so the police can make contact in the event of a suspicious or emergency situation.		
51. There is regular maintenance and/or testing of the entire security alarm system at least every six months.		

52. Are classrooms numbered with reflective material:
    a. Over door
    b. On bottom of door
    c. On an exterior window (visible to emergency personnel)		

53. Has consideration been given to replacing present classroom locks with locks that can be activated from the inside?		

54. Does the PA system work properly:
    a. Can it be accessed from several areas in the school
    b. Can it be heard and understood outside		

55. Has consideration been given to establishing a greeters' window inside the first set of exterior doors (must be manned at all time)?		
56. Are convex mirrors used to see around corners in hallways?		
57. Are convex mirrors used to see up and down stairwells?		
58. Do all exterior doors have signs requiring visitors to report to the main office to sign in and obtain ID?		
59. Has consideration been given to installing proximity readers on certain exterior doors?		

60. How do you communicate during emergencies:
    a. Two-way radios
    b. Cell phones
    c. Pagers
    d. Other
61. Who is issued two-way radios:
    a. Administrators
    b. Custodians
    c. Members of the emergency response team
    d. Other
62. There is a control system in place to monitor keys and duplicates.
63. Mechanical rooms and hazardous storage areas are locked.
64. Fire drills are conducted as required by law.		

DEVELOPMENT / ENFORCEMENT OF POLICIES	**YES**	**NO**
65. A visitor policy is in effect, requiring a sign-in procedure for all visitors, including visible identification. All staff members are trained to challenge any visitor without identification. 66. The school has a crisis management plan in effect that is reviewed and updated annually. 67. The incident command system is an integral part of the safety plan. 68. A chain of command has been established for the school when the principal and/or other administrators are away from the building. 69. The school has implemented pro-active security measures on campus, at school-sponsored activities, and on all school property (i.e., school buses). 70. The policy provides a system(s) whereby staff and students may report problems or incidents anonymously. 71. Specific policies and/or procedures are in place that detail staff members' responsibilities for monitoring and supervising students outside the classroom, such as in hallways, cafeteria, rest rooms, etc. 72. The school has implemented and communicated a pro-active policy regarding parental actions during sporting events.		
PROCEDURES FOR DATA COLLECTION	**YES**	**NO**
73. All violations of state and federal law are reported to law enforcement. 74. An incident reporting procedure for disruptive and violent students and incidents has been established in accordance with the local or state requirements.		
INTERVENTION AND PREVENTION PLANS	**YES**	**NO**
75. Students have access to conflict resolution programs. 76. Students are assisted in developing anger management skills. 77. Diversity awareness is emphasized. 78. Students may seek help without the loss of confidentiality.		

	YES	NO
79. Students and staff are aware of bullying consequences and programs are in place to prevent verbal, physical, and non-physical bullying such as emails, threats, and exclusion.		
STAFF DEVELOPMENT	**YES**	**NO**
80. Administrators and staff (including security and law enforcement personnel) are trained in conflict resolution methods.		
81. Administrators and staff (including security and law enforcement personnel) are trained in implementation of the crisis management plan and have that training updated annually.		
82. Administrators and staff are trained in personal safety.		
83. School resource officers (law enforcement) receive in-service training for their responsibilities.		
84. School volunteers receive training to perform their duties.		
85. Teachers and staff are made aware of their legal responsibilities for the enforcement of safety rules, policies, and state and federal laws.		
86. School safety and violence prevention information is regularly provided as part staff development plan.		
87. Staff development opportunities extend to support staff, including cafeteria workers, custodial staff, secretarial staff, and bus drivers.		
OPPORTUNITIES FOR STUDENT INVOLVEMENT	**YES**	**NO**
88. Students are represented on the school safety team.		
89. The school provides opportunities for student leadership related to violence prevention and safety issues.		
90. The school provides adequate recognition opportunities for all students.		
91. Students are adequately instructed in their responsibility to avoid becoming victims of violence (i.e., by avoiding high-risk situations)		
LEVEL OF PARENT AND COMMUNITY INVOLVEMENT	**YES**	**NO**
92. The community supports the school's programs and activities that teach safety and non-violence.		
93. School activities, services, and curricula reflect the characteristics of the students and the community.		
94. School safety planning reflects the neighborhood, including crime and hazardous conditions.		
95. Parents are an integral part of the school's safety planning and policymaking.		
96. Parents are aware of behavioral expectations and are informed of changes in a timely manner.		
97. Local businesses and other community groups are involved in the school's safety planning.		
ROLE OF LAW ENFORCEMENT	**YES**	**NO**
98. Incidents of crime that occur on school property or at school-related events are reported to law enforcement.		

	YES	NO
99. Law enforcement is consulted on matters that may fall below the threshold of criminal activity.		
100. Law enforcement personnel are an integral part of the school's safety planning process. Law enforcement and fire departments have complete current campus maps, floor plans and diagrams showing the location and use of all rooms and critical materials such as chemicals and utility shut-off. Police and fire departments have had tours of the buildings and opportunities to familiarize themselves with the campus.		
101. The school and local law enforcement have developed a written agreement of understanding, defining the roles and responsibilities of both.		
102. Law enforcement personnel provide a visible presence on campus during school hours and at school-related events.		
103. Local law enforcement provides after-hours patrols of the school site.		
DEVELOPMENT OF A CRISIS MANAGEMENT PLAN	**YES**	**NO**
104. The school has a crisis management plan: a. Reviewed on an annual basis b. Developed by the building safety team and reviewed by management. c. Team membership is open to all employees and student representatives		
105. The school has established a well-coordinated emergency plan with law enforcement and other crisis response agencies.		
106. Categories listed in the plan should include, but may not be limited to, the following: a. Natural disasters b. Accidents c. Acts of violence d. Death e. Loss of power f. Fire g. Earthquake		
SAFETY AND SECURITY TEAM NOTES		

CPTED APPLICATIONS FOR SCHOOLS*

4

Timothy D. Crowe

Lawrence J. Fennelly, CPO, CSS, HLS-III

Security expert witness and consultant, Litigation Consultants Inc.

The proper design on effective use of the built environment can lead to a reduction in the fear and incidence of crime, and to an improvement in the quality of life.

Dr. C. Ray Jeffery

INTRODUCTION

There are many examples of CPTED applications. Those that follow are intended to stimulate readers to think of adaptations to their own environmental setting. Each situation is unique, requiring its own individual application of CPTED concepts. No two environmental settings are exactly the same, even though they serve the same function. Accordingly, the reader must use the strategies that make the most sense within each different location. Paul van Soomeren[1] notes that there are many crime-prevention concepts and theories which would aid the practitioner in reducing the fear of crime:

> In Europe…CPTED-like crime-prevention approaches are also known as the situational approach, designing-out crime (DOC), or to stress the more social and organizational aspects of the approach, the reduction of crime by city maintenance, urban planning and architectural design or the Situational Crime Reduction in Partnership Theory, also known as SCRIPT (van Soomeren, 2001).

SITUATIONAL APPROACHES

I (Fennelly) remember, several years ago, when one of my institution's dormitories was experiencing a high frequency of cash and small items being stolen from unlocked rooms. We addressed the problem in two ways:

---

*Portions of this chapter are excerpted from Crowe T. and Fennelly L. Examples of CPTED Strategies and Applications. Crime Prevention Through Environmental Design. Boston, MA: Butterworth-Heinemann; 2013. Updated by the author, 2014.

[1] van Soomeren, Paul. (2013). *Crime Prevention Through Environmental Design*. Boston: Butterworth-Heinemann.

1. First, we took one of our old police cruisers that was no longer in use and parked it right in front of the building. The midnight-to-8 a.m. watch commander was in charge of moving it up and down the roadway so it appeared to be an active vehicle.
2. Second, we did an educational program to get students to lock their dorm rooms.

The thefts stopped and the fear of crime was reduced among the student body. Consider taking positive actions such as the ones from the above example to help alleviate a negative problem.

OBJECTIVES FOR SCHOOL ENVIRONMENTS

1. *Access controls.* Provide secure barriers to prevent unauthorized access to buildings, grounds, or restricted interior areas.
2. *Surveillance through physical design.* Improve opportunities for surveillance by physical design mechanisms that increase the risk of detection for offenders, enable evasive actions by potential victims, and facilitate intervention by police.
3. *Mechanical surveillance devices.* Provide businesses with security devices to detect and signal illegal entry attempts.
4. *Design and construction.* Design, build, or repair buildings and building sites to enhance security and improve quality.
5. *Land use.* Establish policies to prevent ill-advised land and building uses that have a negative impact.
6. *Owner and management action.* Encourage owners and managers to implement safeguards to make businesses and commercial properties less vulnerable to crime.
7. *User protection.* Implement safeguards to make shoppers less vulnerable to crime.
8. *Social interaction.* Encourage interaction among business people, users, and residents of commercial neighborhoods to foster social cohesion and control.
9. *Private security services.* Determine necessary and appropriate services to enhance commercial security.
10. *Police services.* Improve services to efficiently and effectively respond to crime problems and enhance citizen cooperation in reporting crime.
11. *Police and community relations.* Improve police and community relations to involve citizens in cooperative efforts with police to prevent and report crime.
12. *Community awareness.* Create community crime-prevention awareness to aid in combating crime in commercial areas.
13. *Territorial awareness.* Differentiate private areas from public spaces to discourage trespass by potential offenders.
14. *Neighborhood image.* Develop a positive image of the commercial area to encourage user and investor confidence and increase the economic vitality of the area.

CRIME ENVIRONMENTS

Most places have no crime and most crime is highly concentrated and in a relatively small number of places. If we can prevent crime at these high crime places, then we might be able to reduce total crime.[2]

---

[2]Ronald V. Clarke. Hot Products: Understanding, Anticipating and Reducing Demand for Stolen Goods. Police Research Services Paper 112. The Home Office U.K. 1999.

What follows are descriptions of several high-crime environments, their problems, and the appropriate CPTED strategies and design directives.

CRIME ENVIRONMENT: PARKING LOTS

Crimes that commonly occur in parking lots include:

- Assault;
- Theft;
- Breaking and entering; and
- Vandalism.

Crime environment problem

- Location and design of student parking near bus-loading areas without restricting borders promotes unmanaged pedestrian use of parking areas, promotes preemption of space by groups, and prohibits natural surveillance. Assaults, breaking and entering, thefts and vandalism occur (one half of vandalism are incidents with breaking and entering procedures).
- Design and location of parking lots provide unclear definition of transitional zones and unmanaged access by vehicles and pedestrians and students and nonstudents. Breaking and entering, thefts, vandalism and trespassing occur.
- Location of informal gathering areas designated as smoking zones in open corridors adjacent to parking lots and visible from public thoroughfares prohibits natural surveillance, attracts outsiders, and is an impediment to school policies restricting student use of parking lots during school hours. Breaking and entering, thefts, and vandalism occur.
- Isolation of student parking lots (some locations) prohibits any natural surveillance. Variable student hours limit use of fencing and gates. Breaking and entering, thefts, and vandalism occur.

CPTED strategies

- Relocate and/or redesign bus-loading and parking lot access procedures to reduce the necessity of pedestrian use of the lot, reduce congestion in transition zones, and support strict definition of parking lot use.
- Provide natural border definition and limit access to vehicular traffic in student parking and clearly define transitional zones to reroute ingress and egress during specific periods and to provide natural surveillance.
- Relocate informal gathering areas to places with natural surveillance that are isolated from the view of public thoroughfares and designed to support informal gathering activities.
- Relocate student parking (or part of) to areas with natural surveillance and/or locate safe activities in juxtaposition with student parking to increase natural surveillance.
- Redesign parking lots to provide levels of security consistent with variable access needs of the students.
- Remove graffiti within 24 hours and repair vandalism also within 24 hours.

CPTED design directives

- Switch locations between student parking and driver education range.
- Designate access ways to the student parking lot that avoid the bus-loading zone.
- Install hedges around parking lots less than 3′ high.
- Install aesthetically pleasing gates on vehicular access points.

- Set policies to limit student pedestrian use of the parking lots.
- Organize a student/faculty committee to assist in the design and coordination of the border definition and parking lot access control activities.
- Organize a student/faculty committee to assist in the design and coordination of the mini-plaza activities.
- Switch locations between student parking and the driver education range.

CRIME ENVIRONMENT: SCHOOL GROUNDS

Crimes that commonly occur on school grounds include:

- Assault;
- Breaking and entering of motor vehicles as well as the building;
- Bicycle theft;
- Vandalism;
- Buying of drugs; and
- Bullying/harassment/fighting.

Crime environment problem
- Design of and procedures for bus-loading areas prohibit teacher surveillance, increase supervision ratio, impede pedestrian traffic flow, and cause congestion. Confrontations, thefts, and vandalism occur.
- Location of informal gathering areas (natural and designated) promotes the preemption of space, interferes with traffic flow, and prohibits natural surveillance. Assaults occur.
- Design, use, and location of bicycle compounds or parking areas on school grounds prohibit natural surveillance and limit proper use because of students with variable hours. Thefts of bicycles occur.
- Design, use, and location of facilities have created opportunity for breaking and entering, theft, and vandalism to occur. (One half of vandalisms are incidents with breaking and entering.)

CPTED strategies
- Redesign bus-loading zone and service procedures to increase surveillance area for natural surveillance, control pedestrian flow, and decrease the ratio of students to supervisors.
- Remove vandalism within 24 hours.
- Relocate informal gathering areas near supervision or natural surveillance.
- Redesign informal gathering areas to promote orderly flow and breakup the preemption of space by groups.
- Provide functional activities in unused or misused problem areas to promote natural surveillance, increase safe traffic flow, and attract different types of users.
- Provide clear border definition of transitional zones for access control and surveillance.
- Notify the police if drugs are sold on school grounds.
- Provide functional community activities on school campus (off hours) to increase surveillance through effective use of facilities.
- Overcome distance and isolation by improving communications to create rapid response to problems (and its perception) and more effective surveillance.
- Redesign bicycle parking areas to provide levels of security consistent with variable access needs of students.

CPTED design directives

- Create one zone in the surveillance area for loading and unloading students, limited in size to a maximum of 4-5 buses.
- Require bus drivers to allow students to enter or leave their bus only when in a specified loading zone.
- Create a bus queuing zone for waiting buses that is convenient to the loading zone.
- Require teachers on monitoring assignment at the bus-loading zone to direct the movement of buses and to disperse each group of students from the bus-loading area before allowing another group to load and unload.
- Move benches and physical amenities that support informal gatherings from undefined areas to courtyards.
- Relocate the student smoking zone to the interior courtyards.
- Remove conventional picnic tables and benches.
- Install new tables and benches that physically divide the space and size of groups.
- Position amenities to create multiple access and passageways.
- Place ticket booths in problem areas.
- Create mini-plazas in courtyards.
- Organize a student/faculty committee to assist in the design and coordination of mini-plaza activities.
- Install low hedging no higher than 3′ with flowerbeds or ornamental fencing along borders.
- Organize a student/faculty committee to assist in the design and coordination of border definition activities.
- Create a police "school precinct" office.
- Install audio horns for burglar alarm system. Provide portable radios to deans, school resource persons, custodians, and security or law enforcement.
- Create a fenced bicycle cage parking area (secure area).
- Create an open bicycle parking area located in a place with good natural surveillance (nonsecure area).
- Assign students to either a secure or nonsecure bicycle parking area based on their schedules.
- Install ground-level locking devices in each bicycle parking area.
- Set a policy requiring students to utilize a bicycle locking cable or chain.

CRIME ENVIRONMENT: CORRIDORS

Crimes that commonly occur in corridors include:

- Assault;
- Threats; and
- Extortion.

Crime environment problem

- Design and use of corridors provide blind spots and isolated areas that prohibit natural surveillance. Assaults, threats, and extortions occur.
- Class scheduling promotes congestion in certain areas at shift changing that decreases supervision capabilities and produces inconvenience. Assaults and confrontations occur.

- Location of benches and/or other amenities in corridors creates misused space and congestion. Corridor locations are lacking in natural surveillance because of design. Assaults and confrontations occur.
- Location and use of corridors for functions other than pedestrian passage such as smoking zones promote preemption of space by groups and unsurveillable misused space. This misused space supports behavior that attracts outsiders to the external corridors designated as smoking areas. Assaults, confrontations, and other illegal activities occur.
- Design and definition of corridor areas do not support a clear definition of the dominant function of that space (i.e., passage). Unclear transitional zones produce behaviors conducive to assault and confrontation.

CPTED strategies
- Provide functional activities (or re-designate use) in blind spots or isolated areas to increase natural surveillance (or the perception thereof).
- Remove obstacles to natural surveillance (increase perception of openness).
- Revise class scheduling and management procedures to avoid congestion, to decrease supervision ratio, and to define time transitions.
- Relocate informal gathering areas to areas with natural surveillance that are designed to support the particular activity.
- Relocate activities and functions from misused space to areas designed in support of these activities and to provide natural surveillance.
- Provide clear definition of the dominant function (and the intended use of space) and clearly define transitional zones to increase territorial concerns and natural surveillance.

CPTED design directives
- Relocate teacher planning areas.
- Redesign blind spot areas to provide storage spaces for clubs and/or the school administration.
- Install windows in walls along problem corridors.
- Install windows in walls of exterior stairwells.
- Provide a 3-5 minute shift change hiatus between lunch periods.
- Remove benches and other physical amenities from crowded corridors that are over 3′ tall.
- Provide healthy cafeteria food at the gymnasium snack bar.
- Provide multiple access to the snack bar and install queuing lanes.
- Place graphic designs in stairwells and corridors defining the intended function of these spaces.
- Color code various sections of the school and use graphics and art designs uniquely for each functional component of the school.

CRIME ENVIRONMENT: CLASSROOMS

Crimes that commonly occur in classrooms include:

- Assault; and
- Theft.

Crime environment problem

- Design requirements for classrooms produce isolation of individual classes, resulting in high student-to-teacher ratios and little external natural surveillance (real or perceived) when class is in session. Assaults occur. Theft occurs when class is empty.
- Location and design definition of multiple-purpose classrooms produce unclear transitional zones, decreases territorial concern, and decreases natural surveillance. Thefts occur.

CPTED strategies

- Remove obstacles to natural surveillance to increase risk of detection and to reduce perception of isolation.
- Overcome distance and isolation by improving communications to create rapid responses to problems, the perception of rapid response, and more effective surveillance.
- Extend the identity of surrounding spaces to multiple purpose space to increase territorial concern and natural surveillance.
- Provide functional activity in problem areas to increase territorial concern and natural surveillance.

CPTED design directives

- Install windows in classroom walls and doors.
- Provide portable radios to deans, school resource persons, and custodial personnel.
- Install alarm systems in problem classrooms for after hours.
- Color code and graphically identify multiple-purpose classrooms with adjacent spaces.
- Relocate a teacher planning area to each multi-purpose classroom.

CRIME ENVIRONMENT: RESTROOMS

Crimes that commonly occur in restrooms include:

- Assault; and
- Extortion.

Crime environment problem

- Location of restrooms near external entrances and exits isolates them from normal school-hour traffic flow and prohibits surveillance. Assaults occur.
- Privacy and isolation required for internal design provides blind spots that reduce surveillability on the part of students and supervisory personnel (i.e., exterior door and anteroom wall). Assaults occur.

CPTED strategies

- Limit access to isolated areas during specific times for access control and to reduce the need for surveillance.
- Remove obstacles to natural surveillance to decrease fear, increase use, and increase risk of detection.

CPTED design directives

- Organize student/faculty committees by functional component to select and coordinate the graphic design and color coding activities.
- Install collapsible gates at restroom entrances for locking during problem periods.

- Remove entrance doors to restrooms.
- Eliminate unnecessary portions of anteroom walls.

CRIME ENVIRONMENT: LOCKER ROOMS

Crimes that commonly occur in locker rooms include:

- Theft;
- Breaking and entering; and
- Fights/assaults.

Crime environment problem

- Design and use of lockers (by multiple assignment) disperses students throughout the area, reduces surveillance, and increases territory for teacher supervision. Breaking and entering and thefts occur.
- Similar design of lockers creates confusion and decreases natural surveillance by creating unclear definition of transitional zones. Breaking and entering and theft occur.
- Isolation of locker area while class is in gymnasium or on playing field eliminates natural surveillance. Breaking and entering and thefts occur.

CPTED strategies

- Redesignate use of space to increase territorial concern, to increase the defined purpose of space, and to reduce area requiring surveillance.
- Provide clear definition of transitional zones and use of space for easy recognition of bona fide users.
- Provide functional activities in problem areas to increase natural surveillance.

CPTED design directives

- Assign lockers by section, separately for each class.
- Color code locker sections uniquely for each class.
- Relocate a teacher planning area to the physical education offices.
- Assign teachers to the planning area during all classes.

CONCLUSION

This chapter discusses CPTED strategies and design directives for combating crime in schools. Your objective is always to reduce opportunity for a crime to occur or make it harder for a crime to occur. This is done through risk assessment studies, communication, awareness, target hardening, putting controls in place, access control, surveillance, and proper management of the complex.

Below is a list of four proven tactics for the prevention of crime in schools:

1. Support school staff in their efforts to keep guns, knives, and other weapons out of schools.
2. Encourage students to report any weapons they know about on school property to school authorities or to the police.
3. Involve students in issues. Young people can and do organize events against weapons and violence.
4. Show and teach students how to settle arguments without resorting to violence.

AN OVERVIEW OF SCHOOL SAFETY AND SECURITY

Brad Spicer

Chief executive officer, SafePlans, LLC

INTRODUCTION

Protecting schools from violent intruders is complicated and tragically imperfect. There is no one solution and the goal is to identify and streamline the many strategies that can help leaders better protect those around them from acts of violence. Content of this summary is based on best practices and SafePlans' research and experience, which includes planning and training with local, state, and federal agencies, and work with hundreds of school systems across the nation.

As with most emergencies, violent intruders and active shooters are low-volume but high-impact events. Effective intruder response plans are every bit as necessary in a school's all-hazards plan as are fire and severe weather. In the past, schools have relied on lockdown plans to meet this need, but a lockdown alone does not effectively address the complex nature of these attacks.

Because no plan or system can totally protect schools from a violent intruder, the Department of Homeland Security (DHS) provides a three-option approach. The options are Run, Hide, and as a last resort, Fight.

A lockdown is simply compartmentalization and denying access. Lockdown is a valid security concept, but a lockdown cannot help those having direct contact with an attacker in areas that cannot be secured. Further, most schools treat lockdowns as a very passive response—possibly not the best mindset when confronted by a mass killer.

Building-wide response plans work for fire or severe weather because these threats are less dynamic and fluid than a human-based threat. Compartmentalization (lockdown) certainly helps, because an intruder cannot pose a direct threat to an entire school at once. If the threat is in the cafeteria, compartmentalizing students in classrooms may well be the best response. While a building leader may order a building-wide lockdown, every leader in the school needs to understand their specific response may vary depending on their level of contact and location.

Run-Hide-Fight are response options. It should be noted that "response" is just one element of emergency management. Since its evolution from the civil defense days of World War II, emergency management has focused primarily on preparedness. However, like response, preparedness is also only one phase of emergency management. Current thinking defines four phases of emergency management: Prevention-Mitigation, Preparedness, Response, and Recovery (Figure 5.1). The idea is for each phase to make people and places even safer.

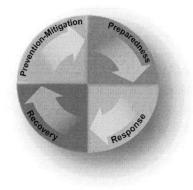

FIGURE 5.1

Four phases of emergency management.

DEFINING THE THREAT

For the purposes of this chapter, attacks may be placed into the category of Insider or Outsider.

- *Insider.* Persons closely affiliated with the target, such as students or former students, carry out Insider attacks. Because of their knowledge of and affiliation with the site, physical security measures can have limited value in preventing Insider attacks. However, this same level of intimacy enables threat assessment programs to be highly effective in preventing Insider attacks.
- *Outsider.* Persons not closely affiliated with the target carry out Outsider attacks. In these instances the site is often viewed as a soft target that is lacking in sufficient physical security measures to dissuade an attack. Because the attacker is not closely affiliated with the site, it is highly unlikely information has been presented to warrant a threat assessment.

Unfortunately, no amount of physical security can stop every Outsider attack and even the most robust threat assessment programs can fail to identify potentially violent behavior in time to stop all Insider attacks. Therefore, it is vital that all facilities implement intruder response plans and training to mitigate the impact of a violent intruder and maximize survivability for occupants.

CORE RECOMMENDATIONS FOR PREVENTION AND MITIGATION
THREAT ASSESSMENT PROGRAMS

Threat assessment is the process of determining the likelihood that any given event will escalate to violence. Threat assessment should be looked upon as one component in an overall strategy to reduce targeted school violence.

All schools should develop a threat assessment team to assess potentially violent behavior. To ensure this behavior is reported, each school should develop a reporting process and provide awareness training to all staff.

PHYSICAL SECURITY

Physical security is a vital component of preventing and mitigating acts or violence and should include multiple layers. While there are many components, considerations for schools include: security assessments, law enforcement, private security, access control (building and classroom), and video surveillance.

CORE RECOMMENDATIONS FOR PREPAREDNESS
MINIMUM SAFETY STANDARDS

Schools should institute formal policies that establish minimum safety standards. This policy should eliminate any ability for staff to allow deviation from accepted best practices, such as securing non-primary entrances or reporting concerning behavior. This policy will also help to shield leaders from pushback regarding inconveniences as a result of these enhanced security measures.

COMMUNITY COLLABORATION

Schools should coordinate with the local emergency management and public safety agencies to coordinate the implementation of emergency plans and establish response protocols.

STANDARDIZE EMERGENCY PLANS

Schools should work with partner agencies to develop and maintain site/building emergency plans that embrace the National Incident Management System (NIMS) guidelines. Minimum requirements include coordination of planning efforts, use of the Incident Command System, planning for special needs populations, and expansion beyond the outdated "lockdown" response to violent intruders.

EMERGENCY TRAINING AND DRILLS

Sites should conduct additional emergency drills that include a minimum of two intruder response drills annually.

CORE RECOMMENDATIONS FOR RESPONSE
BEST PRACTICE INCIDENT RESPONSE PLANS

All sites should develop intruder response plans that expand upon basic lockdown principles and include instruction for evacuation and may include fighting back as a last resort.

TACTICAL SITE MAPPING DATA

First responders should be provided access to tactical site mapping data (i.e., floor plans, images, utility shutoffs, etc.) to improve response times.

VIDEO SURVEILLANCE

Measures should be taken to provide law enforcement remote access to on-site video surveillance to enhance tactical response capabilities.

CORE RECOMMENDATIONS FOR RECOVERY
FAMILY REUNIFICATION

One of the first steps to recovery is safely and efficiently reuniting students with their families. Districts should have detailed plans to accomplish family reunification.

MENTAL HEALTH PLANS

Plans should identify mental health resources and detail how they can be applied to incidents of violence involving students.

CONTINUITY OF OPERATIONS

Plans should identify continuity of operations needs and detail how they can be applied should a violent attack occur.

PREVENTION AND MITIGATION

The Federal Emergency Management Agency's (FEMA) definitions of prevention and mitigation (Figure 5.2) are as follows:

> Prevention: Actions to avoid an incident or to intervene to stop an incident from occurring.
> Mitigation: Activities to reduce the loss of life and property from natural and/or human-caused disasters by avoiding or lessening the impact of a disaster and providing value to the public by creating safer communities.[1]

FIGURE 5.2

Prevention and mitigation.

[1]"Glossary," Federal Emergency Management Agency (FEMA), accessed March 27, 2014, http://training.fema.gov/EMIWeb/emischool/EL361Toolkit/glossary.htm.

When someone hears the words "Columbine" or "Sandy Hook" they are likely to remember school shootings. While both were the scenes of horrible attacks, most similarities stop there. The shooting at Columbine high school was an Insider attack that was carried out by students who were part of the Columbine school community. The shooting at Sandy Hook Elementary School was carried out by someone whose only affiliation with the elementary school appears to have been geographic.

Anything short of federal courthouse-level physical security is unlikely to have stopped the Columbine killings, but there were numerous warning signs. There is no reason to think that the staff at Sandy Hook Elementary could have observed any warning signs from Adam Lanza (the shooter), but more robust physical security could have deterred his attack or, at a minimum, sufficiently delayed his entry to allow the implementation of a more successful intruder response plan.

THREAT ASSESSMENT

The goal of a threat assessment is to determine if someone *poses* a threat, not simply to verify if they have made a threat. This is, perhaps, the most proactive thing a school can do to improve safety. A threat assessment is a proactive approach to assessing, evaluating, and intervening in a potentially violent situation by assigning a degree of dangerousness.

At SafePlans, we have helped hundreds of districts develop formal threat assessment teams using resources such as Gavin de Becker & Associates MOSAIC tool (https://www.mosaicmethod.com) and the Secret Service Safe School Initiative (http://www.secretservice.gov/ntac_ssi.shtml). Both offer a great deal to help schools predict violent behavior and prevent attacks.

In his book *The Gift of Fear*, Gavin de Becker outlines a simple and powerful way to efficiently assess the seriousness and dangerousness of a high stakes prediction. The approach is called JACA and every school leader should consider this approach when trying to determine if a person is truly dangerous.

JACA is an acronym for Justification, Alternatives, Consequences, and Ability. These are elements that exist when there is a serious risk of violent behavior. Apply JACA from the viewpoint of the person you are assessing, not your own, and answer the following questions:

- *Justification.* Does the person feel justified in taking violent action?
- *Alternatives.* Does the person feel there are alternatives to violence?
- *Consequences.* Is the person concerned about the consequences of a violent action?
- *Ability.* Does the person have the ability to carry out an attack?

Indication of dangerousness

0 JACA elements present: No threat
1 JACA elements present: Mild threat (Monitor)
2 JACA elements present: Moderate threat (Refer for Full Assessment)
3 JACA elements present: Severe threat (Refer for Full Assessment)
4 JACA elements present: Profound threat (Refer for Full Assessment)

JACA is simply a snapshot, and in no way replaces the need for school districts to develop a formal and comprehensive threat assessment program that includes student and faculty awareness training, a formal reporting process, a trained multidisciplinary threat assessment team and a case management program.

The Secret service's safe school initiative

After the Columbine shooting, the United States' Secret Service and the Department of Education implemented the Safe School Initiative (SSI) and offered suggestions for schools and parents. According to the *Final Report and Findings of the Safe School Initiative*, "to the extent that information about an attacker's intent and planning is knowable and may be uncovered before an incident, some attacks may be preventable."[2] While the finding may seem innocuous, the fact that acts of targeted violence are not impulsive means there are opportunities to observe behavior and intervene before the attacks are carried out.

10 Core findings of the safe school initiative[3]

1. Targeted school shootings are not impulsive acts.
2. Prior to most incidents, the attacker told someone about his idea and/or plan.
3. Most attackers did not communicate *direct threats* to their targets prior to the attack.
4. There is no accurate or useful profile.
5. Prior to the attack, most shooters were observed engaging in some behavior that caused others concern, or indicated a need for help.
6. Most shooters had difficulty coping with significant personal loss or personal failures.
7. Many attackers felt persecuted or injured by others prior to the attack.
8. Most attackers had access to, and had used, firearms prior to the attack.
9. In many cases, other students were involved in, or had prior knowledge of the attack.
10. Despite prompt responses, most attacks were stopped by means other than law enforcement intervention and were brief in duration.

Conclusion of the safe school initiative

Targeted violence is the end result of an understandable, and oftentimes discernable, process of thinking and behavior.[4]

The fact that most attackers engaged in preincident planning behavior and shared their intentions and plans with others suggests that those conducting threat assessment inquiries or investigations could uncover this type of information.

In order for threat assessment to be effective, concerning behavior must be reported. At SafePlans, we encourage districts to incorporate a See Something-Say Something program to encourage reporting of any behavior that causes concern for your safety or the safety of the others. For example, in the case of immediate danger or threat, faculty should call 911. For nonemergency concerns, faculty, or staff should contact the building principal or other specific person or a dedicated tip line.

---

[2]"The Final Report and Findings of The Safe School Initiative," United States Secret Service and United States Department of Education, May 2002, page 32, http://www.secretservice.gov/ntac/ssi_final_report.pdf.
[3]Ibid, pages 11-12.
[4]"Threat Assessment in Schools: A Guide to Managing Threatening Situations and to Creating Safe School Environments," United States Secret Service and United States Department of Education, May 2002, page 29, http://www.secretservice.gov/ntac/ssi_guide.pdf.

Table 5.1 Behavioral Symptoms That May Cause Concern	
• Noticeable change in quality of work • Significant change in mood • Inappropriate outbursts • Bizarre written or verbal statements • Inappropriate use of violent themes/subjects • Persistent unwanted contact • Feelings of hopelessness or helplessness • Trouble sleeping and/or eating	• Appears disoriented • Depressed or lethargic mood • Hyperactivity or very rapid speech • Verbal or written references to suicide • Isolation from friends, family or classmates • Prepares for death by making a will or final arrangements • Gives away personal belongings and prized possessions

Table 5.2 Signs That May Warrant Intervention	
• Making threats of suicide or statements about hurting one's self • Making threats of violence, directly or implied • Expressing fascination with firearms or asserting ownership of firearms • Having a history of violence or behavior obviously insensitive to others • Preoccupation with television, music, and/or stories about violence • Identify with criminal or terrorist individuals, acts and/or philosophy • Making references and maintain preoccupation with other incidents of publicized violence (collecting articles or photos, showing fascination with perpetrators of these events, etc.)	• Crossing boundaries (e.g., excessive phone calls or emails, impromptu visits, inappropriate gifts) • Being easily provoked, showing sudden or erratic agitation with others • Blaming others for things that go wrong and has no sense of personal responsibility • Marked academic performance decline • Demonstrate notable changes in personality, mood, or behavior • Give away personal possessions • Shows noticeable decline in hygiene • Substance abuse • Family or relationship conflicts • Intimidating others, frequently confrontational

What is meant by concerning behaviors

Although the terms, "concerning," "worrisome," and "threatening" are subjective in nature, the list of examples in Table 5.1 provides some context when assessing whether a student may need additional support.

PREVENTING VIOLENCE

There is no 100% proven method of predicting when someone may become violent. Listed in Table 5.2 are some indicators or signs that may warrant closer attention and possibly intervention. It is important to consider the context of the warning signs, such as tone of voice and your level of familiarity with the person making the troubling statements.

PHYSICAL SECURITY IN SCHOOLS

For the purpose of this chapter, *physical security* describes measures implemented with the goal of protecting people and property inside a school. A primary goal of physical security is managing access to prevent unauthorized or undesired entry. Physical security includes human resources (such as law enforcement), hardware (doors and locks), and electronics (video and electronic access control).

Security cannot be implemented without costs, and security can never eliminate all risks. A balance must be struck to provide a reasonable degree of protection within a sustainable budget. While partial physical security measures can provide some value, security is best achieved with a layered approach. Physical access controls for protected facilities are generally intended to:

- Deter potential intruders (e.g., warning signs and perimeter markings)
- Distinguish authorized from unauthorized people (e.g., using badges and keys)
- Delay, frustrate and ideally prevent intrusion attempts (e.g., minimal number of entrances, law enforcement presence, and door locks)
- Detect intrusions and monitor/record intruders (e.g., intruder alarms and video surveillance systems)
- Trigger appropriate incident responses (e.g., by security and law enforcement).

The tried and true method of evaluating a facility's security is through a security vulnerability assessment. In some states, these are called safety audits or just security assessments. These assessments should help to identify security strengths and vulnerabilities. At SafePlans, we use our web-based Emergency Response Information Portal (www.safeplans.com/about-ERIP) to conduct and manage these assessments. No matter how the assessments are completed, they need to be comprehensive and the party conducting the assessment needs to be an honest broker.

The exact questions in the assessments vary, but in general terms they should touch on the following (Figure 5.3):

- *Building Exterior*
  - Area Hazards
  - Grounds and Location
  - Perimeter

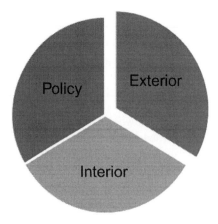

FIGURE 5.3

General areas of security assessments.

  - Exterior Doors and Entrance Ways
  - Trailers/Portable Classrooms
  - Buses, Drop Off and Parking Areas
  - Stadiums & Recreations Areas
- *Building Interior*
  - Building Access
  - Surveillance
  - Communications
  - School-Based Law Enforcement and Security
  - Visitor Procedures
  - Building Layout and Construction
  - Cafeteria
  - Gymnasium
  - Science Lab
  - Materials/Supplies
  - Specialized Areas
  - Hallways and Stairs
  - Restrooms
- *Policy*
  - State Compliance
  - Emergency Operations Plan and Training
  - Specific Procedures for Core Emergencies
  - Drills
  - Parental Reunification
  - School Code of Conduct
  - Information Security
  - Staff and Student Training
  - Health Practices
  - Outsourcing of Security
  - School Climate Interview (Bullying)

Since the Sandy Hook Elementary shooting, more schools are considering physical security updates, especially to main entrances. When considering the overarching security plan for any campus, Crime Prevention Through Environmental Design (CPTED) is a great place to start. CPTED has been around since 1970s and while the term was coined by criminologist C. Ray Jeffery, the principles in practice today are a combination of multidisciplinary efforts. Some key components of CPTED that related to more secure entrances include:

Natural surveillance
People are less likely to commit crimes if they feel they are being observed. Natural surveillance involves designing features to maximize the visibility of areas that should be observed.

Access control
Limiting and regulating entrances reduces opportunities for crime and allows for more efficient screening of persons entering a facility.

Territoriality

Clear delineation of space creates a sense of ownership for legitimate users (staff and students) and creates an environment where intruders are more likely to standout.

CPTED is much broader than these three basic concepts, but they do serve as a strong basis for creating more secure entrances.

Eleven components of more secure school entrances

These 11 items are not a guarantee against forced entry, and a secured main entrance does not a safe school make. Just as there are other elements of CPTED and physical security, there are other considerations, beyond active shooters, that schools must consider when developing security plans and all-hazards emergency plans. It is also important to note that these recommendations do not include the assignment of personnel, such as law enforcement or security.

A full-site security assessment or safety audit is the most effective way to identify security-related strengths and weaknesses of your campus. This assessment should serve as the basis for short- and long-term enhancements. School districts and/or large campuses should implement a standardized assessment process for all facilities in order to prioritize recommendations based on vulnerabilities.

Consider unintended consequences and coordinate all security and emergency planning efforts with and by local public safety agencies. Implementing a new access control system may keep intruders out, but it can also make it difficult for law enforcement to gain rapid entry. The benefits of better access control easily outweigh the highly manageable risk of delaying law enforcement, but a degree of planning is required.

1. *Perimeter fencing to deter trespass and limit access to non-primary entrances.*
   Fencing should encourage entry via highly visible and well-monitored areas, preferably those that are under video surveillance. While fencing does not prevent unauthorized access, it does make persons approaching the facility from undesired areas more obvious (Figure 5.4). The Secret Service will, at times, use theater-style ropes to block off an area. Obviously, a would-be attacker could easily cross the rope line. However, this act would draw the attention of the agents. People should have to make some effort and announce their presence if they enter your perimeter.

FIGURE 5.4

Highly visible fencing.

2. *Single point of entry.*

   Effective access control requires that entry to and from a facility be regulated. A single point of entry allows for such monitoring. Efforts to mitigate forced entry via the primary entrance are marginalized if secondary points of entry are unsecure or easily defeated.

   Some buildings require multiple points of entry. That is understandable; just realize that all points of entry must be regulated. For a point of entry to be regulated, no unauthorized person should pass through without drawing the attention of those responsible for the safety of the building.

   If you cannot regulate all entrances, measures must be taken to regulate access at the campus level (extending the security perimeter) while ensuring each classroom operates with locked doors. Sites that cannot regulate access must be given priority when considering assignment of law enforcement or security personnel.

3. *Staff monitoring of arrival and dismissal times.*

   Arrival and dismissal times require a lower security posture due to the volume of student and staff movement. Properly trained and equipped staff must be assigned to monitor activities during these periods. This requires training on intruder response, reverse evacuation, and how to assist in the arrival of public safety vehicles. Staff should be equipped with a radio to communicate with building/office staff and a phone for calling 911.

4. *Strong visitor management program.*

   Regulating access to a school requires sound visitor management procedures. At a minimum, visitors should not be able to enter the school without registering at the main office. This should require proof of identification and the issuance of a visitor badge, and visitors should be escorted.

   Visitor management programs should include prominent signage on all building entrances (Figure 5.5), visitor parking areas, and even parking lot entrances. Let visitors know your expectations.

5. *Use of a vestibule/double entry system.*

   The intercom/video call box is located outside the school. Visitors are granted access upon approval from the main office. Ideally, visitors granted access through the primary entrance are required to

FIGURE 5.5

Prominent visitor management signage.

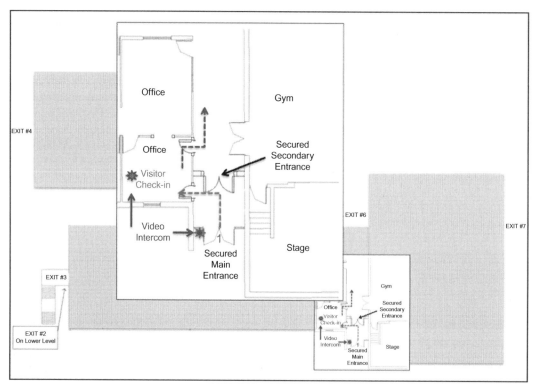

FIGURE 5.6

Visitors must pass through the main office before entering the school.

pass through the main office (Figure 5.6). The office would allow visitors to enter the first entrance but the secondary entrance would remain locked.

6. *Minimal glass.*

   Large windows and vision panels, while visually attractive, are easily defeated. Minimizing glass presents a more secure image and makes forced entry more difficult (Figure 5.7). General guidelines for the use of glass in main entrances are:

   (a) Full windows should be a minimum 72″ off ground.

   (b) Narrow windows/vision panels, below 72″ should be a maximum 12″ wide.

   (c) Install security window film to reinforce glass on main entrances.

7. *Electronic Access Control (EAC).*

   In its simplest form, an EAC system consists of an electronic door lock and some form of electronic verification device. The verification device can be an entry pad, card reader, biometric scanner, or even a video camera. Once a predefined criterion is met (i.e., a code is entered or a secretary looks at the screen and recognizes the person) the verification device communicates with the electronic door lock to allow entry.

   The use of EAC will allow desired users, such as staff with proper access rights, to utilize the entrance without authorization from the main office. It is critical to coordinate with local public safety to ensure they have proper access rights and capabilities.

FIGURE 5.7

Reduced glass on main entrances presents a more secure image.

8. *Video intercoms for visitor screening.*

    A video intercom system allows staff to see and talk with visitors before admitting them into the secured school. By determining a visitor's identity before unlocking the door, staff can avoid face-to-face confrontations with a possibly dangerous individual.

    Staff responsible for this preliminary security screening requires the backing of leadership. They need to know they are expected to ask questions and have the obligation to delay or even deny access to the school if they are not 100% certain the person does not pose a risk.

9. *Door hardware.*

    The center mullion is the vertical element between double doors. A sturdy center mullion is vital to the integrity of locked doors. Door handles and push bars should be flush with the door to prevent them from being tied together to delay law enforcement or prevent emergency egress.

10. *Panic button in office.*

    Panic or duress buttons (Figure 5.8) make it easier for school staff to notify law enforcement than calling 911 and allow more communication efforts to be directed toward safeguarding students.

    If your school is totally dependent upon front office staff to provide notification of an intruder situation, consider expanding the panic button to a full intruder alarm that broadcasts a unique warning to the entire school.

11. *Situational awareness*

    Not all elements of security rely on CPTED or hardware. Situational awareness is the ability to identify, process, and comprehend the critical elements of information about what is happening around you. This generally provides greater opportunities to prevent or at least mitigate the threat.

    Situational awareness is an attitude, not a hard skill. It is something we all have some of the time and something none of us has all of the time. Jeff Cooper pioneered the concept of levels of situational awareness. Cooper was a marine and innovator of tactical training. He developed a color code system to illustrate levels of alertness. This system is called Cooper's Color Codes (Table 5.3) and it has been used to train military and law enforcement personnel for decades.

FIGURE 5.8

Panic button.

Table 5.3 Cooper's Color Codes	
White	Unprepared and unready
Yellow	Prepared, alert and relaxed. Good situational awareness
Orange	Specific alert to probably danger. Ready to take action
Red	Action Mode. Totally committed to the emergency at hand
Black	System overload. Total breakdown of physical and mental performance

Situational awareness is a key element in intruder response. The following hypothetical example illustrates the value of situational awareness:

A person is going to a school to commit carry out an attack. You cannot change that he is coming, but you can determine when you observe his intent. When would you want to make this observation?

At the parking lot or at the front door? The front door or the hallway?
Hallway or classroom?
The sooner you are aware of the danger, the more time and options you have to respond.

PREPAREDNESS

The FEMA definition of preparedness (Figure 5.9) is:

A continuous cycle of planning, organizing, training, equipping, exercising, evaluating, and taking corrective action in an effort to ensure effective coordination during incident response.[5]

[5]"Glossary," Federal Emergency Management Agency (FEMA), accessed March 27, 2014, http://training.fema.gov/EMIWeb/emischool/EL361Toolkit/glossary.htm.

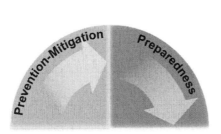

FIGURE 5.9

Preparedness.

The Preparedness phase includes actions that will improve your chances of successfully dealing with an emergency. As noted in FEMA's definition, preparedness is a continuous cycle of planning, organizing, training, equipping, exercising, evaluation, and improvement activities to ensure effective coordination and the enhancement of capabilities to prevent, protect against, respond to, recover from, and mitigate the effects of natural disasters, acts of terrorism, and other man-made disasters.

ALL-HAZARDS PLANS

While active shooter events are rare, more students have died from acts of violence in U.S. K-12 schools over the last 50 years than have died from bus crashes, fires, and severe weather events in U.S. schools combined. Schools absolutely need all-hazards plans, but these plans must contain robust plans to address human-based threats and violent intruders.

RUN/HIDE/FIGHT

If you are ever confronted with a violent intruder or active shooter situation, you will need a plan. While no plan can totally protect schools, the Department of Homeland Security (DHS) provides a three-option approach. The options are Run, Hide, and as a last resort, Fight.

As mentioned earlier, lockdown is simply compartmentalization and denying access. Lockdown is a valid security concept, but a lockdown cannot help those having direct contact with an attacker of those in areas that cannot be secured. A lockdown falls under the Hide category and is a component of intruder response, but a lockdown does not help those at the point of the attack—those at the greatest risk.

The good news about compartmentalization is that an attacker cannot be everywhere. If the threat is in the cafeteria, compartmentalizing students in classrooms may well be the best response. A lockdown should be viewed as an element of the Hide response, not as your only option.

APPLYING RUN-HIDE-FIGHT

Run-Hide-Fight is not a linear progression. A misperception of Run-Hide-Fight is that Run is always your first option. Going back to the shooter in the cafeteria scenario, while the students in the cafeteria should be directed to run, students in classrooms may need to implement a hide. Response is based on two key factors: your proximity to the threat (contact) and your location.

$$Contact + Location = Response$$

Contact

The most critical element in determining your response to an active shooter is your *proximity* to the threat—what's between you and the attacker. Proximity is divided into two types:

- *Direct Contact*. There are no barriers between your location and the intruder and the intruder is close enough to pose an immediate danger.
- *Indirect Contact*. The intruder is inside or near your facility/general area but distance or barriers delay the intruder's ability to harm you.

Location

The next important considerations address your abilities to secure your location and to escape. Obviously there are many different types of locations where attacks can occur; and this chapter classifies all locations into two types—securable and nonsecurable locations:

- *Securable Location*. A location that can provide a degree of protection from an intruder. This includes rooms with doors that may be secured and has minimal interior windows from the hallway to the room. A securable location is conducive to a *Hide* or *lockdown* response. (Note for more rural areas [response time over 5 minutes]: For a location to be deemed securable, it should be able to deny entry for as long as it will take law enforcement to arrive. School planners must coordinate with local law enforcement to estimate response times and analyze the ability to secure rooms.)

- *Nonsecurable Location*. A location that offers no protection from an intruder. This includes hallways or common spaces that do not have doors that could be secured. A nonsecurable location does not deny access and is not conducive to a Hide.

GENERAL INTRUDER RESPONSE GUIDELINES

No plan can cover every scenario. Run-Hide-Fight should be viewed as options (Figure 5.10). Only the exact scenario, your level of contact, and your location can determine your best response (Contact + Location = Response).

Run

Initiate a running evacuation when:

- You have direct contact with the intruder.
- You cannot lock the intruder out of your location.

Hide

Barricade or secure your area to delay the intruder if:

- You have *indirect* contact with the intruder.
- You can deny access/stop the intruder from entering.

Violent Intruder
- **Call 911** (when safe to do so)
- **Alert & Help Others** (as you can)

RUN
- ✓ **Direct Contact** *or*
- ✓ **Can't Secure Area** *or*
- ✓ **Clear Escape Path**

Avoid contact with the intruder.

HIDE
- ✓ **Indirect Contact** *and*
- ✓ **Able to Secure Area**
- ✓ Deny Access!

Lock/tie off/barricade doors.

FIGHT
- ✓ **LAST RESORT**
- ✓ **Direct Contact** *and*
- ✓ **Cannot Run** *and*
- ✓ **Risk to Life**

Lead others, resist & fight back!

© 2013 Safeplans.com

FIGURE 5.10

SafePlans provides these cards following trainings. These cards are a subtle reminder of the training. www.safeplans.com.

Fight

As a last resort, when lives are in immediate danger, FIGHT if:

- You have direct contact, and you are in fear for your safety or the safety of others.
- You CANNOT RUN.

SafePlans does *not* recommend training K-12 students in the Fight option. As with any emergency, schools should prepare themselves on how to provide best direction and control over their students should Fight be required. Some students are physically capable of assisting, but the amount of time needed to train students on *when* to Fight is not easily justified by the risk. Training students in Run and Hide greatly improves upon the basic lockdown, making a Fight scenario even less likely.

RUN

One of the most common questions about Run/Hide/Fight is whether the entire school should always try to run or evacuate as a first response to a violent intruder or active shooter. The short answer is: No.

The Department of Homeland Security (DHS) presents Run-Hide-Fight as individual options, not building-wide action plans. When presenting Run (or evacuate) (Figure 5.11), DHS says to try and evacuate if there is an accessible escape path. A hallway packed with students (and a possible killer) may not be a path of escape. At a minimum it is never *always* a path of escape.

FIGURE 5.11

Run.

FIGURE 5.12

Hide.

During an active shooter attack, some people inside the school will likely need to implement Run. However, a building-wide strategy to Run is only slightly better than a building-wide strategy to Hide (lockdown).

It is understandable why many want to provide one simple instruction in response to a violent intruder. Building-wide action steps work for fire (evacuate) or severe weather (shelter in place), but intruder response plans must have options. Remember, Run-Hide-Fight are options, not a linear system. During an active shooter event, persons in different locations will experience circumstances that require them to implement different actions. For instance, if there is a violent intruder in the cafeteria, Run would be the best response for those in the cafeteria (direct contact). At the same time, the best response for teacher in a classroom (indirect contact) may be to Hide by locking or even barricading the classroom door.

The level of contact with the attacker and the staff member's location determines the best response—not an intercom announcement or mass message. Remember: Contact + Location = Response.

While one-size-fits-all responses are convenient, they simply do not provide occupants the maximum opportunity to survive.

HIDE

The Hide option should be viewed as an active response. In a Hide situation you are trying to deny the attacker access to you and others. A Hide response (Figure 5.12) is not simply hide and seek. It is like hide and seek with no rules. Lock doors whenever you can, but even if you cannot lock doors, there are still ways to deny entry. This is called impromptu target hardening and it can save your life. Embrace your inner MacGyver and deny entry!

If you are in an area where you cannot deny entry, such as a hallway or area with no doors, you should strongly consider implementing the Run response and make every effort to avoid contact with the intruder. Trying to hide under tables or behind curtains may not make you safer. It will create a passive and stationary target for the attacker. Stationary targets are easier to shoot and more likely to receive fatal wounds. Again, if you cannot deny entry, strongly consider the Run option and avoid contact with the attacker.

Barricade

Doors that open inward are typically easy to barricade. A barricade may prevent the door from being opened (Figure 5.13). Place heavy objects in front of the door and never use your body to support the barricade. The contents of the room will likely determine the success of a barricade.

Blockade

For doors that open outward, you may be able to place a blockade in the doorway. Place heavy objects in doorway and never use your body to support the blockade (Figure 5.14). While the intruder may be able to open the door, he will have to contend with the blockade. The contents of the room will likely determine the success of a blockade.

FIGURE 5.13

Barricade the door with heavy objects in the room.

FIGURE 5.14

A blockade may slow down or deny entry to an attacker.

Tie Off

Tie off the door by looping a belt, computer cable, or extension cord (or keep 20 ft of 550/Para cord in your desk) around the door handle. Either tie off to a solid fixed object or pull the door closed (Figure 5.15). Your size and strength may not be enough—so get help.

FIGHT

Violent intruders are very rare and the Hide and Run options greatly improve upon the basic lockdown. However, when it is not possible to Run or Hide, you must Fight (Figure 5.16) back against the attacker. The Fight option is about resisting and not allowing the attacker to have access to passive targets that are easy to shoot and kill. The Fight option is not grabbing a chair and running down a hallway to find the shooter. The Fight option is the last resort of resisting with physical aggression to protect lives when you cannot Run or deny access (Hide).

When fighting back, it is possible that people will be injured or even killed. However, if you do nothing, it is likely that more people will be injured and killed.

When you must Fight, remember the following:

- Commit to fighting back.
- Lead others to help.
- Provide clear and confident instructions.
- Use improvised weapons, such as fire extinguishers, chairs, and books.
- Act with aggression until the threat is incapacitated.

FIGURE 5.15

Tie off a door to prevent entry.

FIGURE 5.16

Fight.

When law enforcement arrives on the scene, remember:

- Their response to an intruder situation is focused on locating and neutralizing the threat.
- **DO NOT** leave a secure area to approach responders.
- All persons may be treated as suspects until determined otherwise.
- Keep hands raised, with your fingers spread.
- Do not make sudden movements.
- Follow law enforcement commands.
- Provide detailed information as appropriate.

OPERATIONAL ENVIRONMENT ANALYSIS

Now that you understand the basic Run-Hide-Fight options, becoming more familiar with your environment will help improve response efficiency. An operational environment analysis is a simple approach to gaining a better understanding of your Run-Hide-Fight options. Every principal should be able to explain how to apply Run-Hide-Fight in every area of his or her school. Teachers should be able to explain Run-Hide-Fight in his or her classroom, hallways, and common areas.

Figure 5.17 shows the K-12 Operational Environment Analysis form we use at SafePlans.

RESPONSE

The FEMA definition of response (Figure 5.18) is:

> Activities that address the short-term, direct effects of an incident. Response includes immediate actions to save lives, protect property, and meet basic human needs.[6]

Organizational response to any significant disaster—natural or terrorist-borne—is based on existing emergency management organizational systems and processes. There is a need for both discipline (structure, doctrine, process) and agility (creativity, improvisation, adaptability) in responding to a disaster.

Emergency plans help educators prepare for and manage critical incidents. However, no emergency plan can cover every possible scenario. Ideally, training programs simulate real emergencies. But too often schools train to do extremely well under reasonable conditions—rather than training to perform reasonably well under extreme conditions. Real emergencies are extreme conditions, and when they occur, the ability to make sound decisions rapidly is imperative.

A valuable system in understanding the importance of *proper* timely decisions in a critical incident is the Observe-Orient-Decide-Act (OODA) loop (sometimes referred to as Boyd's Cycle after its creator, retired U.S. Air Force Col. John Boyd) (Figure 5.19). Being a student of and expert on tactical operations, Boyd detailed that in many of the battles, when one side is not able to keep up with the ever-changing dynamics of a combat situation, that slower-to-react side was almost always defeated.

---

[6]Ibid.

SafePlans

Location & Function	
HIDE	☐ **Area Cannot Be Secured.** **Nearest securable area:** _____ ☐ **Area May Be Secured (Complete Section)**
	Can you lock the room from inside? ☐ Yes. ☐ No.

	Do you need a key?
	☐ Yes.
	☐ No.
	   Do you always have the key?
	     ☐ Yes.
	     ☐ No.

	Can this room serve its purpose while remaining shut and locked? ☐ Yes. Door should remain locked whenever possible ☐ No.
	If it cannot be locked at all times, can the door remain locked, but in the open position? ☐ Yes. Door should remain locked position so when the door is pulled closed it is locked. ☐ No.
	Glass vision panel(s) that can be defeated to gain entry? ☐ Yes. ☐ No.

	Can the door be reinforced with a barricade or tie off?
	☐ **Door swing into room= Barricade**
	   ☐ **Locate desks or heavy objects for barricade.**
	☐ **Door swing into hallway=Tie off**
	   ☐ **Place to stand while holding the tie off that is out of view from the hallway?**
	   ☐ **Locate extension cord or computer cable for tie off**

RUN	**Primary exit from this room/location:** **In a Run/Get Out the nearest securable area is:** **Secondary exit from this room/location:** ☐ **No secondary exit (no other doors or windows)** ☐ **Windows (ensure they can be opened and less than a 10 ft. drop)**
FIGHT	**Available improvised weapons:** ☐ Chairs ☐ Fire Extinguisher ☐ Books ☐ Impact tools (sticks/poles) ☐ Other:

Intruderology™: Operational Environment Analysis
©SafePlans, LLC   www.safeplans.com

FIGURE 5.17

Operational Environment Analysis form.

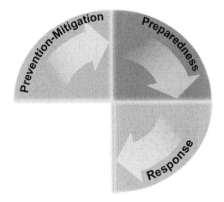

FIGURE 5.18

Response.

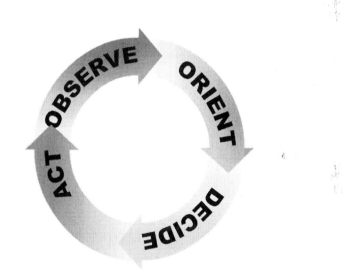

FIGURE 5.19

Observe-Orient-Decide-Act loop.

In observing this, Boyd concluded that timely decision making is critically important and applied the phrase "time-competitive."

According to Boyd's theory, emergency response can be seen as a series of time-competitive, OODA cycles. Response begins by *observing* the overall situation. *Orientation* is next. Orientation is critical because the dynamic nature of an emergency makes it impossible to process information as quickly as it is observed. Orientation can be thought of as a snapshot approach to obtaining perspective. Once orientation is gained, it is time to *decide*. The decision considers all factors that were present during the orientation phase. Lastly, the final process is to *act* on the decision.

The "loop" occurs when our actions have changed the situation. The cycle continues throughout an incident.

OBSERVE

The earlier you can *observe* someone intending to harm you or others, the greater your opportunity to survive. Observations can be visual or audible, anything that alerts you to possible danger. This ties into situational awareness mentioned earlier in this chapter.

ORIENT

Orientation is about making the best connection between your observations and your response options. Unfortunately, the more immediate the threat, the faster you must orient. Fortunately, in an active shooter situation response options are Run, Hide, and Fight. Orientation to which response is most appropriate is based on your level of contact with the intruder and your location.

DECIDE

Your *decision* is based on what you observe and how you orient those observations to your environment and abilities. For those not in direct contact with the shooter, and in a room that can be secured by a locked or barricaded door, Hide is typically the best response. If you are in an area that cannot be secured and you are *not* being attacked, you should Run to an area that offers safety. Persons in direct contact cannot Hide from the shooter. They must either Run or, if running is not an option, Fight as a last resort.

ACT

Once the decision is made, it is time to *act*. Have confidence in knowing your actions are based on the best information available. Do not second-guess yourself, but have the presence of mind to repeat the OODA loop as your observations change. For instance, if you have to Fight as a last resort and the shooter flees, your OODA analysis may very well be to disengage and retreat to a safer area. Conversely, if you decide to Hide in a room and the shooter attempts to defeat the locked or barricaded door, an OODA analysis would prepare you to Run or Fight (Figure 5.20).

RECOVERY

The FEMA definition of Recovery (Figure 5.21) is:

> Encompasses both short-term and long-term efforts for the rebuilding and revitalization of affected communities.[7]

The aim of the **recovery** phase is to restore the affected area to its previous state. It differs from the response phase in its focus; recovery efforts are concerned with issues and decisions that must be made after immediate needs are addressed.

---

[7] Ibid.

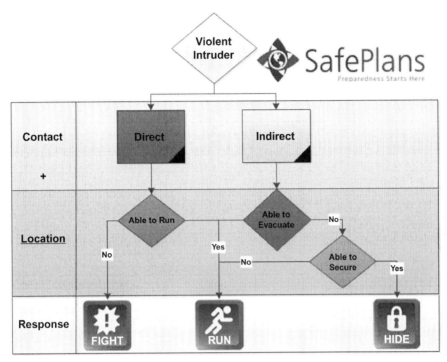

FIGURE 5.20

Decision-making flowchart for violent intruder encounters.

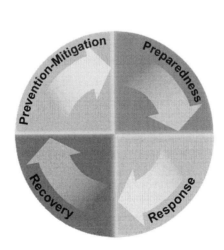

FIGURE 5.21

Recovery.

Planning for recovery is conducted in the Preparedness phase and involves establishing key community partnerships, developing policies, providing training, and developing memorandums of understanding between agencies. Recovery is a vital component of an all-hazards emergency. Certain aspects of recovery are more pertinent to intruder-based events. These include:

- Return to the "business of learning" as quickly as possible.
- Schools and districts need to keep students, families, and the media informed.
- Provide assessment of emotional needs of staff, students, families, and responders.
- Provide stress management during class time.
- Conduct daily debriefings for staff, responders, and others assisting in recovery.
- Take as much time as needed for recovery.
- Remember anniversaries.
- Implement a system to manage receipt of donations.
  - Establish locations for storing and strategies for delivering.
  - Determine what donations will be accepted—for example, gift cards.

Major categories for recovery are:

- Resources
- Mental Health Programs
- Family Reunification
- Business Resumption

RESOURCES

While most school districts have adequate resources to meet daily operations, they are not sufficient to deal with an active shooter incident. It is important to document agreements for services that aid disaster response and recovery efforts. Memorandums of understanding (MOU) and mutual aid agreements (MAA) should be implemented in recovery plans. Note that MOUs should be completed with all agencies or facilities that will assist, but expect nothing in return.

Examples:

- An area transportation system agrees to aid in transporting students under extenuating circumstances.
- A local church agrees to provide shelter and basic relief services.
- The local Department of Mental Health agrees to aid in post-disaster counseling.

At the same time, MAAs should be completed for agencies or facilities that will assist schools, and *do* expect a reciprocal agreement for aid.

Example:

- A nearby church agrees to serve as an off-campus shelter but requests the school provide a location to evacuate their daycare in return.

MENTAL HEALTH

Mental health must be considered in each phase and should be a part of each school's plan and the overall district plan. At a minimum, each district should have a crisis intervention team (CIT) that operates and coordinates district-appointed teams. The crisis intervention team addresses the emotional needs of the students and staff. In that capacity, the team must be able to make rapid assessments of student and staff needs, provide family outreach, plan and carry out appropriate interventions, use individual and group strategies, and make referrals to mental health resources as appropriate. The team is also a key component of the school threat assessment process, helping to identify those who pose a threat to themselves or others, then helping to develop appropriate interventions and responses.

The objectives of crisis intervention are:

- BEFORE THE DISASTER/CRITICAL EVENT:
    - Build community at school.
    - Identify, monitor, and support at-risk students and staff.
    - Develop ties with mental health and other community resources that support the emotional well-being of children.
- DURING THE DISASTER/CRITICAL EVENT:
    - **Protect**—children by shielding them from:
        - Bodily harm
        - Exposure to traumatic stimuli (sights, sounds, smells)
        - Media exposure
    - **Direct**—ambulatory students who are in shock and dissociative:
        - Using kind and firm instruction
        - Away from danger, destruction, and the severely injured
    - **Connect**
        - To you as a supportive presence
        - To caregivers
        - To accurate information
    - Triage for signs of stress that jeopardize safety.
    - Segregate survivors based on exposure level.
    - As appropriate, activate the Regional Homeland Security Mental Health Response System.
    - Begin psychological first aid, including the work to reestablish the perception of security and sense of power.
- AFTER THE DISASTER/CRITICAL EVENT:
    - Reunite students with caregivers as soon as possible.
    - Reestablish a calm routine.
    - Restore the learning environment.
    - Continue with psychological first aid.
    - Provide responsive crisis and grief counseling.
    - Initiate referrals to mental health professionals.
    - Provide information and psychoeducational materials to families and caregivers.
    - Assist in community efforts to provide support for families.

The CIT team may be made up of individuals from a range of school staff who meet the above criteria, including: school counselors, psychologists, social workers, nurses, teachers, special education professionals, language learners, resource officers, or other law enforcement. Also consider that some maintenance and dietary staff form a special bond with students and may be willing to be trained and act in this capacity. This team will be led by a knowledgeable school-based mental health professional, such as the school counselor, social worker, or psychologist.

Timely identification and intervention with students experiencing academic, social, and behavioral difficulty is an integral part of the mitigation effort. Mitigation supports efforts to prevent or reduce violence against self and others.

The CIT will also develop ties with professional mental health resources in the area.

Organizations that provide mental health resources that the district should consider include:

- Supporting schools and neighboring school district teams
- Local community mental health centers
- Local college and university resources
- Private mental health agencies
- Chaplains and pastors with the appropriate training
- NOVA, the National Organization of Victim Assistance:
  - Contact information for the national NOVA headquarters in Washington, DC, is nova@try-nova.org or 202-232-6682. NOVA services include:
    - Immediate assistance within 24 hours
    - Planning coordination with emergency responders
    - On-site, one-to-one companioning
    - On-site community group crisis intervention

The CIT should establish a family assistance center during major catastrophes. A central location provides both a community resource and a focal point for friends and family, relieving response agencies to do their jobs. CIT team members take on information liaison, mental health, and assistance functions in a controlled environment. Friends and families receive continuing updates on rescue or recovery efforts, as well as other information like family companioning, assistance visiting the disaster site, crisis intervention, mental health referrals, assistance filing for victim compensation, assistance with emergency financial needs, and assistance with forms to expedite death certification.

A family assistance center may exist long after a crisis is over, depending on the magnitude of the event. In the aftermath of a hurricane or tornado, where the missing may be counted in thousands, mental health, grieving, and personal paperwork issues could exist for months.

FAMILY REUNIFICATION FUNCTIONS

Throughout crisis evolution the school community is more or less engaged, some up close and some from afar, like parents at home. There is a continuing need for crisis response teams and school administration to track every individual student or staff member, and their community support system, from beginning of the event through to each person's ability to resume education activities. Family reunification functions include the following:

1. *Safe evacuation and full accountability of staff and students.*
   - Alert students and staff of evacuation.
   - Evacuation of the school.
   - Accountability of students after evacuation.
   - Establish bus staging and loading areas.
   - Move and load students and staff onto buses.

2. *Establishing and carrying out a full relocation and reunification process.*
   - Alert and notification of the reunification team.
   - Notification of parents, guardians, and media.
   - Establish and set up the relocation site.
   - Complete a reunification process.
   - Test grief counseling team.
   - Test first aid team.
   - Test ability to handle special needs students.
3. *Activation of a school District level EOC to coordinate these activities.*
   - Alert and notification.
   - Establish the emergency operations center (EOC), proper coordination, and tracking of status of events.
   - Coordinate through Response, Reunification, and Recovery.

BUSINESS RESUMPTION

The following points reflect the priorities, purpose, assumptions, and necessities of the business resumption process (getting the business back up and running normally).

Priorities
- Protect life and safety.
- Secure critical infrastructure and facilities.
- Resume operations.

Purpose
- Provide for continued performance of essential functions under all circumstances.
- Ensure survivability of critical equipment, records, and other assets.
- Minimize business damage and losses.
- Achieve orderly response and recovery from the emergency.
- Ensure succession of key leadership.
- Serve as a foundation for overall program.
- Ensure survivability of the mission in most severe events.

Assumptions
- Access to buildings may be delayed or limited.
- The response and investigation process alone could take weeks (worst case).
- Cleanup and repairs could take much longer.
- *You may be unable to enter your facility for an extended period of time.*

Necessities
- Care of students and faculty.
- Locating temporary space.
- Computing infrastructure.
- Communications protocol.

EMPOWERMENT OF CRISIS MANAGEMENT IN EMERGENCIES

Robert Lang, CPP, CEM
Chief security officer, Kennesaw State University

Don't panic, but a plane just hit the building, there's smoke, and I need you to call 911 or World Trade Center maintenance and give them my cell phone number. Tell them there are people on the 104th floor, we're all O.K., but we need to know what to do.
Transcript from a World Trade Center caller to his wife during the terrorist attacks on Sept. 11, 2001.[1]
(Account by Karen Lee, wife of Richard Lee, victim.)

INTRODUCTION

Knowing what to do has always been the main issue during emergencies. Previously, whether to shelter-in-place or evacuate had been the sole responsibility of the police, fire, or other emergency personnel, now known as first responders. However, with the increasing occurrences related to active shooters and adverse weather incidents, along with increased usage of hazardous materials on campuses, the earlier premise of waiting for someone in an official capacity to tell others what to do is now both outdated and dangerous. What we have learned is that many crisis situations are quick to happen with no foreseeable warnings (active shooters) or are evolving situations such as the 9/11 terrorist incidents, where people were attuned to letting the police, fire, or other emergency personnel tell them what to do. Yet, in emergency situations very quick action is needed to survive. You may not have all the facts readily at hand, but many times doing nothing is worse than doing something. This is where awareness and training can come together to allow people to implement all the tools of survival.

CASE STUDY: KENNESAW STATE UNIVERSITY

Kennesaw State University (KSU) deploys a layered approach to both emergency notifications and crisis response in mitigating its responsibilities to keep the students, faculty, staff, and visitors apprised of crisis situations. They do so by utilizing a cadre of 260 volunteer crisis coordinators to act as immediate responders when these crises occur. The concepts, identification of participants, and resultant

---

[1]"Accounts from the North Tower," *The New York Times*, May 26, 2002, http://www.nytimes.com/2002/05/26/nyregion/26NTOWER.html.

The Handbook for School Safety and Security
© 2014 Elsevier Inc. All rights reserved.

actions are not just applicable to higher education, but are encouraged and promoted to be functional at any level: pre-K, K-12, and higher ed.

WHAT PROMPTED THIS DIRECTIONAL CHANGE?

Prior to 2007, the KSU Campus Public Safety Department was the sole authority to respond to incidents and notify personnel of what to do in an emergency. However, with the shootings at Virginia Tech and Northern Illinois University, it became apparent that police response to an incident did not allow time for anything other than the immediate police action and any notification of the incident was usually made after the event was stabilized. The result was that there was no opportunity for anyone to take shelter, evacuate, or glean any information as to what to do. Just about every after-action report on crisis response has identified "the lack of pertinent communications" as a major issue. The active shooter event at Sandy Hook Elementary School in Newtown, CT identified a real weakness in emergency response time, as well as non-effectual security procedures that were deployed with the intent to keep unauthorized persons from gaining access.

KSU's Crisis Coordinator program is quite unique, not only in its makeup and training but also in its main goal of empowering people to make immediate decisions relative to sheltering-in or evacuation. The empowerment afforded by this program, intended for all levels, is contingent upon school administrators admitting to themselves that a centralized form of action may not always be prudent in a major crisis such as active shooters.

EVOLUTION OF THE PROGRAM

Upon arriving at KSU, I realized that most police departments, including KSU's Public Safety Department, were unable to provide the entire spectrum of response, mitigation, and recovery by themselves and began to identify individual building representatives to assist in providing that immediate help for the occupants. Thirty-five crisis response individuals were identified (some volunteers, some were "volunteered" as they say) and based in the existing 35 buildings on campus. The number then exploded to over 260, all now real volunteers, based on the complexity of the facilities (many different floors and wings) as well as their experience with real incidents that had occurred over the years. The KSU Crisis Manager, Dr. Randy Hinds, who is also the VP of Operations, realized that the communications aspect of any crisis is critical to ensuring the proper support and response for mitigation. He acquired funding for a state-of-the-art radio communication network, migrating to a digital platform with trunking capabilities, and thus ensuring personnel could talk to each other via radio without "stepping on" one another. Many an incident response has failed due to lack of clear and concise communications.

However, just finding people to fill positions is not the final solution. Initial and continued training is at the heart of the program. Crisis coordinators are required to attend comprehensive training that starts with a four-module program consisting of:

1. Overview of the Crisis Coordinator program
2. Operational interface with the Police Department
3. Terrorism awareness and indicators
4. Cardiopulmonary resuscitation (CPR)/first aid/automated external defibrillator (AED) certifications/safety overview and material safety data sheet (MSDS) review

Once a crisis coordinator completes each of the four modules, they then need to take the incident command online course, ICS-100b, Introduction to the Incident Command System, not only to ensure that they are aware of the protocols during an incident but also in order to comply with the National Incident Management System (NIMS) requirements for all personnel responding to an emergency to have this training. Volunteers are then "KSU certified" as crisis coordinators and receive a certificate attesting such. These modules can be calibrated to apply to any environment (e.g., pre-K and K-12) with some minor adjustments to the first and second modules.

CERTIFIED EMERGENCY RESPONSE TEAM

The second in the series of trainings is called the "Challenge Coin" level, open to all certified crisis coordinators and made up of individual disciplines created from the list of NIMS and ICS courses available from the FEMA site for the Emergency Management Institute. Taking at least three other courses after receiving your original certification qualifies for the Challenge Coin created for KSU.

Next in the series, is the "Lapel Pin" level, in which a lapel pin and a retractable logo badge holder is granted those who attain the Crisis Coordinator Certification and the Challenge coin and then obtain 80 additional hours of training approved by the Office of Strategic Security and Safety. Those 80 hours can be acquired by volunteers for special event support, teaching CPR and first aid (many crisis personnel are certified to train based on attending a "train the trainer" course) or attending and being certified as a Certified Emergency Response Team (CERT) member through the County Emergency Management Agency. The ability to obtain PIN status was greatly enhanced with the inclusion of the CERT opportunity. CERT training has no qualifiers, such as higher ed or K-12, and can be taken to support and bring new crisis response awareness to schools.

The last level is Eagle status. A very nice desktop trophy with a spread eagle top and cherry base is for those who obtain all three previous levels plus 500 additional approved training hours. As of this writing, no one has achieved this status, but many are working toward completion of the additional hours. The attainment of these levels and the certifications/coins/pins is not the main driver; what matters more is the continued training these people get to maintain their competency in what we are trying to do: save lives.

TALKING THE TALK IS FINE, BUT WALKING THE WALK IS WHERE THE RUBBER MEETS THE ROAD

KSU has had its share of opportunities to deploy their layered communications methods, consisting of an early warning siren/voiceover system for the initial alert (used only for tornado warnings, HazMat spills or events, and active shooters), short message service (SMS) texting/cell voice and e-mail (Blackboard's ConnectED notification system), a network computer override system for warnings on PCs and Macs, and digital signage to scroll emergency messages in real events. Any school system, regardless of whether higher ed, pre-K, or K-12, can deploy any of the technologies for mass notification, early warnings, or computer override and is only driven by the cost involved and the desire to initiate. Examples of those opportunities include the following scenarios.

In 2009, a prisoner was being transported from Florida to Tennessee when the accompanying police officer stopped at a Waffle House across the street from the campus footprint. While the police officer was inside eating, the prisoner, who came to be known as "little Houdini," escaped his vehicle and entered the campus. Once it was determined that a prisoner, unknown as to whether he was armed or not, had entered the facility, the KSU protocol to notify everyone to shelter in their locations was issued. As it turns out, the notification system didn't work, as the assistant vice president for strategic security and safety was in Tucson, AZ, giving a presentation at a conference. The system alerted his cell phone in both text message and voice message and the AVP was able to direct many of the responses via cell phone. However, protocols in place allowed for instantaneous response through standard operating procedures.

The second real-time incident occurred when a report was received from a crisis coordinator that some Civil War artifacts (cannonballs) had been identified in a glass cabinet within one of the offices in the social sciences building. After a quick review by the security and police officials, it was determined that upon visual identification, fuses could be seen intact on the cannonballs themselves. Therefore, an evacuation was deemed necessary, utilizing the crisis coordinator radio system in order to alert the 25 crisis personnel in the building within the five existing floors. In order to utilize the elevators, the fire alarms were not activated, thus allowing the ability to evacuate handicapped personnel as quickly as possible. All in all, evacuation of 4,000 people within 12 minutes was a great accomplishment. Many K-12 facilities are structured as multilevel buildings and can utilize the same response in dealing with this type of evacuation.

The third incident occurred when the campus, which occupies approximately 300 acres and 37 buildings, suffered a complete power outage. The only power and communication sources that were still intact were the crisis coordinator radio system and the campus police radio system. Most people thought they could just ride out the power outage and remain in their offices if they had windows. However, it was realized that most of the fire panels that controlled the fire alarm systems had only enough battery backup power for approximately 20 minutes. Once this situation was realized, the response team could not afford for anyone to remain in their offices regardless of whether there was light or the ability to do any kind of work. If there happened to be a fire with no fire panel support, no one would know to evacuate the facility. The crisis coordinators were able to advise everyone within all facilities of the need to evacuate while communicating via radio to the official command center located within the office of strategic security and safety.

As with any emergency protocol or any system that supports crisis management, a layered approach to communications as well as response initiatives is integral to any viable emergency plan. Another integral component is the ability for those involved to be empowered to act and confidently save lives as well as the physical assets of the facility. This program is not intended to be solely for the higher education level and is encouraged to be incorporated into all levels of emergency response protocols, including pre-K and K-12.

PREVENTION AND STUDENT SAFETY FOR K-12

Rick Shaw

Founder, CEO, and CDO of Awareity

INTRODUCTION

As a school leader, would you rather your students and staff *react* to a threat at your front door or *prevent* threats from getting to your front door?

Most (if not all) school and college administrators agree that prevention is the best and the right answer. The answer also reveals the difference between *school security* and *student safety*. School security involves reacting to threats at your front door while student safety involves preventing threats from getting to your front door.

All school administrators have a responsibility to create a safe learning environment for all students and staff, but student safety is not about how many alarms, cameras, and locks you have or how much money a school or college spends on security systems and security personnel.

Did you know security system solutions (alarms, cameras, locks, visitor management systems, panic buttons, mass notification systems, etc.) existed in every school and college that has experienced a tragic incident? Did you know a new security system was installed just before the tragic shootings at Sandy Hook Elementary?

SOLUTIONS

Security solutions are designed to record and/or alert people that risks and threats are present on your campus, at your front door and/or inside your building. For example, cameras record incidents that occur in a hallway, classroom or on campus and their primary purpose is recording "data" for post incident investigations in reaction to an incident. Most are not monitored in real-time due to costs and lack of resources. Other security solutions such as locks, safe rooms, and panic buttons serve as a last resort to deter threats.

Security solutions are not designed to proactively prevent student safety-related incidents such as bullying, cyber bullying, harassment, intimidation, abuse, suicide, drugs, alcohol, depression, targeted shooters, and other threats.

Since the Middle Ages and the era of castles and moats, humans have displayed a long-standing habit of reacting to risks and tragic incidents by adding even more reactive security solutions (rather than proactive prevention solutions). Evidence from hundreds and hundreds of incidents clearly reveals status quo (or "castle quo") approaches have not prevented preventable incidents and tragedies:

- After the Columbine tragedy in 1999, school security experts and school officials focused on active shooter training, cameras, guards, emergency response plans, and gun control laws—all reacting to a threat at the front door.
- After the Virginia Tech tragedy in 2007, school security experts and school officials focused on mass notification systems, security systems/door locks and emergency/first responder plans—all reacting to a threat at the front door.
- After the Sandy Hook tragedy in 2012, school security experts and school officials focused on gun control laws, cameras, locks, visitor management systems, armed guards, active shooter training, and crisis response plans—all reacting to a threat at the front door.

The focus after each of the above tragedies and hundreds of others around the world has been to add more "reactive security" devices and more "reactive response" approaches.

The key to proactive prevention is equipping students, faculty, staff, threat assessment teams, and community resources with the right tools to do the right things and to get the right information to the right people, so preventable incidents and tragedies can be proactively prevented. The following misconceptions and questions reveal some common problems with reactive rather than proactive security concepts.

IT WILL NEVER HAPPEN HERE AND WE DON'T HAVE A PROBLEM WITH BULLYING, CYBER BULLYING, SUICIDE, VIOLENCE, AND ABUSE...

School officials and school personnel must be open and honest and admit that no school or college is totally immune to bullying, cyber bullying, suicidal ideation, violence, and numerous other risks and threats.

DO YOU AGREE THAT ONE YOUTH SUICIDE IS ONE TOO MANY?

Student safety must include proactively preventing suicides. You may be shocked by these statistics:

- According to the Centers for Disease Control and Prevention (CDC) nearly 4,600 youth (ages 10-24) commit suicide each year.[1]
- The CDC also reports that, annually, "approximately 157,000 youths between the ages of 10 and 24 receive medical care for self-inflicted injuries at emergency departments across the United States."[2]
- The CDC now considers bullying to be a public health problem.
- The CDC has stated that connectedness is a key strategy to preventing suicides.

DO STUDENTS, FACULTY, STAFF, THIRD PARTIES, AND COMMUNITY MEMBERS KNOW INFORMATION YOUR THREAT ASSESSMENT TEAM DOESN'T KNOW?

Schools and colleges cannot prevent what they don't know about, so school and college leaders must eliminate dangerous awareness gaps and disconnects in order to proactively create a safer learning environment for everyone.

---

[1]"Suicide Prevention: Youth Suicide," Centers for Disease Control and Prevention, last updated January 30, 2013, http://www.cdc.gov/ViolencePrevention/suicide/youth_suicide.html.
[2]Ibid.

A shocking example of students knowing information that a threat assessment team doesn't know was identified in an ongoing student survey effort: 37% of students reported they were aware of a student or an individual that represented a threat to their school.[3]

The best way to understand what is really happening in your school is to survey your students. Student survey results can be shocking for some, but more importantly, student survey results validate that students are witnessing and experiencing numerous risks and threats in their schools and communities, allowing proactive prevention efforts to take place. Give your students a voice and a way to contribute.

OUR SCHOOL HAS AN INCIDENT-REPORTING SYSTEM AND/OR HOTLINE SERVICE SO WE ARE COVERED...

This myth has multiple false notions. Just because your school or college has an incident-reporting option, doesn't mean all of your students, faculty, staff, parents, third parties, and community members:

- Know how to access and use your incident-reporting system
- Trust that your incident-reporting system is really anonymous (voice, text, and e-mails are not)
- Believe reporting incidents will make a difference or make things better
- Will actually report the incidents and concerning behaviors they observe/witness

Based on numerous surveys and studies, students, faculty, and staff observe and/or witness bullying, harassment, sexual abuse, violence, drugs, suicidal ideation, and other concerning behaviors quite often. In fact, over 85% of bullying is witnessed.[4] Is your school's threat assessment team aware of all of these incidents, the aggressors, the targets, and the at-risk individuals, and are they equipped to follow up accordingly?

WHY IS ONLY 1 OR 2 OUT OF EVERY 10 INCIDENTS/CONCERNING BEHAVIORS REPORTED?[5] HOW MANY INCIDENT REPORTS DOES YOUR THREAT ASSESSMENT TEAM RECEIVE PER DAY?

Is your incident-reporting system anonymous? Truly anonymous incident reporting must be web-based and must be configured properly. Schools and colleges can lose the trust of their students, faculty, staff, and community resources if they claim their incident-reporting system is anonymous, but in reality is not. Students (and even most adults) know that texting, e-mails, apps, and phone call approaches are not necessarily anonymous. Adding a third-party vendor as a middle-man does not make incident reporting anonymous. With a truly anonymous reporting solution, people will feel more confident they can report concerning behaviors they observe and be more willing to help others without becoming a target themselves.

---

[3] Awareity 2013 Student Safety Summary Report.
[4] Awareity 2013 Student Safety Summary Report.
[5] Christopher P. Krebs, et al, "Campus Sexual Assault (CSA) Study, Final Report," October 2007, National Institute of Justice: Washington, DC. Available at https://www.ncjrs.gov/pdffiles1/nij/grants/221153.pdf.

DID YOU KNOW NEARLY EVERY POST-EVENT REPORT AFTER A LAWSUIT, SUICIDE, AND TARGETED SHOOTING HAS REVEALED THAT MULTIPLE INCIDENT REPORTS EXISTED?

For example, did you know the Virginia Tech Review Panel Report identified over 60 incident reports about the shooter? However, the incident reports were spread across departments, silos, and locations and not reported to a central secure prevention platform, thus Virginia Tech's Threat Assessment Team was not able to connect all the right dots and prevent this tragic mass shooting.

If your school or college does not have a central secure prevention platform with the right tools to connect all the right dots across departments, silos, and locations…it will be nearly impossible to do so. Dangerous gaps and disconnects with traditional incident-reporting systems are very real and obvious. School officials must understand this and must replace conventional incident-reporting systems with central secure prevention platforms that equip every individual—and especially school safety teams (e.g., behavior intervention teams, threat assessment teams)—with the right tools, so proactive investigations, interventions, monitoring, prevention, and documentation actions can be taken and preventable incidents can actually be prevented.

WE HAVE ARMED GUARDS, SROs, AND/OR OUR POLICE DEPARTMENT SO WE ARE COVERED…

Did you know Columbine had an armed security officer in the school at the time of the mass shooting? Did you know Virginia Tech had multiple armed campus police officers onsite and Fort Hood had armed soldiers all over the base? Yet, even with armed personnel ready to react, each organization still experienced a very expensive, embarrassing, and tragic incident. According to post-event reports, each tragedy was preventable because multiple people were aware of concerning behaviors and threatening comments!

Armed guards, SROs, and police are primarily a "security" solution for protecting and reacting during an incident at a school or college. The reactive security role of armed guards was a hot topic after the Sandy Hook tragedy in December 2012, when many experts suggested all schools should have an armed guard (SRO, school security officer [SSO], police officer, armed teachers, other) to provide protection. Does it make sense to put so much emphasis on a last resort option and hope a "good guy" with a gun can stop a "bad guy" with a gun?

Funding multiple SROs can be difficult for most schools and it is impossible for an SRO to be in multiple locations at once. Making SROs and police officers more proactive in preventing preventable incidents is not difficult and has been proven to work very well if they are equipped with the right prevention tools:

- What if parents and students could easily and anonymously share concerns with SROs in real-time?
- What if an SRO or police officer could be immediately notified when an incident report is made and could view all appropriate incident reports and actions that have been taken (across multiple locations)?
- What if an SRO, police officer, or a safety team could help assess and monitor at-risk students and identify escalation behaviors to prevent potential violence?
- What if an SRO, police officer, or threat assessment team could proactively connect at-risk individuals with mental health resources?
- What if an SRO or police officer, or threat assessment team could securely share information and connect the right dots and prevent incidents?

SROs and police must be "armed" in order to prevent preventable incidents, not just armed to react to risks that show up at your school or college. Arming these personnel with information will go a long way to preventing tragic incidents.

WE HAVE HANDBOOKS, POLICIES, AND PROCEDURES SO WE ARE PREPARED...

Every school and college experiencing an expensive, embarrassing, or tragic incident had student handbooks, employee handbooks, policies, procedures, and plans in place, but unfortunately they were not successful at preventing preventable incidents.

Policies, checklists, plans, guidelines, regulations, state laws, federal mandates, job descriptions, training, and many other procedural documents are essentially "recipes" describing how to "make the best cake ever." You may believe your school or college has the best policies ever, but does every individual have updated and situational awareness based on their roles, accountability for their actions and the right tools to do their part in proactively preventing expensive, embarrassing and tragic incidents? Evidence from previous incidents and tragedies reveals that most individuals do not.

WE HAVE AN ANTIBULLYING PROGRAM SO WE ARE SET...

If you do a web search for antibullying programs, you will find there are hundreds of antibullying programs. Some programs are expensive, some are not, some have a curriculum, some use books, some use CDs, some use checklists, some have people sign a pledge, and some provide posters.

With so many antibullying programs available, and with so much awareness on the news about bullying, why do nearly 85% of students still observe/witness bullying?

Lessons learned reveal that just having an antibullying program is like just having a recipe. To turn the recipe into results, individuals (students, teachers, staff, counselors, principals, threat assessment teams, safety team members, student affairs, SROs, police, nurses, bus drivers, coaches, community resources, and others) need updated situational awareness throughout the year so that every individual understands how prevention works and is held accountable for their roles and responsibilities. Every individual also needs the right tools so they can take action and do the right things to follow the antibullying program recipe and proactively prevent incidents and tragic consequences.

WE DON'T HAVE FUNDING IN OUR BUDGET...

An ounce of prevention is worth a pound of cure. We have all heard this wisdom and it can be applied to student safety, too.

Evidence from previous incidents and tragedies reveal that preventing is less expensive and more effective than reacting to incidents. For example, look at the high costs of the following tragic incidents, where the school was reacting rather than preventing:

- Virginia Tech: $48.2 M[6]
- Penn State: $171.0 M[7]
- Phoebe Prince: $225,000 settlement[8]

---

[6]"Report: Va. Tech Massacre Cost $48.2M," *Campus Safety*, April 12, 2012, http://www.campussafetymagazine.com/Channel/University-Security/News/2012/04/13/Report-Va-Tech-Massacre-Cost-48-2M.aspx?goback=.gde_1836305_member_107786480.
[7]Bill Schackner, "Sandusky scandal costs now top $171 million at Penn State," *Pittsburgh Post-Gazette*, November 18, 2013, http://www.post-gazette.com/local/breaking/2013/11/18/Sanusky-scandal-costs-now-top-171-million/stories/201311180161.
[8]Christine Ng, "Phoebe Prince's Parents Settled School District Lawsuit for $225,000," *ABC News*, December 28, 2011, http://abcnews.go.com/blogs/headlines/2011/12/phoebe-princes-parents-settled-school-district-lawsuit-for-225000/.

In response to the Sandy Hook tragedy, one of the most common reactions has been to add more security guards at schools. However, security-related costs are very expensive:

- $2,500: annual cost of insurance for each armed staff member
- $5,000: annual cost for arming and training one staff member
- $75,000: annual cost of a SRO in salary, benefits, training, and equipment
- $200: cost per student of placing one SRO at each school

At a time when every school and college is facing tighter budgets and government funding cuts, there has never been a better time to equip your school or college with more effective and less expensive prevention solutions. Evidence clearly reveals that prevention is far less expensive than reaction, which is great for schools and colleges and their tight budgets.

Yet, even with these expensive and embarrassing lessons learned, data shows that school and college administrators continue to approve and invest millions and millions of dollars in reactive security devices, while investing almost nothing in proactive prevention solutions.[9]

CAN WE LEARN ABOUT PREVENTION FROM SMOKEY THE BEAR?

Smokey the Bear is all about preventing forest fires. He is famous for saying: "Only *you* can prevent wildfires." Smokey the Bear understands that prevention does not mean we create a law to ban matches. He understands that prevention does not mean that we place armed firefighters at every tree in every forest. Smokey the Bear's prevention strategy focuses on situational awareness, awareness of best practices, awareness of surroundings, accountability for consequences, and for individuals to speak up when they see someone in danger of starting a wildfire. Smokey the Bear understands that preventing wildfires is a better approach than just handing out emergency response plans to all campers on ways to take cover, hide, run, or fight the wildfire.

The first question in this chapter asked whether you would want your students and staff to react to a threat at your front door or prevent threats from getting to your front door. If your answer was that preventing is better than reacting, doesn't it make sense to put more focus on proactive prevention tools and student safety efforts?

---

[9]"Wisc., Va., Ark., Pa., N.J., N.H., Conn. Schools Announce Security Upgrades," *Campus Security*, September 4, 2013, http://www.campussafetymagazine.com/Channel/School-Safety/News/2013/09/05/Wisc-Va-Ark-Pa-N-J-N-H-Conn-Schools-Announces-Security-Upgrades.aspx.

THINK PREVENTION AND THINK SAFETY

Victor Cooper, MSM, CPP
Emergency preparedness program manager, Aria Health System

INTRODUCTION

Much work has been done in the area of facility security for educational institutions post the incidents at Columbine High School, Virginia Tech University, and Sandy Hook Elementary School, and for good reason. There have been over 30 attacks at U.S. schools in the last 10 years resulting in well over 300 deaths. Security practitioners have worked hard to produce and distribute best practices for schools in an effort to reduce the risk of violence. But what has been done to keep our student, teachers, and administrators safe when they leave the school on school business? Not much.

SAFE TRAVEL

Every year, parents send their children off to study abroad or to spend a few weeks in the summer with a host college/family in an effort to gain valuable international experience. Teachers attend conferences all the time for the purpose of overall personal development and to give as well as receive new techniques to better reach their students. The fact is both do so with very little, if any, safety preparation. Safe travel doesn't just happen. As with everything else in business and in life, preparations play a big role in determining the outcome. The key to safe travel is to think about security from the start. It must be a part of your travel strategy. Planning is very important because it gives direction for an expected outcome. Note the use of the word planning and not plans. Dwight D. Eisenhower once said, "Plans are nothing; planning is everything." He wasn't saying that plans are of no value. It's the process of planning that is most important. Planning is where one considers the difficulties and challenges and devises ways to mitigate them. Most plan for safe travel by simply hoping all goes well. Planning involves the steps taken to ensure all goes well. Remember, the primary goal is to reduce the opportunity for crime to occur by avoiding risk. To do this, planning is necessary.

Crime prevention is for everyone. Teachers, students, and administrators would do well to think about prevention of risks and safety when traveling. When motivation, opportunity, and desire come together, crime is nearly unavoidable. To reduce the possibility of this happening, one of the three must be eliminated. Opportunity (dark alley) and motivation (ravenous wolf) are very difficult to eliminate. However, desire (sitting duck) can be controlled, eliminating the potential for crime through education. Educate the duck to avoid the dark alley where the ravenous wolf waits. Control crime through education.

TOP EIGHT STEPS

The following eight steps are not all an individual should do in order to close the window of opportunity for crime, but it is designed to give you a clearer picture of what safe travel looks like:

1. Teachers and students both need city- or country-specific travel briefs that lay out the country and city threat levels, identifying the type of security threats that have occurred in the past in those locations and noting whether the dates of travel will hold any significance in the destination country or city that could affect threat conditions. This is a standard procedure for missionaries who travel to render aid, politicians, military personnel, as well as others, and should be for you too.

   If the threat level warrants it, one should arrange to have a driver and secure ground transportation meet them on arrival. Your name should never be placed on a card and held up for everyone to see. Avoid this tactic altogether. Doing so gives criminals the opportunity to duplicate the card and pose as a driver, which can be the prelude to robbery, rape, kidnapping, and murder. Instead, there should be a secure way for the driver to be identified by the traveling employee. For example, the traveler can get the driver's name and a picture of him/her in advance. Even better, arrange for the hotel shuttle to pick you up. Both the driver's identification and the vehicle's markings will have the hotel's identification on them.

   Travelers should also register with the embassy or consulate's office in the country of their destination so that they can be contacted in the event of an emergency. This should be done on a country-by-country basis as some have a propensity to be corrupt.

   As part of the planning process, you should know how various contingencies should be handled. If your flight is late, how do you contact your host or the driver? If you get sick, have an accident, face a natural disaster, or other problem, what do you do? Knowing what to do when the unexpected happens reduces risk when traveling.

2. The National Crime Victimization Survey (NCVS) reports that between 2004 and 2008 more than 1 in 10 property crimes took place in parking lots or garages.[1] Gary R. Cook, P.E., publisher of Security Design Newsletter, states that roughly 80% of the criminal acts at shopping centers, strip malls, and businesses occur in parking lots.[2] The Supreme Court of Appeals of West Virginia has stated that "a quick review of reported cases reveals that Wal-Mart parking lots are a virtual magnet for crime" (due to it being a 24-h operation with little, if any, security).[3] In 2007, the *East Bay Express* published an article called "Lots of Trouble" that reviewed the explosion of crime in parking lots the previous summer in San Francisco Bay Area, reporting numerous instances of assault.[4]

   Suffice it to say that parking lots and garages by their very nature and poor design provide opportunity for all sorts of crime to occur and many times we are left with very few options and nearly forced to use them.

---

[1] "Location," *Bureau of Justice Statistics*, updated March 5, 2014, http://www.bjs.gov/index.cfm?ty=tp&tid=44.

[2] Gary R. Cook, "Parking Lot Security," *CrimeWise*, accessed March 27, 2014, http://www.crimewise.com/library/parking.html.

[3] Doe v. Wal-Mart Stores, Inc., 558 S.E.2d 663 (W. Va. 2001), filed December 13, 2001, https://www.courtlistener.com/wva/7E3x/doe-v-wal-mart-stores-inc/.

[4] Anneli Rufus, "Lots of Trouble," September 5, 2007, *East Bay Express*, http://www.eastbayexpress.com/oakland/lots-of-trouble/Content?oid=1084127.

The following are a few things to consider when parking in lots or garages:

a. Consider hotel transportation and valet parking when available. It's both convenient and safer. Also, know that mall security will provide escorts from and to vehicles if requested.

b. With parking garages, the key is visibility. High visibility from within and outside the facility can greatly reduce safety risks. It is important to establish lines of sight between exits and parking areas. For example, if a pedestrian walks down the aisle and reaches a point where he/she must turn toward an elevator or stairway, the person should be able to see both the elevator/stairs and the vehicle from that point. Avoid placing yourself in any other position.

c. Lobbies leading to elevators should have as much glass as possible and, if possible, should face a public area, such as a street, so that you are visible from the outside. Glass elevator shafts and cabs are great because they allow others to see who's in the elevator, minimizing the risk of attack.

d. The same need for visibility holds true for stairways. In the past, fire codes required stairways to be entirely enclosed in masonry. Today, codes permit as much glass as possible on the exterior side. Some codes now permit completely open stairs on the outside of the building, enhancing visibility. If the stairway is enclosed, use caution.

e. It is best to park in lots/garages that provide spaces at 90° angles because it results in driving aisles that are up to 26 ft wide, which allows parkers to walk to and from their vehicles without walking too close to the parked cars. Cars parked at a 45° angle have the narrowest aisles at approximately 12 ft. Once parked, the pedestrian should always walk down the center of the aisles (rather than near the vehicles where one could be pulled between the vehicles and assaulted) moving only for vehicular traffic.

3. There are two aspects to hotel safety and security: what the hotel security procedures are, and what the guest should do. Most would not view hotel check-in as a security issue, but I assure you, it is. During the check-in process, valuable information is exchanged between the hotel clerk and the guest. "Hi, I'm Mrs. Brown and I have a reservation for a three night stay here at your hotel." Or, "Mrs. Brown, here is your key to room #345 located on the third floor. Enjoy your stay with us!" This very professional conversation produces very important information. This information in the hands of the wrong person could be quite problematic. Check-in conversation should be as private as possible and not include those milling around in the lobby area. Armed with your name, room number, and length of stay, anyone can pose as an employee of the hotel, knock on your door using your name which will give you a (false) sense of security, and cause you to open the door to a complete stranger.

All people should be vigilant when traveling alone in a foreign country, but since statistically women are at higher risk, included below are some tips designed specifically for females. In selecting lodging, one should choose hotels with a reputation for both safety and security. Females should also look for hotels considered safest for women. For example, many hotels have a designated "women only" floor which could reduce the likelihood of an attacker lurking outside or following a woman to her room. It would be wise to request a room between the second and seventh floor. Individual floors in most buildings are about 12 ft high and many cities have fire trucks with 100-ft. ladders. The 100-ft ladder, the largest in most cities, should be able to get to or near the top of an eight-story building. Rooms above the seventh floor should be avoided because fire ladders may not be able to reach rooms that are higher than that. Street level is not good because it provides easy access for criminals.

Female travelers should stipulate that rooms not be at the end of the hallway where they will be more isolated and vulnerable; they should also request that the room not be across any stairways, because a person could hide in the stairway awaiting for an opportunity to force their way in from behind as the guest enters the room.

Females should accept the service of the bellman. They should wait at the door while the bellman deposits the luggage and walks around the room turning on the lights. When women check into a room unescorted, they should follow the 15-second rule: After looking right and left for anyone who may be lurking in the hall, open the door and lodge the suitcase against the open door. Now, within 15 seconds, turn on all the lights, look behind the drapes and shower curtain, and give a quick kick beneath the bed to determine whether the bed sits on a pedestal (eliminating the possibility of someone hiding underneath). This secures the room. Afterward, quickly close and double lock the door and use the top latch as well. Creating an extra level of security is important because hotel locks are far from unassailable. It is easy for staff to make copies of keys and it has been known, though not often, for one key to fit all doors!

Female travelers may also want to pack a men's shirt or tie or some other article of clothing distinctively male. These items can be spread around the room to give housekeeping the impression that a male is around. This will also help when ordering room service—a situation which exposes female travelers to a degree of risk because they are letting strangers, usually male, into the room. Here's how a women can make room service less risky: With male clothes or other items in plain view, she should run the shower before the delivery person knocks on the door. She should then speak to the shower door saying, "food's here" (or something like that) loud enough to be heard on the other side of the hotel room door. Room service will assume there is more than one person in the room. The woman in the room should have a pen in hand and a place cleared for the waiter to place the food. As she opens the door, she should motion for the waiter to step in, and while standing against the open door (which offers an escape path if a threat arises), she can motion for the waiter to set down the food, return, and step outside at which point she can sign the bill, then close and lock the door.

4. Body posture and eye contact are big! The likely criminal targets are men and particularly women who appear unaware or unfamiliar with their surroundings, and unlikely to fight back. Many people are unaware that they are sending "victim signals" to predators. We've all walked by people and noticed (or didn't notice because we were the one sending the signals) people who refuse to make eye contact. They are rigid or robotic in their walk, walking faster or slower than their normal pace, which affects their gait or normal stride. As you approach them, one can notice them looking straight ahead, as if looking at the person approaching would be offensive. Or, they will become busy with their phone, hands, bag, etc., or even worse, just look down. Predators look for this submissive behavior and gravitate toward it. Instead, one should walk at his or her normal pace with his or her head up. As the individual approaches, note their eye contact. If there is none, feel free to walk by without speaking. However, if there is eye contact, acknowledge them. This should be done with a very confident "hello!" The last thing a predator wants is a confident person because they assume that the confident person will fight to protect their property. This isn't always true, nor am I telling you to fight back. What I am saying is the predator desires an easy target and by walking with confidence, making eye contact, and speaking to him/her, it will more than likely cause him/her to choose another target.

5. Transportation can be a bit problematic as well. As previously stated, hotel transportation is preferred but may not always be available. Other options include renting a vehicle or arranging transportation through a colleague or friend. Busses and trains may not work well if you are

not familiar with the area. That said, taxicabs have become the preferred mode of transportation while traveling on business.

I once loaned a textbook to a student who left the book in the back of a cab. Because my name and number were stamped in the book, the cab driver was kind enough to call and return my book to me. I once found a fifty-dollar bill (which I turned over to the driver) in the back of a cab as I was getting a ride to the airport.

How often does this happen? How often do people leave items in cabs? Well, it turns out that it happens quite often. So often that, for example, in New York City, nycitycab.com has a page on their website dedicated to lost items. Cell phones, wallets, keys, purses, and more are left in cabs daily. In 1999, the *Los Angeles Times* reported that "Musician Yo-Yo Ma forgot his $2.5-million, 266-year-old cello in the trunk of a taxi Saturday, but police tracked it down at a garage in Queens in time for his evening concert."[5]

This issue creates a huge opportunity for one of the, if not the fastest, growing crimes on the planet: identity theft. The United States Department of Justice states, "to victims of identity theft and fraud, the task of correcting incorrect information about their financial or personal status, and trying to restore their good names and reputations, may seem as daunting as trying to solve a puzzle in which some of the pieces are missing and other pieces no longer fit as they once did. Unfortunately, the damage that criminals do in stealing another person's identity and using it to commit fraud often takes far longer to undo than it took the criminal to commit the crimes."[6] It's important that you inspect the passenger area of the taxi cab, bus, train, or any other mode of transportation as you enter it, but more important, as you exit, to ensure personal items are not left behind.

6. Looking like a tourist can certainly ruin your travel plans. It's important to blend in with the locals as much as possible. Nothing screams "I'm a tourist" more than watching a person standing on the corner looking up at a skyscraper commenting on its size or even unfolding a map with a confused look on their face. Every predator will know you're prey. If you're not sure where you are, stop inside a store, any store, and browse just long enough for you to gather your thoughts and develop a plan of action.

For the international traveler, it's wise to dress conservatively. A modest appearance will be necessary in countries with strong religious views. Avoid flashy jewelry and clothing with religious or military symbols. Also, be aware that common western hand gestures like the "thumbs up" and the way we in the west call or summon one another by waving our index finger back and forth are seen as both obscene and offensive.

7. Issues, problems, and emergencies can arise and a proper response to each is necessary. Many either use the terms interchangeably or confuse the three, which could create a worse situation. If you mistake a problem for an emergency, you will overplay the situation causing panic and alarm when it is totally unnecessary. If you underestimate an emergency and treat it as if it were an issue, you could create a disaster. First things first, let's define these three terms:

  a. An issue is an unplanned distraction.
  b. A problem is the cause of one or more issues.
  c. An emergency is an unresolved problem(s) now requiring immediate action.

---

[5] Associated Press, "Yo-Yo Ma's Cello Lost, Found," October 17, 1999, *Los Angeles Times*, http://articles.latimes.com/1999/oct/17/news/mn-23281.

[6] "Identity Theft and Identity Fraud," United States Department of Justice, accessed March 27, 2014, http://www.justice.gov/criminal/fraud/websites/idtheft.html.

Based on the above definitions, an incident is something that needs to be resolved before it becomes a problem or an emergency. This can be either a permanent or a temporary fix. An example of an incident would be a power loss at your hotel which causes a disruption in the normalcy of your morning. Now, because the issue does not affect your day-to-day business, by definition, you do not have a problem. It becomes an incident only when the power outage extends into the hours, affecting your work, comfort, and convenience.

A problem is not an issue. An issue can become a problem, especially if there is a high possibility that the issue might happen again. In the case of a power outage, when the outage extends into the hours in which you would be relaxing or working in your room, there is a problem. This is a problem because if the situation is not resolved, this can become an emergency.

An emergency is far from being a problem and farther from being an issue. An emergency is a serious and often dangerous situation requiring immediate attention. In keeping with the current example, the power outage reaches emergency status when the safety of the guests is compromised. As a result of the outage, there's no access control and a woman could be attacked in her room. Here, immediate attention is needed. Yes, each can happen independent of the other, but my point is that one should not allow a situation to escalate to the next level if it can be avoided.

8. Trust your instincts. Don't take unnecessary chances, lock your car, lock your home or apartment, don't make it easy for criminals, reduce opportunity, and you will not be a victim.

UNDERSTANDING HOW TO USE THE PROCESS HAZARD ANALYSIS (PHA) AND THE LAYERS OF PROTECTION ANALYSIS (LOPA)

Mark H. Beaudry, Ph.D., CPP

Instructor, researcher, and author in security studies at various universities in Massachusetts

INTRODUCTION

In today's society, most security professionals adopt the usage of risk analyses, as a best practice. Typically, a risk analysis will begin with an assessment to determine the likelihood that an unfortunate event may occur with an undesirable consequence. With that, a risk analysis may also require some type of estimation in the event or likelihood that an event will occur. It also assesses this likelihood and provides a comparative analysis in order to determine the probability that the existing protection layers will or will not operate as required (sometimes technology, procedures, or human behavior may not act or perform as predetermined). In addition, a risk is the result of any deviation from the expected operation, process design, failed procedures, or a lax (possibly a nonexistent) site safety and security culture. The risk analysis seeks to identify these deviations and to develop a plan to reduce or mitigate an event should one occur. Once the results of each deviation have been measured and analyzed, the design and previous performance should be included as part of the holistic posture. This of course may result in some of the event deviations being significant enough that a serious hazard may be likely. However, by using the Layers of Protection Analysis (LOPA) concept a security professional can reduce or mitigate the risk as low as reasonably manageable.

PROCESS HAZARD ANALYSIS

As mentioned previously, businesses and agencies that have implemented and use a risk ranking procedure do so in conjunction with a Process Hazard Analysis (PHA) that is supported by a risk matrix comparing the frequency and consequence priorities. The risk ranking procedure is used to determine both the priority and criticality posture in order for the security professional to make recommendations that will additionally reduce or mitigate a risk of any deficiencies specifically within the safety and security measures. In addition, a security professional is then able to provide the rankings of the consequence severity by considering the hazardous situation posed by the event. It is important that the consequence severity ranking be based on the harm that results when everything that could go wrong, either has gone wrong, or may go wrong (training, testing, and any simulations that can be done will assist with finding any deviations). Also, sometimes the historical data can be used to determine previous incidents or difficulties that security professionals may have experienced. Determine if there are any incident records including any safety and security operation safeguards that can reduce the potential harm caused by varied types of hazardous situations (i.e., such as an armed intruder or a failed emergency response procedure). As stated previously, any type of consequence modeling or simulations, role playing, or realistic training that can be practiced can be used to better understand the hazardous situation and impact zones where the situation have or may possibly occur moving forward.[1]

LAYERS OF PROTECTION ANALYSIS

The security professional also may use varied levels of a risk analysis to provide estimates that the event likelihood technique called LOPA. The LOPA also allows the risk to be estimated along various points throughout the incident sequence. In addition, it can provide quantitative estimates of the risk which LOPA can be applied to hazardous events that have a consequence severity involving any type of scenario:

- Any facility or equipment damage or failures that may cause harm (i.e., may be either an internal or external explosion, or a detonation within the facility perimeter)
- Significant operations interruption (i.e., possibly a bomb threat, workplace violence incident, threat via the mail, etc.)
- Serious injury or fatality of an employee or staff (i.e., active shooter, etc.)
- Any external injury or fatality to the community at large
- Significant environmental impact that affects everyone (i.e., gas or chemical exposure)

When LOPA is used by the security professional, they will begin with examining how causes lead to process deviations (or initiating events), this will assist with understanding how they propagate (also called "chain reaction" or domino effect). This evaluation also allows the security professional to determine if any enabling conditions were critical to understanding the failed event, i.e., typically more than one thing must be wrong for the process deviation to occur. In addition, the risk rank procedure that is performed will use a risk matrix for calculation purposes, and then the event risk is compared to the operations risk in order to determine whether additional risk reduction or mitigation techniques are required. According to Summers and Hearn (2010),[2] who argue that when the process risk does not satisfy the chosen risk criteria then an independent protection layer (IPL) is used to close the gap by reducing or mitigating the hazardous or harmful event frequency.[3] Initially, the main purpose of IPLs is to stop propagation of the hazardous event (think of it as a time delayed mechanism) and any probable harm that may result from the event. Generally, most security professionals will utilize an onion-skin concept (sometimes referred to as lines of defense or defense in depth), used to illustrate the typical

---

[1]Summers, Angela, Bill Vogtmann, and Steve Smolen, Consistent Consequence Severity Estimation, American Institute of Chemical Engineers, 2010 Spring Meeting, 6th Global Congress on Process Safety, San Antonio, Texas, March 22-24, 2010.
[2]Summers, Angela E., and Hearn, William H. (2010) Risk Criteria, Protection Layers and Conditional Modifiers. SIS-TECH.
[3]CCPS/AIChE, *Layer of Protection Analysis: Simplified Process Risk Assessment*, Concept Series, New York (2001).

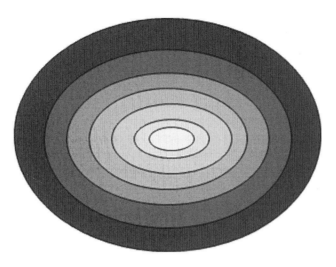

FIGURE 9.1

Typical lines of defense when designing layers of protection.

order of IPL deployment. If the event propagates through the onion skin of IPLs, the impact on the process operation becomes greater as does the uncertainty of the final outcome (typically, the outer lines of defense are physical security measures as opposed to inner measures which may be procedural in nature). Also, a key element of using these types of lines of defense is that it will cause time delays, or difficulties, or the propagation (sometimes called a hard target versus a soft target that doesn't use layers of protection). Using LOPA is exactly represented by the layers of an onion skin (Figure 9.1).

The hope is that the layers will stop or delay (maybe reduce or mitigate) a process deviation from exceeding the safe operations limit. Specifically, providing a safer design, with lines of defense and access control, any supervisory procedures or measures (checks and balance technique), preventive and mitigation layers will ultimately provide proactive measure to reduce or mitigate events from occurring. In addition, a well-designed posture that proactively reduces or mitigates any type of hazardous event can have a high certainty of effectiveness.

Since risk is a function of frequency and consequence, the frequency estimation and the LOPA concept can provide different techniques in evaluating its acceptability. Typically, the consequence severity is used by security professionals to conduct an assessment of the potential likelihood of events for more strict frequency analysis. As mentioned previously, many security professionals may rely on the assessment of operating experience and incident history to make their determination, and they may use holistic factors that influence the severity (i.e., crime rates, types of crime data, etc.), including operating practices, layers of protection, and conditional modifiers that can alert or monitor a situations events. Historically, during the assessments, the security professional may consider reactive and response layers, i.e., actions that facility personnel must take in order to reduce or mitigate harm; this will sometimes be in addition to the proactive layers (i.e., closing and locking a door from the inside of an office or room). One other important issue to keep in mind is that each layer provides protection independent of each other, the use of these layers and the conditional modifiers are critical, since they are often interrelated. For example, an alarm annunciator system may be used to initiate evacuation of personnel, or a lockdown situation for occupants.

USING LOPA

When using risk analysis, the LOPA can also be incorporated to improve implementation of consequence estimation tools (Summers, 2010). In addition to the consequence estimation tool, the risk analysis is also dependent on the estimated frequency of the hazardous event. Additionally, any error associated with the consequence severity estimate directly impacts the risk reduction measures. LOPA can also provide a determined priority based on the estimate of the hazardous event frequency by assessing the frequency of the initiating events that lead to the hazardous event and the possibility that the safety and security measures may fail. Security professionals will use experience to determine the right types of protection layers to utilize, and use best practices to demonstrate the risk reduction or mitigation techniques that have worked when conducting previous risk analysis. Security professionals will also attempt to analyze the root causes (or initiating causes) and determine those enabling conditions that result in process deviations (or initiating events). This is a critical part of a risk analysis since understanding the likelihood of the types of hazards that may occur and the conditions that enable them, security professionals can then estimate the initiating event frequency.

In LOPA, the security professional may recommend independent protection layers (IPL) based on the hazard or threat. Also, an IPL can be a best practice that is known to provide the risk reduction (i.e., fences, gates, guards, police, CCTV, alarms, etc.). Generally, all of the above-mentioned best practices used, however, alarms are typically identified as safety and security tools that are used as an input to identification and notification systems. Basically, these types of alarms are defined as "an audible and/or visible means of indicating to the operator an equipment malfunction, process deviation, or abnormal condition *requiring a response*." Which is different from a safety alarm "an alarm that is classified as critical to process safety or to the protection of human life."[4]

Using the IPL risk reduction method also allows the security professional to estimate the hazardous event frequency based on information and incident data that corresponds to key performance indicators (i.e., it could be alarm logs, CCTV usage determined to view incidents, police reports, staff or visitor information, etc.). LOPA is an excellent tool for assessing a wide variety of threat scenarios and applying protection layers of various types using the appropriate design measure. In addition, LOPA can be utilized as a semi-quantitative analysis as mentioned above with key performances, which will also allow for efficient evaluation of the threat or vulnerability. Realistically, the more that organizations progress with using and implementing LOPA throughout different schools, it will invariably result in similar usage, comparisons, and questions asked on implementation. When similar threats or vulnerabilities are compared from school to school, the LOPA will become more constant, and staff will see the variation in the risk estimate for similar threats. Once we begin to recognize that the LOPA procedures have well-defined methods for estimating the hazardous event frequency, the inconsistency in the risk estimate will generally be due to a variation in the estimated consequence severity.

As security professionals attempt to get consistency in the LOPA methodology by providing schools with varied types of LOPA scenarios, the safety and security measures will improve and eventually reduce or mitigate events. This is especially attractive in organizations with virtually identical facility

---

[4]Stauffer, T., Sands, N.P., and Dunn, D.G. (2010). Get a life (cycle)! Connecting Alarm Management and Safety Instrumented Systems. ISA Safety & Security Symposium (April, 2010); http://www.isa.org.

types or those with multiple locations. Many of the LOPA template scenarios can be useful by providing specific guidance to a school safety and security measures. In many cases, the LOPA best practices utilized by security professionals have guidance on not only the risk analysis, but also the means for risk reduction and mitigation. Finally, many LOPA templates have proven to be difficult to develop, approve, and implement, predominantly because consensus on a school-wide consequence severity ranking is difficult to achieve.

MASS NOTIFICATION REQUIREMENTS FOR OUR CHILDREN'S SCHOOLS

10

Frank J. Davies, CHS-IV, CIPS, CVI
President, Aella Consulting Group, Inc.
Gregory Bernardo, CHS-IV, CDT, CVI
Vice president, Aella Consulting Group, Inc.

INTRODUCTION

Over the past several years, violence has continued to erupt on school and college campuses throughout the United States and around the world. For more than 20 years, numerous regulations and regulating bodies have attempted to address issues related to that violence here in the United States through guidelines, recommendations, and requirements. Recently, "mass notification" has become a common topic of discussion for many of our schools. Mass notification is being redefined with every update of the NFPA 72 code book. Most recently it is defined as a "system used to provide information and instructions to people in a building, area site or other space using intelligible voice communications, visible signals, text, graphics, tactile or other communications methods."

This chapter summarizes our research and experience regarding mass notification as it pertains to educational facilities, including K-12 and higher education institutions.

NOTIFYING THE MASSES

For many years, the activity of mass notification was an on-premise action that could simply involve the public address (PA) system and/or fire alarm, and notice was limited to evacuation of an area or facility. Recently, with advances in technology, mass notification has evolved to include information posted on Websites, updates through email or via social media, automated phone message dialers, mobile phone text messaging, digital signage, and other overlapping information technologies. The changes in mass notification indicate momentum for a different way of looking at notifications as more of a "system of systems" approach where different communication modes are working together to accomplish a number of things.

Today, we can identify over 120 manufacturers who support some aspect of the various methods of mass notification through a host of services, component products, and targeted mass notification systems.

RECENT REGULATORY ACTIVITIES
1990 CLERY ACT

At present, specific regulatory reporting actions are required by the Cleary Act, established in 1990 for all schools (K-12 and higher education). The Clery Act was originally known as the Crime Awareness and Campus Security Act.

The law is named for Jeanne Clery, a 19-year-old Lehigh University freshman who was raped and murdered in her campus residence hall in 1986. The backlash against unreported crimes on numerous campuses across the country led to the Jeanne Clery Disclosure of Campus Security Policy and Campus Crime Statistics Act.[1]

2008-2009 DEPARTMENT OF EDUCATION HIGHER EDUCATION OPPORTUNITY ACT

In October 2009, the Department of Education (DOE) finalized the rules to the Higher Education Opportunity Act amendment that Congress originally passed in 2008. The changes affected many parts of the original act, but significant changes were put in place that specifically affect emergency management and reporting.

Annual security report: reporting

The Annual Security Report required by the DOE is a comprehensive account of virtually everything pertaining to campus safety. This is a clearly defined requirement for transparency of higher educational institutions, but does not apply to K-12 facilities or higher educational facilities not accepting any federal funding.

Some of the key elements required by the DOE are crime statistics and reporting, emergency notification policies and procedures, missing student notification policies and more. Three main groups must receive either a copy of the school's annual security report or notice of the report's availability by October 1st of each year. The reporting requirements began in October of 2010. These groups include:

1. Secretary of the Department of Education
2. All enrolled students and current employees
3. All prospective students and prospective employees

Policy of emergency notification

Institutions of higher education are required to have a policy for emergency notification of the campus community upon "the confirmation of a significant emergency or dangerous situation involving an immediate threat to the health or safety of students or employees occurring on the campus."[2] These timely warnings must be issued when events considered a threat to students and employees are reported to campus security or local police agencies. Institutions must provide descriptions of the process the institution will use to:

- Confirm there is an emergency/dangerous situation
- Determine appropriate segments of the campus to notify
- Determine content of the message
- Initiate the notification system

---

[1]20 U.S.C. § 1092(f) Disclosure of campus security policy and campus crime statistics (Jeanne Cleary Act), last amended 2008, section J(i), http://clerycenter.org/jeanne-clery-act.
[2]Ibid.

To avoid flooding campus recipients with messages, an institutional emergency notification procedure is not required to issue a timely warning based on the same circumstance repeatedly, but must adequately follow up on information provided to the community as needed. In other words, both a warning message and an emergency notification message do not need to be issued.

The new DOE regulations also include a provision that ensures sufficient information is disseminated to the campus in situations where the emergency or investigation is still developing. The new requirement states that an institution uses its emergency notification system to provide follow-up information to the community as needed and that it should not interfere with emergency operations.

Policy of emergency response and evacuation

A statement of policy regarding emergency response and evacuation procedures is the primary element of an annual security report. This statement describes how the institution will immediately notify the campus community upon confirmation of a significant emergency or dangerous situation (unless notification will compromise efforts to contain the emergency).

Testing of emergency response and evacuation

The annual security report must contain a description of how the institution will test its emergency response and evacuation procedures at least annually. Testing should include:

- At least one test per calendar year, which may be announced or unannounced
- Document a description of the exercise, date, time and whether it was announced or unannounced
- Procedures the institution will use to immediately notify the campus community upon confirmation of a significant emergency or dangerous situation involving an immediate threat to the health or safety of students or employees occurring on campus, unless notification will compromise efforts to contain the emergency
- Must provide follow-up information to the community as needed when the emergency notification system is used

Notification required: Unless it compromises efforts to assist victim

The annual security report must also contain a statement that the institution will, without delay, determine the content of the message and initiate the notification system unless notification will compromise efforts to assist a victim or mitigate the emergency. Other items the report must contain include:

1. List the titles of who is responsible for carrying out the actions
2. Procedures for disseminating emergency information to the larger community
3. A statement of the policies regarding missing student notification procedures for the students who reside on campus (in institution-provided student housing facilities).

In an excerpt from the Handbook for Campus Safety and Security Reporting, the DOE states:

> The Department encourages institutions to consider overlapping means of communication in case one method fails or malfunctions...Additionally, institutions have the flexibility to alert only the appropriate segment or segments of the population that they determine to be at risk.[3]

---

[3]The Handbook for Campus Safety and Security Reporting, Department of Education, February 2011, pages 100-01, http://www2.ed.gov/admins/lead/safety/handbook.pdf.

NFPA 72

The National Fire Protection Association (NFPA) has set national standards to be followed when planning for fire safety. The NFPA now has conformance guidelines and requirements for mass notification systems and how they should interface and overlap with other systems specific to mass notification. The NFPA 72 standards are intended to minimize the possibility and effects of fires, emergency events, and the effect of events in virtually every building through a design, installation, and monitoring process.

PLANNING AND IMPLEMENTING MASS NOTIFICATION SYSTEMS

When planning and implementing a mass notification system, institutions should also consider what role fire, life safety, and emergency notification alerts will play in emergency communications. Institutions must take into account the need for targeting specific areas of the campus and accommodating employees and students with disabilities. The most recent change to NFPA 72 allows the mass notification system to reside above and signal different devices attached to the fire alarm system as well as gather more information from outside systems that may provide advanced warning of a potential event.

REDUNDANCY AND RELIABILITY

Redundancy and reliability are two necessary attributes of a holistic approach to mass notification on campuses. Best practices indicate that a mixed media approach with multiple tiers of communication technologies are needed in an emergency. The visual alerts available with programmable digital notification such as smart LED solutions strategically placed in high traffic and gathering areas is a fundamental part of effectively communicating vital information instantly. With the right technology mix, emergency management personnel can save time and save lives while leveraging components of a solution for practical daily use and delivering return on investment.

NATIONAL STANDARDS

NATIONAL INCIDENT MANAGEMENT SYSTEM, THE INCIDENT COMMAND SYSTEM, AND THE NATIONAL RESPONSE FRAMEWORK

Started by presidential order in 2003 and originally intended to address national incidents like the tragic events of 9/11, a series of standards and procedures have been developed to help the United States be better prepared during emergencies. These include the National Incident Management System (NIMS), the Incident Command System (ICS), and the National Response Framework (NRF). These programs are very comprehensive and are administered by DHS under FEMA.

A few states have begun to use the NIMS and ICS structure to address school emergencies and establish programs and guidelines for response. While the interface to federal, state, and local agencies is an important component of any response plan, a well-tailored and comprehensive plan that takes the details of the specific institution or school's needs into account is imperative.

EFFECTIVE PLANNING STARTS WITH RISK ASSESSMENT

Schools, colleges, and universities should begin with a full risk assessment and comprehensive development of an emergency plan. These actions are the first steps in determining the needs of your particular environment and the requirements of the location.

Following the NIMS and DOE guidelines only provides an outline of what is required. A full multidisciplinary team of participants should be utilized. Once the plan is established with the policies for compliance and the emergency responses, then the supporting systems and equipment can be functionally addressed.

COMPLIANCE AND ENFORCEMENT
CLERY ACT AND DOE

As stated earlier, the Clery Act requires all colleges and universities that participate in federal financial aid programs to keep and disclose information about crime on and near their respective campuses. The U.S. Federal DOE requires college campuses to submit yearly updated security and safety plans to address the newly established requirements if they wish to participate in federal financial aid programs.

The methodology for addressing the systems in support of these DOE-required plans is coming into shape in the requirement changes and additions to NFPA 72. Compliance is monitored by the DOE, which can impose civil penalties—up to $27,500 per violation—against institutions for each infraction and can suspend institutions from participating in federal student financial aid programs.

AUTHORITY HAVING JURISDICTION

While there are ever tightening requirements for higher education and mandates associated with fines for noncompliance with safety and security planning, the K-12 school environment is woefully behind.

In some cases, K-12 schools are required to meet state regulations if they exist. Yet even in states that have statutes applicable to K-12 schools, some districts and departments do not have enough funding to comply. A few states have begun to use NIMS to address school emergencies and establish programs and guidelines for response.

The authority having jurisdiction (AHJ) ultimately is responsible for compliance with state and local code enforcement, but in many discussions, we have found that even the AHJ has not kept up with the requirements and recommendations associated with K-12 schools.

Following an incident, civil lawsuits for millions of dollars are prevalent. The basis of these lawsuits is negligence for failing to provide a safe and secure environment. With direction and guidance provided by federal and state levels, individuals, institutions and municipalities have little defense.

Table 10.1 shows the inconstancy and growing disparity of enforcement between K-12 and higher education institutions.

Table 10.1 Inconstancy of Enforcement Between K-12 and Higher Education Institutions		
	K-12	**Higher Ed**
1990 Clery Act—Disclose Crime Information	Does not apply to K-12	Enforced
2003-2008 Federal Guidelines	No Enforcement	Enforced
State Enforced Assessments	Only 20 States	N/A
NFPA 72 and 101	Inconsistently Applied and Enforced	

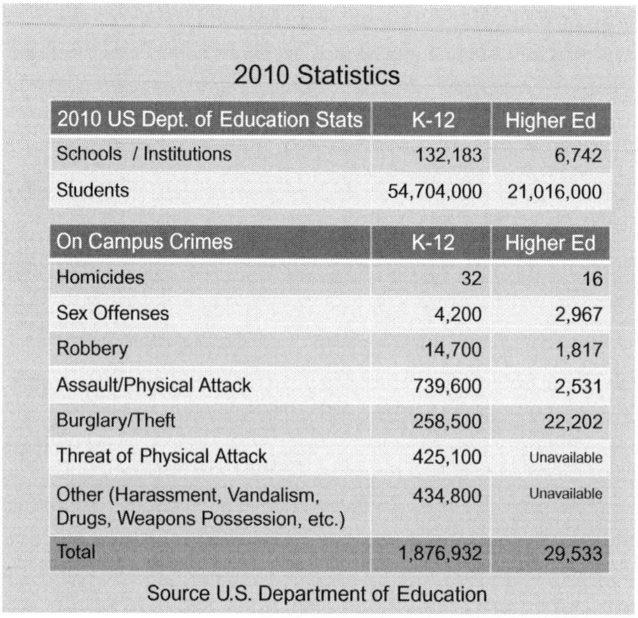

2010 Statistics

2010 US Dept. of Education Stats	K-12	Higher Ed
Schools / Institutions	132,183	6,742
Students	54,704,000	21,016,000

On Campus Crimes	K-12	Higher Ed
Homicides	32	16
Sex Offenses	4,200	2,967
Robbery	14,700	1,817
Assault/Physical Attack	739,600	2,531
Burglary/Theft	258,500	22,202
Threat of Physical Attack	425,100	Unavailable
Other (Harassment, Vandalism, Drugs, Weapons Possession, etc.)	434,800	Unavailable
Total	1,876,932	29,533

Source U.S. Department of Education

FIGURE 10.1

U.S. Department of Education 2010 statistics.

ALARMING STATISTICS FOR K-12

Considering the disparity of enforcement, the following statistics shown in Figure 10.1[4] bear out this disparity and are especially alarming when we consider the ages of the affected students.

The following statistics below (broken out from Figure 10.1) add concern and also help drive the need for completion and assessment of the individual schools in a "holistic" approach.

- In 2009, about 5% of K-12 students avoided a place in school, a school activity, or stayed home because of fear of attack or harm.
- 16% of public schools reported gang activity in 2009-2010.
- K-12 teachers are victims of over 400,000 violent crimes each year.

Risk assessments would produce not only mass notification requirements, but also an entire security and safety plan with the current associated liability.

MASS NOTIFICATION ROLE AND ITS IMPORTANCE

The role of a mass notification system should allow a layered communications strategy for your physical security plan needs. This will address how you alert your security staff, faculty, students, parents, and the public. A holistic approach to protection should be employed to address all possibilities and potential threats.

[4]National Center for Education Statistics—Institute of Education Sciences. Digest of Education Statistics: 2010. http://nces.ed.gov/pubs2011/2011015.pdf.

Mass Notification type events can vary from the severe, "a bomb or terrorist attack," to the informational, such as closings due to weather "a snow day." The intent of Mass Notification Systems is as the name would imply: "to notify the masses" in the case of an event.

As authors in this subject matter, we would be remiss not to caution the reader that Clery Act considerations and changes within NFPA, set expectations and requirements regarding these systems. We advise that these items be given the consideration they deserve. Laws, regulations, and codes have begun to change regarding fire and notification systems. When designing these systems NFPA requirements and recommendations should be followed closely.

In some locales, requirements utilize NFPA as a guide and add requirements to make the requirements more stringent. As you consider these systems, please keep in mind that while State and ultimately local jurisdiction presides, any deviation that is less than the NFPA standard opens the school or institution to potential litigious pursuits.[5]

The principal directives and driving factors for mass notification are described in brief above but should now be evident. The threat to life safety is the most important reason to deploy and utilize mass notification. The standpoint of business continuity and liability is arguably the second greatest reason to utilize a mass notification system.

CONCLUSION: ADDRESSING GAPS

In order to address the gaps and provide for one of the most vulnerable sectors of our population (our children), the K-12 schools should be accountable to the same regulatory standards as higher education institutions. The following points are evident to us as authors, subject matter experts, and parents of school age children:

- Crime statistics are markedly higher in K-12 institutions compared to universities
- This age group is more dependent on guidance in an emergency
- Standardized assessment criteria is needed
- Standardized security administrator training is needed
- Many K-12 schools already receive federal funds

Further development and enacting the requirements of NFPA 72 for mass notification at the K-12 level is required. The educational and awareness efforts for AHJs and other responsible parties will begin the process of providing school assessments and further safety and security for our school-age children. Though we do not encourage more federal involvement, it is our belief that earmarked DOE funds and grants with requirements for assessments and mass notification will improve the K-12 school environment rapidly.

As a final note, it is important to note that the role of the schools in today's communities has increased to include many public functions, including being put into service during times of emergency. It is important to provide these institutions with the necessary tools to handle the emergencies when the demand arises.

---

[5]H.L. Homrighaus, F. J. Davies, & G. Bernardo. (2012). *A Primer on Electronic Security for Schools, Universities & Institutions*. Aella Consulting Group, Inc.

YOU GET WHAT YOU PAY FOR (OR WHEN FREE IS NOT REALLY FREE): COMMENTARY AND INSIGHT ON FREE SECURITY CONSULTING SERVICES FOR SCHOOLS

Frank J. Davies, CHS-IV, CIPS, CVI,
President, Aella Consulting Group, Inc.
Gregory Bernardo, CHS-IV, CDT, CVI
Vice president, Aella Consulting Group, Inc.

THE NEED TO DO SOMETHING

Every time there is an incident that reaches national attention, school officials predictably receive numerous inquiries from a lot of people calling themselves experts or consultants. Often, these school officials are pressured by a moral or political need *to do something*. The immediacy of this pressure may cause normally responsible individuals to fall victim to predatory practices.

"FREE" CONSULTING SERVICES TRAP

One of the most common predatory practices occurs when self-proclaimed consultants offer free services that are simply veiled attempts to prey on responsible individuals who feel a need to do something.

Free or no-cost services (such as security assessments) are typically offered by product manufacturers and product installers (sometimes referred to as integrators). This practice should always be suspected because the primary purpose for these companies is to sell a specific product or service. Pressure to purchase products and services may appear as an unspoken expectation, or the salesman may directly pressure the end user due to "all the free work I [salesman] have done for you." In many cases, the individuals performing the free service will focus on the areas which their product or service fits, leaving other important areas unaddressed or exposed.

QUALIFIED OR UNQUALIFIED?

Another example of free services as a loss leader comes from unqualified and self-proclaimed consultants. In many states, consultants are not required to have a license. In those states, it is your responsibility to perform due diligence and determine if consultants are relevant, current, and qualified for the subject matter on which they profess to be an expert.

The recent economic conditions found many people out of work and forced many others to consider their job security. Having worked in a particular facet of the security industry for a while, some of these individuals may have felt they had the expertise to become a consultant and risk the $50 to file a Doing Business As (DBA) form at the local county clerk or $150 to form an LLC.

However, many of these individuals have worked in only one facet of the industry and are limited in their subject matter expertise and training. For example, a salesperson for a national security provider that specializes in residential security technology likely has no experience in fire systems, mass notification, active shooter, FEMA Incident Command System, and the myriad other priorities of a school or district.

Likewise, individuals from law enforcement often have a myopic view that is focused on response. While law enforcement performs this function well, generally, law enforcement personnel do not have expertise in application of technology or proactive actions.

REALITY—YOU GET WHAT YOU PAY FOR

Truly independent consultants, who make a living solely on consulting, do so based on their subject matter expertise. They will promote their areas of expertise and have certifications or can offer proof of their relevance in the areas that your school needs to address. Generally, a team with complementary disciplines is required to provide a holistic solution. Typically, independent consultants can only afford to do a small amount of discounted work because they have hard overhead costs such as errors and omissions insurance, which protect both the consultant and the client.

By accepting and receiving free services, you may be leaving yourself open to liability if something should happen at your facility. Consider the potential liability for this scenario:

A salesperson wants to increase sales of his or her security cameras. He has sold security cameras for many years and offers to perform security assessments to schools as a loss leader (namely his or her time). Surprise! The report recommends installing security cameras, citing a potential reduction of criminal incidents (i.e., presence of cameras as a deterrent and availability of recorded video as prosecutor forensic evidence).

Subsequently, the school spends their entire security budget and borrows additional money through a bond to install the video system.

Sometime later, the school learns about undisclosed ongoing maintenance costs (such as camera failures, maintenance for video recording servers, and annual software license fees). The school is forced to scramble to shoehorn as much of these unexpected costs as possible into an already tight school budget. As a result, the system is not fully maintained and some cameras go offline for extended periods.

SUSTAINABLE DESIGN

If equipment and systems (such as security cameras, two-way radios, panic buttons, visitor management systems, access control, etc.) are included in the mitigation strategy, these technical components need to be incorporated into school policies and procedures, and sustainable maintenance programs need to be developed to keep the systems updated and functioning.

This creates a new liability for the school because staff, students, and parents now have a false expectation of security and safety in the affected areas.

Should the school inform the populace about the unprotected areas and subsequently alert would-be criminals? Should the school remove cameras from the affected areas? This would have the same result, in that criminals would know the area is unprotected. A more acceptable solution would be to provide security personnel in that area.

In another example, at the same school, a noncustodial parent enters the school and kidnaps their child. This scenario plays out at schools nationwide and sometimes results in life-threatening situations. However, the security camera salesperson's security assessment report did not consider this situation because his primary expertise is myopic to a specific niche of the security industry.

To cover this scenario, the school needs to address how to help stop this type of incident from occurring and how to respond if it does. For example, one way to help prevent a noncustodial kidnapping could be to force all visitors through a single entry and confirm identity with a visitor management system tied to state and federal records system (CORI). Another facet may be to construct a secure entry where the visitor is not allowed to access any larger areas. Cameras can be a part of the check-in process and also be used in response to an incident if they are placed with both considerations in mind. Each of these areas requires specific expertise and disciplines. Schools need to build a team that covers a holistic approach to securing the school, its personnel, and students.

LIABILITY

In the court cases we have reviewed, liability surrounding the expectation of safety was determined by answering "Was the criminal act sufficiently foreseeable to give rise to a duty?"[1]

The term *foreseeable* is generally a major point of debate[2] in lawsuits and relies on a combination of criminal activity statistics for the type of facility, demographics for the location, incidents of local criminal activity,[3] and other criteria. In a higher-education environment, the Clery Act helps to ensure that criminal incidents are accurately reported. K-12 institutions are not bound by the Clery Act, so criminal statistics are less accurate for those facilities and other sources are relied upon.

In a case tried in the District of Columbia in 1995 involving a teenage girl who was shot while trying to leave a cheerleading competition, the court found that the victim was entitled to a heightened duty of protection because she was a young child attending an event at a public school, over which the District

---

[1] *Board of Trustees of the University of the District of Columbia v. Gaciette DiSalvo* (D.C. Court of Appeals 2009).

[2] A US court describes a duty of protection in *District of Columbia v. Doe*, 524 A.2d 30 (D.C. 1987), "where a young student was abducted from inside of her elementary school classroom and raped by an unknown intruder" on the grounds that "crimes against persons in and around the school—an arson in the school and a robbery on the school's playground; sexual assaults and other violent activity in the surrounding area; and deficient school security —the open rear gate, broken doors, malfunctioning intercom, and presence of adult males who freely roamed throughout the school" supported a finding that the particular criminal act was reasonably foreseeable.

[3] *Doe v. Dominion Bank, N.A.*, 295 U.S. App. D.C. 385, 388-89 (D.C. Cir. 1992) (finding a duty where a woman was raped on an unsecured vacant floor of a building where other criminal activity had occurred and tenants had specifically warned the landlord about the potential danger posed by the lack of security, vacant floors, and unauthorized persons in the building). Also, *Novak v. Capital Mgmt. & Dev. Corp.*, 371 U.S. App. D.C. 526, 528 (D.C. Cir. 2006).

of Columbia exercised custodial care; who was "particularly vulnerable to the conduct that befell her"; and was "taken from a place that we would expect to be a safe haven."[4]

By using the wrong resources, schools often fail to address the wide range of known security and safety concerns and create more liabilities than they started with. In the example of the salesperson offering a free assessment, the security salesperson has little, if any, liability because the school relied on his myopic security assessment. The school and the decision maker who relied on this free assessment will be scrutinized and potentially held liable.

THE RIGHT WAY

Truly effective security at our children's schools requires a holistic approach that is not provided by the usual loss leader giveaway services. FEMA describes its five missions that make up a holistic approach: Prevention, Protection, Mitigation, Response, and Recovery. School security requires consideration of a broad range of security risks that are specific to the school, the environment, and demographics.

ASSESSMENT

The starting place for school security planning is a comprehensive risk and vulnerability assessment. This assessment needs to identify not only the physical issues that an equipment-centric salesperson would focus on but also any defects with existing policies, procedures, and plans.

Every facility has a unique layout, purpose of use, and populace which results in a unique list of risks and vulnerabilities.

MITIGATION STRATEGY

Once the risks have been identified, weighted, and prioritized, a mitigation strategy can be developed. The mitigation strategy should incorporate existing guidelines, best practices, and well-refined policies, procedures, and plans specific to the school environment.

There is no magic bullet that will make all the risks go away. Installing cameras does not mean theft and violence will suddenly cease. There are many established best practices, but each one is a starting point that needs to be tailored to the school.

Often, several disciplines are needed to comprehensively address a particular vulnerability. One example restricts access to the interior of the school through a combination of procedural and policy changes, application of crime prevention through environmental design (CPTED),[5] and the introduction of technologies to restrict access and automated positive identification and Criminal Offender Record Information (CORI) inquiry.

Similar to chess strategy, developing a mitigation strategy requires consideration of several steps beyond the obvious starting points. For example:

---

[4]*Bailey v. District of Columbia*, 668 A.2d 817, 821 (D.C. 1995).
[5]Crime Prevention Through Environmental Design (CPTED) is defined by the International CPTED Association "as a multidisciplinary approach to deterring criminal behavior through environmental design. CPTED strategies rely upon the ability to influence offender decisions that precede criminal acts by affecting the built, social and administrative environment."

- In some high-risk environments, a mitigation plan may recommend the installation of magnetometers to screen students and visitors for weapons. The addition of magnetometers will create queue lines that impede the students entering the school each morning. Issues relating to American with Disabilities Act (ADA) compliance and secondary (possibly invasive) searches will need to be addressed.
- School mitigation plans should include provisions for training exercises that help the school deal with unfolding events (such as active shooter) and what should happen after an event. Training sources and coordination with law enforcement will need to be addressed.

Lastly, all risk assessments and mitigation strategies need to be updated on a regular basis. This is a cost of time and money that needs to be considered and planned for as well.

STILL CONSIDERING SO-CALLED FREE SERVICES?

No matter how well intentioned the individual offering a free service is, the old adages hold true: "You get what you pay for," and "Nothing is truly free."

ASK WHY

Understand the motivation and purpose for offering a "free" service. Is it because they live in the district? Do they have children in that school? Do they make a commission for promoting a product or company?

ConsultantRegistry.Org (a free consultant directory and resource used by security professionals) recommends that you choose a consultant who does not have a vested stake in selling you a product.

CHECK REFERENCES AND RELEVANCE

Do they have the credentials and experience necessary to perform the work they are offering (FEMA, DHS, American Board for Certification in Homeland Security, ASIS International, etc.)?

If they are promoting technology solutions, do they attend trade shows and product training so they are knowledgeable about the best solutions available? Do they have experience and current references to back up their claims of expertise?

Do they carry errors and omissions insurance? If not, they are probably not qualified to give advice.

IMPORTANCE OF PROTECTING YOUR INFORMATION

Regardless of the cost of the service, during the assessment, you are giving someone privileged access to your facility, policies, and procedures. In the early part of discussions and contract negotiation, there should be a nondisclosure agreement (NDA) that is signed by the individual you are working with and an officer of the company they work for.

In March 2013, National Union Fire Insurance filed suit against ADT Security Services, Inc. claiming that unique and confidential information in the care of ADT was used by parties to evade and bypass security equipment and monitoring services at locations in Florida, Texas, and Illinois.

If you progress, your contract should specifically spell out the acceptable use and storage of sensitive information and include a requirement for written permission prior to sharing any information with outside parties.

AUTHOR'S RECOMMENDATIONS

A security program that achieves all of your objectives requires a team or partnership. In the educational environment, we suggest at minimum a team with at least one representative from:

- the district and/or school administration,
- local police authority,
- local fire authority and EMS,
- internal security, and
- the information technology (IT) department.

Notice we suggest a team, not a committee. If the group considers itself a committee, it is sometimes difficult to accomplish the required tasks to achieve the desired goals. However, a team conveys common, combined goals and strategies to effectively and decisively deal with this focused issue. It is essential that the team be selected with sufficient knowledge of the institution(s) and the issues so that they can aggressively pursue sources of information. Many of these team members should be the keepers or custodians of the finished product(s).

Your team will need to formulate a plan with the individual components required to implement an effective security and safety solution. Where your team may include some truly motivated individuals, team meetings should be the primary forum for far-reaching decisions regarding assessments, planning, equipment evaluation, preparation of offerings, and any other items dealing with the overall security and safety of the institution(s).

Managing all of the aspects of the security process can appear to be a daunting task. There are so many variables to understand and deal with to give definition, operational guidelines, and compliance to a well-developed security and safety program. This is amplified by all of the different and varying circumstances found within our schools.

There are many FEMA training programs with certifications. These FEMA programs identify standards for incident management and describe responsibilities that school officials should be aware of and plan for (see FEMA: NIMS and ICS[6]). Many of these FEMA programs are free and should be part of minimum credentials for someone to offer advice on school security.

Your team may initially need some professional help, but use it for areas of your team's specific weaknesses, to supplement your team, or for specific tasks. Ultimately, your team remains to take ownership and responsibility for the results.

When hiring professional help, make sure that you hire for your specific area of need and check to ensure that the professional has the appropriate and necessary qualifications for the task you assign to them.

---

[6]FEMA provides training for schools, responders, and industry professionals for the National Incident Management System (NIMS) and the Incident Command System (ICS). These systems provide standards and procedures for responses in the time of incidents, local and national emergencies to insure a common operational environment.

Sometimes schools need help in getting started with this task and need help to define goals and objectives; this is a valid reason to hire a professional security consultant. Another valid reason to hire a professional is to help with the constructs of a comprehensive and legally compliant and responsive plan; or conduct a full safety and security audit or assessment if it has not be done recently or your team does not possess the skills or knowledge.

Through our experience, we have found that a well-defined role or set of tasks performed by an outside professional will pay for the cost of the professional, sometimes many times over.

Please understand, we are not advocating turning this task over to an outsider; rather, utilizing qualified help where it is needed. In our experience, we have taken assignments to "correct" schools where free advice was taken or where a company or individual has offered incorrect, incomplete, or inadequate advice and information. In all cases, the cost to "correct" has far exceeded the cost to provide the right solutions or answers in the first place.

Therefore, we implore you to consider your actions when pressured by a moral or political need *to do something*. Please help to share that this is not just a task; rather, it is a task to be done right, well, and comprehensively. Take your time to lay the groundwork, select your internal team, and be highly selective of your professionals and the tasks they are assigned.

AN ACCESS CONTROL TEMPLATE FOR K-12 SCHOOLS

Donald R. Green, CPP, CEMA

Director of operations, Educational Safety Services

INTRODUCTION

How secure should a public school building be? A small neighborhood school in a farming community might be wide open for parents to drop in anytime. In parts of Israel, razor-wire fencing and concrete barriers surround schools while military personnel maintain machine gun emplacements near the main entrance. I think we can likely agree that for most schools in the United States, somewhere between these two extremes is ideal.

PROPERTY PERIMETER

Like any sensitive facility, physical security and access control for schools can best be examined in concentric rings, from the outside working in. Access control starts at the extreme perimeter of the school property. Do we need a 7-feet-tall chain link fence with three strands of barbed wire angled out at the top? That gives the appearance of overkill, and in this circumstance, it is ineffective. Using the principles of crime prevention through environmental design (CPTED), it is important to delineate the property lines and show territoriality. CPTED also encourages natural access control. We can easily accomplish that with a relatively low, attractive fence or landscaping that guides people to the designated entrance. That avoids a prison-like appearance and the subliminal messaging "this place is unsafe" that a "security" fence suggests. There may be places, such as athletic fields where admission needs to be highly regulated, where a more secure fence might be appropriate.

As the pedestrian traffic gets channeled to the selected entrance, vehicle traffic should be the next concern addressed. From a safety viewpoint, pedestrian traffic should not cross vehicle travel lanes if at all possible. There are five primary considerations: buses, staff, students, visitors/vendors, and student drop-offs/pickups. In an ideal design, these five should be separated. Buses should have their own entrance/exit and be routed so that there is direct access between a bus and school entrance. Staff and students (in high schools) should have a regulated parking section.

There are different ideas about segregating staff and students, reserved or named parking spots, and numbering spaces. I suggest the following as a best practice:

- Staff and students need to register their vehicles with the school.
    - A condition of registration is that vehicles parked on school property are subject to search.
- They receive a mirror hang tag permit that is numbered and recognizable to staff, but does not identify the school to an outsider.
- Staff and student parking is integrated and there are no assigned spots.
    - This incorporates the CPTED principle of natural surveillance—mixing cars ensures that everyone in the school has an interest in keeping an eye on the parking area.
- Signage warns that parking on school property is assumed to be consent to search and that vehicles without a valid permit are subject to towing at the owner's expense.
- Contract with a local towing company to check the lot and tow unpermitted vehicles.
- Encourage staff who plan to work late to move their cars closer to the entrance after dismissal.

Visitor and vendor parking should be well marked and segregated from other areas. The area should be checked periodically for nonvisitors and those cars should be ticketed or removed. Student drop-off/pickup might be collocated with the visitor parking or, if space allows, at a separate location.

BUILDING PERIMETER

It is generally accepted that all building doors should be locked, with the possible exception of the main entrance, but that does not always work. There are doors leading to playgrounds, remote trailer classrooms, open campus buildings, or satellite buildings such as gyms. Depending on the grade levels, there may be need for student access to and from other buildings. Some points to consider are:

- Any door that is not used on a regular basis should be locked and have the exterior handle hardware removed.
- At the main entrance, there may be several doors—only one should be used during the day.
    - There are several ways to control the main entrance:
        - Have it visible to natural surveillance from the main office
        - Have it visible to a digital recording camera system that is monitored in the main office
        - Have it monitored by a staff member or parent volunteer who directs visitors or vendors to the main office
        - A buzzer/intercom/remote unlock device (many include a camera)
- Other doors that get used periodically throughout the day also need to be controlled by locking them.
    - Proximity cards or key scan cards:
        - These can be combined with student or staff ID cards.
        - The card access can be disabled if:
            - An employee is terminated or transferred
            - A student loses privileges
            - A card is lost
        - Other factors include:
            - The times and days that a card will work can be programmed for individual or class needs.
            - It is imperative to deactivate cards when they are no longer needed and to ensure lost cards are immediately reported.

- Cipher/Combination Locks
  - Students (and therefore their families) *will* learn the combinations
  - Need to be changed immediately if compromised
  - Should be changed on a regular basis
  - Best if used on a door that has access to the area restricted such as entering the school from a fenced in trailer classroom group
- Police/Fire Access
  - In an emergency, police or fire/EMS may be more effective when not using the main entrance.
  - A Knox box is a locked case secured to an exterior wall near a door—responders have master keys to all Knox boxes and can retrieve a door key from the box.
  - Some jurisdictions are now installing proximity card readers on doors that are programmed to the local police or fire department ID card readers or giving all police and fire access to the school district's card readers.
- Windows must also be controlled, primarily to limit the ability of students to pass contraband in but also to minimize the risk of after-hours access.
  - Using the CPTED principle of natural surveillance, prune bushes to a height of 3 ft, and trees from the ground up the first branch must be 8 ft off the ground.
  - Make teachers responsible for locking classroom windows at the end of the day.
  - Ensure custodians check behind teachers and lock common area windows.
- Roof access may or may not be a concern, depending on construction.
  - Exterior-installed ladders should have locking cages blocking them.
  - Roof access from inside must have locked hatches or doors.

VISITOR AND VENDOR MANAGEMENT

It behooves a school administrator to know who is in his or her building at all times. If a fire or other disaster happens, we need to be able to say with certainty who was inside and whether or not they are accounted for. We also need to know that the people who are in the building are supposed to be in the building.

Permanent staff seem like they would be the easiest to account for, but with human resource regulations and union rules, they may actually be more difficult to document. The best practice is for all the staff to check in and out of the building in some manner. In a small elementary school, it might be at the main office. A large building might use an electronic time and attendance system. Consider the problem if a teacher left during a planning period to run an errand and did not let anyone know that she was gone. The building catches fire or a tornado strikes, and she is unaccounted for. The lives of others would be at risk trying to rescue someone who does not need rescuing because they are not even there. Staff should wear school or district ID at all times.

Volunteers should be background checked through human resources, the same as any other employee. Once cleared to work with children, they should check in and out at the main office. They should be issued ID that indicates that they are a volunteer.

Contractors or vendors should only be in the school if approved or arranged through district policy. They should check in and out at the main office. They should receive a temporary ID that designates where they should be working. If calling on an employee, that employee should meet the vendor at the office and escort them at all times.

Parents can be a tremendous asset or a headache to a school. Some will happily abide by all access rules while others will treat the rules as if they do not apply to them. Still others may test the rules to try and compromise or embarrass the school. It is important to establish ground rules and expectations at the start of the school year and that the expectations are the same for all parents.

The first step is to ensure that only people allowed to visit a child, classroom, or activity are those who are on a list provided by the parents or guardian. School staff cannot be expected to interpret custody papers or restraining orders. Whoever registers the child for school must list the only people who are allowed to see the child. To ensure that the list is effective, office staff must check the identification of all visitors and confirm that they are on the approved list. To be consistent, they must check every visitor, every visit. Some schools have adopted an automated system of logging visitors, checking sex offender or approved visitor records, and printing visitor passes. These systems are fine, but they do not take the place of an employee physically checking a visitor's ID card and confirming that it identifies the person who is presenting it. After confirming that a parent or visitor is approved for a visit, the office staff (or an automated kiosk) should issue the visitor a temporary ID card or sticker, ideally one that self-expires.

Some typical restrictions a parent visit include:

- Silent classroom observation—when a parent may observe a classroom but not take part in or distract from instruction—should be limited to one class period and no more than two to three times per week
- Teacher conferences—parents must make appointments to meet with teachers outside of instruction time. Teachers will not stop instruction to discuss anything with a parent
- Lunch or breakfast—because mealtime is very social for students, parents should be discouraged from eating with a child unless it is a special circumstance, such as:
  - Child's birthday
  - Some sort of appreciation day
  - Veteran's Day (if the parent or relative is a veteran)
  - As a special reward for the child

Parents eating with a child may be assigned to a separate table or area depending on the circumstances.

HALLWAYS AND CLASSROOMS

It is the responsibility of all staff in a school to assist in access control and to monitor visitors or report those who may not be approved. Teachers should keep their classroom doors locked at all times. The door can be open, but the knob should be locked. In a crisis, fine motor skills deteriorate and it is difficult to manipulate a key to lock a door under stress. With the door open, but locked, all a teacher needs to do in a crisis is slam the door.

If a parent or other visitor comes to a classroom or encounters a staff member in the hall, he should have visitor or other appropriate ID displayed. If not, the staff must be trained and responsible to direct or escort the person to the office and to notify the office that the person is *en route*. Administrators should reprimand staff who allow undocumented visitors or who take measures to negate access control.

CONCLUSIONS

Staff must take ownership of their building and their safety responsibilities. If outside at recess and a teacher sees a trespasser, she should know that she is empowered and trusted to take action without asking permission. If a school board member complains because a custodian made him walk "all the way around" the building to the main entrance rather than letting him in a side door, the custodian should be thanked for his consistency and the board member reminded of the school's access control policies. When a parent gets frustrated and yells at the secretary who made her go back to the car to get her ID, the secretary should be recognized for doing the right thing and the parent counseled about behavior expectations.

There are places where it is extremely difficult to gain access in or out. They are called prisons. We cannot ensure 100% control of a school while still keeping it a positive learning environment. No matter the level and type of access controls in place at a school, consistency is the key to safety. The steps outlined in this chapter can make a school safer and more secure, but it is up to the staff, parents, and yes, even the students to be alert, report suspicious or inappropriate contact, and abide by the rules. Prevention is the responsibility of everyone.

"CRIME RISK" VERSUS "FEELING SAFE" IN SCHOOLS: TRUE AND FALSE RISK ASSESSMENT IN SCHOOLS

Paul van Soomeren

CEO, DSP-groep (http://www.dsp-groep.eu/); director of the board, the International CPTED Association and the European Designing Out Crime Association

INTRODUCTION

The concept of "fear of crime" usually refers to two quite different components: a risk assessment and a feeling. In this chapter, we will focus on the concept of fear of crime and one specific group: young people in high schools in the Netherlands.

RISK ASSESSMENT

In this context, risk assessment refers to the fear of personally becoming a victim of particular types of crime, such as violence, vandalism, theft, or burglary. A person's sense of risk can be measured by including a question in a victim survey that asks respondents how likely they think it is that they will be a victim of violence, vandalism, theft, or some other crime in the coming year. In short, the risk assessment of becoming a victim.

FEELING SAFE

Another type of question often posed in a victim survey in order to measure feelings of insecurity is: "How safe do you feel walking alone in the area after dark? Do you feel very safe, fairly safe, a bit unsafe, or very unsafe?"[1] This question paints a different picture of fear of crime. In response to the question of street safety, women, elderly, and disabled people emerge as more fearful. This may be because the prospect of being out after dark evokes anxiety about a greater and more serious range of mishaps for these groups.

---

[1] For example, the United Nation International Crime Victim Survey started by Jan van Dijk (The Netherlands) and Pat Mayhew (UK). See the website of UNICRI, Turin, Italy.

A related question to look at fear of crime is "How safe do you feel when at home alone after dark." The results of this question sketch a more optimistic picture: The better one knows an environment, the safer one feels. Hence, "at home" (even when you're alone) feels a lot safer compared to walking in an area after dark.

WHY DO PEOPLE FEEL INSECURE?

The degree of fear and the kind of crimes a person is afraid of differ depending on gender and age. The hypothesis is that women, the elderly, and disabled people are more likely to fear crime. They fear for their personal safety and are afraid of street violence and, in particular, sexual assaults. It is far more terrifying to be confronted with crimes like rape, which threaten a person's integrity and dignity, than with the loss of material goods. For this reason, women are usually more affected by this feeling than men.

Though studies of public areas where sexual assaults have occurred show that the type and characteristics of fearful places—for example, poor lightning and the presence of hiding places—correlate with the occurrence of crime, fearful places are not necessarily places where actual crimes occur. Nevertheless, fear influences the way people behave with regard to public or semi-public spaces. In particular, women and the elderly are more likely to use avoidance strategies that keep them away from problematic areas and situations. They tend to restrict their own activities due to their fear of crime. This behavior has effects on neighborhoods, on routes chosen to visit places and on the popularity of schools. Right or wrong, if a school is seen as a high crime risk, people may act accordingly with very real consequences such as avoiding the school as much as possible until the community feels safe by both police presence and a reduction in crime.

Avoidance behavior may also have an effect on the victimization rate: avoiding risk may actually be quite an effective strategy. In that respect, one might also argue that men and youngsters are irrational risk seekers and consequently have a higher victimization risk.

But let's face the facts first. Who are more at risk? Young people or older people? Pupils or staff at school?

QUITE RIGHT TO FEAR CRIME WHEN YOU'RE YOUNG!

Flight and Rietveld[2] (2003) showed for the Netherlands (17 million inhabitants) for the first time that young people are in fact more at risk of becoming a victim of crime compared to adults. Also, young people seemed to be a bit more fearful. These two researchers compared national victim surveys—containing questions on fear of crime as well as victimization rates—with research surveys done in schools in the 1990s (see also Van Soomeren and Boersma elsewhere in this volume). In this chapter, we have replicated this analysis based on the national victim survey and the school survey figures of 2012 for the Netherlands.

---

[2]Sander Flight and Mark Rietveld (2003). Terecht bang, Slachtofferschap en beleving van veiligheid door jongeren. DSP-groep link http://www.dsp-groep.nl/projecten/p1/3825/.

Sources: national and schools

Every year the National Bureau for Statistics in the Netherlands does a survey on crime and safety (Veiligheidsmonitor CBS, random effective sample of 80,000 participants age 15+), which is a great source for all facts and figures on crime and fear of crime.

Separately, and specific for schools, every 2 years research is done on "social safety in and around schools" in schools for primary education as well as high schools (ITS/Regioplan[3]). We will focus on the outcomes for high schools where in the 2012 research sweep about 1,300 staff (teachers and school support officials) and 9,000 pupils have answered questions on crime, safety, and fear of crime.

The research in high schools is not easy to compare with the national crime survey because the questionnaires, the age of the respondents, the context, and the sampling differ. But from a bird's eye view, the results may be more comparable than initially appears and are certainly interesting. We compare the total population, youth 15-25 and pupils (age 12-18) plus staff in high schools.

CRIME RISKS FOR YOUNGSTERS

As already mentioned, the results from the national victim survey and the schools survey are not easy to compare: the age groups studied differ (12-18 versus 15-25) and figures on cybercrime are not yet available for schools. Also, the two categories of property crimes (mainly theft) and vandalism in the national survey are only one category in the school survey. There are also differences in the definition of violence. Therefore, in Table 13.1 we will omit the categories of verbal, social, and light physical violence and only present figures on heavy physical violence.

Table 13.1 Victim Percent Nationally and in High Schools (2012, The Netherlands)				
Type of Crime	**Victim % for the Total Population**[a]	**Victim % Age 15-25**[b]	**Victim % Pupils**[c]	**Victim % Staff**[d]
Violence total	2.6	5.3	16.5	3.9
Sexual violence[f]	*0.1*	*0.2*	*11.6*	*5.3*
Property crimes/theft	13.2	18.5	18.1[e]	5.2[e]
Vandalism	7.7	7.5		
Cybercrime	12.1	19.5	Not available	Not available
Cyber ragging/bullying	*3.1*	*8.0*		

[a] Veiligheidsmonitor CBS 2012, The Hague (National Crime Victim Survey with yearly sweeps and an effective sample of about 80,000 respondents aged 15+).
[b] Veiligheidsmonitor CBS 2012, statline.
[c] Table B6.6 11 ITS/Regioplan 2012, page 134.
[d] Table B6.8 ITS/Regioplan 2012, page 130.
[e] For this category, property crimes/theft and vandalism were seen as one (no distinct figures available).
[f] Italics indicate the item is a subcategory of the preceding category.

---

[3] ITS (Ton Mooij) and Regioplan (2012). Sociale veiligheid rond en in scholen. Comparable research results available for 2006, 2008, 2010 and 2012. Professor Dr. Ton Mooij has done research in Dutch schools on crime and safety since the 1980s. He has also published a lot in the English language.

Table 13.1 shows:

1. Students in age group 15-25 have a substantially higher risk of becoming a victim of violence, theft, and cybercrime compared to the Dutch population (age 15+) as a whole.
2. For pupils in high schools the risks are even higher: Compared to the Dutch population as a whole, the risk of becoming a victim of violence is at least five times as high in schools. But also the risk of theft, property crimes, and vandalism is higher for school pupils.[4]
3. The victim percentages for staff in high schools are lower than the Dutch population as a whole for theft/vandalism, and only slightly higher for violence, but much higher for sexual violence. On the other hand, there is other research also showing that indeed violence—and sexual violence in particular—seems to be a rather high risk for high school staff.[5]

In sum: Being young obviously results in a higher risk of becoming a victim of crime and high schools are a rather risky environment for pupils (and to a lower degree also for staff).

But how well do people assess this risk and how safe do pupils and staff feel in high schools?

CRIME RISK AND FEELING SAFE IN SCHOOLS

In 2011, DSP-groep worked with a group of 40 schools to develop a joint safety organization and policy method for schools. We used the IRIS triple S tool (www.IRIStripleS.com) to do research on the feeling of safety and the actual crime risk within the school premises. The difference between the real crime risk and the feelings of safety were striking:

- The most mentioned location where staff felt unsafe was in the hallways (two times more than in the classroom);
- The number of incidents was more than six times higher in the classrooms than in the hallways.

Obviously, the sound risk assessment of staff in these schools was false. Does the same go for pupils?

FEELING SAFE

Does the higher victim risk for young people in general and school pupils in particular (see Table 13.1) result in higher levels of fear? In fact it hardly does!

The school survey research (ITS/Regioplan) shows that in 2012 more than 90% of the school population felt safe in and around their high schools. This goes for pupils (93%) as well as staff (93%). It

---

[4]Interesting is that the National Crime Survey openly presents victim percentages while the schools survey seems to be more restricted in mentioning victim facts. The victim figures are hidden in difficult to read appendices while the general conclusion of the school survey is: "By far the most pupils and staff (>90%) feel safe at school." As mentioned before: The better you know an environment, the safer you feel. Hence, the conclusion that pupils and staff feel safe in an environment they are in 5 days a week is not very surprising.

[5]In research for the Dutch Ministry of Interior (2007-2009-2011) looking at violence to people exercising a public task the victim percentages for violence and sexual violence against staff in high schools also showed to be high (physical violence/intimidation > 10% and sexual violence 5%) see Flight/DSP-groep 2011, Geweld tegen Publieke Taak afgenomen. Link: http://www.dsp-groep.nl/projecten/p1/5573/).

also goes for specific places in school and outside (parking, around the school): all percentages "feeling safe" rank 90% or more for pupils and staff.[6] In the publicity around the school safety research, this item is bi-yearly publicized in the press: Schools are safe because pupils and staff feel safe!

However, that pupils and staff feel safe in schools is not that special. When asked "How safe do you feel at home?" pupils and staff also feel safe at home (97%); even a bit more safe at home than in and around school. Exactly the same figure is shown by the National Crime Victim survey: Only 2.6% of the whole Dutch population feels unsafe at home. The figure for the age group 15-25 is slightly higher (4.7%) but still that is not a very frightening figure. In fact, almost everyone feels safe at home and also in school. These are environments you know well. It would be strange if people would feel afraid there.

The risk assessment of people about the probability of becoming a victim of crime (in general/not specified) is also rather low in the Netherlands: 3.4% and the age group 15-25 perceives only a slightly higher risk (4.5%). When the question is specified for different environments, as shown in Table 13.2, the age group 15-25 shows also slightly higher levels of fear.

Table 13.2 Percent of People Feeling Unsafe Sometimes/Often (2012, The Netherlands)		
	Total Population (%)	**Age Group 15-25 (%)**
In around leisure spots	25	36
Spots where youngster hang out	44	55
City centers	19	20
Shopping centers	15	15
Public transport	19	25
Source: *National Crime Victim Survey, CBS, The Hague, The Netherlands.*		

In general, the Dutch population feels safe. The age group 15-25 still feels rather safe and pupils and staff at school feel safe too. The differences are extremely small. This might have to do with the fact that research into feelings of safety is still in its infancy. Still, the fact remains that for the three groups—population as a whole, youth 15-25 and high school pupils/staff—the levels of fear are comparable low.

CONCLUSION

The crime risk, especially for pupils in high schools in the Netherlands, is high when compared to the country's population as a whole. It is even higher than the crime victim risk for the age group 15-25.

But when asked about how safe people feel, there is not that much difference in responses. Young people (15-25) feel slightly more fearful of crime, but when asked using a different questionnaire and different procedure, high schools pupils say they feel extremely safe.

---

[6]There is only one very minor exception: feeling safe around school/in the school neighborhood ranks 89.7% for pupils.

In sum, these figures from the Netherlands show that the risk of becoming a crime victim is:

- Higher for young people (15-25)
- Even higher for pupils in high schools

but pupils feel very safe in and around school.

Hence, when looking at crime in schools it is better to focus on the risks of becoming a crime victim than asking pupils about how safe they feel. Though everyone may report to feel very safe, the real crime risks may actually be rather high in schools.

PARTNERING WITH LOCAL FIRST RESPONDERS AND PUBLIC SAFETY OFFICIALS

14

Donald R. Green, CPP, CEMA

Director of operations, Educational Safety Services

INTRODUCTION

Schools are safe places as a rule. The vast majority of students will experience 12 years of education and their experiences with school emergencies will likely be not much more than seeing a fistfight or an asthma attack. That is not always the case, however. Schools are large facilities with a lot of people in them, and any number of large or small emergencies can happen. Illnesses, accidents, criminal attacks, weather events, fires, gas leaks... the list of examples of what could happen is endless. As I wrote this chapter, one of the high schools in my district had an electrical fire in the ceiling and the fire department responded while students and staff were evacuated to the gym and cafeteria. School leaders need to have positive relationships and partnerships with the people who will respond to emergencies, at all levels. For the purposes of this chapter, we will focus on law enforcement (police department or sheriff's office), fire/emergency medical services (EMS) (fire department and rescue squad; in some localities they will be the same agency, in others they will be separate and distinct), and emergency management (disaster planning, response, and recovery). We will examine partnerships at the school and district levels.

LAW ENFORCEMENT

Police are likely the first responders that most school personnel have experience with. Police return truants to school. They serve as school resource officers (SROs) assigned to schools. They work security at football and basketball games. They show up when you find a student with a bag of marijuana.

At the school level, it is important for the local precinct officers to be familiar with your school's floor plan, staff, and students. The local officers are the ones who will respond to your school in a crisis and it is crucial that they know their way around. There are a number of ways to accomplish this.

Invite them to lunch or breakfast. In my district, patrol officers are always welcome in our cafeterias. They know upfront what the cost of a meal for an adult is ($3 for lunch) and come prepared to pay, but often principals or cafeteria managers will "comp" them. This lets the officers learn the layout of the school and gives them positive interaction with students.

The principal should regularly meet or interact with the precinct commander, shift supervisor, or other similar police leaders in the area of the school. It could be formal, scheduled meetings or simply regular phone calls or drop-in visits. The communication should be two-way. The principal needs to know what is happening out in the neighborhood, and the patrol supervisor needs to know what is going on in the school. This is the time to discuss gangs, daytime burglaries, truancy, drug dealers, sex offenders… pretty much any issue that affects people within the school, whether they are actually in school or not.

Trust is a key element of a school/police relationship. The school does not need to get the police involved with every little fight or cell phone theft that happens. The police do not need to arrest every student who breaks any law, but they do need to keep each other informed and involved in major situations. Most states have legislation that specifies which criminal acts must be reported to the police by a school. Most police officers do not have to take a full, official report for everything they come in contact with. A good relationship will allow the school to report what they must, and the police to take action if needed. Virginia law requires a principal to report to police if a student threatens a teacher. There is no gray area or judgment. A threat must be reported. However, with a good relationship, a principal can report a threat, and if it is not substantiated and the victim wishes no further action, the police officer can simply make an intelligence report or even just a "duly noted" comment in some cases. Trust is weakened when the perception exists that the school hides or covers up information, or when the police are overbearing or over-reaching. A school was required to report anything that "may be" a sexual assault. A female student was caught having sexual relations outside the school with two male students. The principals spoke to all three who agreed it was consensual, so he issued discipline and sent them home. When the girl got home, she told her parents she had been assaulted and the school did nothing to the boys. The parents called the police who knew nothing about it, and the immediate perception was that the principal was covering it up. That principal learned that the key phrase was "may be" and he now immediately notifies his SRO of anything sexual, even if it is completely consensual. He still does discipline, but he lets the police and the parents determine if there was a criminal violation. On the other side of the issue, the law required the police to notify the principal if a student was arrested at school. The SRO witnessed a parent being verbally abusive and disruptive in the main office. The parent stopped the behavior and left. However, the SRO went to the magistrate and got a warrant charging the parent with disorderly conduct and the parent was arrested at home that evening. The SRO never told the school, because the law did not require him to. The end result was that the SRO and the principal now have better communications and he notifies her of any arrest or report that is even slightly connected to the school.

Another way to build relationships is for the principal to invite the police to train in the school. K-9s can check the lockers after school as a proactive measure; in doing so the dogs get their training time and the handlers learn the school's floor plan. On a staff development day, teachers can role-play a crisis situation and the patrol units can train on active shooter response. The intelligence analyst can speak at a faculty meeting about how teachers can recognize and report suspicious activity. At a parent teacher association meeting, the crime prevention officer can speak about drug and gang awareness for parents.

At the division level, it is imperative that the district superintendent has direct and regular contact with the police chief or sheriff. If a major crisis happens, they will be at the forefront of the response and recovery, and they have to know and trust each other. If the community size warrants it, the district security director and mid-level captains and assistant chiefs need to communicate regularly. They will be the "boots on the ground" leaders during a major crisis and have to have a preexisting relationship. They are also the ones who can solve problems before they rise to the top levels.

FIRE/EMS

Local structure may vary, but typically the fire marshal and the rescue squad are the two aspects of the fire department and EMS services that a school interacts with on a regular basis. The fire marshal conducts inspections. Are storage rooms safe? Are flammable materials covering walls? Are sprinklers inspected and clear from obstructions? A positive relationship between the school and the fire marshal can make those inspections more productive and less punitive. As homecoming or any other event approaches, the principal should invite the fire marshal to do an informal inspection of the decorations to ensure that they will not be in violation of the fire code. Perhaps the fire marshal would meet with the decorating committees and give them the parameters and rationale for the limits. A new lead custodian would benefit from meeting and working with the fire marshal before a problem develops. The fire marshal investigates false fire alarms and arsons. Even a trash can fire in the bathroom is arson and should be treated seriously by the authorities. A great way to build a positive relationship is for a school's security officer to review video footage of the event with the fire marshal and work together to develop and interview suspects.

The school nurse is likely the employee most involved with responding rescue squads. The nurse should get to know the "first-in" rescue units in the area before they are needed. Invite them to tour the building and ensure they know which doors are closest to the nurse's office. The fire department may respond with the rescue squad, but will definitely respond to alarm activations, the smell of "smoke" or "burning," and for actual fires. I suggest extending an open invitation to the station captain or supervisor for all newly assigned firefighters to come tour the school to learn the floor plan, locations of water sources, and building construction. A principal should also consider inviting fire and rescue staff to bring apparatus to career days and similar events. At the district level, fire and rescue leadership should be part of any safety committees, crisis plan development, and construction design discussions.

EMERGENCY MANAGEMENT

Schools play a vital role in the emergency management plans of most communities. Schools become shelters, buses evacuate residents to safe locations, and cafeterias feed evacuees. There needs to be advanced planning, communication, and a relationship for it to be a positive for all involved. I recommend that schools and emergency management authorities develop memoranda of understanding and outlining exactly how and when school resources will get used, any staffing demands, responsibilities for supplies, cleanup, liability, phone/internet access, and consumables, and funding or reimbursement. There should be one designated school district point of contact with emergency management who makes the arrangements with other school district building or department heads. This person should have a regular and assigned role in the community's emergency operations center during disasters, drills, and training. Conducting shelter set-up drills every year or two helps ensure that school and emergency management staff will be able to work together to serve the public when a disaster does happen.

CONCLUSION

Things happen at school. People get in trouble, people get sick or injured, and people in need come to schools for help. To respond effectively, school and district leaders need to have positive, cooperative relationships with local public safety agencies and staff. The media and public will look much more favorably on a statement such as, "working together with our partners in the school district, a potential disaster was avoided and everyone is safe," rather than, "you'll have to ask the school district spokesperson about that, we manage our responsibilities and they manage theirs." The aftermath of a serious event is not the time for the superintendent to meet the police or fire chief. A first responder should already know the principal and the building floor plan. Blueprints or digital maps of every building on campus should be provided to local responders before there is an emergency situation. These maps can be used by first responders during training exercises on school property to familiarize them with the interior of the buildings as well as the exterior exits. It is vital that local officials know the location of fire and safety equipment, utility services, and HAZMAT storage areas on school property before there is an emergency situation.

Public/private sector partnerships such as those between schools and law enforcement and the fire department and local emergency officials are not new concepts. It is accurate to say that the collaboration between schools and first responders has become more publicized with the recent events at schools nationwide, but these partnerships have proved to be instrumental in keeping our children safe. Partnerships make the entire community safer and involve all of the partners in the problem-solving process. Building trust and the exchange of information is crucial to developing a solid, working relationship between the partners. In order for a partnership to be successful, each of the partners has to realize that they are working toward the same goal—a safer, healthier community and school environment. It is important to reiterate that partnerships should not be used only in a crisis situation, but should develop over time as a proactive measure to be better prepared if the unimaginable does happen at schools.

If you are interested in learning more about partnerships, there is a significant amount of information available. For example:

1. *Reaching out to the Private Sector*, US Dept. of Justice;
2. *Operation Partnership, Trends & Practices, US Dept. of Justice*;
3. *COPS Office, Community Policing Resources*, US Dept. of Justice; and
4. *Partnering with Businesses*, COPS Problem Solving Tools, Series No. 5.

These and other titles can be obtained at no cost from: www.cops.usdoj.gov.

EMERGENCY MANAGEMENT PROCEDURES

15

Inge Sebyan Black, B.A., CPP, CFE, CPOI

Principal consultant and owner, Security Investigations Consulting

Schools are entrusted to provide a safe and secure environment, along with a healthy learning atmosphere. Families and communities expect schools to keep their loved ones and educators safe from all threats, including natural and human-caused emergencies. With the collaboration of their district staff, first responders, public and mental health, local government and community partners, schools should develop a school Emergency Operations Plan (EOP) that is designed for their building's specific needs. This EOP will play a key role in both preventative measures and protective measures to stop an emergency from occurring or reducing the impact of an incident. The EOP should describe the required actions necessary to protect students, faculty and the public from all threats. The EOP will help school administrators and decision makers prepare for responding to a crisis situation along with identifying all types of emergencies, individual roles, and responsibilities. Preparedness should encompass five specific areas: prevention, protection, mitigation, response, and recovery. These five areas align with three timeframes associated with an incident: before, during and after. Prevention, protection, and mitigation typically occur before an incident, although any of these can occur through any of the timeframes, while response occurs during the incident and recovery begins during the incident as well as after the incident.

The EOP must be well written, and automated in a clear and logical order. It is recommended that schools writing their emergency plans use concepts and principles recognized by the National Incident Management System (NIMS). One of these components is the Incident Command System (ICS), which provides a standardized approach for incident management, regardless of the type of incident. These practices help to integrate the efforts of first responders and other key emergency management personnel. They will also help school administrators understand the role that responders will be assuming. The emergency plan must be supported by senior level officials. It must also provide for the access and functional needs of the entire school community, including individuals with disabilities and other needs. In addition to those with disabilities, other needs might include religious, racial, and language barriers. Considerations also need to be made for incidents occurring outside of the school day as well as off the school campus (e.g., field trip).

To begin planning for emergencies, a planning team should be created with the responsibility for developing, implementing, and continually updating their EOP. When a team is identified, each person involved in the development and maintenance of the plan should know his or her role and responsibility in the planning process. The planning process should be an ongoing one that is reinforced with regularly planned meetings. At the onset of the planning process, schools must assess their vulnerability by conducting a security threat assessment. Once the assessment is complete, a matrix should be developed to help forecast possible threats.

In the early planning stages, it will be important to identify agenda/action items. The following list is a start, but it is not inclusive and you will want to incorporate other action items specific to your school. Planning Stage List:

Creating a response team
Identify all threats and hazards
Determine goals and objectives
Developing your emergency plan
Liaison, understanding the emergency management structure within your community
Communications/language access
Mutual aid agreements
Continuity of operations
Emergency notification systems
Evacuation procedures/sheltering
Training
Drills/exercises
Process to review and revise the plan
Grief counseling procedures
Media communications

When developing the plan:

- Identify the course of action and determine how and when each response will be implemented
- Determine the amount of response time anticipated
- Develop course of action to ultimately achieve your goals and objectives

AMERICANS WITH DISABILITIES ACT

Plans must comply with the Americans with Disabilities Act (ADA), among other prohibitions on disability discrimination, through all steps and processes in the emergency management plan, including preparation, testing, notification, alerts, evacuation, sheltering, recover, transportation, and emergency medical care. To comply, the plan must include students, staff, and parents with disabilities. The plan also must address the provision of appropriate auxiliary aids and services to ensure effective communication with all individuals with disabilities. The plan must ensure that individuals with disabilities are not separated from service animals and assistive devices and can receive disability related assistance throughout the emergency. Information and technical assistance on the ADA can be found at http://www.ada.gov.

Essential to both the emergency planning process and the response is the section which addresses individuals with limited English proficiency (LEP), including parents and students. Plans must comply with legal requirements on language access, including *Title VI* of the *Civil Right Act of 1964* and *Title VI* regulation of the *Civil Rights Act of 1964*.

Procedures to include within the EOP include:

- Lockdown procedures. Specifics should identify when to go to a lockdown, which persons make the decision, how it will be announced (over a public address system or other designated system), and by whom. There may be a preselected code word. Provisions for an evacuation should be maintained even in the event of a lockdown.

- Evacuation procedures. Evacuations should be implemented at the discretion of the building administrator or other designee. The plan should include procedures for transporting students and staff to a safe distance away to a designated safe area.
- Sheltering procedures. Sheltering provides refuge for the students, staff, and visitors within the school building in the event of an emergency. This shelter or safe area should maximize the safety of all persons. The area chosen may change depending on the specific emergency.
- Facility diagrams/site plans. These plans should show primary and secondary evacuation routes, exits, designated safe areas, both inside the building and away from the building, fire alarms, fire extinguishers, hoses, and water faucets. These should all be kept on file in the school district office.
- Emergency telephone numbers. Each school should maintain and update all emergency telephone numbers, with names and addresses of local and county personnel who will be involved in any crisis situation. It should include numbers for police, fire, ambulance, hospitals, the poison control center, local, county, and state emergency management agencies, along with the local public works department, local utility companies, the public health office, mental health/suicide contacts, and the county welfare agency. Additional contacts should be listed and updated appropriately.
- Transportation. Maintaining the flow of individuals is critical to minimize panic and injury. Plans for transporting the disabled and handicap staff must be in every plan. Agreements with local support agencies should be made in advance to ensure that when the emergency occurs, transportation is smooth.
- Crisis response teams. This team should be identified by the top management of the school and trained to respond in an emergency. All should be trained on the crisis emergency plan and trained on all procedures, evacuation routes, and safe areas.

The plan should specifically address key issues currently facing crisis teams, such as active shooters and workplace violence. The Department of Homeland Security's (DHS) goal is to enhance preparedness through a "whole community approach." The DHS has developed a series of training materials, including some specifically for schools. One such training awareness program is entitled "run, hide or fight," which encourages individuals to run if there is a safe path available. If it is not possible to run, it encourages individuals to hide. While hiding, if it becomes necessary, the training encourages individuals to work together, through an act of aggression, and with improvised weapons, to fight. Both active shooter and workplace violence incidents are by their nature unpredictable, often spontaneous, and can evolve quickly; there are no patterns or methods, but training should be made to raise awareness of behaviors that represent preincident indicators and characteristics of active shooters. Additional active shooter training is available through the Federal Emergency Management Agency (FEMA), including workshops, presentations, webinars, pamphlets, and online training videos.

Discussion on lessons learned, key terms and definitions, and ways that school administrators can work better with law enforcement should also be included in training programs. Knowing the following terms and definitions will assist the crisis team when working with law enforcement:

- Active shooter: a suspect's actions are immediately causing death and serious bodily injury. The incident is not contained and there is immediate risk of death and serious injury to other potential victims.
- Barricaded suspect: a suspect who is barricaded in a room or a building and is armed and has indicated that he or she will become violent. There may or may not be hostages and there is no indication that the subject's activity is immediately causing death or serious bodily injury.

- Traditional deployment: a tactical concept where officers maintain a secure perimeter while monitoring the armed suspect and waiting while specially trained units (SEB, SWAT, etc.) arrive at the scene.
- Rapid deployment: the swift and immediate deployment of law enforcement personnel to ongoing, life-threatening situations where delayed deployment might result in death or great bodily injury to innocent victims.
- Dynamic situation: the situation is evolving very rapidly with the suspect.
- Static situation: the suspect appears to be contained.

Training and testing every emergency plan is the key to success. Testing will identify areas of weakness and allow for modifications to the plan. As important are the emergency plan updates and continual audits.

POLICY AND PROCEDURES FOR SCHOOLS

16

Mark H. Beaudry, Ph.D., CPP

Instructor, researcher, and author in security studies at various universities in Massachusetts

INTRODUCTION
EMPLOYEE MANUAL

The policy and procedure manual(s) and employee handbooks are essential to the consistent, productive, and efficient administration of any business. This is especially true in the area of school security, where there are many diverse services offered, numerous departments with different goals and responsibilities, and a myriad of problems that could arise. It is therefore recommended that in addition to a school-wide policy and procedure manual, each school should have its own security manual. Chances are that the school-wide manual covers policies and procedures that are general for the entire community, which may sometimes include vital, yet fundamental, practices and procedures for each department within a school. This type of manual is usually referred to only as a guideline, which allows the individual facility to develop its own section within the manual and handbook based on their geographic location. Most school facilities may also have a detailed manual for each department with an emphasis on its operational departments.

SECURITY MANUAL

In the event that there is a school-generated "security manual," it should be used as an outline for the facility security manual. A separate manual specifically for security is an indispensable tool for assuring that all school personnel have been given the same information regarding the purpose, functions, and procedures carried out by school personnel. Security manuals typically consist of a series of policies and procedures, directives, and references to information that may be critical, or at least helpful, to school personnel.

Manuals should be designed for quick reference whenever a need arises and they should also be readily accessible. Little is accomplished when a well-written and well-designed security manual is locked up in an office after regular business hours. Ideally, every school staff member and local resource/police officer is given their own copy of the manual, and all manuals are updated, as it becomes necessary, generally on an annual basis. The contents of a manual should have three basic categories:

1. General Information
2. Department Policies
3. Emergency Procedures

The *General Information* section could include a description of the school's mission, organizational chart, dress code, and job descriptions for school personnel. *Department Polices* is written statements that indicate the objective of the policy and any relevant procedures that school staff are expected to follow. Finally, the *Emergency Procedures* section would include detailed information on the steps to be taken by school staff and other school resource/police personnel during an emergency. For example, an emergency procedure for a fire would state the responsibilities of school staff and indicate the roles expected of other school personnel.

Manuals are, however, meant to be used as a guideline for expected behavior during a given situation. No one has yet written a policy, procedure, or directive that covers every situation that could arise, as well as a definitive procedure to prevent a situation.

CONSTRUCTING POLICY AND PROCEDURES

Policies and procedures for every aspect of the school operation need to be developed. By using a generic outline format, you can fill in the pertinent information as you develop your manual. This ensures that there is a set way to deal with specific tasks and situations as outlined in the following sections.

Patrolling: Check all areas around the school, including locker rooms, the gym, and service areas to include the kitchens. Check all areas deemed important and utilize a checkpoint in all of these areas. Maintain a visible presence throughout the school checking all doorways, stairways, and so forth. Check all floors for suspicious persons, vandals, and trespassers. Check all fire exits, fire exit signs, lights, pipes, restrooms, classroom doors, and so forth to ensure a safe and secure environment. Again, utilize checkpoints to your advantage to ensure that school staff is checking areas.

Everyone should, however, have a general school-wide policy and procedure manual that includes a variety of essential documents. As stated at the beginning of this section, the fundamental policies and procedures of each department need to be covered in the school-wide manual.

This is especially true for topics on security. Many people think security policies only involve how to patrol the premises or the methods employed when conducting an investigation. However, there are many areas that fall under the realm of security, and all employees of the school need to be aware of the appropriate steps to be taken in an all situations that are likely to arise. Such situations may include:

- Dealing with student or employee theft;
- Implementing emergency fire evacuation procedures;
- Actions to take/avoid during strikes or collective bargaining negotiations;
- Access control and badging (visitors, vendors, staff, etc.);
- Sexual harassment or assault involving employees/teachers;
- Lost and found;
- Escorting terminated employees or expelled students;
- Conducting first aid, CPR/AED, and blood-borne pathogens training (29 CFR 1910. 151) and repeat recertification as required;
- Crisis intervention;
- Key management (hard key and electronic keys);
- Confidentiality procedures and privacy issues;
- Suicide;

- Alcohol and drug-related incidents;
- Crisis management; and
- Many other related topics.

By including the essential steps to take in certain situations in the school-wide manual, it can be assured that proper policies will be followed, and staff throughout the school will act in a similar and consistent manner.

REPORT WRITING

The school staff members are an integral part of an operation; therefore, school management should think and act likes a business manager. This includes generating various types of reports that disclose and describe the issues, problems, and concerns encountered by the school staff. By producing reports as simply and clearly as possible, the school staff will:

- Have an accurate record of the number and types of incidents it deals with, it may determine trends which may exist, and it also establishes a record for the school;
- Learn how to most efficiently allocate manpower;
- Determine areas of weaknesses and potential security violations; and
- Ascertain which policies and procedures need modification and be able to identify new areas of concern for which there may not have been policy.

CONCLUSION

Every school district assumes that a security manual is in place. Unfortunately, this is not the case, and some schools have to step into a position and start from scratch. Technically, if a school has been operating without a security manual the hard part is not writing the manual, it is implementing it. School managers need guidance just like other managers, and who better to get a manual from than a security manager. Finally, every year all policies should be reviewed and updated by a team of school staff. That way, school administrators will be aware of the latest developments and trends, e.g. the recent shift away from the phrase, "zero tolerance" to "Guidelines for Criminal Acts."

APPROACHES TO PHYSICAL SECURITY

AN OVERVIEW OF PHYSICAL SECURITY TECHNOLOGY FOR SCHOOLS: WHAT SECURITY TECHNOLOGIES TO CONSIDER FOR SCHOOLS—FINDING A DIRECTION

17

Frank J. Davies, CHS-IV, CIPS, CVI
President, Aella Consulting Group, Inc.
Gregory Bernardo, CHS-IV, CDT, CVI
Vice president, Aella Consulting Group, Inc.

INTRODUCTION

This chapter is intended to introduce school practitioners to the various types of physical security technologies that should be considered for incorporation into their operational school security plans. The information we provide is intentionally high level in order not to burden you with information overload. This way you will be aware of the most commonly applied technical tools at your disposal before you commit to a specific direction.

OVERARCHING CONCERNS AND CONSIDERATIONS

Security technology applied correctly can be a massive force multiplier,[1] while saving you time and making your facility safer. There are important considerations you will want to keep in mind as you learn about applying these technologies.

RECENT LAWS (PASSED AND PENDING)

Between the horrific events of the school shooting in Newtown, Connecticut and the time of this writing, state legislatures have introduced over 470 bills intended to improve school security. Not all of the introduced bills will become law, but the ones that do will need to be considered in your plans.

---

[1] A force multiplier refers to something that increases (hence "multiplies") the effectiveness of an item, individual, or group. For example, a camera system can allow one security resource officer to monitor the front lobby and all the hallways at the same time.

Some of the pending and signed bills focus on improving emergency response. Many of the security technologies described in this chapter can make emergency response more efficient when interfaced with other systems. For example, cameras placed in the area of a panic button can automatically display on a monitor and provide immediate insight to that area. Initially, you may have looked at installing cameras for other reasons and the panic button to protect staff, but the two systems work together when you plan well and consider all of the uses of your equipment in conjunction with your plan.

MASS NOTIFICATION REGULATIONS

Prior to the above-noted legislative bills, the National Fire Protection Association (NFPA) 72 bill (which references ANSI/UL 2572) added requirements for mass notification that can apply to schools. Languages in new legislative bills reinforce, and sometimes duplicate, requirements found in NFPA 72. While not enforced uniformly nationwide, we recommend caution with regard to mass notification. This is because NFPA 72 has over-the-cliff (must be compliant with all requirements) verbiage that creates a liability for schools that attempt to "step into" mass notification. We recommend that you become familiar with the changing regulations, specifically NFPA 72, or consult with a knowledgeable expert who can help prepare your planning in this area. It is important to keep open designs in mind when planning so that additions to meet compliance do not require starting over.

DAILY TRAINING AND INCIDENT MODES

Another consideration is different modes of use for technology. You may be adding technology like access control so that you do not have to post staff at every door during different parts of the day. That may be its intended primary function, but it may be helpful if that product also has a training mode or an incident mode like "lockdown." For example, a training mode would allow staff to train with some or all of the on-site alarms and notifications but not alert authorities. In a lockdown mode, a single action (panic button) could automatically initiate multiple "lockdown" actions such as locking all doors, initiating mass notification messaging, and increasing video-recording quality or frame rate.

MOVIES AND TELEVISION SHOWS LIE

Physical security technologies, like those that you see in the movies and on television, are not all real. The technology often does not exist or is misrepresented in its effectiveness (remember: television is for entertainment). Most security industry veterans recognize the limitations of security hardware from years of exposure. Ask many questions when you evaluate technologies and do not overestimate what a system can do based on a fancy marketing presentation.

DOES IT PLAY NICELY WITH IT?

Today, schools rely heavily on IT networks that are shared by hundreds of computers, voice-over IP desk phones, tablets, and a host of other connected devices. Physical security technology is yet another demand that schools are adding to their network infrastructure and network administrators.

Many of the physical security technologies you may want to add to a facility can be connected to the network. If not designed and implemented correctly, digital video surveillance systems can clog up a network to the point that nothing works. Likewise, other systems may require exacting data speeds or response times when communicating across your network.

Beyond the network, many of the security technologies you might consider implementing will have one or more computer servers that need a home. The obvious place to put these servers is with your existing servers and in the capable hands of your IT team. However, doing this takes up rack space, uses power, and adds heat. In short, make sure to bring in your IT people early and allow them to evaluate the proposed equipment and the impact new technologies will have on IT infrastructure and subsequent maintenance before you make a purchase.

NEW CLOUD SERVICE OPTIONS

Cloud computing has garnered notoriety as more and more businesses take advantage of its benefits. This is also the case in the physical security market.

The costs of accessing security software through a cloud provider can offset the costs associated with purchasing and hosting software locally. However, online storage costs can be more restrictive versus what you can achieve under a onetime cost with local storage.

Just as with every other decision, there are benefits and drawbacks to using cloud-based physical security technologies. As you evaluate cloud service options, consider the following benefits and drawbacks.

Benefits
Flexibility
The cloud promises and often delivers flexibility that can increase productivity and efficiency. Access to cloud-based systems can be made through browsers on existing desktop and mobile devices.

Limited maintenance
As with consumer and business cloud solutions, support and maintenance of software, servers, and storage devices is managed by the cloud service provider. Facilities with little or no on-site IT presence may find an acceptable solution using cloud services.

Drawbacks
Limited interfaces
Cloud-based physical security technologies currently have limited interfaces to complementary on-site or cloud-based systems. This means the convenience and flexibility benefits of a cloud-based access control solution may restrict your ability to interface with a video system.

Security
Security is paramount to your physical security technology plan. Can your cloud provider ensure the level of security that you require? Make sure to perform due diligence as part of your decision making. In our security technology primer,[2] we identified that a leader in consumer cloud storage was reported as having an application-wide security incident due to employee error.

---

[2]*A Primer on Electronic Security for Schools, Universities and Institutions*, 2nd Edition, March 2012.

Internet connection/bandwidth

Uninterrupted access to your physical security system is crucial. Many of the cloud service providers offer high availability levels and high-issue resolution response levels. However, the Internet connection in between can be interrupted or slowed due to Internet attacks. Even if you have a stable Internet connection, the number of cameras your facility needs may demand more constant bandwidth than is available through your Internet connection.

DATA, DATA, EVERYWHERE!

A primary concern in designing the security system is how it will handle all of the associated information produced by the various physical security systems. For example:

- Alarms from the intrusion and fire systems,
- Alerts from the access control system, and
- Video from the video surveillance system.

Recognize that each of these individual systems has evolved separately under different companies, and as a result, they present information differently. We will discuss more about ways to control disparate data sources in the next section.

The rest of this chapter is dedicated to the types of physical security technologies. As you continue reading and reflect on these technologies, consider whether they will meet the short- and long-term needs of your facility and how you would want to access or see the information that these systems can deliver.

PHYSICAL SECURITY TECHNOLOGIES
TIERED TECHNOLOGY APPROACH

There is no standard template for security technology that fits every application. In our primer, we refer to a "tiered" method of constructing a physical security system. This proven method creates multiple hierarchal layers of physical security technologies, thereby delivering layers of autonomy, redundancy, and backup.

PHYSICAL SECURITY INFORMATION MANAGEMENT/COMMAND AND CONTROL

A well-designed, comprehensive security plan is not just about sensing and reporting alarms or recording and displaying video, it is about collecting and presenting all of the information in a coherent fashion so that it can be effectively used by security and safety personnel.

Physical security information management (PSIM) systems, previously known as command and control, allow disparate information from different manufacturers' products to become interoperable on a standard platform or "user interface." Most PSIM manufacturers are system agnostic; therefore, most other manufacturers do not see them as a competitor and will be willing to cooperate and work with them.

One of the major advantages of utilizing a PSIM system is to provide a "big picture" or "situational awareness." While this certainly provides an everyday benefit, it can also be extremely important in the most critical of emergency times. Most PSIMs can deliver an additional benefit to the common operating picture with the ability to present a "live" campus system map. This map displays the systems in real time, as well as the operational status of all the lower-tier systems by using icons to indicate the status of doors, sensors, cameras, and other system attributes.

Smaller educational facilities may not warrant the addition and cost of a PSIM system. However, a PSIM system is a good place to start our discussion because smaller, independent facilities are often brought into a campus-wide plan.

On the following pages, we will discuss lower-level systems that can function both independently or as tier 2 systems under a PSIM system.

VIDEO MANAGEMENT SYSTEMS

On the surface, many video management systems (VMSs) look the same. At the most basic level, video management software products route and/or record compressed video from cameras and encoders and display video to monitors. These systems also provide camera and user administration and access rights. Most of today's VMSs display live video in a graphical user interface (GUI) or a standard Windows Internet browser on an operator's PC. Some systems offer video "decoders" to display the video directly on dedicated monitors or "video walls," without requiring a PC.

A close examination of available VMS reveals a wide variety of product features, functionality, and price. VMS manufacturers oftentimes vary in maturity and market focus, resulting in product differences in scalability, network management, fault tolerance, operating systems, software clients, and the availability of standard conventions and protocols (interfaces).

At a minimum, VMSs require cameras, a PC platform with servers and storage equipment, and the manufacturer's software. Some manufacturer's designs are proprietary and require you to use their hardware and/or software. Other manufacturers feature more open-design platforms, which provide the opportunity for easier system additions and support.

You may hear references to CCTV, digital video, video surveillance, security cameras, and the "mystical" digital video analytics. We would like to point out that these terms are not interchangeable. Video surveillance is a rapidly changing segment of security that is much like computers: Whatever you buy today will no longer be state-of-the-art tomorrow. This rapid change and transition in the market (often referred to as "convergence") requires a well-thought design concept to ensure the long-term viability of your installation.

Today, video surveillance is making a shift from analog cameras (based on the original one-signal-per-cable design) to network (IP) cameras (where many cameras can transmit on the network cable). There are still many analog cameras being installed because integrators are comfortable with their installation and troubleshooting. However, they will be obsolete in the near future.

The key to extending the life of your video system is to install a platform that supports open protocols. This term means that the purchaser will not be limited to proprietary technical components from a single vendor. In theory, future incremental enhancements then will be cost-effective and take advantage of new technologies without having to incur sweeping replacement costs for major system components.

CAMERAS

Cameras are the most basic and critical elements of video surveillance and predetermine operational characteristics of the entire system. The cameras you install predetermine certain system-wide operational characteristics such as:

- Fixed position versus pan/tilt/zoom (can the camera be remotely controlled?)
- Standard resolution or megapixel (how wide of an area can I see or can I digitally zoom?)
- Built-in storage (does video recording impact my network all the time?)

- Built-in video analytics (do I get alarms from my camera that other systems can use?)
- Built-in processing power for future video analytics (do I replace the camera or add hardware to use video analytics on a camera?)

Most recently, the cost for night-vision and low-light cameras has become economical enough to be used in commercial and educational applications to detect and capture images not previously available in older systems.

MONITORS

Video surveillance monitors come in an assortment of sizes and technical functions. Monitors can be applied differently as your monitoring layout and overall design strategy requires. Many VMSs utilize one or more flat panel monitors of larger size to view multiple images. Often VMS, access control, or PSIM systems display additional system information as well as video.

Multiple monitors may be used, but you need to consider how your security personnel will use them. It is also important to remember that the more monitors security personnel are required to watch, the faster they develop monitor fatigue and are more likely to miss critical events. However, multiple monitors with important cameras displayed enable security personnel to assess critical areas at a glance.

RECORDING

Today's digital video recorders (DVRs) and network video recorders (NVRs) allow security system designers to use any combination of the previously discussed features of analog and IP security cameras.

DVRs are computers or purpose-built devices that use internal video capture hardware with specific channel capacities of 4, 8, 9, 16, 24, 32, and 64 (with each channel being a camera). These devices are close ended with a predetermined storage size, thus requiring the need for additional devices if the system is expanded.

NVRs are designed to work with network edge devices (IP cameras and IP encoders) rather than directly connect with analog (non-IP) cameras. An NVR is a PC server or specialized embedded device with video management software/firmware. NVR capacities vary substantially depending on the VMS and server specifications.

There are some hybrid recorders that offer both DVR (video capture hardware) and NVR (IP only), but they typically have a reduced total capacity of IP and analog video streams.

Both DVRs and NVRs are easy concepts for IT directors and tech-savvy consumers, but build-your-own systems are something to be avoided. "Build your own" is the practice of adding video capture cards and software to regular PCs and building your own DVR or NVR.

Recording systems vary tremendously in scalability (as we touch on above). Evaluation of camera types (standard versus megapixel), calculation of the quantity of camera types, and the anticipated system growth must be considered carefully in your purchasing decision.

ANALOG, DIGITAL, STANDARDS COMPLIANT?

Decisions regarding video systems invariably include decisions regarding analog cameras, digital cameras, or a combination of both. The differences are discussed later, but the important thing to know is that they use different wiring. Additionally, digital cameras can be proprietary (only work on one

Table 17.1   Typically Found Analytic Functions
• Motion detection • Object classification and tracking • Object removed • Object left behind • Wrong way detection and object counting • License plate detection • Facial recognition

system), open standard (their communication standard is openly shared), or standards compliant (uses a communications standard promoted by an independent standards organization). Typically, the VMS you choose will limit your camera choices.

DIGITAL VIDEO ANALYTICS

Though they have been around for some time, video analytics are still not well understood by all for the correct use and implementation. New advances and product offerings are available each year, but should be evaluated very carefully.

We are typically interested in video analytics as a way to monitor multiple cameras without concern for operator fatigue and to free up staff to do other things. However, video analytics have not progressed to the point where they can replace human decision making or make judgment calls. Table 17.1 shows analytic functions that are typically found in security cameras.

In every video analytics deployment, camera placement and properties have a profound effect on performance. Proper expectations and adequate design are critical to ensure a successful deployment.

MASS NOTIFICATION SYSTEMS

The intent of mass notification systems is, as the name would imply, to notify the masses in the case of an event. Mass notification type events can vary from the severe (terrorist attack) to the informational, such as closings due to weather (snow day).

As authors in this subject matter, we would be remiss not to caution the reader that the Clery Act considerations and changes within NFPA, Underwriters Laboratory (UL), and the Department of Education set certain expectations and requirements regarding these systems. We advise that these items be given the consideration they deserve. Laws, regulations, and codes regarding fire and notification systems have begun to change. When designing these systems, NFPA and UL requirements and recommendations should be followed closely.

Many voice-based systems come preprogrammed with English, Spanish, or French messages, and often are able to use customized message(s) recorded by the customer. The power of the human voice added to the typical bell, siren, and flashing lights makes a system highly effective. However, too often, systems are installed that are less than adequate, making annunciation of voice wholly unintelligible, for which there are now established standards.

Mass notification systems should include or consider the requirements unique to your setting in the following lists.

At a minimum:

- Public address system
- Posted notices
- Emergency call-in hotline
- SMS/text messaging
- Website/portal
- Outdoor public address system/warning sirens
- Voicemail notification system
- Visually/audibly impaired warning system

Recommended:

- Digital signage
- Desktop alerting in each classroom and throughout the campus/school
- Voice-enabled programmable fire alarm
- Mobile loudspeaker system(s)
- Blue light towers
- Staff radio system with alerting
- Outdoor emergency phones
- Utilization of social media, blogs, etc.

These lists are not all encompassing, but rather a starting point to identify and evoke a discussion regarding the responsibilities and the tools available in your unique circumstance to protect the students, faculty, and staff of the institution.

ACCESS CONTROL, BADGING, AND VISITOR MANAGEMENT

When access control is paired with visitor management and a badging system (credentials), the result is a more complete accounting and control of the entire school population. These systems should work in unison but not impair the functions of one another to create, access, or provide information.

Access control

The purpose of an access control system is to limit access and create a record of accountability. Employees can only access areas where they are authorized and during the times they are authorized to be there. Likewise, students and visitors can be kept out of areas they are not supposed to access.

The most basic component of security access systems is a keypad or card reader or some combination of both located at entry points you wish to secure. The door access devices are wired to control panels and from there to a computer system (server or other manufacturer-specific PC) to run software. These panels are generally proprietary to the manufacturer. Access control systems typically allow the supplemental tie in and monitoring of multiple systems; that is, fire, perimeter alarms, interior alarms, video system motion detection, and other alarms.

All access control manufacturers' software is proprietary and therefore this decision is of paramount importance. Examine all of the performance details of the equipment to determine if and how they meet your institutional requirements now, and for the future.

Badging system

Most mature access control systems have an integral badging system component allowing the creation of credentials (picture) on an access control card. However, the quantity and type of cards may dictate a badge product from a manufacturer that is different but integrated with the access system.

Card readers (credential readers) utilizing magnetic strips, RFID technology, and traditional Wiegand swipe technology are the most prevalent access control devices. RFID technologies include prox (short for proximity) and smart cards, which are similar to prox, but house additional data other than just the user's ID.

As you evaluate these choices, you may be tempted to tie in your cafeteria or other card-based purchasing program (sometimes referred to as the One Card system). Our experience is that combining security and commerce is generally problematic because each area is specialized.

Visitor management

Visitor management in school is a valuable extension of a well-designed access control plan and is intended to let the right people in and keep the wrong people out. Software-based visitor management systems can quickly verify a visitor's credentials against a blacklist or a white list (a Criminal Offender Record Information [CORI] check is essential here) and provide an audit trail that is easy to create and access. Beyond the obvious security improvement, visitor management can be part of a program that makes your entire staff accountable for visitors while on site.

The policy of making faculty and staff "known" by prominently wearing their ID credential will make visitors stand out through their lack of such a credential. This can be improved by making visitors wear temporary badges with a distinctive overall color, which can be seen from a distance, and text, to identify their area or reason to be in the school. Through proper training of faculty and staff, a visitor or unknown person can be challenged or identified, thereby increasing awareness, accountability, and safety.

Ties between the access control system and the VMS can aid in accountability if the building must be evacuated. Most robust VMSs can be used to determine the presence of visitors within the facility or provide a "muster list" to account for all evacuated guests.

FIRE AND INTRUSION CENTRAL MONITORING

There are several ways to approach the monitoring of your security and fire alarms systems. Keep in mind, as we have stated earlier, the best system designs incorporate layered redundancy, which in the case of fire and intrusion systems lends itself to supplemental monitoring by a hierarchal system.

All state-of-the-art fire and intrusion systems contain digital communicators capable of transmitting to a central station or monitoring center in a variety of formats. However, you will have to make sure your systems support a format that is compatible with whatever central station or monitoring method you elect to use.

In conventional configurations, digital receivers are assigned to dedicated telephone lines and integrated with the central station software. Field security panels send alarms, open and closing signals, supervisory signals, and test signals of all systems to central station receivers. The central station software deciphers this information and displays it on computer terminals for action by the central station operator.

There is a growing segment of security systems equipment that can be centrally monitored over the Internet. Only specific equipment has been listed or approved to date.

User-owned central station or monitoring center

There is a significant expense to operating your own central station. It is only reasonable to consider your own central station if you have your own police, fire, and security forces deployed 24 hours a day, 7 days a week, 365 days a year, and are willing to hire full-time dispatchers.

Independent third-party central station

The third-party central station will usually be UL approved, thereby providing all of the assurances of outside-unbiased supervision and having all of the electrical, physical, ventilation, and software requirements met. Third-party central stations are in the business to provide this type of monitoring, so they assume all the burdens of insurance, training, and any licensing requirements.

This solution usually is best for the school, university, or institution that does not have a fulltime police or security officer program to mitigate all of the associated costs. It has the most flexibility with the least associated risk, and it provides some sharing of the risk and liability.

Security-supplier-owned central station

In some instances where a school district, university, or institution contracts their security services to a security systems supplier, including monitoring, it is the responsibility of the security systems supplier to assume all of the previously discussed burdens of cost, insurance, training, licensing, and UL approval.

Whichever monitoring solution you ultimately adopt, we strongly recommend that you do not rely solely on unsupervised telephone lines as your sole source of communication with the central station. We highly recommend that you employ backup solutions involving cellular communication backup, telemetry, long-range radio, or a network-deployed application to facilitate the delivery of emergency signals during telephone outages.

INTRUSION DETECTION SYSTEMS

Intrusion detection is an integral part of your physical security technology. Intrusion detection can be a standalone intrusion detection system (IDS), but is often part of an access control system. The descriptions below apply to both applications of the technology.

IDS sensors (described below) are connected using dedicated wiring. This wiring is often protected by a metal conduit to prevent tampering or rendering a device inoperable by simply cutting the wire. In many cases, these sensors will be "supervised" to detect tampering or make the sensors inoperable.

Rather than run wire from every device back to a central point, IDSs usually have control panels located throughout the building in secure locations. As with the device wiring, IDS panels should also be monitored for tampering.

Balanced magnetic contacts

Balanced contacts are used on all types of indoor and outdoor doors and windows to detect when they are opened or closed.

Motion detection

The use of long-range combination passive infrared (PIR) and microwave detectors in corridors and hallways is commonplace. These represent two different technologies, which can be applied to detect motion in different areas. PIR detectors measure infrared (IR) light radiating from objects in its field of view. While very accurate, these devices can create false alarms from items that change temperature, such as heating radiators and electronics.

Microwave detectors send out pulses of ultrasonic waves and measure the reflection off a moving object to detect motion. The technology works similarly to a police radar gun. These devices are also very accurate, but they can be bothered by electrical "noise."

Some motion detectors use a combination of both PIR and microware technologies; when the PIR sensor is tripped, it activates a microwave sensor to confirm the motion detection.

OTHER ALARM SYSTEM FEATURES

The security system can be used for a host of other supervisory tasks capable of alerting school personnel of potentially damaging events. For example, monitoring food storage temperatures in coolers and freezers, power outages and generator failure to start, HVAC systems, and in colder climates, monitoring boilers used for heating is a frequent application.

The security system can also be used to monitor the building fire alarm system (provided it meets the UL listing).

In addition to the protection provided by the security systems, a well-documented deterrent is signage deployed throughout the facility identifying that these premises are monitored and protected.

FIRE ALARM SYSTEMS

Fire alarm manufacturers are regulated and scrutinized by ULs, the NFPA, Factory Mutual, insurance risk carriers, federal and state agencies, ADA Security, and many others. They are tested routinely in order to ensure reliability. However, if fire alarms are so reliable, then what is the concern?

For fire alarm systems to be of any value, they must be designed, installed, and maintained correctly. If you already have a fire alarm system, the following information can help you to understand where you might lower some of your maintenance costs and how to integrate your fire system into your overall physical security plan.

Conventional versus addressable

Fire alarm architecture is described as conventional or addressable. Your choice of architecture determines the devices you can attach and some of your system's core functionality. In both cases, there are two functional sides of a fire alarm system: detection and annunciation. The detection side of a fire alarm system is comprised of detectors and pull stations that are connected to a fire alarm panel. Similarly, the annunciation (or alarming) side of the system is comprised of the same fire alarm panel and is connected to strobe lights and alarm sounders. Fire alarm architecture also determines how specific your system can be regarding what area "zone" that an alarm is coming from or that you want to annunciate to. Depending on the local code and the fire alarm panel design, these zones may refer to an area of the building such as the "south hallway classrooms" or the "auditorium."

Fire alarm components

Smoke and heat detectors are your primary fire detection devices and should be installed according to code and located throughout the structure. Manual pull stations should also be located according to code and protected with covers that sound an audible alarm if the manual pull station cover is opened. This deters false alarms and class disruption.

It is also important to remember that all horns/strobes must be located in compliance with the fire code, authority having jurisdiction (AHJ), and Americans with Disabilities Act (ADA).

There are many types of fire detection devices on the market today and most do a great job for their intended area of specialization. There are also many mainstream and specialized detectors available; we recommend that you follow code requirements when deciding which of them you need.

SCHOOL BUS SECURITY TECHNOLOGY

Technology has advanced rapidly to the point where it is economically feasible to track and provide two-way communication and private or public addressing to each school bus. This technology will handle an array of potential hazards that may be faced during the day while a bus is in transit. Video recording of events helps to deter and defend against bullying, assaults, and accidents.

In addition to the information that can be transmitted to the buses, information can be gathered *from* the buses and utilized by state and local law enforcement, even in real time from a mobile platform. Handoff of video and data from buses can be efficiently handled and coordinated to work in harmony with school security and notification.

Some important considerations that exist when presenting and detailing the need for the technology inclusion within your bus fleet are as follows:

- Is the technology designed for a mobile/transportation environment?
- Does it contain hardened equipment with power backup?
- Does it have recording mechanisms that are hardened or solid state?
- Is it protected from extremes of heat and cold?
- Is the wireless technology incorporated in the hardware?
- How are updates delivered to the hardware and software (directly or wirelessly)?
- How does the system report faults?
- Are the cameras designed for rigors of environment?
- What other peripheral devices (lights, panic switches, and geolocation) can be added to the system?

Physical security technology on school buses and public transportation is currently a specialty niche serviced primarily by companies specializing in transportation. Only a few of these systems can interface with other physical security systems.

SUMMARY

Physical security technology cannot and will not provide you with security in a school, but rather is part of a holistic approach and a well-crafted security and safety plan. Security technology applied correctly can be a huge force multiplier, while saving you time and making your facility safer.

This chapter was intended only to introduce you to the technologies that should be considered by school practitioners for incorporation into their operational school security plans. The information we included was intentionally high level to provide awareness of the most commonly applied technical tools at your disposal before you commit to a specific direction. We highly recommend that a multidisciplinary team address the needs of your school to insure that you have all of the components of a complete security plan.

HARDWARE FUNCTION CHOICES AND LOCKDOWN PROCEDURES: K-12 AND UNIVERSITY CLASSROOMS

18

Jim Harper, CRL, CIL

K-12 and university specialist, ASSA ABLOY

INTRODUCTION

Historically, schools used a single-sided *classroom function* lock on doors leading into classrooms. This function allowed the first person in to insert their key, rotate it 360°, and put the lockset into "passage function" or unlocked for the day. During a lockdown, the staff had to open the door, then insert their key to lock the door, putting them at risk.

Some schools would use an *office function* lock, which has a turn button on the inside that can lock or unlock the outer trim. The difficulty with this is that students can lock the door as a prank. The school could also have a liability issue with this function if one student forces another into the room, locks the door, and does harm to the other person.

Another option is using a *storeroom function* lock, which is always locked and the door is left open all day. This would require teachers to carry their classroom key with them at all times and lead to interruptions every time someone wants to come in when the door is closed. In larger schools with multiple classroom keys (keyed to departments), the teacher could be in an area where their key does not allow access to the classrooms they want to bring students into as a place of safe haven, thus leaving them exposed.

The *classroom intruder function* lock acts as the traditional classroom function lock but has a keyed cylinder on the inside that locks the outside trim. In a lockdown, the staff uses their lockdown key on the inside to lock the door without exposing themselves to potential harm. Teachers in any part of the building can go into any unlocked room and use this key to secure the room.

Any brand names mentioned in this chapter should not be considered endorsements, but rather suggestions from the author's own experience of products that have proven to be high quality.

THEORETICAL DISCUSSION ON CLASSROOM INTRUDER FUNCTION: KEYING OPTIONS

EXTERIOR-SIDE KEYING

There are several different ways of keying the inside cylinder on the intruder function lock, and in my experience, the level of school (K-6, middle school, and high school) changes the way these locks are keyed. When consulting with a school about safety, I will discuss in depth the various options with the school administration or superintendent and let them make the decision of which option best suits their operational and lockdown procedures.

In the K-6 elementary school setup, the teachers generally stay in their assigned rooms. In most cases, the classrooms are all keyed alike (e.g., exterior / hallway side). You need to ask if the classrooms are ever really locked by the staff during the day or only secured at night by the custodians for after-hours security reasons. You should also ask if teaching staff need to carry an exterior side classroom key. Suggestion: Use a second combination for all interior lockdown cylinders and require staff to carry this key at all times. The reason for using a second combination is that this lockdown key does not unlock locks from the hallway side; rather, it only locks doors from the inside of the classroom. A second combination would prevent an intruder from taking keys away from a staff hostage to gain entry into secured rooms.

In the middle and high school environments, the teachers do move around to various classrooms. Therefore, in middle schools, there may be a need for several different keys: a common general classroom key, an art key, a gym key, a music key, and so on. In high schools and university settings, there may be a need to key by department and there may be up to 20 different department masters. Further, under these there could be a common department classroom key, a department head admin office key, a department storage key, or a computer lab key.

INTERIOR-SIDE KEYING

The physical layout of the building may affect the keying, such as keying all classrooms by building wings rather than by class discipline. Each school is different in layout and department structure and operational policy.

Since the shooting at Virginia Tech, I recommend that the lockdown key be a separate combination and that *all* school personnel (teachers, aides, custodians, administrators, nurses, food services personnel, etc.) carry this key with them at all times. Schools will need to consider their policy on sign-out keys for substitute teachers and staff that travel between schools such as PE or special education teachers. Ideally, the teachers will carry two keys: a regular exterior-side classroom key (which can be kept in their pocket or in their desk) and the lockdown key, which *must be on their person at all times*. Some school districts will purchase lariats for this key (and ID card) to be worn at all times. In this case, I will key the teacher lounges, copy rooms, and rest rooms to this key to force teachers to carry the lockdown key with them at all times. Under this concept this key only operates the inside lockdown cylinder. Therefore, if a perpetrator does incapacitate or take a staff member hostage, this key will not unlock the doors from the exterior side. As part of the lockdown procedures, the school could inform students as to how this key works so they could take the key from an incapacitated teacher and go into an unlocked room and lock themselves in.

In some cases where the school administration does not want the teachers to carry two keys, I have cross-keyed the inside cylinder to be operated by all classroom keys. Under this concept, there is no lockdown key and the teaching staff must take steps to protect their keys. This allows any teacher to enter any unlocked classroom during a lockdown and be able to close any of these doors and lock them with their key from the inside.

In this scenario, the place of exposure now becomes the connecting doors. In most schools, classrooms are left unlocked during operating hours. If a perpetrator gains access into the school, he or she could go into an unlocked classroom and gain access into other rooms through the connecting doors. These doors now need to be viewed as part of the lockdown procedure and a decision made on how to secure them during a lockdown. These doors are not required by code as a secondary means of egress unless the room is designed for more than 50 students, or under NFPA 101, if on a second or third floor there is a designated fire escape window, the door(s) leading to this escape cannot be locked. One option on these is using double-sided deadbolts keyed to the lockdown key only on both sides (the 10G26 function). Again, a policy needs to be established and the local authorities (fire and police) need to be brought in to confer.

This brings up a point on exterior door keying: Ensure that each side of the building(s) has an access point for emergency responders and that there is a policy in place for getting keys to them (for example: Knox boxes, keys in cruisers, or at predetermined locations).

An in-depth discussion with the local authority having jurisdiction, school department administration, school facilities management, and local fire and police representatives should be held before the final design stage of the project. In addition, an in-depth discussion on patented keys should be started in these conversations to educate the end user so they can make an informed decision on the type of key system to use.

POINTS TO CONSIDER ON HARDWARE/FUNCTION

Some lock companies offer several different options with the intruder function. Discussion with the end user in preplanning is critical to get the desired operation and level of protection (such as latch only, deadbolt, key operation, etc.). The intruder function is also available on some companies' exit devices. These can be used for places of assembly, such as the library, gym, auditorium, and multipurpose rooms. However, this does mean that mullions will be needed on each pair of doors so that ADA opening requirements are maintained. The lockdown cylinder is used on the inside of these just as in a classroom.

All exterior exit devices should use a cylinder dogging so that only authorized staff can leave these doors in the unlocked position. All exterior doors should have door-propped-open alarms (alarms that will sound when a door has been propped open) that alert a central manned location, as well as an established response policy.

Cross-corridor doors with exits need to be reviewed when these are to be used to lock off an area after hours while school events are going on and the building is occupied. Again, it is a good idea to use cylinder dogging so that only authorized staff can leave the doors in the unlocked position.

Staff restrooms or workrooms are another area where it is important to have a discussion with the end user in the predesign stage in order to ascertain the desired function. They should be secured to reduce risk of vandalism. Some options include hotel function, occupancy indicators, and combination locks (Sargent KP mortice is recommended). If using a lockdown key, these should be keyed to it to force staff to carry the key with them at all times.

Some newer locks come with an antimicrobial finish. This option should be reviewed with the school district as an added feature to increase student health. This feature is even available for the surface on some thermal fused wood doors.

PROS AND CONS OF OFFICE FUNCTION LOCKS

Pros

The classroom can be left unlocked during operating hours so students do not interrupt the classroom when returning during classroom time.

Cons

The door could be locked by students, thus locking staff out.

If multiple department keys are used, there is the possibility of a scenario where a staff person is escorting students to other areas in the building during a lockdown and find themselves in a corridor where all doors are locked and their key does not allow access into the classrooms.

PROS AND CONS OF STOREROOM FUNCTION

Pros

Classroom doors are always locked.

Cons

Locked doors become a distraction during class when students return to the room, as someone has to allow them in, disturbing the class. Over time, staff will block doors open, or tape latches or strike plates to avoid the class disturbance, thus defeating the purpose of the locked doors.

All staff have to carry their keys with them. In a hostage situation, their key would allow access to some classrooms. However, if, for example, in an elementary school all doors are keyed alike, then all classrooms become vulnerable.

CLASSROOM INTRUDER FUNCTION

This lock acts as the traditional classroom function, but has a keyed cylinder on the inside that locks the outside trim. During a lockdown the staff uses their lockdown key on the inside to lock the door without exposing themselves to potential harm. Teachers in any part of the building can go into any unlocked room and use this key to secure the room. It is recommended that this lockdown key is the same on all doors in the school or district.

The culture change that is required with this function is that all staff must carry the lockdown key with them at all times. In a hostage situation, this key does NOT unlock doors from the corridor side.

ELECTRONIC LOCK FUNCTIONS

Various options of electronic locks are available, from stand-alone battery locks to hard-wired and wireless versions.

Each has its own capabilities depending on software options. Stand-alone locks require yearly battery changes. Initial costs would be higher than for mechanical locks and the school would need to require staff to carry access credentials at all times. One should also consider the administrative time required to maintain the software.

When upgrading to new lever-style classroom security function locksets, you will receive an extra benefit of being in compliance with the ADA, which states that door locks must be operable with a closed fist (Figure 18.1).

New classroom security function

Being able to lock the door from the inside during a lockdown avoids exposure of staff to physical risks. Conventional classroom function locks require you to lock the door from the corridor side, which could expose the teacher or student to potential physical risk.

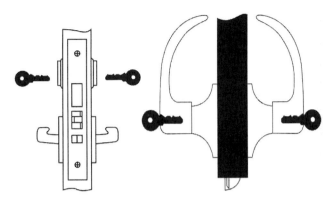

FIGURE 18.1

Classroom security function. During a lockdown, staff use the key on the inside lever to lock the outside lever, thus reducing their exposure.

Several well-known lock companies (e.g., Sargent, Corbin Russwin, and Yale) have provided a solution to this dilemma with their classroom intruder function locks available in cylindrical and mortise applications. For some of the devices this helps to alleviate a panic situation where the person may actually unlock the door in the heat of the moment. This function is also available for some exit devices so that areas of assembly such as cafeterias, auditoriums, and gymnasiums can be secured in a lockdown situation by authorized staff.

SCHOOL SECURITY DOOR HARDWARE UPGRADE PROJECT
STEP 1: WHAT DO YOU HAVE ALREADY?

You have to conduct a physical inventory or survey of all your facilities. At the same time, start reviewing your philosophy on security and procedures. Doors, frames, door hardware, locking devices, and access control systems should all be looked at as components of your physical security system. Each part plays an important role in providing barriers to unauthorized access to your facilities. A well-designed security philosophy will provide protection of students, staff, and assets and reduce your liability.

Physical locking devices

As stated above, take inventory of what you have for existing hardware products, including product brands and product types per school (this is a simple survey). Older schools may still have knob-style handles, so updating these to newer lever styles will comply with ADA regulations.

A door-by-door survey is a listing of the locking hardware on every door opening in every school. This survey is necessary because once completed you will have a list of the exact quantities of what materials will be needed to upgrade each school. These figures will be helpful in other ways as well. They will be used to process bids for the project. They will be used by the installers to verify that correct hardware is installed on the proper opening. After the installation, they will become a time management (time saving) tool on future service requests and can be used to conduct preventative maintenance schedules.

Once you have completed the survey, determine if a particular brand is the most predominant one in use in your schools. The Builders Hardware Manufacturers Association (BHMA) evaluates and grades commercial hardware. Determine if the hardware used in your school is evaluated and graded by the BHMA. Then evaluate commercial BHMA-certified grade 1 products on the market and establish a hardware standard for your school system. Creating a standard for door hardware will help reduce future operating costs by reducing multiple product inventories, and allow staff to become familiar with maintenance and repairs for just one system, thus reducing labor costs.

Master key system(s)

While you are surveying your school's hardware, ask the following questions:

1. How many different master key systems are in use?
2. How old are they?
3. What level of key control is in place?
4. Are there records for who has keys to school property?
5. Do any of these systems offer protection against unauthorized duplication?

Master keying gives you the convenience of carrying fewer keys to operate your facilities. It also allows you to segment access to individuals to areas where they need access. This allows a better sense of controlling access but does not offer time zones or auditing capabilities that newer electronic access control devices offer.

Mechanical key systems offer several different levels of protection for you from unauthorized duplication. Plain old conventional keys can be easily duplicated without your authorization. There are "restricted" key sections in which the manufacturers restrict use by geographical boundaries, but key blanks could be made by other companies once economically feasible. There are high-security systems which offer the benefit of patent protection. The highest level of protection is with products that hold a utility patent.

You also have to decide what physical type of product you want to use: conventional, interchangeable, or removable core. These products all have different price points, which will affect the cost of the project. An interchangeable or removable core product has higher initial costs but offers future labor savings when rekeying is required.

During the time the survey is being done you have to create a conceptual schematic of how you want the new master key system designed. There must be a completed design by the time an order for a product is entered.

Access control

Are there any access control systems in use? If so, are they expandable? Are there any intercom or cameras systems in use? New standalone or wireless products will greatly reduce your initial product and installation costs.

You need to establish a plan of action on the implementation of an access control system. Card access systems offer many levels of protection not obtainable with mechanical keys. Access control systems allow you to establish time zones, which assign times of operation for individual cardholders. These systems also provide you with the benefit of reporting when an individual tried to or gained access to your facilities.

The door hardware industry is exploding with new types of products which work with traditional systems or are their own access systems. Newer standalone systems may make more sense in a multiple school system and be less expensive than traditional hard-wired systems. In the near future, wireless products will allow end users all the features and benefits of traditional hard-wired systems at a substantially lower investment. Lay the ground work now for a system-wide access control system (e.g., have teachers who historically possessed keys for exterior doors issued ID cards and channeled into using a single point staff entry door).

STEP 2: WHAT DO YOU WANT TO GET?

Once the survey is completed you will have an idea of what type of hardware you are using. Now is the time to identify what you want for the future. Usually the most pressing issues are to upgrade older worn-out hardware, replace out of control master key systems, and start an expandable access control system.

In identifying what you want for the future, list what you want to achieve; some examples follow.

Classrooms, gyms, libraries, multipurpose rooms, cafeterias, and auditoriums

For these areas, provide locking capability from the interior side. This is so that during a lockdown condition school staff can secure their areas from the inside of doors without having to expose themselves by opening the door to secure it.

Exterior doors

For exterior doors, you may want a locked trim, interior side locked by a key cylinder dog so that students cannot leave doors unlatched by using an Allen wrench. Use local door alarms to indicate doors that have been propped open so school staff can investigate. Upgrade older style crossbar-type exits with newer rail-style units to prevent doors from being chained closed from the interior side. Reduce exterior doors with pulls that can be chained or otherwise secured from the exterior side.

Key system(s)

Only patented systems that offer a higher degree of protection from unauthorized key duplication should be used. You may want a new single district-wide patented master key system to regain key control on all school buildings. Establish a district policy on key control policy which will outline the in-house procedures to issue, track, and retrieve keys. Establish procedures for requesting keys, serially stamping of keys, key agreement forms, issuing and tracking keys. This policy should:

- Identify the key system administrator;
- Set guidelines on issuing keys by operational need and not convenience;
- Set procedures on tracking all keys;
- Set disciplinary actions for violations of the policy; and
- Set collection of keys, and yearly audits of all keys.

(See Appendix A for a sample employee key request form and sign-out sheet.)

Access control

Identify exterior door controls. You may want a main entry intercom system(s) with remote door release. Consider establishing staff entry points using card access; also establish procedures for delivery of foodstuffs and other vendors. Identify areas that are opened to the public for functions and then create barriers to the rest of the school. Focus on products that require less maintenance and offer low lifecycle operating costs.

STEP 3: HOW DO YOU GET THERE?

After the completion of surveys and designing the systems you want to implement, you then need to request costs from vendors. Then you need to decide upon the scope of work to be done and establish budgets and timelines.

Some work can be done in house, some by contractors on bids. Funding may come from yearly maintenance budgets or have to be assigned to capital budgets. You may have to develop a capital improvement project budget with monies designated over several years. There are funds available from federal programs (e.g., Homeland Security) as well as state grants for upgrading school security.

STEP 4: MAINTAIN SYSTEMS

Most importantly, establish an in-house product guide spec to be maintained and issued for use on new construction and renovation projects to keep continuity of products and services. Educate all staff, including maintenance, new construction planning, and facilities management as to the importance and cost savings incurred by adhering to these standards.

Once you start an upgrade project there is one other critical component to establish. You need to view doors, frames, door hardware, locksets, master key systems, and access control systems all together as one workable system. Historically these components are viewed independently of each other, but they all need to be given the same priority and maintenance attention as your other systems, such as HVAC and fire detection systems. You need to establish yearly maintenance procedures and budgets to properly maintain all these components. Doors, frames, fire door assemblies, locks, and keys all are part of your life safety and security systems. They all require regular inspection and attention to insure they offer you the degree of functionality they were originally designed for.

CONCLUSION

To aid the reader's understanding of the terminology used in this chapter, I have attached a set of definitions (Appendix B).[2]

APPENDIX A: SAMPLE EMPLOYEE KEY REQUEST FORM AND SIGN-OUT SHEET

North Crockett Public Schools[1]
John Wood Administration Building
6 Morse Street
North Crockett, Massachusetts 02760

---

[1]Fictitious school name.
[2]For more information, the author of this chapter can be contacted at: 1-774-571-1351 or jharper@kelaher.net

Employee Key Request Form

Name (please print):
Work Phone Number:
Request for Area/Office(s):

Key Requested:

Key Set # :	Serial #	Key Set # :	Serial #
Key Set # :	Serial #	Key Set # :	Serial #
Key Set # :	Serial #	Key Set # :	Serial #
Key Set # :	Serial #	Key Set # :	Serial #

►*Statement of Intent* Access control devices for North Crockett Public Schools are controlled by mechanical and electronic locking systems designed at considerable costs to the facility. All combinations for these systems are controlled by the Director of Facilities and Grounds, and are structured for the convenience of employees and departments and for the purpose of maintaining departmental physical security.

►*Policy* Unauthorized duplication or distribution of a key, access card or access code is strictly prohibited by the North Crockett Public Schools. Any employee who duplicates, alters, or divulges any key, access card, or access code to another person or organization without first receiving the necessary authorization from the Director of Facilities and Grounds may be held financially responsible for any expenses incurred by the North Crockett Public Schools as a result of such disclosure or duplication. In addition, the employee may be subject to discipline up to and including termination for such actions.

►*Financial Responsibility* The cost of rekeying or combination changes due to a loss or unauthorized distribution of combinations shall be borne by the department authorizing the issuance of said key(s), access cards, or access codes. North Crockett Public Schools will determine whether and under what circumstances all or part of these costs will be passed to an individual department member who has lost or made unauthorized distribution of key(s), access cards, or access codes. Determination of the requirement to re-key or change accesses cards or codes shall be made by the Director of Facilities and Grounds or his/her designee.

I, hereby declare that I need access requested to assist me in the performance of my assigned job duties. I affirm that I will not attempt to have, or allow, any keys, access cards, or access codes issued to me to be duplicated, altered or distributed to others. If I am transferred or leave the employment of North Crockett Public Schools, I will return the key(s), access cards, and access codes issued to me to the Director of Facilities and Grounds or his/her designee. Further, should I lose a key(s), access card, or access code, issued to me I will report the loss immediately to the Director of Facilities and Grounds at the following number:

Signature (your name): _____ Date: _____

Departmental Approval: I have received this request and approve the issuance of the key(s), access card or access code requested.

Signature (principal): _____ Date: _____ Phone #: _____

Director of Facilities and Grounds: Date:

North Crockett Public Schools, High School Key System

Key Administrator: Keith Cwiekowski

Name of Key	Location	Department	Phone#	508-999-9999
AB-4	**Campus Custodial**	**Facilities**		

Hook 111   High school campus cust. closet, cross corridor, cylinder dogs, restrooms key

Serial Number	Name of Person Carrying Key (Please print)	Date	ID#	Initials
1	In Key Cabinet on Hook 111	9/6/2009		KC
2	In Key Cabinet on Hook 111	9/6/2009		KC
3	Glenn McWilliams	9/2/2009		KC
4	Tony Sousa	9/8/2009		KC
5	Wayne Medeiros	9/8/2009		KC
6	Manuel Rebelo	9/8/2009		KC
7	Maria Furtado	9/8/2009		KC
8	Maria Amaral	9/8/2009		KC
9	Lorin Gosling	9/8/2009		KC
10	Laurette Gonzaga	9/8/2009		KC
11	James Dawicki	9/9/2009		KC
12	Donald Skidmore	9/8/2009		KC
13	John Laffan (Temp.)	11/2/2009		KC
14	Maria DaSilva	10/5/2009		KC
15	Gary Wilmoth	9/8/2009		KC
16	PARKER SPARE	10/19/2009		KC
17				
18				
19				
20				
21				
22				
23				
24				
25				
26				

FIGURE A1

This is an example sign-out sheet that would be maintained by a department head and sent to the key control office.

APPENDIX B: GLOSSARY OF TERMS AND DEFINITIONS

Some of the terms defined in this appendix may not be commonly used in a school environment. However, this appendix is meant as a resource for the reader should a locksmith need to be called in to address a lock issue in a school.

All-section key blank The key section that enters all keyways of a multiplex system.

Bitting 1. The number(s) that represent(s) the dimensions of the key; 2. The actual cut(s) or combination of a key.

Bitting list A listing of all the key combinations used within a system. The combinations are usually arranged in order of the blind code, direct code, and/or key symbol.

Bow The portion of the key that serves as a grip or handle.

Bumping One of many methods used to open locks with the use of "bump keys" that leave no sign of physical attack.

Cam 1. A lock or cylinder component that transfers the rotational motion of a key or cylinder plug to the bolt works of a lock. 2. The bolt of a cam lock.

Change key 1. A key that operates only one cylinder or one group of keyed-alike cylinders in a keying system. 2. Any device that is used to mechanically or electronically allow resetting of certain key or combination locks.

Combinate To set a combination in a lock, cylinder, or key.

Composite keyway A keyway that has been enlarged to accept more than one key section, often key sections of more than one manufacturer.

Construction core An interchangeable or removable core designed for use during the construction phase of a building. The cores are normally keyed alike and, upon completion of construction, they are to be replaced by the permanent system's cores.

Construction master key (CMK) A key normally used by construction personnel for a temporary period during building construction. It may be rendered permanently inoperative without disassembling the cylinder.

Control key 1. A key whose only purpose is to remove and/or install an interchangeable or removable core. 2. A bypass key used to operate and/or reset some combination-type locks. 3. A key that allows disassembly of some removable cylinder locks.

Controlled cross keying A condition in which two or more different keys of the same level of keying and under the same higher level key(s) operate one cylinder by design: e.g., XAA1 operated by AA2. Note: This condition could severely limit the security of the cylinder and the maximum expansion of the system when (1) more than a few of these different keys operate a cylinder or (2) more than a few differently cross-keyed cylinders per system are required.

Core A complete unit, often with a figure eight shape, which usually consists of the plug, shell, tumblers, springs, plug retainer, and spring cover(s). It is primarily used in removable and interchangeable core cylinders and locks.

Cross keying The deliberate process of combining a cylinder (usually in a master key system) to two or more different keys which would not normally be expected to operate it together. See also *controlled cross keying* and *uncontrolled cross keying*.

Cut key A key that has been bitted or combinated.

Day key 1. The key for a day gate or day operation of a safe or vault lock. 2. A cash register key that does not allow audit or reset functions. 3. See *change key*.

Disposable construction core Used with interchangeable core keying, where nonessential locking doors are used within a construction project. Locks are supplied with disposable plastic cores.

Dummy cylinder A nonfunctional facsimile of a rim or mortise cylinder used for appearance only, usually to conceal a cylinder hole.

High security cylinder A cylinder that offers a greater degree of resistance to any two or more of the following: picking, impressioning, key duplication, drilling, or other forms of forcible entry.

Housing The part of a locking device that is designated to hold a core.

Interchangeable core A key removable core that can be used in all or most of the core manufacturer's product line. No tools (other than the control key) are required for removal of the core.

Key bitting array (KBA) A matrix (graphic) display of all possible bittings for change keys and master keys as related to the top master key.

Key cabinet A cabinet with hooks, Velcro, or other means designed to store keys systematically.

Key changes The total possible number of different keys available for a given type of tumbler mechanism.

Key control Any method or procedure that limits unauthorized acquisition of a key and/or controls distribution of authorized keys. A systematic organization of keys and key records.

Key interchange An undesirable condition, usually in a master key system, whereby a key unintentionally operates a cylinder or lock.

Key section The exact cross-sectional configuration of a key blade as viewed from the bow toward the tip.

Key symbol A designation used for a key combination in the standard key coding system, e.g., A, AA, AA1, etc.

Key system schematic A drawing with blocks utilizing keying symbols, usually illustrating the hierarchy of all keys within a master key system. It indicates the structure and total expansion of the system.

Keyed alike (KA) Of or pertaining to two or more locks or cylinders which have or are to have the same combination. They may or may not be part of a keying system.

Keyed different (KD) Of or pertaining to a group of locks or cylinders, each of which is or is to be combinated differently from the others. They may or may not be part of a keying system.

Keying Any specification for how a cylinder or group of cylinders are or are to be combinated in order to control access.

Keying schedule A detailed specification of the keying system listing how all cylinders are to be keyed and the quantities, markings, and shipping instructions of all keys and/or cylinders to be provided.

Keyway 1. The opening in a lock or cylinder that is shaped to accept the key bit or blade of a proper configuration. 2. The exact cross-sectional configuration of a keyway as viewed from the front. It is not necessarily the same as the key section.

Large format interchangeable core (LFIC) 1. A key removable core that can be used in all or most of the core manufacturer's product line. No tools (other than the control key) are required for removal of the core. Recognized as a core having a universal figure 8 shape, and is generally unique in size to a specific manufacturer. An interchangeable core that is too large to fit into a small format interchangeable core housing.

Levels of keying The divisions of a master key system into hierarchies of access.

Master key 1. A key that operates all the master keyed locks or cylinders in a group, each lock or cylinder usually operated by its own change key. 2. To combinate a group of locks or cylinders such that each is operated by its own change key as well as by a master key for the entire group.

Master key system 1. Any keying arrangement that has two or more levels of keying. 2. A keying arrangement that has exactly two levels of keying.

Master keyed Of or pertaining to a cylinder or group of cylinders that are or are to be combinated so that all may be operated by their own change key(s) and by additional key(s) known as master key(s).

Multiplex key system 1. A series of different key sections that may be used to expand a master key system by repeating bittings on additional key sections. The keys of one key section will not enter the keyway of another key section. This type of system always includes another key section that will enter more than one, or all of the keyways. 2. A keying system that uses such keyways and key sections.

NMK A notation used to indicate "not master keyed" and is suffixed in parentheses to a regular keying symbol. It indicates that the cylinder is not to be operated by the master key(s) specified in the regular keying symbol, e.g., AB6 (NMK).

Pattern key 1. An original key kept on file to use in a key duplicating machine when additional keys are required. 2. Any key that is used in a key duplicating machine to create a duplicate key.

Pin tumbler Usually a cylindrical-shaped tumbler. Three types are normally used: bottom pin, master pin and top pin.

Plug The part of a cylinder that contains the keyway, with tumbler chambers usually corresponding to those in the cylinder shell.

Removable core A key removable core that can only be installed in one type of cylinder housing, e.g., rim cylinder or mortise cylinder or key-in-knob lock.

Selective master key An unassociated master key that can be made to operate any specific lock(s) in the entire system in addition to the regular master key(s) and/or change key(s) for the cylinder without creating key interchange. Examples include: (ENG) engineering key, (HSKP) housekeeping key, (JAN) janitor's key, (SEC) security key, (GRND) grounds key.

Shear line A location in a cylinder at which specific tumbler surfaces must be aligned, removing obstruction(s) that prevent the plug from moving.

Shell The part of the cylinder that surrounds the plug and usually contains tumbler chambers corresponding to those in the plug.

Simple key section A single independent key section which cannot be used in a multiplex key system.

Single key section An individual key section which can be used in a multiplex key system.

SKD Symbol for "single keyed," normally followed by a numerical designation in the standard key coding system, e.g., SKD1, SKD2, etc. It indicates that a cylinder or lock is not master keyed but is part of the keying system.

Small format interchangeable core (SFIC) 1. A key removable core that can be used in all or most of the core manufacturer's product line. No tools (other than the control key) are required for removal of the core. 2. Recognized as a core having a universal figure 8 shape, and is small in size.

Standard key coding system An industry standard and uniform method of designating all keys and/or cylinders in a master key system. The designation automatically indicates the exact function and keying level of each key and/or cylinder in the system, usually without further explanation.

Surreptitious entry The use of entry or bypass techniques that cannot be detected via disassembly and detailed inspection of lock components.

Tailpiece An actuator attached to the rear of the cylinder, parallel to the plug, typically used on rim, key-in-knob or special application cylinders.

Top master key (TMK) The highest level master key in a master key system.

Uncontrolled cross keying A condition in which two or more different change keys under different higher level keys operate one cylinder: e.g., XAA1, OB (operated by) AB, AB1.

Note: This condition severely limits the security of the cylinder and the maximum expansion of the system, and often leads to key interchange.

Visual key control (VKC) A specification that all keys and the visible portion of the front of all lock cylinders be stamped with standard keying symbols. Symbol used in hardware schedules to indicate a cross-keyed condition for a particular cylinder: e.g., XAA2, OB (operated by) AA3, AA4, AA, A.

Zero bitted Of or pertaining to a cylinder which is or is to be combinated to keys cut to the manufacturer's reference number "0" bitting.

SECURITY LIGHTING FOR SCHOOLS*

Philip P. Purpura, CPP, Lawrence J. Fennelly, CPO, CSS, HLS-III,
Gerard Honey, and James F. Broder, CPP

INTRODUCTION

Over the years, a lot has been written about lighting and return on investment (ROI). We suggest that school administrators contact their electric providers, to conduct an assessment of their lights in and around the school for the purpose of installation of lighting that will give an ROI as well as meeting the proper levels of lighting for cameras and safety issues.

As security consultants we see a variety of hodge-podge lighting in and around schools. We see lights on during the day, broken covers or lenses, a bird's nest inside a lantern fixture with broken glass, and lens covers that have turned brown from the heat of the bulb. In addition, we see fixtures that are not cost-effective.

COST AND ROI

Cost is broken down into three categories: (1) energy cost (usually 88%), (2) capital cost (8%), and (3) maintenance cost (4%). ROI is broken down into (1) efficiency and energy savings payback, (2) reduce costs by shutting off unnecessary units, and (3) the concept of going green.

From a safety perspective, lighting can be justified because it improves and promotes safety and prevents lawsuits, improves employee morale and productivity, and enhances the value of real estate. From a security perspective, two major purposes of lighting are *to create a psychological deterrent to intrusion* and *to enable detection.* Good lighting is considered such an effective crime control method that the law, in many locales, requires buildings to maintain adequate lighting.

One way to analyze lighting deficiencies is to go to the building at night and study the possible methods of entry and areas where inadequate lighting aids a burglar. Before the visit, contract local police as a precaution against mistaken identity and recruit their assistance in spotting weak points in lighting.

---

*Originally from Purpura P., et al. Security Lighting. *The Handbook of Loss Prevention and Crime Prevention.* Boston, MA: Butterworth-Heinemann; 2012. Updated by the editor, Elsevier, 2014.

The Handbook for School Safety and Security

159

What lighting level aids an intruder? Most people believe that, under conditions of darkness, a criminal can safely commit a crime. But this view may be faulty, in that one generally cannot work in the dark. Three possible levels of light are bright light, darkness, and dim light. *Bright light* affords an offender plenty of light to work but enables easy observation by others; it deters crime. Without light, in *darkness*, a burglar finds that he or she cannot see to jimmy a good lock, release a latch, or do whatever work is necessary to gain access. However, *dim light* provides just enough light to break and enter while hindering observation by authorities.

Although much case law supports lighting as an indicator of efforts to provide a safe environment, security specialists are questioning conventional wisdom about lighting.[1] Because so much nighttime lighting goes unused, should it be reduced or turned off? Does an offender look more suspicious under a light or in the dark with a flashlight? Should greater use be made of motion-activated lighting? How would these approaches affect safety and cost-effectiveness? These questions are ripe for research.

ILLUMINATION[2]

Lumens (of light output) per watt (of power input) is a measure of lamp efficiency. Initial lumens per watt data are based on the light output of lamps when new; however, light output declines with use. *Illuminance* is the intensity of light falling on a surface, measured in foot-candles (English units) or lux (metric units). The *foot-candle* (fc) is a measure of how bright the light is when it reaches 1 foot from the source. One lux equals 0.0929 fc. The light provided by direct sunlight on a clear day is about 10,000 fc, an overcast day would yield about 100 fc, and a full moon gives off about 0.01 fc. A sample of outdoor lighting illuminances recommended by the Illuminating Engineering Society of North America are as follows: self-parking area, 1 fc; attendant parking area, 0.20-0.90 fc; covered parking area, 5 fc; active pedestrian entrance, 5 fc; and building surroundings, 1 fc. It generally is recommended that gates and doors, where identification of persons and things takes place, should have at least 2 fc. An office should have a light level of about 50 fc.

Care should be exercised when studying fc. Are they horizontal or vertical? Horizontal illumination may not aid in the visibility of vertical objects such as signs and keyholes. (The preceding fc are horizontal.) The fc vary depending on the distance from the lamp and the angle. If you hold a light meter horizontally, it often gives a different reading that if you hold it vertically. Are the fc initial or maintained?

David G. Aggleton, CPP, stated in an article in *Security Technology Executive* (March 2011) that "A quick rule of thumb for minimum reflected light is: (A) Detection: 0.5 fc, (B) Recognition: 1.0 fc, (C) Identification: 2.0 fc are required."

Maintenance and bulb replacement ensure high-quality lighting.

[1] Berube, H. (1994). New notions of night light. *Security Management* (December).
[2] National Lighting Bureau. Lighting for safety and security. Washington, DC: National Lighting Bureau; n.d. pp. 1–36; Smith MS. Crime prevention through environmental design in parking facilities. Washington, DC: National Institute of Justice; 1996, pp. 1-4; Bowers DM. Let there be light. Security Management 1995; pp. 103-111; Kunze DR, Schiefer J. An illuminating look at light. Security Management 1995; pp. 113-116.

TYPES OF LAMPS[3]

The following lamps are applied outdoors:

- *Incandescent.* These are commonly found at residences. Passing electrical current through a tungsten wire that becomes white-hot produces light. These lamps produce 10-20 lumens per watt, are the least efficient and most expensive to operate, and have a short lifetime of 9000 hours.
- *Halogen and quartz halogen lamps.* Incandescent bulbs filled with halogen gas (like sealed-beam auto headlights) provide about 25% better efficiency and life than ordinary incandescent bulbs.
- *Fluorescent lamps.* Pass electricity through a gas enclosed in a glass tube to produce light, yielding 40-80 lumens per watt. They create twice the light and less than half the heat of an incandescent bulb of equal wattage and cost 5-10 times as much. Fluorescent lamps do not provide high levels of light output. The lifetime is 9000-20,000 hours. They are not used extensively outdoors, except for signs. Fluorescent lamps use one-fifth to one-third as much electricity as incandescent with a comparable lumen rating and last up to 20 times longer. They are cost-effective with yearly saving per bulb of $9.00-25.00.
- *Mercury vapor lamps.* They also pass electricity through a gas. The yield is 30-60 lumens per watt and the life is about 20,000 hours.
- *Metal halide lamps.* They are also of the gaseous type. The yield is 80-100 lumens per watt, and the life is about 10,000 hours. They often are used at sports stadiums because they imitate daylight conditions and colors appear natural. Consequently, these lamps complement video surveillance systems, but they are the most expensive light to install and maintain.
- *High-pressure sodium lamps.* These are gaseous, yield about 100 lumens per watt, have a life of about 20,000 hours, and are energy efficient. These lamps are often applied on streets and parking lots, and through fog are designed to allow the eyes to see more detail at greater distances. They also cause less light pollution then mercury-vapor lamps.
- *Low-pressure sodium lamps.* They are gaseous, produce 150 lumens per watt, have a life of about 15,000 hours, and are even more efficient than high-pressure sodium. These lamps are expensive to maintain.
- *LED (light emitting diodes).* These are small lights, such as Christmas bulbs, and spotlights. They use very low energy consumption and are long lasting up to 50,000-80,000 hours. This rapidly growing light source maybe the light of the future. Currently they are used in many applications such as in garages, street lighting, and rear tail-lights in motor vehicles. These lights are considered *the bulb of the future.*
- *Quartz lamps.* These lamps emit a very bright light and snap on almost as rapidly as incandescent bulbs. They are frequently used at very high wattage—1500-2000 watts is not uncommon in protective systems—and they are excellent for use along the perimeter barrier and in troublesome areas.
- *Electroluminescent lights.* These lights are similar to their florescent cousins; however, they do not contain mercury and are more compact.

---

[3]National Lighting Bureau. Lighting for safety and security. Washington, DC: National Lighting Bureau; n.d. pp. 1-36; Smith MS. Crime prevention through environmental design in parking facilities. Washington, DC: National Institute of Justice; 1996, pp. 1-4; Bowers DM. Let there be light. Security Management 1995; pp. 103-111; Kunze DR, Schiefer J. An illuminating look at light. Security Management 1995; pp. 113-116.

Each type of lamp has a different *color rendition index* (CRI), which is the way a lamp's output affects human perception of color. Incandescent, fluorescent, and halogen lamps provide an excellent color rendition index of 100%. Based on its high CRI and efficiency the preferred outdoor lamp for video surveillance systems is metal halide. Mercury vapor lamps provide good color rendition but are heavy on the blue. Low-pressure sodium lamps, which are used extensively outdoors, provide poor color rendition, making things look yellow. Low-pressure sodium lamps make color unrecognizable and produce a yellow-gray color on objects. People find they produce a strange yellow haze. Claims are made that this lighting conflicts with aesthetic values and affects sleeping habits. In many instances, when people park their vehicles in a parking lot during the day and return to find their vehicle at night, they are often unable to locate it because of poor color rendition from sodium lamps; some even report their vehicles as stolen. Another problem is the inability of witnesses to describe offenders accurately.

Mercury vapor, metal halide, and high-pressure sodium take several minutes to produce full light output. If they are turned off, even more time is required to reach full output because they first have to cool down. This may not be acceptable for certain security applications. Incandescent, halogen, and quartz halogen have the advantage of instant light once the electricity is turned on. Manufacturers can provide information on a host of lamp characteristics including the "strike" and "re-strike" time.

The following sources provide additional information on lighting:

- National Lighting Bureau (http://www.nlb.org): Publications.
- Illuminating Engineering Society of North America (http://www.iesna.org): Technical materials and services; recommended practices and standards; many members are engineers.
- International Association of Lighting Management Companies (http://www.nalmco.org): Seminars, training, and certification programs.

LIGHTING EQUIPMENT

Incandescent or gaseous discharge lamps are used in streetlights. Fresnel lights have a wide flat beam that is directed outward to protect a perimeter and glares in the faces of those approaching. A floodlight "floods" an area with a beam of light, resulting in considerable glare. Floodlights are stationary, although the light beams can be aimed to select positions. The following strategies reinforce good lighting:

1. Locate perimeter lighting to allow illumination of both sides of the barrier.
2. Direct lights down and away from a facility to create glare for an intruder. Make sure the directed lighting does not hinder observation by the patrolling officer.
3. Do not leave dark spaces between lighted areas for burglars to move in. Design lighting to permit overlapping illumination.
4. Protect the lighting system. Locate lighting inside the barrier, install protective covers over lamps, mount lamps on high poles, bury power lines, and protect switch boxes.
5. Photoelectric cells enable light to go on and off automatically in response to natural light. Manual operation is helpful as a backup.
6. Consider motion-activated lighting for external and internal areas.
7. If lighting is required in the vicinity of navigable waters, contact the U.S. Coast Guard.

8. Try not to disturb neighbors by intense lighting.
9. Maintain a supply of portable, emergency lights and auxiliary power in the event of a power failure.
10. Good interior lighting also deters burglars and allows passing patrol officers to view the property.
11. If necessary, join Neighborhood Watch Programs to petition local government to install improved street lights.

TWENTY-FIVE THINGS YOU NEED TO KNOW ABOUT LIGHTING FOR YOUR SCHOOL[4]

1. *Watts*: Measures the amount of electrical energy used.
2. *Foot-candle:* Measure of light on a surface 1 square foot in area on which one unit of light (lumen) is distributed uniformly.
3. *Lumen:* Unit of light output from a lamp.
4. *Lamp:* Term that refers to light sources that are called *bulbs.*
5. *Lux:* Measurement of illumination.
6. *Illuminare:* Intensity of light that falls on an object.
7. *Brightness:* Intensity of the sensation from light as seen by the eye.
8. *Foot-lambert:* Measure of brightness.
9. *Glare:* Excessive brightness.
10. *Luminaire:* Complete lighting unit; consists of one or more lamps joined with other parts that distribute light, protect the lamp, position or direct it, and connect it to a power source.
11. *Ballast:* Device used with fluorescent and high-intensity discharge lamps to obtain voltage and current to operate the lamps.
12. *High-intensity discharge (HID):* Term used to identify four types of lamps—mercury vapor, metal halide, and high- and low-pressure sodium.
13. *Coefficient of utilization:* Ratio of the light delivered from a luminaire to a surface compared to the total light output from a lamp.
14. *Contrast:* Relationship between the brightness of an object and its immediate background.
15. *Diffuser:* Device on the bottom or sides of a luminaire to redirect or spread light from a source.
16. *Fixture:* A luminaire.
17. *Lens:* Glass or plastic shield that covers the bottom of a luminaire to control the direction and brightness of the light as it comes out of the fixture or luminaire.
18. *Louvers:* Series of baffles arranged in a geometric pattern. They shield a lamp from direct view to avoid glare.
19. *Uniform lighting:* refers to a system of lighting that directs the light specifically on the work or job rather than on the surrounding areas.
20. *Reflector:* Device used to redirect light from a lamp.
21. *Task or work lighting:* Amount of light that falls on an object of work.

[4]Tyska, L. A., and Fennelly, L. J. (2000). *Physical security, 150 things you should know.* Boston, MA: Butterworth-Heinemann; pp. 155-156.

22. *Veiling reflection:* Reflection of light from an object that obscures the detail to be observed by reducing the contrast between the object and its background.
23. *Incandescent lamps:* Produce light by passing an electric current through a tungsten filament in a glass bulb. They are the least efficient type of bulb.
24. *Fluorescent lamps:* Second most common source of light. They draw an electric arc along the length of a tube. The ultraviolet light produced by the arc activates a phosphor coating on the walls of the tube, which causes light.
25. *HID lamps:* Consist of mercury vapor, metal halide, and high- and low-pressure sodium lamps. The low-pressure sodium is the most efficient, but has a very low CRI of 5.

ENERGY MANAGEMENT

The efficiency and management of lighting is becoming a high priority in commissioning new buildings and upgrading existing systems. Indeed, the subject of energy management is expected to become one of the most important considerations within the building regulation documents and have a tremendous impact on the way the construction industry looks at energy. It is apparent that serious measures must now be taken to reduce energy use and waste. This will have an impact on security lighting and the way it is applied. Lighting experts show an increasing urge to work alongside electrical contractors and installers to help them increase their business opportunities by identifying the roles and applications in which energy-efficient lighting should be installed. Electrical contractors are becoming better educated in lighting design that is effective and energy efficient.

Lighting design personnel need to:

- Recognize inefficient installations.
- Appreciate the environmental, cost, and associated benefits of energy-efficient lighting schemes.
- Estimate energy cost savings and calculate the payback period.
- Recognize the situations in which expert and specialist knowledge is needed in the design of management systems.
- Think in terms of increasing business trying to preserve the environment.

At certain points in time, it was said that lighting any system brighter was advantageous. However, we are now seeing a trend away from large floodlights illuminating the night sky with a strong white glare, as exterior lighting is becoming much more focused on the minimum lux levels required. We are also seeing a move toward directional beams.

The lighting industry wants to remove itself from a proliferation of public and private external lighting schemes to counter the light pollution problem and become more energy and cost conscious in its makeup. There must be a mechanism to tackle the problem of countless floodlights, up lighters, spotlights, decorative installations, and an array of security lighting forms that are badly installed and specified, create light pollution, and use high energy levels.

Lighting pollution is now at the forefront of debates for two main reasons:

(a) Light pollution spoils the natural effect of the night skies.
(b) The greater the light pollution, the greater is the power consumption.

Unfortunately, a certain degree of light pollution is needed to satisfy safety and security applications. Equally, there is always the desire to have purely decorative lighting installations, so the answer lies in a compromise. Systems must be designed with a degree of thought given to the avoidance of light pollution and energy waste. External lighting must provide minimal light pollution, a safe environment, and an attractive feature. For attractive features, we can see a greater use of fiber optic solutions with color-changing effects and lighting engineered to direct the illumination downward. Bollards or recessed ground luminaries can be set into walkways so there is no spill into the night sky. Intelligently designed schemes can ensure that lighting is reflected only in a downward direction so that pedestrians are better guided and the lighting has a pleasing effect with little overspill.

Therefore, within the lighting industry, there is a need is to raise standards in all aspects associated with light and lighting, in particular when it comes to energy management and light pollution. We need to define and harness the pleasures of lighting but at the same time promote the benefits of well-designed energy-efficient schemes among the public at large. There must also be miniaturization and increased lamp life. Energy management must therefore be a part of security lighting.

LIGHTING CHECKLIST

1. Is the entire perimeter well lit?
2. Is there a strip of light on both sides of fence?
3. Is the illumination sufficient to detect human movement easily at 100 yards?
4. Are lights checked for operation daily prior to darkness?
5. Is extra lighting available at entry points and points of possible intrusion?
6. Are lighting repairs made promptly?
7. Is the power supply for lights easily accessible (for tampering)?
8. Are lighting circuit drawings available to facilitate quick repairs?
9. Are switches and controls
   (a) Protected?
   (b) Weatherproof and tamper resistant?
   (c) Accessible to security personnel?
   (d) Inaccessible from outside the perimeter barrier?
   (e) Equipped with centrally located master switch(es)?
10. Is the illumination good for guards on all routes inside the perimeter?
11. Are the materials and equipment in receiving, shipping, and storage areas adequately lighted?
12. Are bodies of water on perimeter adequately lit?
13. Is an auxiliary source of power available for protective lighting?

PROTECTIVE LIGHTING CHECKLIST

1. Is protective lighting adequate on perimeter?
2. What type of lighting is it?
3. Is the lighting of open areas within the perimeter adequate?
4. Do shadowed areas exist?
5. Are outside storage areas adequately lighted?
6. Are inside areas adequately lighted?
7. Is the guard protected or exposed by the lighting?

8. Are gates and boundaries adequately lighted?
9. Do lights at the gates illuminate the interior of vehicles?
10. Are critical and vulnerable areas well illuminated?
11. Is protective lighting operated manually or automatically?
12. Do cones of light on the perimeter overlap?
13. Are perimeter lights wired in series?
14. Is the lighting at shipping and receiving docks or piers adequate?
15. Is the lighting in the parking lots adequate?
16. Is an auxiliary power source available with backup standby units?
17. Is the interior of buildings adequately lighted?
18. Are parking lots adequately lighted?
19. Are guards equipped with powerful flashlights?
20. How many more and what type of lights are needed to provide adequate illumination? In what locations?
21. Do security personnel report light outages?
22. How soon are burned-out lights replaced?
23. Are open areas of a campus sufficiently lighted to discourage illegal or criminal acts against pedestrians?
24. Are any areas covered with high-growing shrubs or woods where the light is insufficient?
25. Are the outsides of buildings holding valuable or critical activities or materials lighted?
26. Are interiors of hallways and entrances lighted when buildings are open at night?
27. Are areas surrounding women's dormitories well lighted? Within a college setting?
28. Are campus parking lots lighted sufficiently to discourage tampering with parked cars or other illegal activities?
29. Are areas where materials of high value are stored well lighted? Safes, libraries, bookstores, food storage areas, and so forth?
30. Lamp life versus efficiency?
31. Lamp CRI?
32. Continuous levels of light at night?
33. Provide specific levels of light for CCTV units? We are in the age of HD cameras and HD television monitors as well as low light cameras, all of which are crime deterrents in some cases.
34. Required light for evening patrols?
35. Complex should have an even and adequate distribution of light?

LIGHTING LEVELS FOR YOUR SCHOOL COMPLEX

By definition a foot-candle is a unit of illuminance or light falling into a surface. It stands for the light level on a surface one foot from a standard candle. One foot-candle is equal to one lumen per square foot.

0.50 fc for perimeter of outer area
0.4 fc for perimeter of restricted area

10.0 fc for vehicular entrances
5.0 fc for pedestrian entrance
0.5-2 fc for roadways
0.2 fc for open years
0.20-5 fc for decks on open piers
10-20 fc for interior sensitive structures

Open parking light levels are a minimum of 0.2 fc in low-level activity areas and 2 fc in high-vehicle activity areas. If there is cash collection, the light level is a minimum of 5 fc.

- Loading docks: 15 fc
- Loading docks interior: 15 fc
- Shipping and receiving: 5 fc
- Security gate house: 25-30 fc
- Security gate house interior: 30 fc
- For pedestrians or normal CCTV cameras the minimum level of light for:
- Detection is 0.5 fc
- Recognition is 1 fc
- Identification is 2 fc
- Parking structures: 5 fc
- Parking areas or open spaces: 2 fc
- Loading docks: 0.20-5 fc
- Loading dock parking areas: 15-30 fc
- Piers and docks: 0.20-5 fc

LIGHTING DEFINITIONS
LUMENS

The quantity or flow of light emitted by a lamp is measured in lumens. For example, a typical household bulb rated at 100 watts may output about 1700 lumens.

Illuminance is the concentration of light over a particular area and is measured in lux, representing the number of lumens per square meter or foot-candles. One foot-candle is equal to 10.76 lux (often approximated to a ratio of 1:10).

Note: When evaluating the amount of light needed by a particular video surveillance camera (or the eye) to perceive a scene, it is the amount of light shining over the area of the lens iris (camera or eye), or its luminance, that is critical.

REFLECTANCE

When you see an object our eyes are sensing the light reflected from that object. If there is no light reflected from the object, we only see a silhouette in contrast to its background. If the object is illuminated by other than white light we will see the object in colors that are not true. The color of the surface also impacts reflectance; a light surface, such as a parking lot paved in concrete, will have higher reflectance than a dark surface (a parking lot paved in asphalt or black-top). The measure of reflectance of an object is the ratio of the quantity of light (measured in lumens) falling on it to the light reflected from it, expressed as a percentage.

CRI

The ability of a lamp to faithfully reproduce the colors seen in an object is measured by the CRI. Security personnel need the ability to accurately describe color. It is an important aspect in the apprehension of criminals who are caught on CCTV displays and recordings. CRI is measured on a scale of 1-100. A CRI of 70-80 is considered good, above 80 is considered excellent, and 100% is considered daylight.

CORRECTED COLOR TEMPERATURE

A measure of the warmth or coolness of a light is the corrected color temperature (CCT). It has a considerable impact on mood and ambiance of the surroundings.

LIGHTING SYSTEMS

A lighting system consists of a number of components, all of which are important to the effectiveness of a lighting application. Below is a list of the major components and their function.

- *Lamp (also known as a light bulb).* Manufactured light source that includes the filament or an arc tube, its glass casing, and its electrical connectors. Types of lamps include incandescent and mercury vapor, which describe the type of technologies used to create the light.
- *Luminary (also known as fixture).* Complete lighting unit consisting of the lamp, its holder, and the reflectors and diffusers used to distribute and focus the light.
- *Mounting hardware.* Examples are a wall bracket or a light pole used to fix the correct height and location of the luminary.
- *Electrical power.* Operates the lamp, ballasts, and photocells. Some lamp technologies are sensitive to reduced voltage, in particular the HID family of lamps (metal halide, mercury vapor, and high-pressure sodium).

WEB SITES

The following organizations provide valuable information about lighting:

National Lighting Bureau: www.nlb.org
Illuminating Engineering Society: www.iesna.org
International Association of Light Management Companies: www.nalmco.org

APPENDIX: LIGHTING DESCRIPTION

Table A1   Types of Lighting

Type	CRI	Color of Light
Incandescent	100	White Reflects all light
Fluorescent	62	Bluish/white Good color rendition
Mercury vapor	15	Blue/green Fair color rendition When used as a streetlight, there will be a blue label indicating wattage
High-pressure sodium	22	Golden/white Poor color rendition When used as a streetlight, there will be a yellow label indicating wattage
Low-pressure sodium	44	Yellow Very low color rendition
Metal halide	65-90	Bright white Very high color rendition When used as a streetlight, there will be a white label indicating wattage
Halogen/quartz halogen	100	White
LED	95-98	White
Induction	80-100	White

Table A2   Operational Costs (10 year)

Technology	Wattage	Lamp Changes	Energy	Maintenance	Material	Cost of Operation
High-pressure sodium	70	3.7	$927	$201	$73	$1201
High-pressure sodium	150	3.7	$1971	$201	$73	$2245
High-pressure sodium	250	3.7	$3154	$201	$73	$3427
High-pressure sodium	400	3.7	$4878	$201	$73	$5151
High-pressure sodium	1000	3.7	$11,563	$201	$224	$11,988
Induction	40	0	$429	$0	$0	$429
Induction	80	0	$858	$0	$0	$858

Continued

Technology	Wattage	Lamp Changes	Energy	Maintenance	Material	Cost of Operation
Induction	100	0	$1072	$0	$0	$1072
Induction	120	0	$1287	$0	$0	$1287
Induction	200	0	$2144	$0	$0	$2144
Metal halide (V)	150	5.8	$1971	$321	$187	$2479
Metal halide (V)	175	8.8	$2,263	$482	$278	$3,022
Metal halide (V)	250	8.8	$3101	$482	$280	$3863
Metal halide (V)	400	8.8	$4793	$482	$280	$5556
Metal halide (V)	1000	7.3	$11,248	$402	$365	$12,014
Metal halide (H)	150	7.8	$1971	$428	$249	$2648
Metal halide (H)	175	11.7	$2263	$642	$370	$3275
Metal halide (H)	250	11.7	$3101	$642	$374	$4117
Metal halide (H)	400	11.7	$4793	$642	$374	$5810
Metal halide (H)	1000	9.7	$11,248	$535	$487	$12,270
Low-pressure sodium	180	5.5	$2308	$301	$345	$2954
Low-pressure sodium	135	5.5	$1873	$301	$257	$2432
Low-pressure sodium	90	5.5	$1306	$301	$203	$1809
Low-pressure sodium	55	4.9	$838	$268	$161	$1267
Low-pressure sodium	35	4.9	$629	$268	$161	$1057

Based on 24 hours of on-time, 0.12 kW/hour, and $55/hour Labor Charge. U.S. Energy Technologies, 2007

Formula to determine the cost to operate a light source

Watts × Hours = Watts Hours

Watts Hours ÷ 1,000 = Kilowatts

Kilowatts × Rate = Cost

Information for the Formula

Watts: On the bulb or fixture of the light source

Watt Hours ÷ 1000 = Kilowatts

Kilowatts × Rate = Cost

U.S. Energy Technologies (2009).

INTRUSION DETECTION SYSTEMS FOR SCHOOLS*

20

Michael D. Brown, CPP, PCI, PSP
Founder and director, MDB Consulting Agency

INTRODUCTION

Burglary is a big business. Moreover, crime figures show a staggering rate of increase in burglaries of private homes, businesses, and schools. It is no wonder then that so many property owners are giving serious consideration to electronic alarm protection. These operators/thieves are in the market to make a fast dollar, and the unwary customer who buys what seems to be a bargain too often ends up being cheated.

The concept of an alarm for a school is no different that the alarms in a corporate setting or even for the home.

THREAT OR RISK

The selection of a proper alarm system is not a simple matter, because the needs of each school are different, like a set of fingerprints. Some factors that determine the requirements of an individual alarm system and the questions that must be answered when selecting a system include:

- The threat or risk. What is the system to protect against?
- The type of sensors needed. What will be protected?
- What methods are available to provide the level of protection needed?
- The method of alarm signal transmission. How is the signal to be sent and who will respond?

Most of the confusion regarding intrusion detection systems is a result of the variety of methods available to provide the protection needed. The combinations of detection methods are in the thousands. An intrusion detection system may deter a would-be intruder. However, the primary function of the alarm system is to signal the presence of an intruder. An intrusion detection system can be just a portion of the overall protection needed. Some schools supplement these systems with security guards or SRO. The successful operation of any type of an alarm system depends on its proper installation and maintenance by the alarm-installing company and the proper use of the system by the customer.

---

*Originally from McKinnon S. Intrusion Detection Systems. *The Handbook of Loss Prevention and Crime Prevention.* Boston, MA: Butterworth-Heinemann; 2012. Updated by the author, Elsevier, 2013.

COMPONENTS OF ALARM SYSTEMS

Sensing devices are used in the actual detection of an intruder (see Figures 20.1 and 20.2). Each has a specific purpose and can be divided into three categories: perimeter protection, area/space protection, and object/spot protection.

PERIMETER PROTECTION

Perimeter protection is the first line in the defense to detect an intruder. The most common points equipped with sensing devices for premise perimeter protection are doors, windows, vents, skylights, or any opening to a business or home. Since over 80% of all break-ins occur through these openings, most

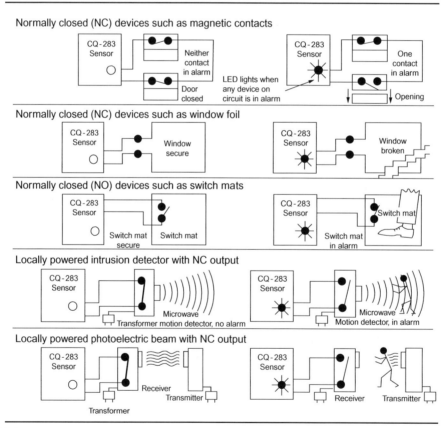

FIGURE 20.1

Typical application of the use of magnetic contacts, window foil, switch mats, motion detection, and photoelectric beam.

(Courtesy of Aritech Corporation)

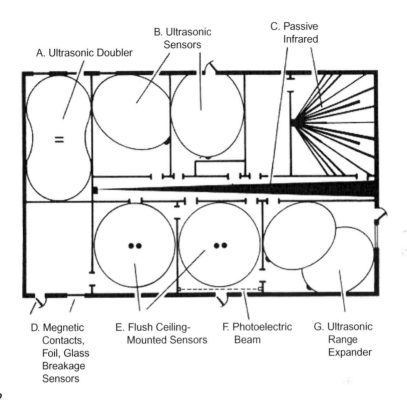

A. Ultrasonic Doubler

B. Ultrasonic Sensors

C. Passive Infrared

D. Megnetic Contacts, Foil, Glass Breakage Sensors

E. Flush Ceiling- Mounted Sensors

F. Photoelectric Beam

G. Ultrasonic Range Expander

FIGURE 20.2

Sensors. (a) Ultrasonic doubler: Back-to-back ultrasonic transceivers provide virtually double the coverage of single detectors at almost the same wiring and equipment cost. With more than 50×25 ft of coverage, the doubler is the best value in space protection. (b) Ultrasonic sensors: Easy to install, no brackets needed. Can be mounted horizontally, vertically, or in a corner; surface, flush, or with mounting feet on a shelf. Each UL-listed sensor protects a three-dimensional volume up to 30 ft wide and high. (c) Passive infrared: For those zones where the lower-cost ultrasonic sensor is inappropriate, there is no need to buy a complete passive infrared system as both ultrasonic and passive infrared can be used in the same system. (d) Magnetic contacts, foil, glass breakage sensors: The building's perimeter protection detectors can be wired into the system via universal interface sensor. There is no need for running a separate perimeter loop. (e) Flush-ceiling-mounted sensors: Only the two small 2-inch-diameter transducer caps are visible below the ceiling tiles. Designed for where minimum visibility is needed for aesthetic or security purposes. (f) Photoelectric beam: The universal interface sensor allows the connection of any NO or NC alarm device into the system for zoned annunciation. It can be used with photoelectric beams, switch matting, microwave motion detectors, and many other intrusion detectors. (g) Ultrasonic range expander: Adding an ultrasonic range expander can increase the coverage of an ultrasonic sensor by 50-90%, depending on where it is positioned and the surrounding environment.

(Courtesy of Aritech Corporation)

alarm systems provide this type of protection. The major advantage of perimeter protection is its simple design. The major disadvantage is that it protects only the openings. If the burglar bursts through a wall, comes through the ventilation system, or stays behind after closing, perimeter protection is useless.

1. *Door switches.* These are installed on a door or window in such a way that opening the door or window causes a magnet to move a contact switch away, which activates the alarm. They can be surface mounted or recessed into the door and frame. A variety of switches are manufactured for all types of doors or windows. The switches are both wide gap type and magnetic standard type.
2. *Glass break detectors.* These detectors are attached to the glass and sense the breakage of the glass by shock or sound. Glass breakage sensors use microphone transducers to detect the glass breakage. A ceiling sensor over a window covers a 30° radius.
3. *Wooden screens.* These devices are made of wooden dowel sticks assembled in a cage-like fashion no more than 4 inches from each other. A very fine, brittle wire runs in the wooden dowels and frame. The burglar must break the doweling to gain entry and thus break the low-voltage electrical circuit, causing the alarm to sound. These devices are used primarily in commercial applications.
4. *Window screens.* These devices are similar to regular wire window screens in a home except that a fine, coated wire is a part of the screen. When the burglar cuts the screen to gain entry, the flow of low-voltage electricity is interrupted and sounds the alarm. These devices are used primarily in residential applications.
5. *Lace and panels.* The surfaces of door panels and safes are protected against entry by installing a close lace-like pattern of metallic foil or a fine brittle wire on the surface. Entry cannot be made without first breaking the foil or wire, thus activating the alarm. A panel of wood is placed over the lacing to protect it.
6. *Interior sensors.* They come in many shapes and sizes depending upon the application; for example, interior motion detector units and proximity and boundary penetration.

AREA/SPACE PROTECTION

Area/space protection devices (Table 20.1) protect the interior spaces of a school, business, or home. They protect against intrusion whether or not the perimeter protection is violated. It is particularly effective against a stay-behind intruder or a burglar who cuts through the roof or breaks through a block wall. Space protection devices are only a part of the complete alarm system.

They should always be supplemented with perimeter protection. The major advantage of space protection devices is that they provide a highly sensitive, invisible means of detection. The major disadvantage is that improper application and installation by the alarm company can result in frequent false alarms.

The types of area/space protection include:

1. *Photoelectric eyes (beams).* These devices transmit a beam across a protected area. When an intruder interrupts the beam, the beam circuit is disrupted and the alarm initiated. Photoelectric devices use a pulsed infrared beam that is invisible to the naked eye. Some units have a range of over 1000 ft and can be used outdoors, although they are rarely used today.
2. *Ultrasonics.* They (although rarely used today) work on a low-frequency sound wave projected from the unit. The frequency is in kilohertz (23-26) and its area of coverage

Table 20.1 Motion Sensor Survey Checklist

Environmental and Other Factors Affecting Sensor Usage	Circle One	Ultrasonics	Microwave	PIR	Recommendation and Notes
1. If the areas to be protected are enclosed by thin walls or contain windows, will there be movement close to the outside of this area?	Yes/No	None	Major	None	Avoid using a microwave sensor unless it can be aimed away from thin walls, glass, etc., which can pass an amount of microwave energy
2. Will protection pattern see sun, moving headlamps, or other sources of infrared energy passing through windows?	Yes/No	None	None	Major	Avoid using a PIR sensor unless the pattern can be positioned to avoid rapidly changing levels of infrared energy
3. Does area to be protected contain HVAC ducts?	Yes/No	None	Moderate	None	Ducts can channel microwave energy to other areas; if using a microwave sensor, aim it away from duct openings
4. Will two or more sensors of the same type be used to protect a common area?	Yes/No	None	None	None	Adjacent units must operate on different frequencies
5. Does area to be protected contain fluorescent or neon lights that are on during protection-on period?	Yes/No	None	Major	None	Microwave sensor, if used, must be aimed away from any fluorescent or neon light within 20 ft
6. Are incandescent lamps cycled on and off during protection-on period included in the protection pattern?	Yes/No	None	None	Major	If considering use of PIR sensor, make a trial installation and, if necessary, redirect protection pattern away from incandescent lamps
7. Must protection pattern be projected from a ceiling?	Yes/No	None, but only for ceiling heights up to 15 ft	Major	Major	Only ultrasonic sensors can be used on a ceiling, but height is limited to 15 ft; at greater ceiling heights, use rigid ceiling brackets to suspend sensor to maintain 15 ft limitation or, in large open areas, try a microwave sensor mounted high on a wall and aimed downward

Continued

Table 20.1 Motion Sensor Survey Checklist—Cont'd

Environmental and Other Factors Affecting Sensor Usage	Circle One	Effect on Sensor				Recommendation and Notes
		Ultrasonics	Microwave	PIR		
8. Is the overall structure of flimsy construction (corrugated metal, thin plywood, etc.)?	Yes/No	Minor	Major	Minor		Do not use a microwave sensor; if considerable structural movement can be expected, then use a rigid mounting surface for ultrasonic or PIR sensor
9. Will protection pattern include large metal objects or wall surfaces?	Yes/No	Minor	Major	Minor (major if metal is highly polished)		Use ultrasonic sensor or use PIR sensor
10. Are any radar installations nearby?	Yes/No	Minor	Major when radar is close and sensor is aimed at it	Minor		Avoid using a microwave sensor
11. Will protection pattern include heaters, radiators, air conditioners, or the like?	Yes/No	Moderate	None	Major when rapid changes in air temperature are involved		Use ultrasonic sensor, but aim it away from sources of air turbulence (desirable to have heaters, etc., turned off during protection-on period) or use microwave sensor
12. Will area to be protected be subjected to ultrasonic noise (bells, hissing sounds)?	Yes/No	Moderate, can cause problems in severe cases	None	None		Try muffling noise source and use an ultrasonic sensor, use a microwave sensor, or use PIR sensor
13. Will protection pattern include drapes, carpet, racks of clothing, or the like?	Yes/No	Moderate, reduction in range	None	Minor		Use ultrasonic sensor if some reduction in range can be tolerated or use microwave sensor
14. Is the area to be protected subject to changes in temperature and humidity?	Yes/No	Moderate	None	Major		Use an ultrasonic sensor unless changes in temperature and humidity are severe or use a microwave sensor
15. Is there water noise from faulty valves in the area to be protected?	Yes/No	Moderate, can be a problem	None	None		If noise is substantial, try correcting faulty valves and use an ultrasonic sensor; use a microwave sensor, or use a PIR sensor
16. Will protection pattern see moving machinery, fan blades, or the like?	Yes/No	Major	Major	Minor		Have machinery, fans, and the like turned off during protection-on period, carefully place ultrasonic sensor, or use PIR sensor

Question				
17. Will drafts or other air movement pass through protection pattern?	Yes/No	Major	None	None, unless rapid temperature changes are involved	If protection pattern can be aimed away from air movement or air movement can be stopped during protection-on period, use an ultrasonic sensor, use a microwave sensor, or use a PIR sensor
18. Will protection pattern see overhead doors that can be rattled by wind?	Yes/No	Major	Major	Minor	If protection pattern can be aimed away from such doors, use an ultrasonic sensor or use a PIR sensor
19. Are there hanging signs, calendar pages, or the like that can be moved by air currents during protection-on period?	Yes/No	Major	Major	Moderate, can be a problem	Use ultrasonic sensor, but aim pattern away from objects that can move or remove such objects or use PIR sensor
20. Are adjacent railroad tracks used during protection-on period?	Yes/No	Major	Minor	Minor	A trial installation is required if using an ultrasonic sensor
21. Can small animals (or birds) enter protection pattern?	Yes/No	Major	Major	Major (particularly rodents)	Install a physical barrier to prevent intrusion by animals or birds
22. Does area to be protected contain a corrosive atmosphere?	Yes/No	Major	Major	Major	None of these sensors can be used

can be anywhere from 5 to 40 ft in length. The pattern is volumetric and cannot be aimed, although the pattern may be directed by the use of deflectors. Deflectors come in 90° or 45° angles. A doubler type uses two 45° angles back to back. Ultrasonics work on a change in frequency, called the *Doppler effect*. A motion detector has two transducers; the transmitter sends out a signal that is bounced back to the receiver by immobile objects in the protected area. If an intruder moves toward or away from the unit, the change in its reflected frequency signals an alarm. Ultrasonics may be found as stand-alone units or part of what is called a *master system*. The stand-alone units compare the reflected signal within the unit and trip the control panel by opening or closing a relay contact. Master systems work by sending the signal back to a main processing unit. The main processing unit compares the signal and trips the relay contacts of the processor. False alarms result from three types of sources:

a. *Motion.* Objects that move in the path of protection and air turbulence are seen as motion because of the frequency of the unit.

b. *Noise.* Ultrasonic noise is present when audible noises are heard; hissing (such as from high-pressure air leaking or steam radiators) or bells ringing can be a source of these noises.

c. *Radio or electrical interference.* Induced electrical signals or radio frequency (RF) interference from radio transmitters can cause false alarms.

Grounding and shielding are both very important in a master system. If an earth ground is required, it should be a cold water pipe. The length of the ground wire should be as short as possible and with a minimum number of bends. Potential problems include:

a. Turbulence and draft, hanging displays, moving draperies, and small pets;

b. Noise caused by air hissing, bells, and telephones; and

c. Temperature or humidity that can affect the range of the ultrasonic unit.

Carpets, furniture, and draperies may absorb some of the signal, decreasing the unit's sensitivity. Ultrasonic energy does not penetrate most objects. The signal may be reflected off some smooth surfaces.

3. *Microwave.* Microwave detectors are a volumetric type of space protection and are based on a Doppler shift. They detect intruders by the use of a radiated RF electromagnetic field. The unit operates by sensing a disturbance in the generated RF field, called the Doppler effect. The frequency range is between 0.3 and 300 GHz (1 GHz = 1 billion cps). Any type of motion in the protected area creates a change in frequency, causing an alarm condition. Because the power output from the unit is relatively low, the field radiated is harmless. Microwave energy penetrates most objects and reflects off of the metal. One of the most important considerations in placement of these units is vibration. The microwave must be mounted on a firm surface: Cinder block, brick, or main support beams are ideal mounting locations. Never mount two microwave units with identical frequencies in the same room or area where the patterns may overlap. This could cause cross talk between the units, causing false alarms. Microwave units draw excessive current; so the proper gauge of wire should be used and the length of the wire run should also be taken into consideration. Current readings should be taken at the end of an installation or while troubleshooting units to ensure that the maximum current of the control panel has not been exceeded. Fluorescent lights may be a problem because the radiated ionization from the lights may be seen as motion by the detector. Potential problems include:

a. Vibrations or movement of mounting surface, mounts on a wall, and sense change in electrical current;

b. Reflection of pattern or movement of metal objects in a protected area, such as moving fan blades or movement or overhead doors;

c. Penetration of thin walls or glass if motion or large metal objects, such as trains or cars, are present;

d. Radio frequency interference (RFI), radar, or AC line transients in severe cases; and

e. A potential interference as a result of water movement in plastic or PVC storm drains if located close to the unit. Most microwave units provide a test point, where the amplifier output voltage can be read. By following the manufacturer's recommended voltage settings the microwave can be set up properly and the unit environment examined.

4. *Passive infrared motion detectors.* These detectors are passive sensors because they do not transmit a signal for an intruder to disturb. Rather, a source of moving infrared radiation (the intruder) is detected against the normal radiation/temperature environment of the room. Passive infrared detectors (PIRs) detect a change in the thermal energy pattern caused by a moving intruder in the field of view of the detector. The field of view of an infrared unit must terminate on an object to ensure its proper operation and stability. An infrared unit should never be set up to look out into midair. Potential problems include:

a. Turbulence and drafts are a problem if the air is blowing directly on the unit or causes a rapid change in temperature of objects in the path of protection.

b. Stray motion (i.e., drapes blowing, hanging objects or displays, small animals).

c. Changing temperatures (i.e., hotspots in machinery, sunlight) may cause false alarms. The temperature of the background infrared level may also affect the unit's sensitivity: PIRs become less sensitive as the temperature increases.

d. Lightning or bright lights, such as halogen headlights. The infrared radiation pattern is blocked by solid objects as it is unable to penetrate most objects. The pattern of protection may also be affected by reflection off smooth surfaces.

5. *Pressure mats.* These mats are basically mechanical switches. Pressure mats are most frequently used as a backup system to perimeter protection. When used as traps, they can be hidden under the carpet in front of a likely target or in hallways where an intruder would travel.

6. *Sound sensors.* These sensors detect intrusion by picking up the noise created by a burglar during an attempt to break into a protected area. These sensors consist of a microphone and an electronic amplifier/processor. When the sound level increases beyond the limit normally encountered, the unit signals an alarm. Some units have pulse-counting and time-interval features. Other types can actually listen to the protected premises from a central monitoring station.

7. *Dual-techs.* Dual-technology sensors, commonly referred to as *dual-techs*, are a combination of two types of space-protection devices. The principle of the unit is that both sections of the detectors must be tripped at the same time to cause an alarm. A dual-tech unit could be a combination of passive/microwave or a combination of passive/ultrasonic. By using a dual-technology device, an installer can provide space protection in areas that may have presented potential false alarm problems when a single-technology unit was used. Repair people can replace units sending false signals because of environment or placement.

Dual-techs are not the solution to all false alarm problems, and unless careful consideration is used in installing or replacing a device, the false alarm problems may persist. Since these contain two different types of devices, there is much more to consider. Dual-techs draw much more current than conventional detectors. Current readings are essential and additional power supplies may be necessary to provide enough operating current and standby power. Until recently, if one section of the unit stopped working or was blocked off in some way by the end user, the unit was rendered inoperable. Manufacturers are only now working on supervising the microwave section of these units. If the unit is located or adjusted so that one section of the unit is continuously in an alarm condition, the dual-technology principle is worthless.

8. *Interior sensors.* These sensors are generally active or passive, covert or visible, or volumetric or line applications.

FALSE ALARMS

There are three reasons for false alarms, and the secret to reducing them is to clearly identify the cause and make proactive corrections. They are:

1. Lack of proper education on how to enter and exit the complex, such as improper arming and disarming of the keypad;
2. Weather; and
3. Equipment failure (dead batteries) and installation problems.

APPLICATION

For all practical purposes, the reason we use space protection is as a backup to the perimeter system. It is not necessary to cover every inch of the premises being protected. The best placement is as a trap in a high-traffic area or spot protection for high-value areas. The worst thing an installer can do is overextend the area being protected by an individual unit (e.g., trying to cover more than one room with a detector or trying to compensate for placement or environment by over adjusting the sensitivity). By using a little common sense and checking for all possible hazards, you can ensure a trouble-free installation. Make sure that the units have adequate power going to each head and the standby batteries are working and charging properly. Be sure to adjust for pets and brief customers and any problems they may create, such as leaving fans or machinery on, and not to open windows in the path of protection. Before leaving an installation, make sure that all units have been walk-tested and the areas in question have been masked out. One of the most important considerations in setting up a number of space protection devices is *zoning*. Never put more than two interior devices in one zone if at all possible. The majority of false alarms are caused by interior devices. Breaking up the interior protective circuits as much as possible gives the service person a better chance of solving a false alarm problem (even with two heads in one zone you have a 50/50 chance of finding the trouble unit). Zoning a system correctly helps with troubleshooting, makes the police department feel better about the company and the company feel better about the installer, and ensures good relations with the customer.

OBJECT/SPOT DETECTION FOR SCHOOLS

Object/spot detection is used to detect the activity or presence of an intruder at a single location. It provides direct security for objects. Such a detection method is the final stage of an in-depth system for protection. The objects most frequently protected include safes, filing cabinets, desks, art objects, models, statues, and expensive equipment. The types of object/spot protection are:

1. *Capacitance/proximity detectors.* The object being protected becomes an antenna, electronically linked to the alarm control. When an intruder approaches or touches the object/antenna, an electrostatic field is unbalanced and the alarm is initiated. Only metal objects can be protected in this manner.
2. *Vibration detectors.* These devices utilize a highly sensitive, specialized microphone called an *electronic vibration detector* (EVD). The EVD is attached directly to the object to be protected. It can be adjusted to detect a sledgehammer attack on a concrete wall or a delicate penetration of a glass surface. It sends an alarm only when the object is moved, whereas capacitance devices detect when the intruder is close to the protected object. Other types of vibration detectors are similar to tilt switches used in pinball machines.

ALARM CONTROL

All sensing devices are wired into the alarm control panel that receives their signals and processes them. Some of the most severe burglary losses are caused not by a failure in equipment but simply by someone turning off the alarm system. The type of control panel needed depends on the sophistication of the overall intrusion alarm system. Some control panels provide zoning capabilities for separate annunciation of the sensing devices. Others provide the low-voltage electrical power for the sensing devices.

Included in the control panel is the backup or standby power in the event of an electrical power failure. Batteries are used for standby power. Some equipment uses rechargeable batteries; the control has a low-power charging unit (a trickle charger) and maintains the batteries in a fully charged condition.

Modern control panels use one or more microprocessors. This allows the control panel to send and receive digital information to the alarm station. An alphanumeric pad can display zone information as well as supervisory conditions. Each user can also have a unique code, allowing restriction during specified times or limiting access into certain areas. By using individual code numbers, the alarm control panel can track activity as well as transmit this information off-site.

If the alarm control panel is connected to a central monitoring station, the times that the system is turned on and off are recorded and logged. When an administrator of the school enters the building in the morning, a signal is sent. If this happens at a time prearranged with the central station, it is considered a normal opening. If it happens at any other time, the police are dispatched.

The administrator of the school or other authorized persons can enter the building during the closed times. The person entering must first call the central station company and identify himself or herself by a special coding procedure. Records are kept at the central station company for these irregular openings and closings.

Tamper protection is a feature that generates an alarm signal when the system is compromised in any way. Tamper protection can be designed into any or all portions of the alarm system (control panel, sensing devices, loop wiring, alarm transmission facilities).

ALARM TRANSMISSION/SIGNALING

The type of alarm transmission/signaling system used in a particular application depends on the location of the business or residence, the frequency of police patrols, and the ability of the customer to afford the cost. Remember, after deterrence, the purpose of an alarm is to summon the proper authorities to stop a crime during its commission or lead to the apprehension of the intruder. It is very important that the response by proper authorities to the alarm comes in the shortest possible time. Two types of alarm signaling systems are in general use:

- *Local alarm.* A bell or light indicates that an attempted or successful intrusion has taken place. The success of the system relies on someone hearing or seeing the signal and calling the responsible authorities. The local alarm also notifies burglars that they have been detected. This may be advantageous in frightening off the less experienced intruder.
- *Central station system.* The alarm signal is transmitted over telephone lines to a specially constructed building called the central station. Here, trained operators are on duty 24 hours a day to supervise, record, and maintain alarms. On receipt of an alarm, the police are dispatched and, in some cases, the alarm company guard or runner. The record-keeping function and guard response ensure thorough documentation of any alarm signal. There are seven types of alarm transmissions to the central station. Each type of transmission has certain advantages and disadvantages that must be considered in determining the risk. Transmission of an alarm signal to the Underwriters Laboratories (UL)-listed central station is generally regarded as the most reliable method for reducing the burglary losses.
  - *Direct wire systems.* High-risk locations (like the music or computer lab) are generally protected with a direct wire system. A single dedicated telephone line is run from the protected premises to the central station or police station, where a separate receiver supervises only that alarm. A fixed DC current is sent from the central station to the protected premises and read on a meter at the central station. The advantage of a direct wire system is that problems can be traced very quickly to a specific alarm system. This makes compromising the alarm signal by a professional burglar more difficult. The disadvantage of such a system is the higher cost of leased telephone lines. This becomes a more serious economic factor as the distance from the central station to the protected premises increases. Proper transmission of the alarm signal to the central station is essential. Problems can result on these telephone lines from shorts and broken wires. Most central stations expect these problems and are well equipped to rapidly make repairs. However, some of today's burglars are more sophisticated. They know they can prevent the transmission of the alarm signal to the central system by shunting or jumpering out the leased telephone line. Special methods are used by the alarm company to protect against jumpering of the alarm signal. Alarm systems having this special line security are classified as AA Grade Central Station alarms by UL.
  - *Circuit (party line) systems.* Alarm signals transmitted over circuit transmission systems can be compared to a party line where several alarm customers defray the cost of the telephone line by sharing it. With a circuit transmission system, as many as 15 alarm transmitters may send alarm signals to a single receiving panel at the central station over the same line or loop. The alarm signals at the central station are received on strips of paper. Each alarm has a distinct code to identify it from others. The advantage of a circuit-loop alarm transmission

system is the lower telephone line cost. Thus, a central station can make its services available to more customers by subdividing the cost of the telephone line among different users. The disadvantage of circuit-loop alarm transmission systems is that problems on a leased telephone line are more difficult to locate than with a direct wire system.

- *Multiplex systems.* The multiplex system is designed to reduce leased telephone line charges while providing a higher degree of line security than circuit-loop alarms. Multiplex systems introduced data processing (computer-based techniques) to the alarm industry.

- *Digital communicators.* This computer-based type of alarm transmission equipment sends its signal through the regular switch line telephone network. The alarm signal transmitted is a series of coded electronic pulses that can be received only on a computer terminal at the central station.

- *Telephone dialer.* The dialer delivers a prerecorded verbal message to a central station, answering service, or police department when an alarm is activated. Many of the earlier tape dialers were a source of constant problems to police departments because of their lack of sophistication. Basically, they were relabeled tape recorders. It was not uncommon for the tape dialer to play most of the message before the police could answer the phone. The police knew that an alarm signal had been sent, but did not know its location. The newer, modern tape dialers have solved these problems.

- *Radio signal transmission.* This method takes the alarm signal from the protected premises and sends it via radio or cellular phone to either a central station or police dispatch center. Additionally, the alarm signal can be received in a police patrol car.

- *Video verification.* Along with standard alarm transmissions, video images are sent to the central station. This provides for a higher level of protection while helping to eliminate false alarms by allowing central station operators to see what is happening inside the protected area. With the increase of the false police dispatches, video verification is playing a major role in the battle against false alarms.

ALARMS DETER CRIME

False alarms waste police resources and alarm company resources. The police and alarm industry are acutely aware of this, and both have initiated efforts across the country to relieve the dilemma.

The National Crime Prevention Institute has long endorsed alarm systems as the best available crime deterrent. This education institution realizes that most criminals fear alarm systems; they much prefer to break into an unprotected building rather than risk capture by a hidden sensor.

Problem deterrence is the alarm business, a field that, in fact, extends far beyond protecting premises from burglary. The crisis prevention duties of alarm firms range from monitoring sprinkler systems and fire sensors and watching temperature levels in buildings to supervising industrial processes such as nuclear fission and the manufacturing of dangerous chemicals.

To alarm companies, deterrence is a sophisticated, specialized art. In the area of crime prevention, companies take pride in spotting potential weaknesses in a building and designing an alarm system that confounds the most intelligent criminals.

Crime prevention is the area where police need the most help. The rise in burglary and other crimes has often put police officers in a response posture.

FALSE ALARMS IN YOUR SCHOOL

The full crime prevention potential in alarm systems has yet to be realized. Relatively speaking, the number of premises not protected by alarms is greater, although those schools or buildings holding the most valuable goods are thoroughly guarded by the most sophisticated sensor systems.

Yet the main drag on the potential of alarms, as industry leaders and police are aware, remains the false alarm problem. A modern instance of the boy who cried "wolf," false alarms erode the effectiveness of alarm systems. They are costly to alarm companies and police agencies.

It is a fact that alarm systems prevent crime. These electronic and electrical systems deter burglars, arsonists, vandals, and other criminals. They are both the most effective and most economical crime prevention tool available.

Police budgets have been reduced in most locales and frozen in others, while private investment in alarm security is growing yearly.

The National Burglary and Fire Alarm Association (NBFAA) asked its members to rank their priorities on association activities. The outstanding response asked for a comprehensive program to help member companies reduce false alarms. Moreover, while researching possible programs, the NBFAA learned that many members had already embarked on significant reduction efforts.

Some police departments initiated a written letter program from the police chief to those who have an excessive number of alarm runs. Others have the crime prevention officer make a follow-up visit to the business or residence. After the other steps have failed, many police departments are assessing false alarm fines.

By protecting such places as hospitals, office buildings, and schools, alarm systems free up police resources and enable patrol officers to spend more time in areas with high crime rates and fewer premises protected by alarm systems. Police may also dedicate more officers to apprehending criminals. In this manner, police and alarm companies work together, complementing one another and waging a mutual war on crime.

ALARM EQUIPMENT OVERHAUL

A California alarm station undertook a major overhaul. The effort began with a false alarm inventory, in which subscribers whose systems produced four or more false alarms per week were weeded out. Service workers then replaced—virtually reinstalled—the alarm systems for those subscribers. New sensors, new batteries, new wiring, and new soldering jobs were required in many instances. The process was costly, but it paid off in the long run. The office then had fewer service calls and an improved relationship with the local police that increased business.

Many NBFAA member companies instituted training programs for their sales, installation, and service personnel. Also, subscribers are educated on the operation of their systems three times: by salespeople, by installers, and by supervisors when they inspect newly installed systems.

One member company weeded out and entirely rebuilt its problem systems. This approach is the most feasible way for smaller firms to attack the problem. Lacking sufficient capital to initiate a comprehensive program, such companies can, nevertheless, cut down the number of false alarms by renovating the relatively few systems that cause the majority of problems.

Police chiefs and crime prevention officers working in areas troubled by false alarms should meet with the heads of the firms in their areas and discuss reduction programs like these.

together to detect and report the existence of an undesirable condition such as an intrusion, a fire, an unsafe condition in an industrial manufacturing process, and so on.

Annunciator A device, typically a small horn or light, used to attract the attention of someone close-by.

Area protection 1. A detector that is sensitive over a two-dimensional space, such as a strain gauge sensor or a seismic detector. 2. A misnomer for "volumetric protection" (which is three-dimensional).

Armed The condition of an alarm system when it is on, ready to be tripped when an intrusion is detected.

Armed light A light or light-emitting diode, usually red, or other device that indicates the alarm system is armed or set.

Audible alarm An alarm that makes noise (as opposed to a silent alarm) using a bell or horn.

Audio alarm A detection device that is triggered upon detecting noises, such as the sounds of breaking and entering. See "vault alarm" and "sonic detector."

Balanced magnetic contact See "high security" and "magnetic contact."

Battery An assembly of two or more cells used to obtain higher voltages than that available from a single cell.

Capacitance detector A device that detects an intruder's touching of or close approach to a protected metal object. Often used to protect safes and file cabinets. Protected objects must be metal, well insulated from the ground, and not too large. Also called safe alarm or proximity alarm. See "E-field detector."

Casement window A type of window that hinges outward and is usually opened with a crank. It is often difficult to mount contacts on casement windows. Tamper switches are sometimes used successfully.

Central station 1. A central location where an alarm company monitors a large number of its own accounts. 2. A company that specializes in monitoring the alarm signals for many alarm companies for a fee.

Certificated alarm system An alarm system that is installed by a UL-certified alarm company and that meets certain requirements for installation, service, and extent of coverage.

Circuit breaker An electrical safety valve; a device designed to interrupt dangerously high currents. Unlike a fuse, a circuit breaker can be reset to be used again; thus, no replacements are needed. Some circuit breakers can also be used as switches.

Closed-circuit television (CCTV) An on-premises TV system used to enable a guard to "watch" one or more critical areas such as entrances, high-value areas, and so on. The TV signal is used to transmit by a coaxial cable or fiber optic cable and is usually limited to distances of a few hundred to a few thousand feet.

Closing signal A signal transmitted by an alarm system to the central station when the proprietor (user) secures and leaves the premises at the close of business. Usually done on a prearranged time schedule.

Coaxial cable A special kind of shielded cable that has one center conductor surrounded by relatively thick insulation, which in turn has a shield (usually braided wires or sometimes spirally laid wires) over it. An outer plastic jacket is usually included. Used primarily for RF work such as antenna lead-in and for CCTV cameras.

Commercial alarm An alarm installed in a commercial or business location, as opposed to a residential alarm.

Day-night switch A switch located at the subscriber's premises used by the subscriber to signal the central station of opening and closing of the premises. Used only on direct-wire, supervised accounts (the milliamp signal method), and multiplex systems.

Dedicated line or circuit A phone line or circuit that is dedicated solely to the transmission of alarm signals. Examples are direct wire, McCulloh, multiplex, and derived channel.

Door switch See "magnetic contact."

Doppler shift The apparent frequency shift due to motion of an intruder in ultrasonic and microwave detection.

Double-hung window A type of window popular in older construction. The lower sash (window) can be raised and the upper sash can be lowered. Two contacts are usually used to protect both sashes.

Dry cell A type of battery that is not rechargeable. Dry cells are occasionally used in alarm work, but because of the required periodic replacement, rechargeable batteries are usually favored. (Rechargeable batteries also have to be replaced periodically, but not as often as dry cells.)

Dual alarm service Protection of one premise by two separate alarm systems, usually serviced by different alarm companies. Thus protected, there is less likelihood that both systems could be successfully compromised and less chance of collusion among dishonest employees of the two alarm companies. Use is limited to high-risk applications because of the cost.

Duress switch A special type of key switch that can be turned in either of two directions or can be operated with two different keys. One direction (or key) operates the alarm systems in a normal manner. The other direction (or key) signals the central station that the owner of the protected premises is under duress (i.e., has a gun in his back). By comparison, a holdup switch is activated secretly, whereas a duress switch is activated openly, and the burglar is unaware of its duress signaling function. (The burglar thinks it is a regular control switch.)

Electronic siren An electronic device with speaker, used to simulate the sound of a motor-driven siren.

Environmental considerations Factors that must be considered in the proper application of alarm detectors to reduce false alarms, particularly with motion sensors. Such factors include rain, fog, snow, wind, hail, humidity, temperature, corrosion, moving or swaying objects, vegetation growth, animals, and many others. They depend on the type(s) of detectors that is considered and where they are to be located.

Exit-entry delay A feature of some alarm systems, particularly in residential applications, that permits locating the on/off station inside the protected premises. When exiting, the user turns the system on, which starts the exit time delay cycle (typically 30-120 seconds). He can then exit through a specific, protected door without tripping the alarm during this delay. Later, when the user returns, the system is tripped when the specific door is opened. This action starts an entry delay cycle but does not cause an immediate alarm (although a small pre-alert alarm may sound as a reminder). The user then has, typically, 15-60 seconds to turn the system off. An intruder would not have a key or would not know the secret code to turn the system off; therefore, the alarm would ring or a silent signal be transmitted after the entry delay expired.

Holdup alarm A means of notifying a remote location, such as an alarm central station or police station, that a holdup is in progress. Holdup alarms are always silent and are actuated secretly; otherwise, the noise of a local alarm or the obvious pushing of an alarm button could prompt the holdup man to acts of violence. A holdup alarm should not be confused with a panic alarm or with a duress alarm.

Indicator light Any light, either incandescent or LED, which indicates the status of an alarm system, such as the "ready" light.

Infrared detector 1. Passive type is one that detects an intruder by his body heat (which is infrared energy). This type does not emit any infrared energy, it only detects it. 2. Active type is a photoelectric beam that uses infrared instead of visible light. This kind does emit infrared energy.

Intrusion alarm An arrangement of electrical and/or electronic devices designed to detect the presence of an intruder or an attempt to break into a protected location, and to provide notification by making a loud noise locally (bell, siren, etc.) or by transmitting an alarm signal to some remote monitoring location or both.

Key pad A collection of push buttons mounted on a plate, used to enter a secret code to arm and disarm alarm systems. Often resembles a touchtone phone pad. Used to replace key-operated switches. Decoding of the correct combination is done by electronics mounted behind the pad. Also called a stand-alone key pad. Compare "system pad."

Line security The degree of protection of the alarm transmission path against compromise. Usually implies the application of additional measures to improve security. See "line supervision."

Line supervision An arrangement where a known current, AC, DC, pulses, or a combination, is present on the line to the central station. Cutting or shorting the line will change this current, signaling an alarm. In high-security systems, complex line supervision systems are used to detect attempts to defeat the system.

Line voltage 1. 120 V AC "house power." 2. The voltage on a telephone line used for alarm service.

Magnetic contact A magnetically operated switch, typically used on doors and windows to detect opening. The switch is mounted on the frame or fixed part while the magnet is mounted on the movable door or window. Generally much easier to use than earlier, mechanically actuated switches. Available in NO, NC, or SPST contact forms.

Mat switch A very thin, pressure-sensing switch placed under carpets (and carpet padding) to trip an alarm when an intruder steps on it. Typical size is 30×36 inches. Typical thickness is 3/32 to 1/8 inch. Runner mat is 30 inches wide $\times 25$ ft long and is cut to the desired length with scissors. With one exception, all mat switches are normally open. Supervised mats have two sets of leads. For damp or wet locations, sealed type mats should be used.

Medical alert An alarm system by which an invalid, elderly, or sick person can push a button near his bedside to alert someone that a doctor, ambulance, or other medical assistance is required.

Microprocessor A computer on a microchip, the heart of all personal computers. This is now used as the heart of alarm control panels. With a microprocessor designed into a control, it is possible to obtain features that would be prohibitively expensive otherwise. Some examples are dozens of zones, information displays in English (or other language), and zone parameters (e.g., speed of response, perimeter/interior/entry-exit/instant response, etc.) assignable for each zone. Most important, these features can be changed, often without requiring a service call to the premises. First introduced by Ron Gottsegen of Radionics in 1977.

Microwave detector A device that senses the motion of an intruder (and of other things) in a protected area by a Doppler shift in the transmitted RF energy. Microwave detectors generally operate at 10.525 GHz. Older units operated at 915 MHz. Both have largely been replaced by PIR detectors, which are less susceptible to false alarms.

Money trap A special switch placed in the bottom of a cash drawer. It is activated during a holdup by pulling out the bottom bill of the stack, which has been previously inserted into a trap. To prevent a false alarm, care must be taken not to remove that bottom bill at any other time.

Motion detector Any of several devices that detects an intruder by his motion within a protected area or protected volume. See "ultrasonic," "microwave," "passive IR," "area protection," and "volumetric protection."

Multiplex 1. In general, any method of sending many signals over one communications channel. 2. Specifically, any method of sending alarm signals from many subscribers over one pair of wires to a monitoring location. (Technically, a McCulloh circuit does this, but the term multiplex is generally used to refer to the newer, electronic techniques using polling computers and similar methods.)

Open and closed loop A combination of an open loop and a closed loop, used on some controls. Note that, unlike the double closed loop, the open loop conductor in this system is not supervised. That is, cutting this wire will disable part of the system without causing an alarm condition.

Opening 1. Any possible point of entry for an intruder, such as windows, doors, ventilators, roof hatches, and so on. 2. Any such point that is protected by an alarm detection device. 3. See "opening signal." 4. See "scheduled opening" and "unscheduled opening."

Panic alarm A local bell alarm, triggered manually, usually by pushing a button (as opposed to being tripped by some kind of detection device). Usually found only in residential systems. The panic button permits the owner/subscriber to trigger the alarm manually in case of intrusion, even though the alarm system happens to be turned off at the time. A panic alarm (which is audible) should not be confused with a holdup alarm, which is always silent.

Power supply Any source of electrical energy. More specifically, power supply usually refers to an electronic device that converts AC to DC for use by alarm equipment. It may also reduce the voltage from 120 V to the voltage needed by the alarm equipment. Some power supplies have provision for connecting a standby battery. Others will accommodate a rechargeable battery and will provide the necessary charging current for that battery.

Preventive maintenance Testing and checking out alarm systems on a regularly scheduled basis to locate and repair potential problems before false alarms or system failures result. Unfortunately, preventive maintenance is usually forgotten until trouble occurs.

Reversing relay 1. A method of transmitting an alarm signal over a telephone wire by reversing the DC polarity. In the secure mode, a voltage is sent over the phone line from the protected premises to the monitoring location to provide line supervision. An alarm signal is transmitted by reversing the polarity, usually by operating a DPDT relay in the subscriber's control. 2. The relay used to reverse the polarity.

Shunt switch A key-operated switch located outside the protected premises that allows the subscriber to bypass usually just one door to permit entry without tripping the alarm system. He will normally proceed to the control or transmitter to turn off the entire system with the on/off switch, usually using the same key. Upon closing the premises, the procedure is reversed.

Silent alarm An alarm system that does not ring a bell or give any other indication of an alarm condition at the protected premises; instead it transmits an alarm signal to an alarm central station or other monitoring location.

Siren 1. Traditionally, a motor-driven noisemaker used on police cars, fire trucks, ambulances, and so on. 2. An electronic replacement for (1) that produces a very similar sound.

Sonic detector 1. A Doppler-principle detection device much like ultrasonic except that it uses an audible frequency. Not very common. 2. A misnomer for ultrasonic.

Subscriber error A false or loss of alarm protection caused by the subscriber not following the correct procedures in the use of the alarm system.

Switch A mechanically or magnetically operated device used to open and close electrical circuits.

Tamper-proof box This term is somewhat of a misnomer because few things are "proof" against attack. The term is usually used to indicate that a control, bell, or equipment box is equipped with a tamper switch to signal an alarm when the door is opened. Tamper switches are preferably connected to a 24-hour protective circuit. Bell boxes or other boxes outside the protected area should also be equipped with a double door. Opening the outer door triggers the tamper switch, while the inner door denies the attacker immediate access to the bell or its wiring.

Transmitter 1. A device that sends an alarm signal to a remote point, such as a McCulloh transmitter. 2. The unit at the end of a photoelectric beam that sends out the light or invisible infrared energy. 3. The ultrasonic transducer that sends out the ultrasonic energy.

UL-listed alarm company An alarm company that meets the requirements of Underwriters Laboratories and is so designated by appearing on UL's published list.

UL standard for alarms Underwriters Laboratories publishes many standards outlining the requirements that must be met by alarm equipment/alarm companies in order to obtain UL listing. The most important of these is UL 681, which outlines alarm system installation requirements. Many others cover various kinds of equipment. It is important to bear in mind that there are many UL listings for many UL standards, many of which are unrelated to security (such as electrical safety). Therefore, the term UL listed is meaningless unless the exact nature of the "list" is detailed. UL 639 outlines transient protection requirements. UL 611 outlines central station units and systems.

Ultrasonic detector A device that senses motion of an intruder (and of other things) in a protected area by a Doppler shift in the transmitted ultrasonic energy (sound is too high a frequency to be heard by humans). Rarely used anymore.

Unscheduled opening Opening of a protected premise at an unscheduled time, that is, not a scheduled opening time. For a silent alarm, supervised account subscribers notify the monitoring alarm company in advance of their standard opening (and closing) times. If the owner or authorized person wishes to enter at any other time, he has to make special arrangements with the alarm company by phone and prearranged secret code word or, preferably, by letter.

Vault alarm An alarm system used to protect a vault such as a bank vault or storage vault. This is a special type of audio alarm and usually has a test feature via the ring-back circuit, which can be actuated from the alarm central station.

Walk test A procedure of actually walking through the area protected by a motion detector to determine the actual limits of its coverage. Indication is usually provided by an LED mounted on the detection unit. This indicator should be disabled or covered when not used for walk-testing. This will prevent a would-be burglar from doing his own walk-testing during open-for-business hours to determine holes in the coverage.

Zone Large protected premises are divided into areas or zones, each having its own indicator or annunciator. This helps pinpoint the specific area of intrusion and is a great aid in narrowing down a problem when troubleshooting. Today's control units may have 16, 30, 48, or more zones.

Zone light A light, LED, or other device used to indicate the status of each zone in a multiple-zone system. One or more indicators can be provided per zone to indicate any of the following: ready, armed, alarmed, and zoned out.

APPENDIX B: SMOKE DETECTORS

The following was extracted from 3/6/2002: GE Interlogix eCommunity message addresses a common question regarding smoke sensors. For information on ESL fire and safety products, visit http://www.sentrol.com/products/firesafety.asp. The question and answer provided courtesy of the Moore-Wilson Signaling Report (vol. 9, no. 5), a publication of Hughes Associates, Inc. For subscription information, e-mail tm-wsr@haifire.com.

Q: I have heard a lot of controversial comments about the use of ionization-type smoke detectors versus photoelectric-type smoke detectors. Where would one specifically choose to use ionization-type smoke detectors?

A: Proper selection of a type of detector begins with an understanding of the operating principles of each type of detector.

In an ionization smoke detector, "a small amount of radioactive material is used to ionize the air between two differently charged electrodes to sense the presence of particles. Smoke particles entering the ionization volume decrease the conductance of the air by reducing ion mobility. The reduced conductance signal is processed and used to convey an alarm condition when it meets present criteria."

In a photoelectric light-scattering detector, "a light source and photosensitive sensor are arranged so that the rays from the light source do not normally fall onto the photosensitive sensor. Then smoke particles enter the light path; some of the light is scattered reflection and refraction onto the sensor. The light signal is processed and used to convey an alarm condition when it meets preset criteria."

The appendix further explains that photoelectric light-scattering detectors respond more to visible particles, larger than 1 μ in size, produced by most smoldering fires. They respond somewhat less to the smaller particles typically produced by flaming fires. They also respond less to fires yielding black or darker smoke, such as fires involving plastics and rubber tires.

Ionization detectors tend to exhibit somewhat opposite characteristics. In a fire yielding "invisible" particles of a size less than 1 μ, an ionization detector will more likely respond than will a photoelectric light-scattering detector. Particles of this size tend to more readily result from flaming fires. Fuel in flaming fires burns "cleaner," producing smaller particles.

Thus, the answer to whether you should use one type of detector over another lies in understanding the burning characteristics of the particular fuel. An ionization-type smoke detector will likely detect a fire that produces flaming combustion more quickly, and a photoelectric-type detector will likely detect a low-energy fire that produces larger particles during combustion more quickly.

Finally, keep in mind that both types of smoke detectors successfully pass the same battery of tests at the nationally recognized testing laboratories. For example, UL-listed ionization smoke detectors and UL-listed photoelectric smoke detectors pass the same tests under UL 268, Standard for Safety for Smoke Detectors for Fire Protection Signaling Systems.

APPENDIX C: ALARM CERTIFICATE SERVICES GLOSSARY OF TERMS
CERTIFICATE TYPES[2]

The Fire Alarm System Certificate Types are:

Central Station (NFPA 71 or 72)—Central Station Fire Alarm System Certificate
Local (NFPA 72)—Local Fire Alarm System Certificate
Auxiliary (NFPA 72)—Auxiliary Fire Alarm System Certificate
Remote Station (NFPA 72)—Remote Station Fire Alarm System Certificate
Proprietary (NFPA 72)—Proprietary Fire Alarm System Certificate

The Burglar Alarm System Certificate Types are:

Central Station—Central Station Burglar Alarm System Certificate
Mercantile—Mercantile Burglar Alarm System Certificate
Bank—Bank Burglar Alarm System Certificate
Proprietary—Proprietary Burglar Alarm System Certificate
Residential—Residential Burglar Alarm System Certificate
National Industrial Security—National Industrial Security System Certificate

DEFINITIONS

Alarm Service Company The listed company responsible for maintaining the alarm system under UL's Certificate Service programs.

Alarm System A fire alarm signaling system that is considered to be the combination of interrelated signal-initiating devices, signal-transmitting devices, signal-notification devices, and control equipment and interconnecting wiring installed for a particular application.

Category Control Number (CNN) An alphanumeric system used by UL to designate and identify the individual grouping of products that have common functional and/or design features to facilitate the application of uniform requirements as the basis of UL listing, Classification, Recognition, or Certificate Service.

Coverage A term that identifies the extent of coverage provided by automatic fire detectors.

Total Coverage Detectors are installed in all areas, rooms, and spaces, as defined in NFPA 72 (National Fire Alarm Code).

Selected Area Coverage Same as total coverage but only for specified area(s) of the protected property.

Partial Coverage Deviations from total or selected coverage. Number of devices and their locations are specified.

File Number Alarm service company's file number. A number assigned by UL to identify a file for a listee within a specific product category.

Protected Property The alarm user, business, residence, location, and/or area protected by the alarm system.

Runner A person other than the required number of operators on duty at a central, supervising, or runner stations (or otherwise in contact with these stations) available for prompt dispatching, when necessary, to the protected premises.

Service Center Number A number, code, or distinctive identification, assigned either by the listee or UL, which when used in association with a client's file number uniquely defines a central station, service center, satellite station, monitoring station, or other service location of the listee.

Standard Criteria used by UL as the primary basis for determining the eligibility of a product to use the UL's Listing, Classification, or Recognition Mark and other markings or certificates that may be required.

---

[2]This material was originally complied by Lawrence J. Fennelly, Mike Rolf, and James Culley.

STANDARDS

UL 681—Installation and Classification of Burglar and Holdup-Alarm Systems

UL 827—Central Station Alarm Services

UL 1023—Household Burglar Alarm System Units

UL 1076—Proprietary Burglar Alarm Units and Systems

UL 1641—Installation and Classification of Residential Burglar Alarm Systems

UL 1981—Central Station Automation Systems

UL 2050—National Industrial Security Systems for the protection of Classified Materials

NFPA 71—Standard for the Installation, Maintenance, and Use of Signaling Systems for Central Station Service

NFPA 72—Standard for the Installation, Maintenance, and Use of Protective Signaling Systems. (1990)

APPENDIX D: FIRE CLASSIFICATIONS

A fire is very dangerous, but it can be even more so if the wrong equipment is used in fighting it. Because of this, a fire classification system has been established that has made it easy to match the correct fire extinguisher to the correct type of fire.

Fires are divided into five types. It is important to use the correct fire extinguisher in combating the blaze. The five classifications include:

CLASS A: This fire is distinguishable by the fact that it leaves an ash. Some of the materials that burn in a Class A fire are wood, cloth, leaves, or rubbish (e.g., this is the class of fire that people have in their fireplaces).

CLASS B: This fire is ignited by flammable liquids. Examples are gasoline, oil, or lighter fluid (e.g., a charcoal grill is started by class B fires).

CLASS C: These are electrical fires. They are common in fuse boxes.

CLASS D: Metals that are flammable cause class D fires. Examples are sodium, magnesium, or potassium.

CLASS K: In recent years, studies have found that some cooking oils produce too much heat to be controlled and extinguished by traditional Class B extinguishing agents. Class K fires and extinguishers deal with cooking oil fires.

USE OF FIRE EXTINGUISHERS

When combating a fire, the extinguisher used must be the same class as the fire. If a Class A extinguisher is used to put out a class C fire, it could cause an explosion if the electrical current is still flowing. The following is an explanation of the contents and purposes of each type of extinguisher.

Class A Extinguishers will put out fires in ordinary combustibles, such as wood and paper. The numerical rating for this class of fire extinguisher refers to the amount of water the fire extinguisher holds and the amount of fire it will extinguish.

Class B Extinguishers should be used on fires involving flammable liquids, such as grease, gasoline, oil, and so forth. The numerical rating for this class of fire extinguisher states the approximate number of square feet of a flammable liquid fire that a nonexpert can expect to extinguish.

Class C Extinguishers are suitable for use on electrically energized fires. This class of fire extinguishers does not have a numerical rating. The presence of the letter "C" indicates that the extinguishing agent is nonconductive.

Class D Extinguishers are designed for use on flammable metals and are often specific for the type of metal in question. There is no picture designator for Class D extinguishers. These extinguishers generally have no rating and there is no multipurpose rating for use on other types of fires.

Class K extinguishers are suitable for cooking oil fires. Studies have found that some cooking oils produce too much heat to be controlled and extinguished by traditional Class B extinguishing agents. Class K extinguishers are polished stainless steel cylinders, and these wet chemical extinguishers are the best restaurant kitchen appliance hand-portable fire extinguishers you can purchase.

VIDEO TECHNOLOGY OVERVIEW FOR SCHOOLS*

Herman Kruegle

OVERVIEW

Digital security surveillance systems for schools are similar to those used in corporate America. The second half of the 2000s witnessed a quantum jump in video security technology. This technology has manifested with a new generation of video components, such as digital cameras, multiplexers, DVRs, HD, and so forth. A second significant activity has been the integration of security systems with computer-based local area networks (LANs), wide area networks (WANs), wireless networks (WiFi), intranets, and the Internet.

Although today's video security system hardware is based on new technology that takes advantage of the great advances in microprocessor computing power, solid-state and magnetic memory, digital processing, and wired and wireless video signal transmission (analog, digital over the Internet, etc.), the basic video system still requires the lens, camera, transmission medium (wired cable, wireless), monitor, recorder, and so forth. This chapter describes current video security system components and is an introduction to their operation.

The primary function of any video security or safety system is to provide remote eyes for the security force located at a central control console or remote site. The video system includes the illumination source, the scene to be viewed, the camera lens, the camera, and the means of transmission to the remote monitoring and recording equipment. Other equipment often necessary to complete the system includes video switchers, multiplexers, video motion detectors (VMDs), housings, scene combiners and splitters, and character generators.

This chapter describes the technology used to (1) capture the visual image, (2) convert it to a video signal, (3) transmit the signal to a receiver at a remote location, (4) display the image on a video monitor, and (5) record and print it for permanent record. Figure 21.1 shows the simplest video application requiring only one video camera and monitor.

The printer and video recorder are optional. The camera may be used to monitor employees, visitors, or people entering or leaving a building. The camera could be located in the lobby ceiling and pointed at the reception area, the front door, or an internal access door. The monitor might be located hundreds or thousands of feet away, in another building, or another city or country with the security personnel viewing that same lobby, front door, or reception area. The video camera/monitor system

---

*Originally from Kruegle H. Video Technology Overview. *The Handbook of Loss Prevention and Crime Prevention*. Boston, MA: Butterworth-Heinemann; 2012. Updated by the editor, Elsevier, 2014.

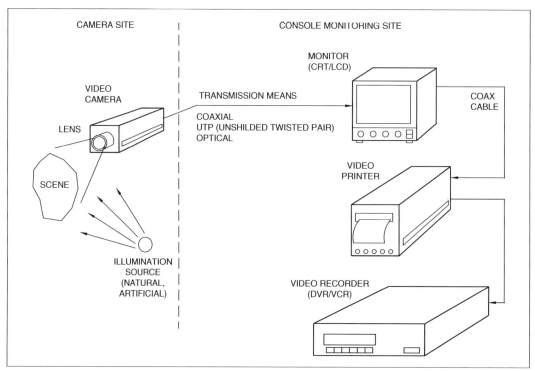

FIGURE 21.1

Single camera video system.

effectively extends the eyes, reaching from observer location to the observed location. The basic one-camera system shown in Figure 21.1 includes the following hardware components:

- *Lens*. Light from the illumination source reflects off the scene. The lens collects the light from the scene and forms an image of the scene on the light-sensitive camera sensor.
- *Camera*. The camera sensor converts the visible scene formed by the lens into an electrical signal suitable for transmission to the remote monitor, recorder, and printer.
- *Transmission link*. The transmission media carries the electrical video signal from the camera to the remote monitor. Hard-wired media choices include: (a) coaxial, (b) two-wire unshielded twisted-pair (UTP), (c) fiber optic cable, (d) LAN, (e) WAN, (f) intranet, and (g) Internet network. Wireless choices include: (a) radio frequency (RF), (b) microwave, or (c) optical infrared (IR). Signals can be analog or digital.
- *Monitor*. The video monitor or computer screens display (cathode ray tube (CRT), liquid crystal display (LCD), HD, or plasma) the camera image by converting the electrical video signal back into a visible image on the monitor screen.
- *Recorder*. The camera scene is permanently recorded by a real-time or time-lapse (TL) VCR onto a magnetic tape cassette or by a DVR using a magnetic disk hard drive.
- *Hard-copy printer*. The video printer produces a hard-copy paper printout of any live or recorded video image, using thermal, ink-jet, laser, or other printing technology.

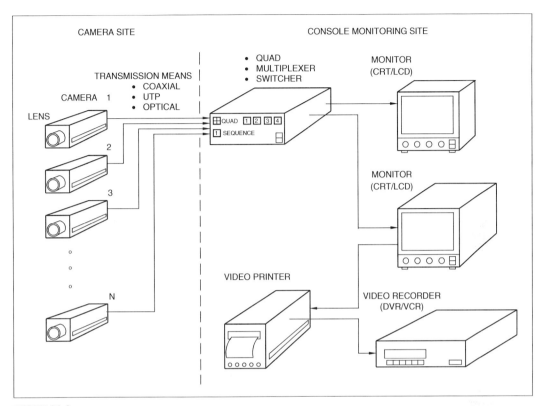

FIGURE 21.2

Comprehensive video security system.

The first four components are required to make a simple video system work. The recorder and/or printer is required if a permanent record is required.

Figure 21.2 shows a block diagram of a multicamera analog video security system using these components plus additional hardware and options to expand the capability of the single-camera system to multiple cameras, monitors, recorders, and so forth, providing a more complex video security system.

Additional ancillary supporting equipment for more complex systems includes: camera switchers, quads, multiplexers, environmental camera housings, camera pan/tilt mechanisms, image combiners and splitters, and scene annotators.

- *Camera switcher, quad, and multiplexer.* When a closed-circuit television (CCTV) security system has multiple cameras, an electronic switcher, quad, or multiplexer is used to select different cameras automatically or manually to display the images on a single or multiple monitors, as individual or multiple scenes. The quad can digitally combine four cameras. The multiplexer can digitally combine 4, 9, 16, and even 32 separate cameras.
- *Housings.* The many varieties of camera/lens housings fall into three categories: indoor, outdoor, and integral camera/housing assemblies. Indoor housings protect the camera and lens from tampering and are usually constructed from lightweight materials. Outdoor housings protect the camera and lens from the environment such as precipitation, extremes of heat and cold, dust, dirt, and vandalism.

- *Dome housing.* The dome camera housing uses a hemispherical clear or tinted plastic dome enclosing a fixed camera or a camera with pan/tilt and zoom lens capability.
- *Plug and play camera/housing combination.* To simplify surveillance camera installations, many manufacturers are now packaging the camera-lens-housing as a complete assembly. These plug-and-play cameras are ready to mount in a wall or ceiling and to connect the power in and the video out.
- *Pan/tilt mechanism.* When a camera must view a large area, a pan and tilt mount is used to rotate it horizontally (panning) and to tilt it, providing a large angular coverage.
- *Splitter/combiner/inserter.* An optical or electronic image combiner or splitter is used to display more than one camera scene on a single monitor.
- *Annotator.* A time and date generator annotates the video scene with chronological information. A camera identifier puts a camera number (or name such as Front Door, etc.) on the monitor screen to identify the scene displayed by the camera.

The digital video surveillance system includes most of the devices in the analog video system. The primary differences manifest in using digital electronics and digital processing within the video devices. Digital video components use digital signal processing (DSP), digital video signal compression, digital transmission, recording, and viewing. Figure 21.3 illustrates these devices and signal paths and the overall system block diagram for the digital video system.

THE VIDEO SYSTEM

Figure 21.4 shows the essentials of the CCTV camera environment: illumination source, camera, lens, and the camera-lens combined field of view (FOV), that is, the scene the camera-lens combination sees.

THE ROLE OF LIGHT AND REFLECTION

A scene or target area to be viewed is illuminated by natural or artificial light sources. Natural sources include the sun, the moon (reflected sunlight), and starlight. Artificial sources include incandescent, sodium, metal-arc, mercury, fluorescent, IR, and other man-made lights.

The camera lens receives the light reflected from the scene. Depending on the scene to be viewed, the amount of light reflected from objects in the scene can vary from 5% or 10% to 80% or 90% of the light incident on the scene. Typical values of reflected light for normal scenes such as foliage, automobiles, personnel, and streets fall in the range of about 25-65%. Snow-covered scenes may reach 90%.

The amount of light received by the lens is a function of the brightness of the light source, the reflectivity of the scene, and the transmission characteristics of the intervening atmosphere. In outdoor applications, there is usually a considerable optical path from the source to the scene and back to the camera; therefore, the transmission through the atmosphere must be considered. When atmospheric conditions are clear, there is generally little or no attenuation of the reflected light from the scene. However, when there is precipitation (rain, snow, or sleet, or when fog intervenes) or in dusty, smoky, or sand-blown environments, this attenuation might be substantial and must be considered. Likewise, in hot climates, thermal effects (heat waves) and humidity can cause severe attenuation and/or distortion of the scene. Complete attenuation of the reflected light from the scene (zero visibility) can occur, in which case no scene image is formed.

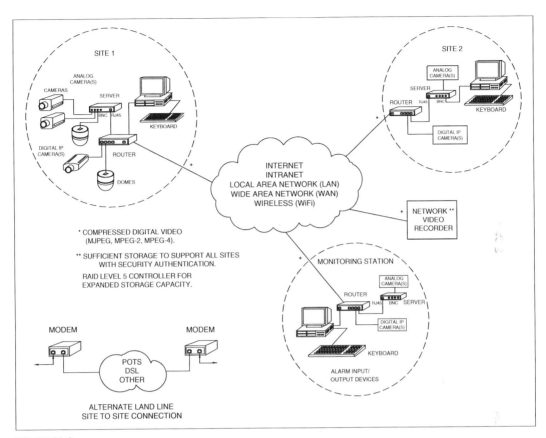

FIGURE 21.3

Networked digital video system block diagram.

Since most solid-state cameras operate in the visible and near-IR wavelength region, the general rule of thumb with respect to visibility is that if the human eye cannot see the scene, neither can the camera. Under this situation, no amount of increased lighting will help; however, if the visible light can be filtered out of the scene and only the IR portion used, scene visibility might be increased to some degree.

This problem can often be overcome by using a thermal IR imaging camera that works outside of the visible wavelength range. These thermal IR cameras produce a monochrome display with reduced image quality and are much more expensive than the charge-coupled device (CCD) or complementary metal oxide semiconductor (CMOS) cameras. Figure 21.5 illustrates the relationship between the viewed scene and the scene image on the camera sensor.

The lens located on the camera forms an image of the scene and focuses it onto the sensor. Almost all video systems used in security systems have a 4×3 aspect ratio (4 units wide $\times$ 3 units high) for both the image sensor and the FOV. The width parameter is designated as h, and H, and the vertical as v, and V. Some cameras have a 16×9 units high-definition television (HDTV) format.

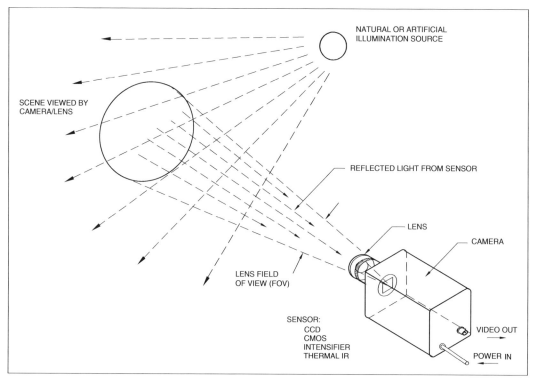

FIGURE 21.4

Video camera, scene, and source illumination.

THE LENS FUNCTION

The camera lens is analogous to the lens of the human eye (Figure 21.6) and collects the reflected radiation from the scene much like the lens of your eye or a film camera. The function of the lens is to collect reflected light from the scene and focus it into an image onto the CCTV camera sensor. A fraction of the light reaching the scene from the natural or artificial illumination source is reflected toward the camera and intercepted and collected by the camera lens. As a general rule, the larger the lens diameter, the more the light will be gathered, the brighter the image on the sensor, and the better the final image on the monitor. This is why larger aperture (diameter) lenses, having a higher optical throughput, are better (and more expensive) than smaller diameter lenses that collect less light. Under good lighting conditions—bright indoor lighting, outdoors under sunlight—the large-aperture lenses are not required and there is sufficient light to form a bright image on the sensor by using small-diameter lenses.

Most video applications use a fixed-focal-length (FFL) lens. The FFL lens, like the human eye lens, covers a constant angular FOV. The FFL lens images a scene with constant *fixed* magnification. A large variety of CCTV camera lenses are available with different focal lengths (FLs) that provide different FOVs. Wide-angle, medium-angle, and narrow-angle (telephoto) lenses produce different magnifications and FOVs. Zoom and varifocal lenses can be adjusted to have variable FLs and FOVs.

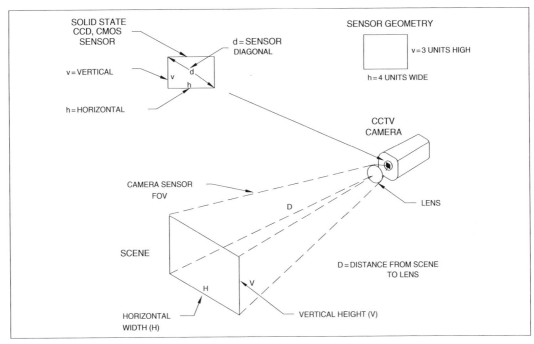

FIGURE 21.5

Video scene and sensor geometry.

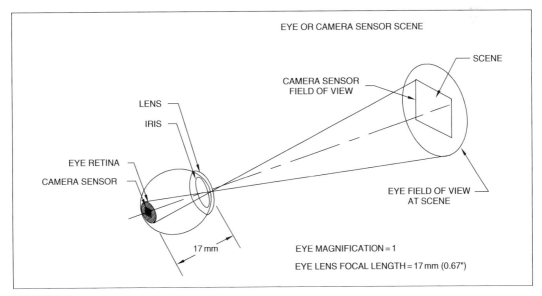

FIGURE 21.6

Comparing the human eye to the video camera lens.

Most CCTV lenses have an iris diaphragm (as does the human eye) to adjust the open area of the lens and change the amount of light passing through it and reaching the sensor. Depending on the application, manual- or automatic-iris lenses are used.

In an automatic-iris CCTV lens, as in a human eye lens, the iris closes automatically when the illumination is too high and opens automatically when it is too low, maintaining the optimum illumination on the sensor at all times. Figure 21.7 shows representative samples of CCTV lenses, including FFL, varifocal, zoom, pinhole, and a large catadioptric lens for long-range outdoor use (which combines both mirror and glass optical elements).

(a)   MOTORIZED ZOOM

(b)   CATADIOPTRIC LONG FFL

(c)   FLEXIBLE FIBER OPTIC

(d)   WIDE FOV FFL

(e)   RIGID FIBER OPTIC

(f) NARROW FOV (TELEPHOTO) FFL

(g)   MINI-LENS

(h) STRAIGHT AND RIGHT-ANGLE PINHOLE LENSES

FIGURE 21.7

Representative video lenses.

THE CAMERA FUNCTION

The lens focuses the scene onto the camera image sensor, which acts like the retina of the eye or the film in a photographic camera. The video camera sensor and electronics convert the visible image into an equivalent electrical signal suitable for transmission to a remote monitor. Figure 21.8 is a block diagram of a typical analog CCTV camera.

The camera converts the optical image produced by the lens into a time-varying electric signal that changes (modulates) in accordance with the light-intensity distribution throughout the scene. Other camera electronic circuits produce synchronizing pulses so that the time-varying video signal can later be displayed on a monitor or recorder or printed out as a hard copy on a video printer. While cameras may differ in size and shape depending on specific type and capability, the scanning process used by most cameras is essentially the same. Almost all cameras must scan the scene, point by point, as a function of time (an exception is the image intensifier). Solid-state CCD or CMOS color and monochrome cameras are used in most applications. In scenes with low illumination, sensitive CCD cameras with IR illuminators are used. In scenes with very low illumination and where no active illumination is permitted (i.e., covert), low-light-level (LLL)-intensified CCD (ICCD) cameras are used. These cameras are complex and expensive.

Figure 21.9 shows a block diagram of an analog camera with (a) DSP and (b) the all-digital Internet protocol (IP) video camera.

In the early 2000s, the nonbroadcast, tube-type color cameras available for security applications lacked long-term stability, sensitivity, and high resolution. Color cameras were not used much in security applications until solid-state color CCTV cameras became available through the development of solid-state color sensor technology and widespread use of consumer color CCD cameras used in camcorders. Color cameras have now become standard in security systems and most CCTV security cameras in use today are color. Figure 21.10 shows representative CCTV cameras including monochrome and color solid-state CCD and CMOS cameras, a small single board camera, and a miniature remote head camera.

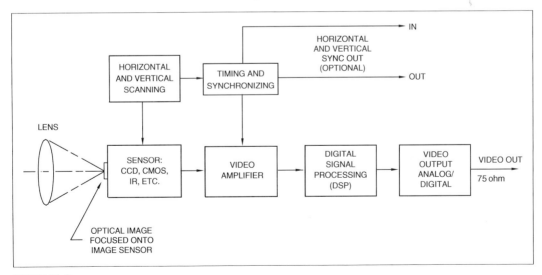

FIGURE 21.8

Analog CCTV camera block diagram.

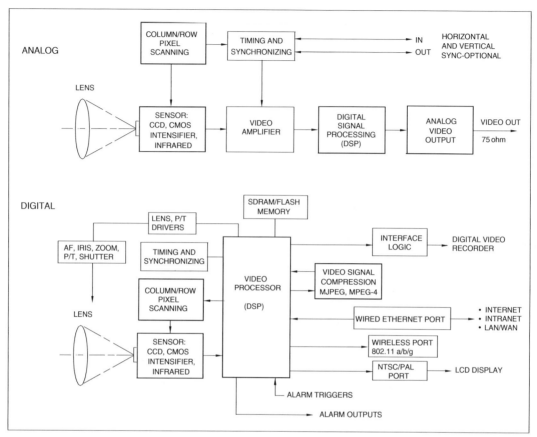

FIGURE 21.9

Analog camera with DSP and all-digital camera block diagram.

THE TRANSMISSION FUNCTION

Once the camera has generated an electrical video signal representing the scene image, the signal is transmitted to a remote security-monitoring site via some transmission means: coaxial cable, two-wire twisted-pair, LAN, WAN, intranet, Internet, fiber optics, or wireless techniques. The choice of transmission medium depends on factors such as distance, environment, and facility layout.

If the distance between the camera and the monitor is short (10-500 feet), coaxial cable, UTP, and fiber optics or wireless is used. For longer distances (500 feet to several thousand feet) or where there are electrical disturbances, fiber optic cable and UTP are preferred. For very long distances and in harsh environments (frequent lightning storms) or between separated buildings where no electrical grounding between buildings is in place, fiber optics is the choice. In applications where the camera and monitor are separated by roadways or where there is no right of way, wireless systems using RF, microwave, or optical transmission are used. For transmission over many miles or from city to city, the only choice

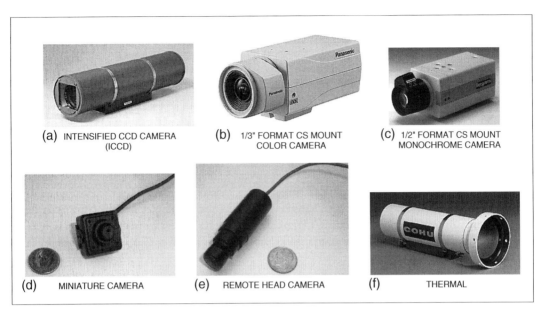

(a) INTENSIFIED CCD CAMERA (ICCD)   **(b)** 1/3" FORMAT CS MOUNT COLOR CAMERA   **(c)** 1/2" FORMAT CS MOUNT MONOCHROME CAMERA

(d) MINIATURE CAMERA   **(e)** REMOTE HEAD CAMERA   **(f)** THERMAL

FIGURE 21.10

Representative video cameras.

is the digital or Internet IP camera that uses compression techniques and transmits over the Internet. Images from these Internet systems are not real time but sometimes come close to real time.

THE MONITOR FUNCTION

At the monitoring site, CRT or LCD, HD, or plasma monitor converts the video signal back into a visual image on the monitor face via electronic circuitry similar but inverse to that in the camera.

The final scene is produced by a scanning electron beam in the CRT in the video monitor. This beam activates the phosphor on the CRT, producing a representation of the original image onto the faceplate of the monitor. Alternatively, the video image is displayed point by point on an LCD or plasma screen. A permanent record of the monitor video image is made using a VCR tape or DVR hard disk magnetic recorder and a permanent hard copy is printed with a video printer.

THE RECORDING FUNCTION

For decades, the VCR has been used to record monochrome and color video images. The real-time and TL VCR magnetic tape systems have been a reliable and efficient means for recording security scenes.

Beginning in the mid-1990s, the DVR was developed using a computer hard disk drive and digital electronics to provide video image recording. The availability of large memory disks (hundreds of megabytes) made these machines available for long-duration security recording. Significant advantages of the DVR over the VCR are the high reliability of the disk as compared with the cassette tape, its ability to perform high-speed searches (retrieval of images) anywhere on the disk, and absence of image deterioration after many copies are made.

SCENE ILLUMINATION

A scene is illuminated by either natural or artificial illumination. Monochrome cameras can operate with any type of light source. Color cameras need light that contains all the colors in the visible spectrum and light with a reasonable balance of all the colors to produce a satisfactory color image.

NATURAL LIGHT

During daytime, the amount of illumination and spectral distribution of light (color) reaching a scene depends on the time of day and atmospheric conditions. The color spectrum of the light reaching the scene is important if color CCTV is used. Direct sunlight produces the highest contrast scene, allowing maximum identification of objects. On a cloudy or overcast day, less light is received by the objects in the scene resulting in less contrast. To produce an optimum camera picture under the wide variation in light levels (daytime to nighttime), an automatic-iris camera system is required. Table 21.1 shows the light levels for outdoor illumination under bright sun, partial clouds, and overcast day down to overcast night.

Scene illumination is measured in foot-candles (fc) and can vary from 10,000 to 1 (or more). This exceeds the dynamic operating range of most camera sensors for producing a good-quality video image. After the sun has gone below the horizon and if the moon is overhead, reflected sunlight from the moon illuminates the scene and may be detected by a sensitive monochrome camera. Detection of information in a scene under this condition requires a very sensitive camera, since there is very little light reflected into the camera lens from the scene. As an extreme, when the moon is not overhead or is obscured by cloud cover, the only light received is ambient light from (1) local man-made lighting sources; (2) nightglow caused by distant ground lighting reflecting off particulate (pollution), clouds, and aerosols in the lower atmosphere; and (3) direct light caused by starlight. This is the most severe lighting condition and requires (1) ICCD, (2) monochrome camera with IR light-emitting diode (LED) illumination, or (3) thermal IR camera. Table 21.2 summarizes the light levels

Table 21.1   Light Levels Under Daytime and Nighttime Conditions

| Condition | Illumination | | Comments |
	fc	lux	
Direct sunlight	10,000	107,500	Daylight range
Full daylight	1000	10,750	
Overcast day	100	1075	
Very dark day	10	107.5	
Twilight	1	10.75	
Deep twilight	0.1	1.075	
Full moon	0.01	0.1075	LLL range
Quarter moon	0.001	0.01075	
Starlight	0.0001	0.001075	
Overcast night	0.00001	0.0001075	

Note: 10.75 lux = 1 fc.

Table 21.2 Camera Capability Under Natural Lighting Conditions and Camera Requirement per Lighting Conditions

Illumination Condition	Illumination		Vidicon[a]	CCD	CMOS	ICCD	ISIT[b]
	fc	lux					
Overcast night	0.00001	0.0001075					
Starlight	0.0001	0.001075					
Quarter moon	0.001	0.01075					
Full moon	0.01	0.1075					
Deep twilight	0.1	1.075					
Twilight	1	10.075	Operating range of typical cameras				
Very dark day	10	107.5					
Overcast day	100	1075					
Full daylight	1000	10,750					
Direct sunlight	10,000	107,500					

ISIT, intensified silicon intensified target.
[a] For reference only.

occurring under daylight and these LLL conditions and the operating ranges of typical cameras. The equivalent metric measure of light level (lux) compared with the fc is given. One fc is equivalent to approximately 9.3 lux.

ARTIFICIAL LIGHT

Artificial illumination is often used to augment outdoor lighting to obtain adequate video surveillance at night. The light sources used are tungsten, tungsten-halogen, metal-arc, mercury, sodium, xenon, IR lamps, and LED IR arrays. Figure 21.11 illustrates several examples of these lamps.

The type of lighting chosen depends on architectural requirements and the specific application. Often a particular lighting design is used for safety reasons so that personnel at the scene can see better and for improving the video picture. Tungsten and tungsten-halogen lamps have by far the most balanced color and are best for color cameras. The most efficient visual outdoor light types are the low- and high-pressure sodium-vapor lamps to which the human eye is most sensitive. These lamps, however, do not produce all colors (missing blue and green) and therefore are not good light sources for color cameras. Metal-arc lamps have excellent color rendition. Mercury-arc lamps provide good security illumination but do not produce the color red; therefore, they are not as good as the metal-arc lamps at producing excellent-quality color video images. Long-arc xenon lamps with excellent color rendition are often used in outdoor sports arenas and large parking areas.

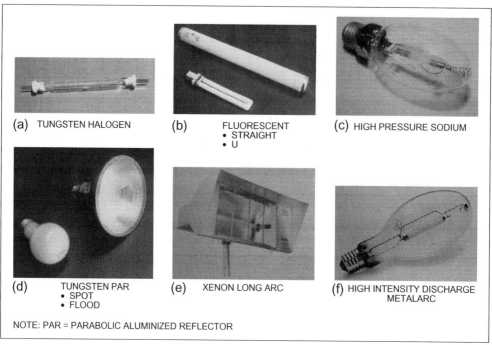

(a) TUNGSTEN HALOGEN

(b) FLUORESCENT
• STRAIGHT
• U

(c) HIGH PRESSURE SODIUM

(d) TUNGSTEN PAR
• SPOT
• FLOOD

(e) XENON LONG ARC

(f) HIGH INTENSITY DISCHARGE METALARC

NOTE: PAR = PARABOLIC ALUMINIZED REFLECTOR

FIGURE 21.11

Representative artificial light sources.

LED IR illumination arrays mounted in monochrome video cameras or located near the camera are used to illuminate scenes when there is insufficient lighting. Since they only emit energy in the IR spectrum, they can only be used with monochrome cameras. They are used at short ranges (10-25 feet) with wide-angle lenses (50-75° FOV) or at medium long ranges (25-200 feet) with medium to narrow FOV lenses (5-20°).

Artificial indoor illumination is similar to outdoor illumination, with fluorescent lighting used extensively in addition to the high-pressure sodium, metal-arc, and mercury lamps. Since indoor lighting has a relatively constant light level, automatic-iris lenses are often unnecessary. However, if the CCTV camera views a scene near an outside window or a door where additional light comes in during the day, or if the indoor lighting changes between daytime and nighttime operation, then an automatic-iris lens or electronically shuttered camera is required. The illumination level from most indoor lighting is significantly lower by 100-1000 times than that of sunlight.

SCENE CHARACTERISTICS

The quality of the video image depends on various scene characteristics that include: (1) the scene lighting level, (2) the sharpness and contrast of objects relative to the scene background, (3) whether objects are in a simple, uncluttered background or in a complicated scene, and (4) whether objects are stationary or in motion. These scene factors will determine whether the system will be able to detect, determine orientation, recognize, or identify objects and personnel. As will be seen later, the scene illumination—via sunlight, moonlight, or artificial sources—and the actual scene contrast play important roles in the type of lens and camera necessary to produce a quality image on the monitor.

TARGET SIZE

In addition to the scene's illumination level and the object's contrast with respect to the scene background, the object's apparent size, that is, its angular FOV as seen by the camera, influences a person's ability to detect it. (Try to find a football referee with a striped shirt in a field of zebras.)

The requirements of a video system are a function of the application. These include: (1) detection of the object or movement in the scene; (2) determination of the object's orientation; (3) recognition of the type of object in the scene, that is, adult or child, car or truck; or (4) identification of the object (Who is the person? Exactly what kind of truck is it?). Making these distinctions depends on the system's resolution, contrast, and signal-to-noise ratio (S/N). In a typical scene, the average observer can detect a target about one-tenth of a degree in angle. This can be related to a standard video picture that has 525 horizontal lines (from the National Television System Committee; NTSC) and about 350 TV line vertical and 500 TV line horizontal resolution. Figure 21.12 and Table 21.3 summarize the number of lines required to detect, orient, recognize, or identify an object in a television picture. The number of TV lines required will increase for conditions of poor lighting, highly complex backgrounds, reduced contrast, or fast movement of the camera or target.

REFLECTIVITY

The reflectivity of different materials varies greatly depending on its composition and surface texture. Table 21.4 gives some examples of materials and objects viewed by video cameras and their respective reflectivity.

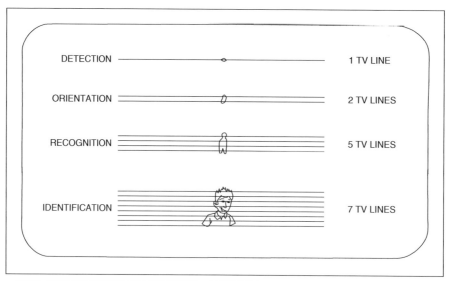

NOTE: 1 TV LINE (BRIGHT AND DARK LINE) = 1 LINE PAIR

FIGURE 21.12

Object size versus intelligence obtained.

Table 21.3   TV Lines Versus Intelligence Obtained

Intelligence	Minimum TV Lines[a]
Detection	1 ± 0.25
Orientation	1.4 ± 0.35
Recognition	4 ± 0.8
Identification	6.4 ± 1.5

[a] *One TV line corresponds to a light and dark line (one TV line pair).*

Since the camera responds to the amount of light reflected from the scene, it is important to recognize that objects have a large range of reflectivity. The objects with the highest reflectivity produce the brightest images. To detect one object located within the area of another the objects must differ in reflectivity, color, or texture. Therefore, if a red box is in front of a green wall and both have the same reflectivity and texture, the box will not be seen on a monochrome video system. In this case, the total reflectivity in the visible spectrum is the same for the green wall and the red box. This is where the color camera shows its advantage over the monochrome camera.

The case of a color scene is more complex. While the reflectivity of the red box and the green wall may be the same as averaged over the entire visible spectrum from blue to red, the color camera can distinguish between green and red.

It is easier to identify a scene characteristic by a difference in color in a color scene than it is to identify it by a difference in gray scale (intensity) in a monochrome scene. For this reason, the target size

Table 21.4   Reflectivity of Common Materials

Material	Reflectivity[a] (%)
Snow	85-95
Asphalt	5
Plaster (white)	90
Sand	40-60
Trees	20
Grass	40
Clothes	15-30
Concrete-new	40
Concrete-old	25
Clear windows	70
Human face	15-25
Wood	10-20
Painted wall (white)	75-90
Red brick	25-35
Parking lot and automobiles	40
Aluminum building (diffuse)	65-70

[a] *Visible spectrum: 400-700 nm.*

required to make an identification in a color scene is generally less than it is to make the same identification in a monochrome scene.

EFFECTS OF MOTION

A moving object in a video image is easier to detect, but more difficult to recognize than a stationary one provided that the camera can respond to it. LLL cameras produce sharp images for stationary scenes but smeared images for moving targets. This is caused by a phenomenon called "lag" or "smear." Solid-state sensors (CCD, CMOS, and ICCD) do not exhibit smear or lag at normal light levels; therefore, they can produce sharp images of both stationary and moving scenes. Some image intensifiers exhibit smear when the scene moves fast or when there is a bright light in the FOV of the lens.

When the target in the scene moves very fast, the inherent camera scan rate (30 frames per second; fps) causes a blurred image of this moving target in the camera. This is analogous to the blurred image in a still photograph when the shutter speed is too slow for the action. There is no cure for this as long as the standard NTSC television scan rate (30 fps) is used. However, CCTV snapshots can be taken without any blurring using fast-shuttered CCD cameras. For special applications in which fast-moving targets must be imaged and tracked, higher scan rate cameras are available.

SCENE TEMPERATURE

Scene temperature has no effect on the video image in a CCD, CMOS, or ICCD sensor. These sensors do not respond to temperature changes or temperature differences in the scene. On the other hand,

IR thermal imaging cameras do respond to temperature differences and changes in temperature in the scene. Thermal imagers do not respond to visible light or the very near-IR radiation like that produced by IR LEDs. The sensitivity of IR thermal imagers is defined as the smallest change in temperature in the scene that can be detected by the thermal camera.

LENSES

A lens collects reflected light from the scene and focuses it onto the camera image sensor.

This is analogous to the lens of the human eye focusing a scene onto the retina at the back of the eye (Figure 21.6). As in the human eye, the camera lens inverts the scene image on the image sensor, but the eye and the camera electronics compensate (invert the image) to perceive an upright scene. The retina of the human eye differs from any CCTV lens in that it focuses a sharp image only in the central 10% of its total 160° FOV. All vision outside the central focused scene is out of focus. This central imaging part of the human eye can be characterized as a medium FL lens that is of 16-25 mm. In principle, Figure 21.6 represents the function of any lens in a video system.

Many different lens types are used for video surveillance and safety applications. They range from the simplest FFL manual-iris lenses to the more complex varifocal and zoom lenses, with an automatic iris being an option for all types.

In addition, pinhole lenses are available for covert applications, split-image lenses for viewing multiple scenes on one camera, right-angle lenses for viewing a scene perpendicular to the camera axis, and rigid or flexible fiber optic lenses for viewing through thick walls, under doors, and so forth.

FFL LENS

Figure 21.13 illustrates three fixed FFL or fixed FOV lenses with narrow (telephoto), medium, and wide FOVs and the corresponding FOV obtained when used with a 1/3-inch camera sensor format.

Wide FOV (short FL) lenses permit viewing a very large scene (wide angle) with low magnification and therefore provide low resolution and low identification capabilities. Narrow FOV or telephoto lenses have high magnification with high resolution and high identification capabilities.

ZOOM LENS

The zoom lens is more versatile and complex than the FFL lens. Its FL is variable from wide-angle to narrow-angle (telephoto) FOV (Figure 21.14).

The overall camera/lens FOV depends on the lens FL and the camera sensor size as shown in Figure 21.14. Zoom lenses consist of multiple lens groups that are moved within the lens barrel by means of an external zooming ring (manual or motorized), changing the lens FL and angular FOV without having to switch lenses or refocusing. Zoom FL ratios can range from 6:1 up to 50:1. Zoom lenses are usually large and used on pan/tilt mounts viewing over large areas and distances (25-500 feet).

VARIFOCAL LENS

The varifocal lens is a variable FL lens used in applications where an FFL lens would be used. In general, they are smaller and cost much less than zoom lenses. Like the zoom lens, the varifocal lens is

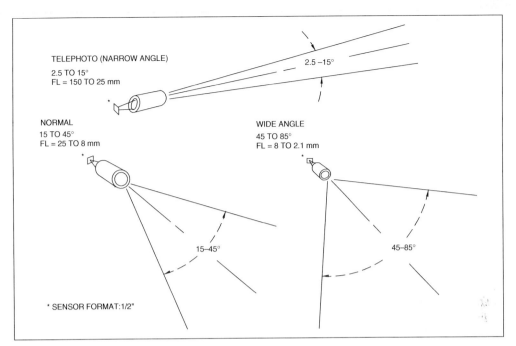

FIGURE 21.13

Representative FFL lenses and their FOVs.

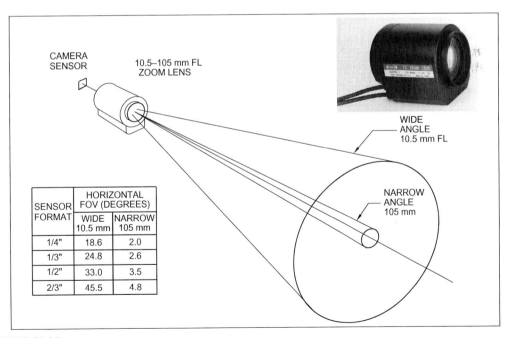

SENSOR FORMAT	HORIZONTAL FOV (DEGREES)	
	WIDE 10.5 mm	NARROW 105 mm
1/4"	18.6	2.0
1/3"	24.8	2.6
1/2"	33.0	3.5
2/3"	45.5	4.8

FIGURE 21.14

Zoom video lens horizontal FOV.

used because its FL (angular FOV) can be changed manually or automatically, using a motor, by rotating the barrel on the lens. This feature makes it convenient to adjust the FOV to a precise angle when installed on the camera. Typical varifocal lenses have FLs of 3-8, 5-12, and 8-50 mm. With just these three lenses, FLs from 3 to 50 mm (91-5° horizontal FOV) can be covered on a 1/3-inch format sensor. Unlike zoom lenses, varifocal lenses must be refocused each time the FL and the FOV are changed. They are not suitable for zoom or pan/tilt applications.

PANORAMIC—360° LENS

There has always been a need to see "all around," i.e., an entire room or other location, seeing 360° with *one* panoramic camera and lens. In the past, 360° FOV camera viewing systems have only been achieved by using multiple cameras and lenses and combining the scenes on a split-screen monitor.

Panoramic lenses have been available for many years but have only recently been combined with digital electronics and sophisticated mathematical transformations to take advantage of their capabilities. Figure 21.15 shows two lenses having a 360° horizontal FOV and a 90° vertical FOV.

The panoramic lens collects light from the 360° panoramic scene and focuses it onto the camera sensor as a donut-shaped image. The electronics and mathematical algorithm convert this donut-shaped panoramic image into the rectangular (horizontal and vertical) format for normal monitor viewing.

COVERT PINHOLE LENS

This special security lens is used when the lens and CCTV camera must be hidden. The front lens element or aperture is small (from 1/16 to 5/16 of an inch in diameter). Although this is not the size of a pinhead, it nevertheless has been labeled as such. Figure 21.16 shows examples of straight and right-angle pinhole lenses used with C or CS mount cameras. The very small mini-pinhole lenses are used on the low-cost, small board cameras.

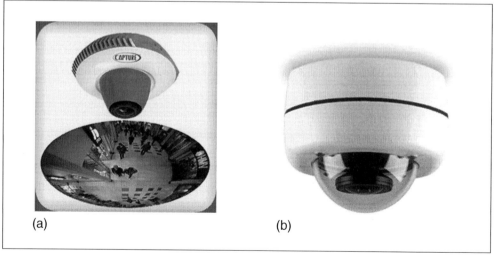

(a)   (b)

FIGURE 21.15

Panoramic 360° lens.

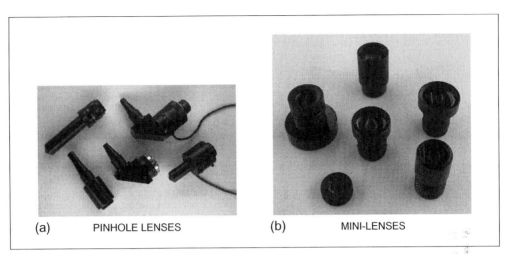

(a)   PINHOLE LENSES   (b)   MINI-LENSES

FIGURE 21.16

Pinhole and mini-pinhole lenses.

SPECIAL LENSES

Some special lenses useful in security applications include split-image, right-angle, relay, and fiber optic lenses (Figure 21.17).

The dual-split and tri-split lenses use only one camera to produce multiple scenes. These are useful for viewing the same scene with different magnifications or different scenes with the same or different magnifications. Using only one camera can reduce cost and increase reliability. These lenses are useful when two or three views are required and only one camera was installed.

The right-angle lens permits a camera using a wide-angle lens installed to view a scene that is perpendicular to the camera's optical axis. There are no restrictions on the FLs, so they can be used in wide- or narrow-angle applications.

The flexible and rigid coherent fiber optic lenses are used to mount a camera several inches to several feet away from the front lens as might be required to view from the opposite side of a wall or in a hazardous environment. The function of the fiber optic bundle is to transfer the focused visual image from one location to another. This may be useful for (1) protecting the camera and (2) locating the lens in one environment (outdoors) and the camera in another (indoors).

CAMERAS

The camera lens focuses the visual scene image onto the camera sensor area point by point, and the camera electronics transforms the visible image into an electrical signal. The camera video signal (containing all picture information) is made up of frequencies from 30 cycles per second, or 30 Hz, to 4.2 million cycles per second, or 4.2 MHz. The video signal is transmitted via a cable (or wireless) to the monitor display.

Almost all security cameras in use today are color or monochrome CCD with the rapid emergence of CMOS types. These cameras are available as low-cost single printed circuit board cameras

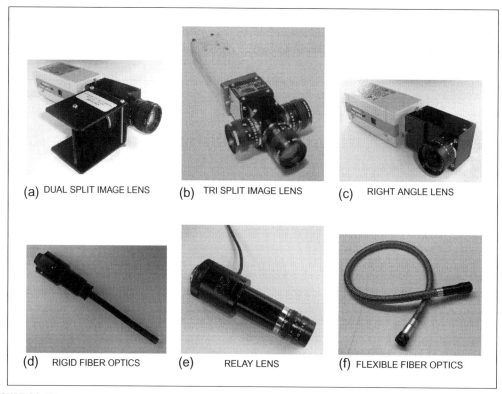

FIGURE 21.17

Special video lenses.

with small lenses already built in, with or without a housing used for covert and overt surveillance applications. More expensive cameras in a housing are larger and more rugged and have a C or CS mechanical mount for accepting any type of lens. These cameras have higher resolution and light sensitivity and other electrical input/output features suitable for multiple camera CCTV systems. The CCD and CMOS cameras with LED IR illumination arrays can extend the use of these cameras to nighttime use. For LLL applications, the ICCD and IR cameras provide the highest sensitivity and detection capability.

Significant advancements in camera technology have been made in the last few years particularly in the use of DSP in the camera and development of the IP camera. All security cameras manufactured between the 1950s and 1980s were the vacuum tube type, either vidicon, silicon, or LLL types using silicon-intensified target (SIT) and intensified ISIT. In the 1980s, the CCD and CMOS solid-state video image sensors were developed and remain the mainstay in the security industry. Increased consumer demand for video recorders using CCD sensors in camcorders and the CMOS sensor in digital still-frame cameras caused a technology explosion and made these small, high-resolution, high-sensitivity, monochrome, and color solid-state cameras available for security systems.

The security industry now has both analog and digital surveillance cameras at its disposal. Up until the mid-1990s, analog cameras dominated, with only rare use of DSP electronics, and the digital Internet camera was only being introduced to the security market. Advances in solid-state circuitry, the demand from the consumer market, and the availability of the Internet were responsible for the rapid use of digital cameras for security applications.

THE SCANNING PROCESS

Two methods used in the camera and monitor video scanning process are *raster* scanning and *progressive* scanning. In the past, analog video systems have all used the raster scanning technique; however, newer digital systems are now using progressive scanning. All cameras use some form of scanning to generate the video picture. A block diagram of the CCTV camera and a brief description of the analog raster scanning process and video signal are shown in Figures 21.8, 21.9, 21.18, and 21.19.

The camera sensor converts the optical image from the lens into an electrical signal. The camera electronics process the video signal and generate a composite video signal containing the picture information (luminance and color) and horizontal and vertical synchronizing pulses.

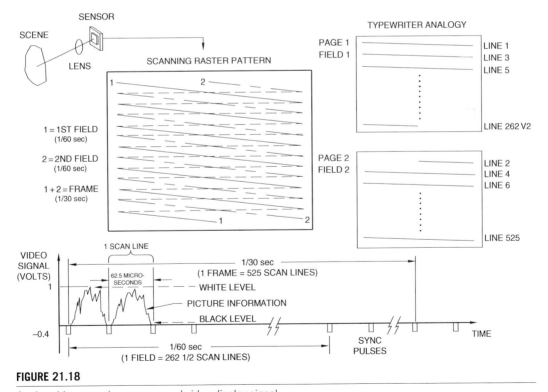

FIGURE 21.18

Analog video scanning process and video display signal.

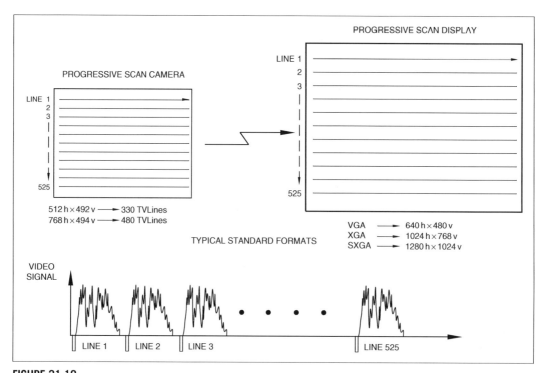

FIGURE 21.19

Digital and progressive scanning process and video display signal.

Signals are transmitted in what is called a *frame* of picture video, made up of two *fields* of information. Each field is transmitted in 1/60 of a second and the entire frame in 1/30 of a second, for a repetition rate of 30 fps. In the United States, this format is the Electronic Industries Association (EIA) standard called the NTSC system. The European standard uses 625 horizontal lines with a field taking 1/50 of a second and a frame 1/25 of a second and a repetition rate of 25 fps.

Raster Scanning

In the NTSC system, the first picture field is created by scanning 262½ horizontal lines. The second field of the frame contains the second 262½ lines, which are synchronized so that they fall between the gaps of the first field lines thus producing one completely interlaced picture frame containing 525 lines. The scan lines of the second field fall *exactly* halfway between the lines of the first field resulting in a 2-to-1 *interlace* system. As shown in Figure 21.18, the first field starts at the upper left corner (of the camera sensor or the CRT monitor) and progresses down the sensor (or screen), line by line, until it ends at the bottom center of the scan.

Likewise, the second field starts at the top center of the screen and ends at the lower-right corner. Each time one line in the field traverses from the left side of the scan to the right it corresponds to one horizontal line as shown in the video waveform at the bottom of Figure 21.18. The video waveform consists of negative synchronization pulses and positive picture information. The horizontal and vertical synchronization pulses are used by the video monitor (and VCR, DVR, or video printer) to synchronize the video picture and paint an exact replica in time and intensity of the camera scanning function onto the monitor face. Black picture information is indicated on the waveform at the bottom (approximately 0 V) and the white picture information at the top (1 V). The amplitude of a standard NTSC signal is 1.4 V peak to peak. In the 525-line system, the *picture* information consists of approximately 512 lines. The lines with no picture information are necessary for vertical blanking, which is the time when the camera electronics or the beam in the monitor CRT moves from the bottom to the top to start a new field.

Random-interlace cameras do not provide complete synchronization between the first and the second fields. The horizontal and the vertical scan frequencies are not locked together; therefore, fields do not interlace exactly. This condition, however, results in an acceptable picture, and the asynchronous condition is difficult to detect. The 2-to-1 interlace system has an advantage when multiple cameras are used with multiple monitors and/or recorders in that they prevent jump or jitter when switching from one camera to the next.

The scanning process for solid-state cameras is different. The solid-state sensor consists of an array of very small picture elements (pixels) that are read out serially (sequentially) by the camera electronics to produce the same NTSC format—525 TV lines in 1/30 of a second (30 fps)—as shown in Figure 21.19.

The use of digital cameras and digital monitors has changed the way the camera and monitor signals are processed, transmitted, and displayed. The final presentation on the monitor looks similar to the analog method, but instead of seeing 525 horizontal lines (NTSC system), individual pixels are seen in a *row* and *column* format. In the digital system, the camera scene is divided into rows and columns of individual pixels (small points in the scene) each representing the light intensity and color for each point in the scene. The digitized scene signal is transmitted to the digital display be it LCD, plasma, or other, and reproduced on the monitor screen pixel by pixel providing a faithful representation of the original scene.

Digital and Progressive Scan

The digital scanning is accomplished in the 2-to-1 interlace mode as in the analog system, or in a *progressive* mode. In the progressive mode, each line is scanned in a linear sequence: line 1, then line 2, line 3, and so forth. Solid-state camera sensors and monitor displays can be manufactured with a variety of horizontal and vertical pixels formats. The standard aspect ratio is 4:3 as in the analog system and 16:9 for the wide screen. Likewise, there are many different combinations of pixel numbers available in the sensor and display. Some standard formats for color CCD cameras are 512 h × 492 v for 330 TV line resolution and 768 h × 494 v for 480 TV line resolution, and for color LCD monitors it is 1280 h × 1024 v.

SOLID-STATE CAMERAS

Video security cameras have gone through rapid technological changes during the last half of the 1980s to the present. For decades, the vidicon tube camera was the only security camera available. In the 1980s, the more sensitive and rugged silicon-diode tube camera was the best available. In the late

1980s, the invention and development of the digital CCD and later the CMOS cameras replaced the tube camera. This technology coincided with rapid advancement in DSP in cameras, the IP camera, and use of digital transmission of the video signal over LAN, WANs, and the Internet.

The two generic solid-state cameras that account for most security applications are the CCD and the CMOS.

The first generation of solid-state cameras available from most manufacturers had 2/3-inch (sensor diagonal) and 1/2-inch sensor formats. As the technology improved, smaller formats evolved. Most solid-state cameras in use today are available in three image sensor formats: 1/2, 1/3, and 1/4 inch. The 1/2-inch format produces higher resolution and sensitivity at a higher cost. The 1/2-inch and smaller formats permitted the use of smaller, less expensive lenses as compared with the larger formats. Many manufacturers now produce 1/3-inch and 1/4-inch format cameras with excellent resolution and light sensitivity. Solid-state sensor cameras are superior to their predecessors because of their (1) precise, repeatable pixel geometry, (2) low power requirements, (3) small size, (4) excellent color rendition and stability, and (5) ruggedness and long life expectancy. At present, solid-state cameras have settled into three main categories: (1) analog, (2) digital, and (3) Internet.

Analog

Analog cameras have been with the industry since CCTV has been used in security. Their electronics are straightforward and the technology is still used in many applications.

Digital

Since the second half of the 1990s, there has been an increase in the use of DSP in cameras. It significantly improves the performance of the camera by (1) automatically adjusting to large light level changes (eliminating the automatic iris), (2) integrating the VMD into the camera, and (3) automatically switching the camera from color operation to higher sensitivity monochrome operation, as well as other features and enhancements.

Internet

The most recent camera technology advancement is manifest in the IP camera. This camera is configured with electronics that connects to the Internet and the WWW network through an Internet service provider. Each camera is provided with a registered Internet address and can transmit the video image anywhere on the network. This is really remote video monitoring at its best. The camera site is viewed from anywhere by entering the camera Internet address (ID number) and proper password. Password security is used so that only authorized users can enter the Web site and view the camera image. Two-way communication is used so that the user can control camera parameters and direct the camera operation (pan, tilt, zoom, etc.) from the monitoring site.

LLL-INTENSIFIED CAMERA

When a security application requires viewing during nighttime conditions where the available light is moonlight, starlight, or other residual reflected light and the surveillance must be covert (no active illumination like IR LEDs), LLL-ICCD cameras are used. The ICCD cameras have sensitivities between 100 and 1000 times higher than the best solid-state cameras. The increased sensitivity is obtained by the use of a *light amplifier* mounted in between the lens and the CCD sensor. LLL cameras cost between 10 and 20 times more than CCD cameras.

THERMAL IMAGING CAMERA

An alternative to the ICCD camera is the thermal IR camera. Visual cameras see only visible light energy from the blue end of the visible spectrum to the red end (approximately 400-700 nm). Some monochrome cameras see beyond the visible region into the near-IR region of the spectrum up to 1000 nm. This IR energy, however, is not thermal IR energy. Thermal IR cameras using thermal sensors respond to thermal energy in the 3-5 and 8-14 μm range. The IR sensors respond to the changes in *heat* (thermal) energy emitted by the targets in the scene. Thermal imaging cameras can operate in complete darkness, as they require no visible or IR illumination whatsoever. They are truly passive nighttime monochrome imaging sensors. They can detect humans and any other warm objects (animals, vehicle engines, ships, aircraft, warm/hot spots in buildings) or other objects against a scene background.

PANORAMIC—360° CAMERA

Powerful mathematical techniques combined with the unique 360° panoramic lens have made a 360° panoramic camera possible. In operation, the lens collects and focuses the 360° horizontal by up to 90° vertical scene (one-half of a sphere; a hemisphere) onto the camera sensor. The image takes the form of a "donut" on the sensor (Figure 21.20).

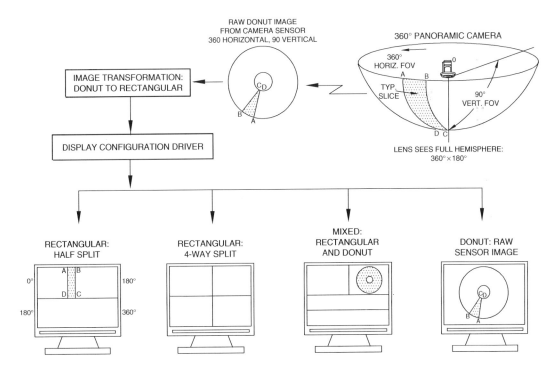

FOUR TYPICAL DISPLAY FORMATS

FIGURE 21.20

Panoramic 360° camera.

The camera/lens is located at the origin (0). The scene is represented by the surface of the hemisphere. As shown, a small part (slice) of the scene area (A, B, C, D) is "mapped" onto the sensor as a, b, c, d. In this way, the full scene is mapped onto the sensor. Direct presentation of the donut-ring video image onto the monitor does not result in a useful picture.

That is where the use of a powerful mathematical algorithm comes in. Digital processing in the computer using the algorithm transforms the donut-shaped image into the normal format seen on a monitor, that is, horizontal and vertical.

All of the 0-360° horizontal by 90° vertical images cannot be presented on a monitor in a useful way—there is just too much picture "squeezed" into the small screen area. This condition is solved by computer software by looking at only a section of the entire scene at any particular time.

The main attributes of the panoramic system include: (1) capturing a full 360° FOV, (2) the ability to digitally pan/tilt to anywhere in the scene and digitally zoom any scene area, (3) having no moving parts (no motors, etc., that can wear out), and (4) having multiple operators that can view any part of the scene in real time or at a later time.

The panoramic camera requires a high-resolution camera since so much scene information is contained in the image. Camera technology has progressed so that these digital cameras are available and can present a good image of a zoomed-in portion of the panoramic scene.

TRANSMISSION

By definition, the camera must be remotely located from the monitor and therefore the video signal must be transmitted by some means from one location to another. In security applications, the distance between the camera and the monitor may be from tens of feet to many miles or, perhaps, completely around the globe. The transmission path may be inside buildings, outside buildings, above ground, underground, through the atmosphere, or in almost any environment imaginable. For this reason, the transmission means must be carefully assessed and an optimum choice of hardware made to satisfactorily transmit the video signal from the camera to the monitoring site. There are many ways to transmit the video signal from the camera to the monitoring site. Figure 21.21 shows some examples of transmission cables.

The signal can be analog or digital. It can be transmitted via electrical conductors using coaxial cable or UTP, by fiber optics, by LAN or WAN, and intranet or Internet.

Particular attention should be paid to transmission means when transmitting color video signals, since the color signal is significantly more complex and susceptible to distortion than monochrome. There are advantages and disadvantages of all of the transmission means and the hardware available to transmit the video signal.

HARD-WIRED

There are several hard-wired means for transmitting a video signal: coaxial cable, UTP, LAN, WAN, intranet, Internet, and fiber optic cable.

Fiber optic cable is used for long distances and when there is interfering electrical noise. LANs and Internet connections are digital transmission techniques used in larger security systems and where the signal must be transmitted over existing computer networks or over long distances.

Coaxial cable

The most common video signal transmission method is the coaxial cable. This cable has been used since the inception of CCTV and is still in use today. The cable is inexpensive, easy to terminate at the

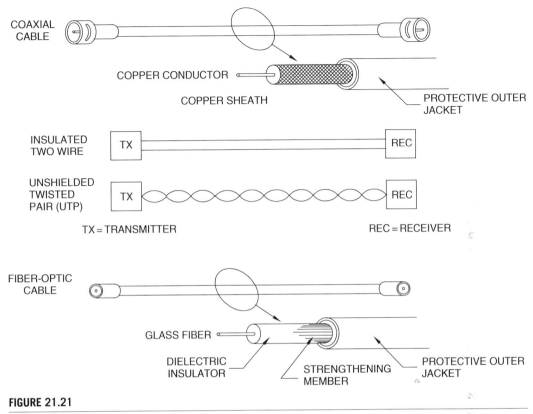

FIGURE 21.21

Hard-wired copper and fiber optic transmission means.

camera and monitor ends, and transmits a faithful video signal with little or no distortion or loss. It has a 75-ohm electrical impedance, which matches the impedance of the camera and monitor, ensuring a distortion-free video image. This coaxial cable has a copper electrical shield and center conductor that works well over distances up to 1000 feet.

UTP

In the 1990s, UTP video transmission came into vogue. The technique uses a transmitter at the camera and a receiver at the monitor with two twisted copper wires connecting them. Several reasons for its increased popularity are that (1) it can be used over longer distances than coaxial cable, (2) it uses inexpensive wire, (3) many locations already have two-wire twisted-pair installed, (4) it uses a low-cost transmitter and receiver, and (5) it has higher electrical noise immunity as compared to coaxial cable. The UTP using a sophisticated electronic transmitter and receiver can transmit the video signal to 2000-3000 feet.

LAN, WAN, intranet, and internet

The evolution of the LAN, WAN, intranet, and Internet revolutionized the transmission of video signals in a new form (digital) which significantly expanded the scope and effectiveness of video for security systems. The widespread use of business computers and consequent use of these networks provided an existing digital network protocol and communications suitable for video transmission. The Internet attained widespread use in the late 1990s and truly revolutionized digital video transmission. This global computer network provided the digital backbone path to transmit digital video, audio, and command signals from anywhere on the globe.

The video signal transmission techniques described so far provide a means for real-time transmission of a video signal, requiring a full 4.2-MHz bandwidth to reproduce real-time motion. When these techniques cannot be used for real-time video, alternative digital techniques are used. In these systems, a non-real-time video transmission takes place, so that some scene action is lost. Depending on the action in the scene, the resolution, from near real time (15 fps) to slow scan (a few fps) of the video image is transmitted. The digitized and compressed video signal is transmitted over a LAN or Internet network and decompressed and reconstructed at the receiver/monitoring site.

WIRELESS

In legacy analog video surveillance systems, it is often more economical or beneficial to transmit the real-time video signal without cable (wireless) from the camera to the monitor using an RF or IR atmospheric link. In digital video systems using digital transmission, the use of wireless networks (WiFi) permits routing the video and control signals to *any* remote location. In both the analog and the digital systems, some form of video scrambling or encryption is often used to remove the possibility of eavesdropping by unauthorized personnel outside the system. Three important applications for wireless transmission include: (1) covert and portable rapid deployment video installations, (2) building-to-building transmission over a roadway, and (3) parking lot light poles to building. The Federal Communications Commission (FCC) restricts some wireless transmitting devices using microwave frequencies or RF to government and law enforcement use but has given approval for many RF and microwave transmitters for general security use. These FCC-approved devices operate above the normal television frequency bands at approximately 920 MHz and 2.4 and 5.8 GHz. The atmospheric IR link is used when a high-security link is required. This link does not require an FCC approval and transmits a video image over a narrow beam of visible light or near-IR energy. The beam is very difficult to intercept (tap). Figure 21.22 illustrates some of the wireless transmission techniques available today.

FIBER OPTICS

Fiber optic transmission technology has advanced significantly in the last 5-10 years and represents a highly reliable, secure means of transmission. Fiber optic transmission holds several significant advantages over other hard-wired systems: (1) very long transmission paths up to many miles without any significant degradation in the video signal with monochrome or color; (2) immunity to external electrical disturbances from weather or electrical equipment; (3) very wide bandwidth, permitting one or more video, control, and audio signals to be multiplexed on a single fiber; and (4) resistance to tapping (eavesdropping) and therefore a very secure transmission means.

While the installation and termination of fiber optic cable requires a more skilled technician, it is well within the capability of qualified security installers. Many hard-wired installations requiring the optimum color and resolution rendition use fiber optic cable.

SWITCHERS

The video switcher accepts video signals from many different video cameras and connects them to one or more monitors or recorders. Using manual or automatic activation or an alarming signal input, the

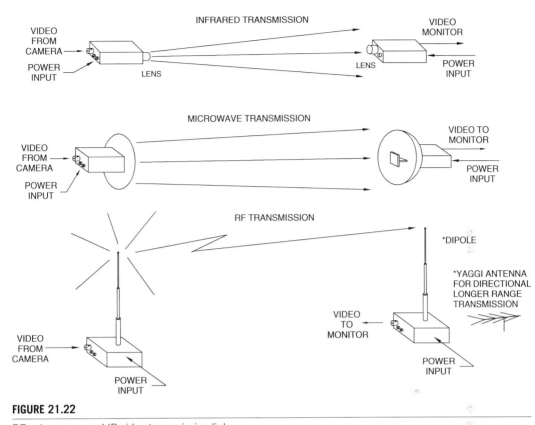

FIGURE 21.22

RF, microwave, and IR video transmission links.

switcher selects one or more of the cameras and directs its video signal to a specified monitor, recorder, or some other device or location.

STANDARD

There are four basic switcher types: manual, sequential, homing, and alarming. Figure 21.23 shows how these are connected into the video security system.

The manual switcher connects one camera at a time to the monitor, recorder, or printer. The sequential switcher automatically switches the cameras in sequence to the output device. The operator can override the automatic sequence with the homing sequential switcher. The alarming switcher connects the alarmed camera to the output device automatically, when an alarm is received.

MICROPROCESSOR CONTROLLED

When the security system requires many cameras in various locations with multiple monitors and other alarm input functions, a microprocessor-controlled switcher and keyboard is used to manage these additional requirements (Figure 21.24).

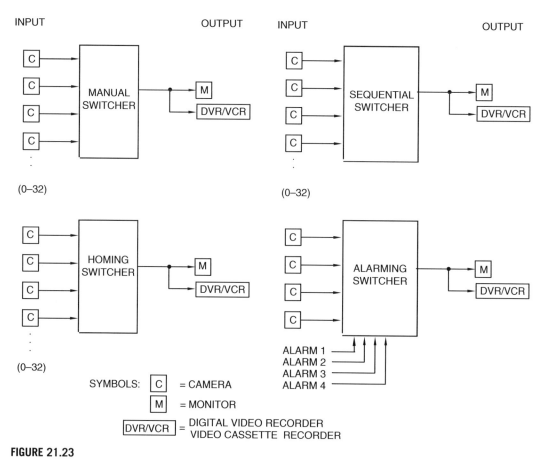

FIGURE 21.23

Basic video switcher types.

In large security systems, the switcher is microprocessor controlled and can switch hundreds of cameras to dozens of monitors, recorders, or video printers via an RS-232 or other communication control link. Numerous manufacturers make comprehensive keyboard-operated, computer-controlled consoles that integrate the functions of the switcher, pan/tilt pointing, automatic scanning, automatic preset pointing for pan/tilt systems, and many other functions. The power of the software-programmable console resides in its flexibility, expandability, and ability to accommodate a large variety of applications and changes in facility design. In place of a dedicated hardware system built for each specific application, this computer-controlled system can be configured via software for the application.

QUADS AND MULTIPLEXERS

A quad or a multiplexer is used when multiple camera scenes need to be displayed on one video monitor. It is interposed between the cameras and the monitor, accepts multiple camera inputs, memorizes

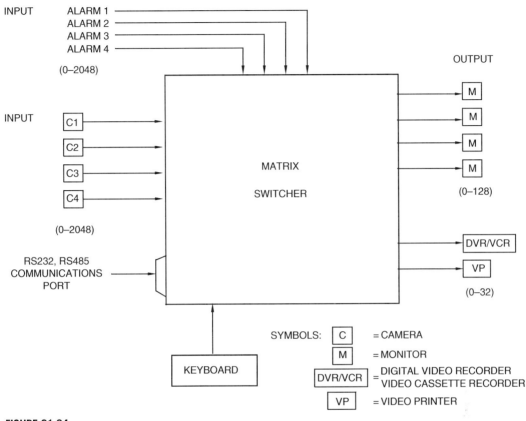

FIGURE 21.24

Microprocessor-controlled switcher and keyboard.

the scenes from each camera, compresses them, and then displays multiple scenes on a single video monitor. Equipment is available to provide 2, 4, 9, 16, and up to 32 separate video scenes on one single monitor. Figure 21.25 shows a block diagram of quad and multiplexer systems.

The most popular presentation is the quad screen showing four pictures. This presentation significantly improves camera-viewing ability in multicamera systems, decreases security guard fatigue, and requires three fewer monitors in a four-camera system. There is a loss of resolution when more than one scene is presented on the monitor with resolution decreasing as the number of scenes increases. One-quarter of the resolution of a full screen is obtained on a quad display (half in horizontal and half in vertical). Quads and multiplexers have front panel controls so that: (1) a full screen image of a camera can be selected, (2) multiple cameras can be displayed (quad, 9, etc.), or (3) the full screen images of all cameras can be sequentially switched with dwell times for each camera, set by the operator.

MONITORS

Video monitors can be divided into several categories: (1) monochrome, (2) color, (3) CRT, (4) LCD, (5) plasma, and (6) computer display. Contrary to a popular misconception, larger video monitors do not

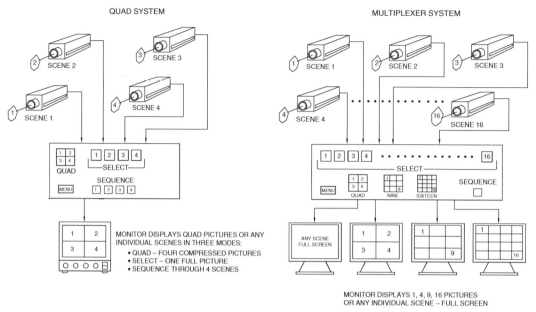

FIGURE 21.25

Quad and multiplexer block diagrams.

necessarily have better picture resolution or the ability to increase the amount of intelligence available in the picture. All U.S. NTSC security monitors have 525 horizontal lines; therefore, the vertical resolution is about the same regardless of the CRT monitor size. The horizontal resolution is determined by the system bandwidth. With the NTSC limitation, the best picture quality is obtained by choosing a monitor with resolution equal to or better than the camera or transmission link bandwidth. With the use of a higher-resolution computer monitor and corresponding higher-resolution camera and commensurate bandwidth to match, higher-resolution video images are obtained. Figure 21.26 shows representative examples of video monitors.

MONOCHROME

Until the late 1990s, the most popular monitor used in CCTV systems was the monochrome CRT monitor. It is still used and is available in sizes ranging from a 1-inch diagonal viewfinder to a large 27-inch diagonal CRT. By far, the most popular monochrome monitor size is the 9-inch diagonal that optimizes video viewing for a person seated about 3 feet away. A second reason for its popularity is that two of these monitors fit into the standard EIA 19-inch wide rack-mount panel. Figure 21.26b shows two 9-inch monitors in a dual rack-mounted version. A triple rack-mount version of a 5-inch diagonal monitor is used when space is at a premium. The triple rack-mounted monitor is popular, since three fit conveniently into the 19-inch EIA rack. The optimum viewing distance for the triple 5-inch diagonal monitor is about 1.5 feet.

COLOR

Color monitors are now in widespread use and range in size from a 3- to 27-inch diagonal and have required viewing distances and capabilities similar to those of monochrome monitors. Since color

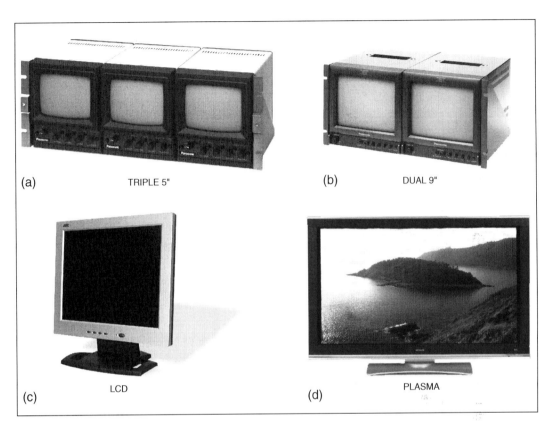

(a)   TRIPLE 5"   (b)   DUAL 9"

(c)   LCD   (d)   PLASMA

FIGURE 21.26

Standard 5- and 9-inch single/multiple CRT, LCD, and plasma monitors.

monitors require three different colored dots to produce one pixel of information on the monitor, they have lower horizontal resolution than monochrome monitors. Popular color monitor sizes are 13, 15, and 17 inch diagonal.

CRT, LCD, PLASMA, HD, DISPLAYS

The video security picture is displayed on three basic types of monitor screens: (1) CRT, (2) LCD, and most recently, (3) the plasma display. The analog CRT has seen excellent service from the inception of video and continues as a strong contender providing a low-cost, reliable security monitor. The digital LCD monitor is growing in popularity because of its smaller size (smaller depth)—2-3 inches versus 12-20 inches for the CRT. The LCD is an all solid-state display that accepts the VGA computer signal. Most small (3-10 inch diagonal) and many large (10-17 inch diagonal) LCD monitors also accept an analog video input. The most recent monitor entry into the security market is the digital plasma display. This premium display excels in resolution and brightness and viewing angle and produces the highest quality image in the industry. It is also the most expensive. Screen sizes range from 20 to 42 inches diagonal. Overall depths are small and range in size from 3 to 4 inches. They are available in 4:3 and HDTV 16:9 format.

AUDIO/VIDEO

Many monitors have built-in audio channel with speakers to produce audio and video simultaneously.

RECORDERS

The video camera, transmission means, and monitor provide the remote eyes for the security guard, but as soon as the action or event is over, the image disappears from the monitor screen forever. When a permanent record of the live video scene is required, a VCR, DVR, network recorder, or optical disk recorder is used (Figure 21.27).

The video image can be recorded in real time, near real time, or TL. The VCRs record the video signal on a magnetic tape cassette with a maximum real-time recording time of 6 hours and near real time of 24 hours. When extended periods of recording are required (longer than the 6-hour real-time cassette), a TL recorder is used. In the TL process, the video picture is not recorded continuously (real time) but rather "snapshots" are recorded. These snapshots are spread apart in time by a fraction of a second or even seconds so that the total elapsed time for the recording can extend for hundreds of hours. Some present TL systems record over an elapsed time of 1280 hours.

The DVR records the video image on a computer magnetic hard drive (HD) and the optical disk storage on optical disk media. The DVR and optical disk systems have a significant advantage over the VCR with respect to retrieval time of a particular video frame. VCRs take many minutes to fast forward or fast rewind the magnetic tape to locate a particular frame on the tape. Retrieval times on DVRs and optical disks are typically a fraction of a second. The VCR cassette tape is transportable and the DVR and optical disk systems are available with or without removable disks. This means that the video images (digital data) can be transported to remote locations or stored in a vault for safekeeping. The removable DVR and optical disks are about the same size as VHS cassettes.

VCR

Magnetic storage media have been used universally to record the video image. The VCR uses the standard VHS cassette format. The 8-mm Sony format is used in portable surveillance equipment because of its smaller size. Super VHS and Hi-8 formats are used to obtain higher resolution. VCRs can be subdivided into two classes: real time and TL. The TL recorder has significantly different mechanical and electrical features permitting it to take snapshots of a scene at predetermined (user-selectable) intervals. It can also record in real time when activated by an alarm or other input command. Real-time recorders can record up to 6 hours in monochrome or color. TL VCRs are available for recording TL sequences up to 720 hours.

(a) SINGLE CHANNEL DVR   (b) 16 CHANNEL DVR   (c) 32 CHANNEL NVR

FIGURE 21.27

DVR and network video recorder (NVR) videodisk storage equipment.

DVR

The DVR has emerged as the new generation of magnetic recorder of choice. A magnetic HD like those used in a microcomputer can store many thousands of images and many hours of video in digital form. The rapid implementation and success of the DVR has resulted from the availability of inexpensive digital magnetic memory storage devices and the advancements made in digital signal compression techniques. Present DVRs are available in single channel and 4 and 16 channels and may be cascaded to provide many more channels.

A significant feature of the DVR is the ability to access (retrieve) a particular frame or recorded time period anywhere on the disk in a fraction of a second. The digital technology also allows many generations (copies) of the stored video images to be made without any errors or degradation of the image.

OPTICAL DISK

When very large volumes of video images need to be recorded, an optical disk system is used. Optical disks have a much larger video image database capacity than magnetic disks given the same physical space they occupy. These disks can record hundreds of times longer than their magnetic counterparts.

HARD-COPY VIDEO PRINTERS

A hard-copy printout of a video image is often required as evidence in court, as a tool for apprehending a vandal or thief, or as a duplicate record of some document or person. The printout is produced by a hard-copy video printer, which is a thermal printer that "burns" the video image onto coated paper or an ink-jet or laser printer. The thermal technique used by many hard-copy printer manufacturers produces excellent quality images in monochrome or color. Figure 21.28 shows a monochrome thermal printer and a sample of the hard-copy image quality it produces. In operation, the image displayed on the monitor or played back from the recorder is immediately memorized by the printer and printed out in less than 10 seconds. This is particularly useful if an intrusion or unauthorized act has occurred and been observed by a security guard. An automatic alarm or a security guard can initiate printing the image of the alarm area or of the suspect and the printout can then be given to another guard to take action. For courtroom uses, time, date, and any other information can be annotated on the printed image.

ANCILLARY EQUIPMENT

Most video security systems require additional accessories and equipment, including: (1) camera housings, (2) camera pan/tilt mechanisms and mounts, (3) camera identifiers, (4) VMDs, (5) image splitters/inserters, and (6) image combiners. The two accessories most often used with the basic camera, monitor, and transmission link are camera housings and pan/tilt mounts. Outdoor housings are used to protect the camera and lens from vandalism and the environment. Indoor housings are used primarily to prevent vandalism and for aesthetic reasons. The motorized pan/tilt mechanisms rotate and point the system camera and lens via commands from a remote control console.

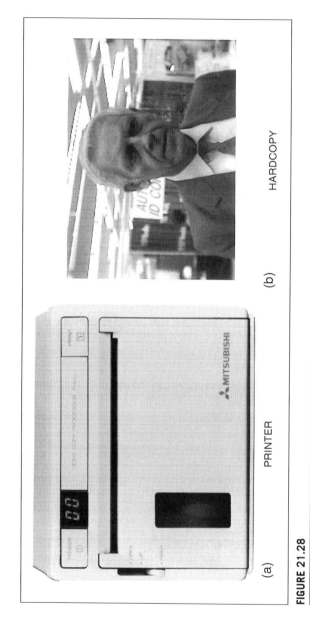

PRINTER   HARDCOPY

(a)   (b)

FIGURE 21.28

Thermal monochrome video printer and hard copy.

CAMERA HOUSINGS

Indoor and outdoor camera housings protect cameras and lenses from dirt, dust, harmful chemicals, the environment, and vandalism. The most common housings are rectangular metal or plastic products, formed from high-impact indoor or outdoor plastic, painted steel, or stainless steel (Figure 21.29). Other shapes and types include cylindrical (tube), corner-mount, ceiling-mount, and dome housings.

Standard rectangular

The rectangular type housing is the most popular. It protects the camera from the environment and provides a window for the lens to view the scene. The housings are available for indoor or outdoor use with a weatherproof and tamper-resistant design. Options include heaters, fans, and window washers.

Dome

A significant part of video surveillance is accomplished using cameras housed in the dome-housing configuration. The dome camera housing can range from a simple fixed monochrome or color camera in a hemispherical dome to a "speed-dome" housing having a high-resolution color camera with remote-controlled pan/tilt/zoom/focus. Other options include presets and image stabilization. The dome-type housing consists of a plastic hemispherical dome on the bottom half. The housing can be clear, tinted, or treated with a partially transmitting optical coating that allows the camera to see in any direction. In a freestanding application (e.g., on a pole, pedestal, or overhang), the top half of the housing consists of a protective cover and a means for attaching the dome to the structure. When the dome housing is mounted in a ceiling, a simpler housing cover is provided and mounted above the ceiling level to support the dome.

Specialty

There are many other specialty housings for mounting in or on elevators, ceilings, walls, tunnels, pedestals, hallways, and so forth. These special types include explosion proof, bullet proof, and extreme environmental construction for arctic and desert use.

Plug and Play

In an effort to reduce installation time for video surveillance cameras, manufacturers have combined the camera, lens, and housing in one assembly ready to be mounted on a ceiling, wall, or pole and plugged into the power source and video transmission cable. These assemblies are available in the form of domes, corner mounts, ceiling mounts, and so forth, making for easy installation in indoor or outdoor applications.

PAN/TILT MOUNTS

To extend the angle of coverage of a CCTV lens/camera system a motorized pan/tilt mechanism is often used. Figure 21.30 shows three generic outdoor pan/tilt types: top-mounted, side-mounted, and dome camera.

The pan/tilt motorized mounting platform permits the camera and lens to rotate horizontally (pan) or vertically (tilt) when it receives an electrical command from the central monitoring site. Thus, the camera lens is not limited by its inherent FOV and can view a much larger area of a scene. A camera mounted on a pan/tilt platform is usually provided with a zoom lens. The zoom lens varies the FOV in the pointing direction of the camera/lens from a command from the central security console. The combination of the pan/tilt and zoom lens provides the widest angular coverage for video surveillance. There is one disadvantage with the pan/tilt/zoom configuration compared with the fixed camera installation.

FIGURE 21.29

Standard indoor/outdoor video housings: (a) corner, (b) elevator corner, (c) ceiling, (d) outdoor environmental rectangular, (e) dome, and (f) plug and play.

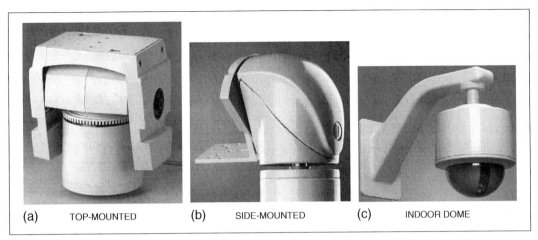

(a)   TOP-MOUNTED   **(b)**   SIDE-MOUNTED   **(c)**   INDOOR DOME

FIGURE 21.30

Video pan/tilt mechanisms: top-mounted, side-mounted, indoor dome.

When the camera and lens are pointing in a particular direction via the pan/tilt platform, most of the other scene area the camera is designed to cover is not viewed. This dead area or dead time is unacceptable in many security applications; therefore, careful consideration should be given to the adequacy of their wide FOV pan/tilt design. Pan/tilt platforms range from small, indoor, lightweight units that only pan, up to large, outdoor, environmental designs carrying large cameras, zoom lenses, and large housings. Choosing the correct pan/tilt mechanism is important since it generally requires more service and maintenance than any other part of the video system.

VMD

Another important component in a video surveillance system is a VMD that produces an alarm signal based on a change in the video scene. The VMD can be built into the camera or be a separate component inserted between the camera and the monitor software in a computer. The VMD electronics, analog or digital, store the video frames, compare subsequent frames to the stored frames, and then determine whether the scene has changed. In operation, the VMD digital electronics decides whether the change is significant and whether to call it an alarm to alert the guard or some equipment, or declare it a false alarm.

SCREEN SPLITTER

The electronic or optical screen splitter takes a part of several camera scenes (two, three, or more), combines the scenes, and displays them on one monitor. The splitters do not compress the image. In an *optical* splitter, the image combining is implemented optically at the camera lens and requires no electronics. The *electronic* splitter/combiner is located between the camera output and the monitor input.

CAMERA VIDEO ANNOTATION

Camera ID

When multiple cameras are used in a video system, some means must be provided to identify the camera. The system uses a camera identifier component that electronically assigns an alphanumeric code and/or name to each camera displayed on a monitor, recorded on a recorder, or printed on a printer. Alphanumeric and symbol character generators are available to annotate the video signal with the names of cameras, locations in a building, and so forth.

Time and date

When time and date is required on the video image, a time/date generator is used to annotate the video picture. This information is mandatory for any prosecution or courtroom procedure.

IMAGE REVERSAL

Occasionally, video surveillance systems use a single mirror to view the scene. This mirror reverses the video image from the normal left-to-right to a right-to-left (reversed image). The image reversal unit corrects the reversal.

SUMMARY

Video surveillance serves as the remote eyes for management and the security force. It provides security personnel with advance notice of breaches in security, hostile, and terrorist acts, and is a part of the plan to protect personnel and assets. It is a critical subsystem for any comprehensive security plan. In this chapter, an introduction to most of the current video technology and equipment has been described.

Lighting plays an important role in determining whether a satisfactory video picture will be obtained with monochrome and color cameras and LLL ICCD cameras. Thermal IR cameras are insensitive to light and only require temperature differences between the target and the background.

There are many types of lenses available for video systems: FFL, varifocal, zoom, pinhole, panoramic, and so forth. The varifocal and zoom lenses extend the FOV of the FFL lens. The panoramic 360° lens provides entire viewing of the scene. The proper choice of lens is necessary to maximize the intelligence obtained from the scene.

Many types of video cameras are available, such as color, monochrome (with or without IR illumination), LLL intensified, thermal IR, analog and digital, simple and full featured, and daytime and nighttime. There are cameras with built-in VMD to alert security guards and improve their ability to detect and locate personnel and be alerted to activity in the scene.

An important component of the video system is the analog or digital video signal transmission means from the camera to the remote site and to the monitoring and recording site. Hard wire or fiber optics is best if the situation permits. Analog works for short distances and digital for long distances. The Internet works globally.

In multiple camera systems, the quad and multiplexers permit multicamera displays on one monitor. Fewer monitors in the security room can improve guard performance.

The CRT monitor is still a good choice for many video applications. The LCD is the solid-state digital replacement for the CRT. The plasma display provides an all solid-state design that has the highest resolution, brightness, and largest viewing angle, but at the highest cost.

Until about the year 2000, the only practical means for recording a permanent image of the scene was the VCR real-time or TL recorder. Now, new and upgraded systems replace the VCR with the DVR recorder with its increased reliability and fast search and retrieval capabilities to distribute the recorded video over LAN, WAN, intranet, or Internet or wirelessly with WiFi using one of the 802.11 protocols.

Thermal, ink-jet, and laser hard-copy printers produce monochrome and color prints for immediate picture dissemination and permanent records for archiving.

All types of camera/lens housings are available for indoor and outdoor applications. Specialty cameras/housings are available for elevators, stairwells, dome housings for public facilities, casinos, shopping malls, extreme outdoor environments, and so forth.

Pan/tilt assemblies for indoor and outdoor scenarios significantly increase the overall FOV of the camera system. Small, compact speed domes have found widespread use in many indoor and outdoor video surveillance environments.

Plug-and-play surveillance cameras permit quick installation and turn-on and are available in almost every housing configuration and camera type.

The video components summarized above are used in most video security applications including: (1) retail stores, (2) manufacturing plants, (3) shopping malls, (4) offices, (5) airports, (6) seaports, (7) bus and rail terminals, (8) government facilities, and (9) schools and universities.

There is widespread use of small video cameras and accessories for temporary covert applications. The small size and ease of deployment of many video components and the flexibility in transmission means over short and long distances has made rapid deployment equipment for portable personnel protection systems practical and important. It is clear that the direction the video security industry is taking is the integration of the video security function with digital computing technology and the other parts of the security system: access control, intrusion alarms, fire, and two-way communications. Video security is rapidly moving from the legacy analog technology to the digital automatic video surveillance technology.

Keep in mind also that recording should be kept for 30 days unless your standards or guidelines are different.

APPENDIX: GLOSSARY OF TERMS

Many terms and definitions used in the security industry are unique to CCTV surveillance; others are derived from the electrooptical-optical and information-computer industries. This comprehensive glossary will help the reader better understand the literature, interpret manufacturers' specifications, and write bid specifications and requests for quotation. These terms encompass the OCTV, physical computer and communications industries, basic physics, electricity, mechanics, and optics.

Access control Used to control overall access, people's assets to a building complex, schools, and even transportation companies.

Analog signal Representation of data by continuously variable quantities in digital format as opposed to a finite number of discrete quantities. The electrical signal that varies continuously and does not have discrete values.

Analog television The "standard" television broadcast. Analog signals vary continuously representing fluctuations in color and brightness of a visual scent.

Aperture Opening that will pass light, electrons, or other forms of radiation. In an electron gun, the aperture determines the size of, and has an effect on, the shape of the electron beam. In television optics, the aperture is the effective diameter of the lens that controls the amount of light reaching the image sensor.

Automatic-iris control Electrooptic accessory to a lens that measures the video level of the camera and opens and closes the iris diaphragm to compensate for light changes.

Automatic light control Process by which the illumination incident upon the face of a pickup device is automatically adjusted as a function of scent brightness.

Bandwidth Data-carrying capacity of a device or network connection. The number of hertz (cycles per second) expresses the difference between the lower and upper limiting frequencies of a frequency band. Also the width of a band of frequencies.

Cable A number of electrical conductors (wires) bound in a common sheath. These may be video, data, control, or voice cables. They may also take the form of coaxial or fiber optic cables.

Camera format Video cameras have 1/6-, 1/4-, 1/3-, 1/2-, and 2/3-inch sensor image formats. The actual scanned areas used on the sensors are $3.2\,h \times 2.4\,mm$ vertical for the 1/4 inch, $4.8\,h \times 3.6\,mm\,v$ for the 1/3 inch, 6.4 horizontal $\times 4.8\,mm$ vertical for the 1/2 inch, and $8.8\,h \times 6.6\,mm\,v$ for the 2/3 inch.

Camera housing Enclosure designed to protect the video camera from tampering or theft when indoors or outdoors or from undue environmental exposure when placed outdoors.

Camera, television Electronic device containing a solid-state sensor or an electronic image tube and processing electronics. The image formed by a lens ahead of the sensor is clocked out for a solid-state sensor or rapidly scanned by a moving electron beam in a tube camera. The sensor signal output varies with the local brightness of the image on the sensor. These variations are transmitted to a CRT, LCD, or other display device, where the brightness of the scanning spot is controlled. The scanned location (pixel) at the camera and the scanned spot at the display are accurately synchronized.

Camera tube Electron tube that converts an optical image into an electrical current by a scanning process. Also called a pickup tube or television camera tube.

Candle power (cp) Light intensity expressed in candles. One foot-candle (fc) is the amount of light emitted by a standard candle at a 1-foot distance.

Closed-circuit television (CCTV) Closed television system used within a building or used on the exterior of a building or complex to visually monitor a location or activity for security or industrial purposes. CCTV does not broadcast consumer TV signals, but transmits in analog or digital form over a closed circuit via an electrically conducting cable, fiber optic cable, or wireless transmission. *CCTV monitor* is part of the CCTV system that receives the picture from the CCTV camera and displays it. *CCTV's role in security (psychological)* includes:

1. Serves as a deterrent
2. Records as a witness to various events
3. Recognition and detection
4. Connect active usage
5. Capable of watching many areas at same time
6. Records and transmits
7. Camera can pan and tilt, zoom, and be in color
8. ROI makes it worthwhile

Covert surveillance In television security, the use of camouflaged (hidden) lenses and cameras for the purpose of viewing a scene without being seen.

Digital 8 Sony format that uses Hi-8 or 8-mm tapes to store digital video.

Digital signal Video signal that is comprised from bits of binary data, otherwise known as ones and zeros (1, 0). The video signal travels from the point of its inception to the place where it is stored, and then on to the place where it is displayed as an analog or digital presentation.

Fiber optic bundle, coherent Optical component consisting of many thousands of hair-like fibers coherently assembled so that an image is transferred from one end of the bundle to the other. The length of each fiber is much greater than its diameter. The fiber bundle transmits a picture from one end of the bundle to the other, around curves, and into otherwise inaccessible places by a process of total internal reflection. The positions of all fibers at both ends are located in an exact one-to-one relationship with each other.

Fiber optic transmission Process in which light is transmitted through a long, transparent, flexible fiber, such as glass or plastic, by a series of internal reflections. For video, audio, or data transmission over long distances (thousands of feet, many miles), the light is modulated and transmitted over a single fiber in a protective insulating jacket. For light *image* transmission, closely packed bundles of fibers can transmit an entire coherent image where each single fiber transmits one component of the whole image.

Fiberscope Bundle of systematically arranged fibers that transmits a monochrome or full-color image that remains undisturbed when the bundle is bent. By mounting an objective lens on one end of the bundle and a relay or magnifying lens on the other, the system images remote objects onto a sensor.

Foot-candle (fc) Unit of illuminance on a surface 1 square foot in area on which there is incident light of 1 lumen. The illuminance of a surface placed 1 foot from a light source that has a luminous intensity of 1 candle.

Foot-lambert A measure of reflected light in a 1-foot area. A unit of luminance equal to 1 candela per square foot or to the uniform luminance at a perfectly diffusing surface emitting or reflecting light at the rate of 1 lumen per square foot.

H.264 Powerful MPEG compression algorithm standard developed through the combined effort of the ITU and MPEG organizations providing excellent compression efficiency and motion detection attributes.

Internet Protocol (IP) Method by which data are sent from one computer to another over the Internet. Each computer, known as a host on the Internet, has one address that uniquely identifies it from all other computers on the Internet. A Web page or an e-mail is sent or received by dividing it into blocks called packets. Each packet contains both the sender's Internet address and the receiver's address. Each of these packets can arrive in an order different from the order from which they were sent in. The IP just delivers them and the Transmission Control Protocol (TCP) puts them in the correct order. The most widely used version of the IP is IP Version 4 (IPv4).

IP address On the Internet, each computer and connected appliance (camera switcher, router, etc.) must have a unique address. This series of numbers functions similarly to a street address, identifying the location of both sender and recipient for information dispatched over the computer network. The IP address has 32 bits in an 8-bit quad format. The four groups in decimal format are separated by a period (.). The quad groups represent the network and the machine or host address. An example of an IP address is 124.55.19.64.

Iris Adjustable optical-mechanical aperture built into a camera lens to permit control of the amount of light passing through the lens.

Iris diaphragm Mechanical device within a lens used to control the size of the aperture through which light passes. A device for opening and closing the lens aperture to adjust the f-stop of a lens.

ISO Worldwide federation of national standards bodies from over 130 countries to promote the worldwide standardization of goods and services. The ISO has international agreements that are published as international standards. The scope of ISO covers all technical fields except electrical and electronic engineering, which is the responsibility of IEC. Among well-known ISO standards is the ISO 9000 business standard that provides a framework for quality management and quality assurance.

Joint Photographic Experts Group (JPEG) Standard group that defined a compression algorithm commonly called JPEG that is used to compress data in portrait or still video images. The JPEG file format is the ISO standard 10918 that includes 29 distinct coding processes. Not all must be used by the implementer. The JPEG file type used with the GIF format is supported by the WWW protocol, usually with the file suffix "jpg."

Lens Transparent optical component consisting of one or more optical glass elements with surfaces curved (usually spherical) so that they converge or diverge the transmitted rays of an object, thus forming a real or virtual image of that object.

Lens, Fresnel Figuratively, a lens that is cut into narrow rings and flattened out. In practice, it is a thin plastic lens that has narrow concentric rings or steps, each acting to focus radiation into an image.

Lens system Two or more lenses arranged to act in conjunction with one another.

Local Area Network (LAN) Digital network or group of network segments confined to one building or campus. Consists of a series of PCs that have been joined together via cabling so that resources can be shared, including file and print services.

Liquid Crystal Display (LCD) Solid-state video display created by sandwiching an electrically reactive substance between two electrodes. LCDs can be darkened or lightened by applying and removing power. Large numbers of LCD pixels group closely together act as pixels in a flat-panel display.

Motion J-PEG (M-JPEG) Digital video compression format developed from JPEG, a compression standard for still images. When JPEG is extended to a sequence of pictures in the video stream, it becomes M-JPEG.

Monitor CRT-based monochrome or color display for viewing a television picture from a camera output. The monitor does not incorporate a VHF or UHF tuner and channel selector and displays the composite video signal directly from the camera, DVR, VCR, or any special effects generator. Monitors take the form of a CRT, LCD, or plasma.

Multiplexer High-speed electronic switch that combines two or more video signals into a single channel to provide full-screen images up to 16 or 32 displayed simultaneously in split image format. Multiplexers can play back everything that happened on any one camera without interference from the other cameras on the system.

Pan and tilt Camera-mounting platform that allows movement in both the azimuth (pan) and the elevation (tilt) planes.

Pan, panning Rotating or scanning a camera around a vertical axis to view an area in a horizontal direction.

Pixel Short for Picture element. Any segment of a scanning line, the dimension of which along the line is exactly equal to the nominal line width. A single imaging unit that can be identified by a computer.

Radio frequency (RF) Frequency at which coherent electromagnetic radiation of energy is useful for communication purposes. The entire range of such frequencies includes the AM and FM radio spectra and the VHF and UHF television spectra.

Time-lapse recorder VCR that extends the elapsed time over which it records by recording user-selected samples of the video fields or frames instead of recording in real time. For example, recording every other field produces a 15 field per second recording and doubles the elapsed time recorded on the tape. Recording every 30th field produces a 1 field per second recording and provides 30 times the elapsed recording time.

WiFi wireless, fidelity The Institute of Electrical and Electronic Engineers (IEEE) 802.11 wireless standard for transmitting video images and other data over the airwaves between computers, access points, routers, or other digital video devices.

ACCESS CONTROL, ACCESS BADGES, AND BIOMETRICS CHARACTERISTICS FOR SCHOOLS*

22

Joseph Nelson, CPP

Vice president of global security, State Street Corporation

INTRODUCTION

More and more schools today are getting involved with access control and biometrics. In this chapter, I will be discussing the concepts of access control, badges, photo identification badges, and visitor and vendor badges.

ACCESS CONTROL

Perimeter barriers, intrusion detection devices, and protective lighting provide physical security safeguards; however, they alone are not enough. An access control system must be established and maintained to preclude unauthorized entry. Effective access control procedures also prevent the introduction of harmful devices, materials, and components. They minimize the misappropriation, pilferage, or the compromise of material or recorded information by controlling packages, material, and property movement. Access control rosters, personal recognition, ID cards, badge exchange procedures, and personal escorts all contribute to an effective access control system.

DESIGNATED RESTRICTED AREAS

The school principal or school district is responsible for designating and establishing restricted areas. A restricted area is any area that is subject to special restrictions or controls for security reasons. Restricted areas may be established for the following reasons:

- The enforcement of security measures and the exclusion of unauthorized personnel,
- Intensified controls in areas requiring special protection, and
- The protection of classified information or critical equipment or materials.

---

* Originally from Nelson J. Access Control, Access Badges, and Biometrics Characteristics. *Handbook of Loss Prevention and Crime Prevention.* Boston, MA: Butterworth-Heinemann; 2012. Updated by the author, Elsevier, 2013.

DEGREE OF SECURITY FOR YOUR SCHOOL

The degree of security and control required depends upon the nature, sensitivity, or importance of the confidential information. Restricted areas are classified as controlled, limited, or exclusion areas as follows:

- A controlled area is that portion of a restricted area usually near or surrounding a limited or exclusion area. Entry to the controlled area is restricted to personnel with a need for access. Movement of authorized personnel within this area is not necessarily controlled since mere entry to the area does not provide access to the security interest. The controlled area is provided for administrative control, for safety, or as a buffer zone for in-depth security for the limited or exclusion area. The commander establishes the control of movement.
- A limited area is a restricted area within close proximity of a security interest. Uncontrolled movement may permit access to the item. Escorts and other internal restrictions may prevent access within limited areas.
- An exclusion area is a restricted area containing a security interest. A restricted area must be designated in writing by the school principal or school district and must be posted with warning signs. In areas where English is one of two or more languages commonly spoken, warning signs will be posted in English and in the local language. Different areas of the school may have varying degrees of security. It may be designated in its entirety as a restricted area, with no further restrictions, or it may be subdivided into controlled, limited, or exclusion areas with restrictions of movement and specific clear zones, depicting a simplified restricted area and the degrees of security.

CONSIDERATIONS

There are other important considerations concerning restricted areas and their lines of division. These considerations include the following:

- *A survey and analysis of the school and its security interests.* This can determine immediate and anticipated needs that require protection. Anticipated needs are determined from plans for the future.
- *The size and nature of the school being protected.* Safes may provide adequate protection for classified documents and small items; however, large items may have to be placed within a secure enclosure.
- *Some security interests are more sensitive to compromise than others.* Brief observation or a simple act by an untrained person may constitute a compromise in some cases. In others, detailed study and planned action by an expert may be required.
- *All security interests should be evaluated according to their importance.* This may be indicated by a security classification such as confidential.

PERIMETER ACCESS CONTROL

Parking areas for the privately owned vehicles (POVs) of faculty, staff, visitors, and students should be established. Vehicle entrances must be kept to a minimum for safe and efficient control. Consider physical protective measures (such as fences, gates, and window bars).

EMPLOYEE SCREENING

Screening faculty, staff, contractors, and volunteers to eliminate the potential for crime and other security risks is important. Personnel screenings must be incorporated into standard personnel policies. An applicant should be required to complete a personnel security questionnaire, which is then screened for completeness and used to eliminate undesirable applicants. A careful investigation should be conducted to ensure that the applicant's character, associations, and suitability for employment are satisfactory.

The following sources may be helpful in securing employment investigative data:

- State and local police (including national and local police in overseas areas)
- Former employers
- Public records
- Credit agencies
- Schools attended (all levels)
- Information and data protection (records, examinations, etc.)
- References (These references should include those names not furnished by the applicant. These are known as throw-offs, and they are obtained during interviews of references furnished by applicants.)

Once an applicant has been identified for employment, he/she is placed on an access control roster.

IDENTIFICATION SYSTEM

An ID system is established at each school to provide a method of identifying personnel. The system provides for personal recognition and the use of security ID cards or badges to aid in the control and movement of personnel activities.

Standard ID cards are generally acceptable for access into areas that are unrestricted. Personnel requiring access to restricted areas should be issued a security ID card or badge. The design of the card/badge must be simple and provide for adequate control of personnel.

ID METHODS

Four of the most common access control ID methods are the personal recognition system, the single card/badge system, the card or badge exchange system, and the multiple card/badge system.

PERSONAL RECOGNITION SYSTEM

The personal recognition system is the simplest of all systems. A SRO, security officer, or receptionist responsible for providing access control visually checks the person requesting entry. Entry is granted based on:

1. The individual being recognized;
2. The need to enter being established; and
3. The presence of the person on an access control roster.

SINGLE CARD/BADGE SYSTEM

This system reflects permission to enter specific areas by the badge depicting specific letters, numbers, or particular colors. Because the ID cards/badges frequently remain in the employee's possession while not at school, it affords the opportunity for alteration or duplication.

CARD/BADGE EXCHANGE SYSTEM

In this system, two cards/badges contain identical photographs. Each card/badge has a different background color, or one card/badge has an overprint. One card/badge is presented at the entrance to a specific area and exchanged for the second card/badge, which is worn or carried while in that area. Individual possession of the second card/badge occurs only while the employee is in the area for which it was issued. When leaving the area, the second card/badge is returned and maintained in the access control area. This method provides a greater degree of security and decreases the possibility of forgery, alteration, or duplication of the card/badge. This level of protection requires multiple access control elements as the levels of protection increase. In the case of badge exchange, this system counts as two access control elements.

MULTIPLE CARD/BADGE SYSTEM

This system provides the greatest degree of security. Instead of having specific markings on the cards/badges denoting permission to enter various restricted areas, the multiple card/badge system makes an exchange at the entrance to each security area. The card/badge information is identical and allows for comparisons. Exchange cards/badges are maintained at each area only for individuals who have access to the specific area.

MECHANIZED/AUTOMATED SYSTEMS

An alternative to using security officers to visually check cards/badges and access rosters is to use building card access systems or biometric access readers. These systems can control the flow of personnel entering and exiting a school. Included in these systems are:

- Coded devices such as mechanical or electronic keypads or combination locks,
- Credential devices such as magnetic stripe or proximity card readers, and
- Biometric devices such as fingerprint readers or retina scanners.

Access control and ID systems base their judgment factor on a remote capability through a routine discriminating device for positive ID. These systems do not require security officers or a receptionist at entry points; they identify an individual in the following manner:

- The system receives physical ID data from an individual.
- The data are encoded and compared to stored information.
- The system determines whether access is authorized.
- The information is translated into readable results.

Specialized mechanical systems are ideal for highly sensitive situations because they use a controlled process in a controlled environment to establish the required database and accuracy. One innovative technique applied to ID and admittance procedures involves dimension comparisons. The dimension of a person's full hand is compared to previously stored data to determine entry authorization. Other specialized machine readers can scan a single fingerprint or an eye retina and provide positive ID of anyone attempting entry.

An all-inclusive automated ID and access control system reinforces the security in-depth ring through its easy and rapid change capability. The computer is able to do this through its memory. Changes can be made quickly by the system's administrator.

The commercial security market has a wide range of mechanized and automated hardware and software systems. Automated equipment is chosen only after considering the security needs and the school environment in which it operates. These considerations include whether the equipment is outdoors or indoors, the temperature range, and weather conditions. Assessment of security needs and the use of planning, programming, and budgeting procedures greatly assist a security director in improving the security posture.

CARD/BADGE SPECIFICATIONS

Security cards/badges should be designed and constructed to meet the necessary requirements. Upon issuing a card/badge, security personnel must explain to the employee that they must wear the badge and about the authorizations that are allowed with the card/badge. This includes:

- Designation of the areas where an ID card/badge is required
- A description of the type of card/badge in use and the authorizations and limitations placed on the individual
- The required presentation of the card/badge when entering or leaving each area during all hours of the day
- Details of when, where, and how the card/badge should be worn, displayed, or carried
- Procedures to follow in case of loss or damage of the card
- The disposition of the card/badge upon termination of employment, investigations, or personnel actions
- Prerequisites for reissuing the card/badge

VISITOR IDENTIFICATION AND LOBBY CONTROL IN YOUR SCHOOL

Procedures must be implemented to properly identify and control personnel. This includes visitors and vendors presenting their cards/badges to receptionist, security officer, or SRO at entrances of restricted areas. Visitors are required to stay with their assigned escort. Receptionists, security officers, or SROs must ensure that visitors stay in areas relating to their visit; an uncontrolled visitor, although conspicuously identified, could acquire information for which he is not authorized.

Approval for visitors should be obtained at least 24 hours in advance (if possible). Where appropriate, the school should prepare an agenda for the visitor and designate an escort individual. Measures must be in place to recover visitor cards/badges on the visit's expiration or when they are no longer required.

Physical security precautions against pilferage and other crimes require the screening, ID, and control of visitors. Further information about visiting requirements and procedures should be in your school policy and procedures.

Visitors or vendors are generally classed in the following categories:

- Persons with whom every school in the district has business (such as a supplier or vendor).
- Individuals or groups who desire to visit a school for personal or educational reasons. Such visits may be approved by the principal, faculty, or staff.
- Guided tours to selected areas of the school in the interest of public relations. The ID and control mechanisms for visitors must be in place. They may include the following:
  - Methods of establishing the authority for admitting visitors and any limitations relative to access should be used.
  - Positive ID of visitors by personal recognition, visitor permit, or other identifying credentials. Contact the principal, faculty, or a staff member to validate the visit.
  - The use of visitor registration forms. These forms provide a record of the visitor and the time, location, and duration of his visit.
  - The use of visitor ID cards/badges. The cards/badges bear serial numbers, the area or areas to which access is authorized, the individual's name, and escort requirements.

Individual groups entering the school must meet specific prerequisites before being granted access. The following guidance is for group access into a school:

VISITORS

Before allowing visitors into a school, contact the person or activity being visited. After verifying the visitor's identity, issue a badge, complete the registration forms, and assign an escort (if required). Visitors may include public utility and commercial service representatives.

CLEANING TEAMS

Schools using contractors for cleaning services must seek advice from the principal or school district. This may include providing escorts.

STUDENTS, FACULTY, AND STAFF IN THE SCHOOL AFTER NORMAL OPERATING HOURS

The principal must establish internal controls based on coordination with the SRP or security officer. They also must notify security personnel about the date when an activity or event will be held and for what duration.

ENFORCEMENT MEASURES

The most vulnerable link in any ID system is its enforcement. Security officers must be proactive in performing their duties. Positive enforcement measures must be prescribed to enhance security. Some of these measures may include the following:

ACCESS CONTROL

- Designate alert and tactful SROs, security officers, or receptionists at entry control points.
- Ensure that access control personnel possess quick perception and good judgment.
- Require entry control personnel to conduct frequent irregular checks of their assigned areas.
- Formalize standard procedures for posting and relieving security personnel. These measures will prevent posting of unqualified personnel and a routine performance of duty.
- Prescribe a uniform method of handling or wearing security ID cards/badges. If carried on person, the card must be removed from the wallet (or other holder) and handed to security personnel. When worn, the badge will be worn in a conspicuous position to expedite inspection and recognition from a distance.
- Designate entry and exit control points of the school to force individuals to pass in a single file in front of security personnel. In some instances, the use of turnstiles may be advisable to assist in maintaining positive control.
- Provide lighting at control points. The lighting must illuminate the area to enable access control personnel to compare the individual with the ID card/badge.
- Enforce access control measures by educating students, faculty, staff, vendors, contractors, and visitors. Enforcement of access control systems rests primarily with the SRO, security officer, or receptionist; however, it is essential that they have the full cooperation of everyone. Students, faculty, and staff must be instructed to consider each unidentified or improperly identified individual as a trespasser and report this to the office.
- Position ID card/badge racks or containers at entry control points so they are accessible only to the SRO, security officer, or receptionist.
- Appoint a responsible custodian to accomplish control procedures of cards/badges according to policy manual. The custodian is responsible for the issue, turn in, recovery, and renewal of security ID cards/badges as well as monthly verification of individuals in various areas and the deletion of terminated faculty or staff badges.

The degree of compromise tolerable in the ID system is in direct proportion to the degree of security required. The following control procedures are recommended for preserving the integrity of a card/badge system:

- Maintenance of an accurate written record or log listing (by serial number) all cards and badges and showing those on hand, to whom they are issued, and their disposition (lost, mutilated, or destroyed)
- Authentication of records and logs by the custodian
- A periodic inventory of records by the security manager or principal
- The prompt invalidation of lost cards/badges and the conspicuous posting at security control points of current lists of lost or invalidated cards/badges
- The establishment of controls within the school to enable the SRO, security officer, or receptionist to determine the number of persons in the school
- The establishment of the two-person rule (when required)
- The establishment of procedures to control the movement of visitors. A visitor control record will be maintained and located at entry points.

DURESS CODE

The duress code is a simple word or phrase used during normal conversation to alert other personnel that an authorized person is under duress. A duress code requires planning and rehearsal to ensure an appropriate response. This code is changed frequently to minimize compromise.

ACCESS-CONTROL ROSTERS

Admission of personnel to a restricted area is granted to those identified and listed on an access control roster. Pen-and-ink changes may be made to the roster. Changes are published in the same manner as the original roster.

Rosters are maintained at access control points. They are kept current, verified, and accounted for by an individual designated by a manager. This manager or their designated representatives authenticate the rosters. Admission of persons other than those on the rosters is subject to specific approval by the principal or another specific member of the faculty or staff. These personnel may require an escort according to the local SOP.

METHODS OF CONTROL

There are a number of methods available to assist in the movement and control of personnel in schools. The following paragraphs discuss the use of escorts and the two-person rule.

ESCORTS

Escorts are chosen because of their ability to accomplish tasks effectively and properly. They possess knowledge of the area being visited. Escorts may be an SRO or security officer. The SOPs of the individual school will determine if a visitor requires an escort while in the building. Individuals on the access list may be admitted to restricted areas without an escort.

TWO-PERSON RULE

The two-person rule is designed to prohibit access to areas where confidential information or high-value equipment are stored. Two authorized persons must be present at all times in these areas. They should be familiar with applicable safety and security requirements of the area. When application of the two-person rule is required, it is enforced consistently by those who make up the team.

The two-person rule is applied in many other aspects of physical security operations, such as the following:

- When uncontrolled access to student records and personal identifying information might provide opportunity for intentional or unintentional damage
- When uncontrolled access to funds could provide opportunity for diversion by falsification of accounts
- When uncontrolled delivery or receipt for materials could provide opportunity for pilferage through "short" deliveries and false receipts

The two-person rule is limited to the creativity of the school district or the principal of the school. They should explore every aspect of physical security operations in which the two-person rule would provide additional security and assurance and include all appropriate recommendations and provisions of the physical security plan. An electronic entry control system may be used to enforce the two-person rule. The system can be programmed to deny access until two authorized people have successfully entered codes or swiped cards.

SECURITY CONTROLS OF PACKAGES, PERSONAL PROPERTY, AND VEHICLES

A good package control system helps prevent or minimize pilferage or theft. The SOP of the school may allow the entry of packages with proper authorization into the school. A package-checking system is used at the access control point. When practical, inspect all outgoing packages except those properly authorized for removal. When a 100% inspection is impractical, conduct frequent unannounced spot checks. A good package control system assists in the movement of authorized packages, material, and property.

Property controls are not limited to packages carried openly, and they include the control of anything that could be used to conceal property or material. Faculty and staff should *not* be routinely searched, except in unusual situations. Searches must be performed according to the school SOP.

All POVs on the campus should be registered with the school's physical security office. Security personnel should assign a temporary decal or other temporary ID tag to visitors' vehicles to permit ready recognition. The decal or the tag should be distinctly different from that of school students, faculty, or staff.

The best control is provided when all of these elements are incorporated into access control procedures. Simple, understandable, and workable access control procedures are used to achieve security objectives without impeding school operations. When properly organized and administered, access control procedures provide a method of positively identifying school students, faculty, staff, contractors, vendors, or visitors.

BUILDING DESIGN

When designing, building, and installing engineered security controls, security practitioners must consider a variety of factors to ensure optimum results. While not doing so can leave access control systems prone to nuisance alarms, it can also lead to limited or no authorization controls at all. Your objective should be to prevent penetration and provide authorized access through layered levels of security on your campus.

LAYERED LEVELS OF SECURITY

The outer perimeter/outer protective layer can be a man-made barrier controlling both traffic and people flow. The inner layer contains the interior lobby and main entrance, turnstiles, revolving doors, handicap gates, elevators, emergency door alarms, and private occupied space. The inner protective layer contains biometrics, mirrors, and video surveillance applications. The middle layer consists of exterior parts of the building.

High-security areas are laid within the inner layer with limited access to a select few. Reducing opportunity within your complex's design must be tailored to the specific area's environment.

When designing administrative controls for access control, one must consider the tolerance for process errors. This means we should consider the percentage of unauthorized transactions we can allow with minimal consequence. While engineered controls make a significant difference controlling access capabilities, our tolerance for mistakes or errors in access control often equally relate to the administrative controls that rule the measurement of results and prove our access control levels are operating at the desired levels.

ACCESS CARDS

1. *Proximity cards.* Proximity access cards are often used for schools. They work via the use of passively tuned circuits that have been embedded in a high-grade fiberglass epoxy card. One can gain access when the cardholder holds the card within two to four inches from a card reader. The reader's sensor detects the pattern of the frequencies programmed in the card, and it communicates with the sensor by electromagnetic, ultrasound, or optical transmission. This pattern is then transmitted to the system's computer. If the pattern matches that of the reader, the reader unlocks the door and records the transaction. If the pattern does not match, no access is granted and this transaction is recorded.

2. *Magnetic stripe cards.* Magnetic cards use various kinds of materials and mediums to magnetically encode digital data onto cards. To gain access, the card user inserts or "swipes" (passes the badge through) the card reader. As the card is withdrawn from the reader, it moves across a magnetic head, similar to that in a tape recorder head, that reads the data programmed in the card. The information read from the card is sent to the system's computer for verification. If verification is made, the computer sends a signal to the card reader to grant or deny access, and if access is granted, the door is unlocked. Magnetic cards look like regular credit cards. The most popular medium for this type of access card is a magnetic stripe on which a pattern of digital data is encoded. This type of card is relatively inexpensive and a large amount of data can be stored magnetically compared to other kinds of magnetic media. These cards tend to chip and break, however, through excessive use.

3. *Weigand cards.* Weigand-based access control cards use a coded pattern on magnetized wire embedded within the card. When this card is inserted into a reader, the reader's internal sensors are activated by the coded wire. This type of card is moderately priced and will handle a large amount of traffic. It is less vulnerable to vandalism and weather effects than other types of cards, but it does stand up to a considerable amount of wear and tear.

4. *Biometrics access control.* Biometrics is most accurate when using one or more fingerprints, palm prints or palm scan, hand geometry, or retina and iris scan. Remember deterrent controls delay unauthorized access. Think *proactive management.*

5. *Biometric ID systems operate locks to doors.* Used in high-security areas where limited access is maintained, this system checks physical characteristics that verify and allow access/entry.

6. *Smart cards.* These contain an integrated chip embedded in them. They have coded memories and microprocessors; hence, they are like computers. The technology in these cards offers many possibilities, particularly with proximity card access control systems. Optical cards have a pattern of light spots that can be read by a specific light source, usually infrared. Capacitance cards use coded capacitor-sensitive material that is enclosed in the card. A current is induced when the card activates a reader that checks the capacitance of the card to determine the proper access code. Some access devices come in the shape of keys, disks, or other convenient formats that provide users with access tools that look attractive and subdued but at the same time are functional.

7. *Dual technology card.* Some cards have dual technology, such as magnetic stripe/proximity card and a radio frequency identification (RFID)/proximity card.

8. *Card readers.* Card Readers are devices used for reading access cards. Readers come in various shapes, sizes, and configurations. The most common reader is the type where the card user inserts the card in a slot or runs or "swipes" the card through a slot. The other type of reader uses proximity technology where the card user presents or places the card on or near the reader. Some insertion-type card readers use keypads; after the user inserts the card, the user enters a unique code number on the keypad. This action then grants access.

9. *Electronic access control (EAC) systems applications.* Ideally used as part of a fully integrated facility management system. In such a system, EAC is interfaced and integrated with fire safety/ life safety systems, video surveillance systems, communication systems, and nonsecurity systems such as heating, ventilation, and air conditioning (HVAC). In an integrated system, EAC systems allow users access to various areas or limited areas. They can track access and provide attendance records. As a safety feature and for emergency response situations, they can determine where persons are located in facilities. In general, EAC systems are very flexible and strides in technology have made them even more so.

This section barely covers all that you need to know about EAC. The best way to learn about EAC is to actually work with EAC systems. Take advantage of every opportunity to work with EAC systems. Seek assignments where EAC systems are used and ask questions to control room operators, your supervisors, and EAC vendors and service technicians. There are many excellent sources where you can read about EAC and related systems.

BADGES

There are many types of badges. Badges with color coding can be used for various reasons that may include designating years of service, clearance levels, departments, and/or locations. In addition, there is video badging, which displays a school logo or a special design and may be color coded and there are badges incorporating digitized data or a photograph.

When badges are initially introduced to a school's security system, it would appear to be a simple process, until some of the questions and concerns we have identified below arise:

1. If an individual loses their badge, it costs $10 to replace. Some schools allow one "free" replacement easily.

2. When a faculty or staff member is terminated, who retrieves the badge, keys, or other school property? Are all school badges deleted if not used in 30 days?

3. If a badge is stolen, what is the process to render it useless?
4. If a badge is borrowed or used by an unauthorized person(s), has sufficient data been included? Height, weight, and color of eyes and hair can be included by using both sides of the card.
5. Database for badges? Are principals required to give written permission before access is granted?
6. Identify access levels and authorization process.
7. Consider all potential vulnerabilities and the risk of threats.

BIOMETRICS CHARACTERISTICS[1]

Biometrics characteristics are often classed in two main categories:

1. *Physiological Biometrics.* Features notably identified through the five senses and processed by finite calculable differences: sight (how a person looks including things like hair and eye color, teeth, or facial features), sound (the pitch of a person's voice), smell (a person's odor or scent), taste (the composition of a person's saliva or DNA), and touch (such as fingerprints or handprints).
2. *Behavioral Biometrics.* Based on the manner in which people conduct themselves, such as writing style, walking rhythm, typing speed, and so forth.

In order for any of these characteristics to be used for sustained identification encryption purposes, they must be reliable, unique, collectable, convenient, long term, universal, and acceptable.

TYPES OF BIOMETRICS DEVICES

Iris cameras. They perform *recognition* detection of a person's identity by mathematical analysis of the random patterns that are visible within the iris of an eye from some distance. It combines computer vision, pattern recognition, statistical inference, and optics.

Iris recognition. This is rarely impeded by glasses or contact lenses and can be scanned from 10 cm to a few meters away. The iris remains stable over time as long as there are no injuries, and a single enrollment scan can last a lifetime.

Fingerprints. Formed when the friction ridges of the skin come in contact with a surface that is receptive to a print by using an agent to form the print, such as perspiration, oil, ink, grease, and so forth. The agent is transferred to the surface and leaves an impression which forms the fingerprint.

Hand scanner and finger reader recognition systems. These measure and analyze the overall structure, shape, and proportions of the hand, such as length, width, and thickness of hand, fingers, and joints and characteristics of the skin surface such as creases and ridges.

Facial recognition device. This views an image or video of a person and compares it to one in the database. It does this by comparing structure, shape, and proportions of the face; distance between the eyes, nose, mouth, and jaw; upper outlines of the eye sockets; the sides of the mouth; location of the nose and eyes; and the area surrounding the cheek bones. The main *facial recognition* methods are feature analysis, neural network, eigenfaces, and automatic face processing.

---

[1] Biometrics Characteristic, www.findBiometrics.com.

Voice recognition voiceprint. This is a spectrogram, which is a graph that shows a sound's frequency on the vertical axis and time on the horizontal axis. Different types of speech create different shapes on the graph. Spectrograms also use color or shades of gray to represent the acoustical qualities of sound.

Smart card. A pocket-sized plastic card with an embedded chip that can process data. It is used in industries such as education, health care, banking, government, and *biometrics*. Smart cards can process data via input and output of information and is essentially a mini processor. They can provide identification, authentication, data storage, as well as other services in an educational setting.

Digital biometrics signature. This is equivalent to a traditional *handwritten* signature in many respects because a properly implemented signature is more difficult to forge than the traditional type. Digital signature schemes are *cryptographically* based and must be implemented properly to be effective. Digital signatures can be used for e-mail, contracts, or any message sent via some other *cryptographic protocol*.

Vein recognition. This is a biometric method for recognizing individual people based on unique physical and behavioral traits. Physiological biometrics is one class of biometrics that deals with physical characteristics and attributes that are unique to individuals. Vein recognition is a type of biometrics that can be used to identify individuals based on the vein patterns in the human finger.

FIRE ALARM SYSTEMS FOR SCHOOLS

Jack Poole, PE, FSFPE
Principal, Poole Fire Protection, Inc.

INTRODUCTION

A school fire alarm system is a key element of its overall fire protection features. Fire alarm systems that are properly designed, installed, operated, tested, and maintained can help save lives and limit property loss, regardless of the occupancy. The fire alarm system is generally intended to indicate and warn personnel of abnormal conditions, summon appropriate emergency responders, and control occupant features to enhance the protection of life.

FIRE CODES

As a result of several well-publicized tragic fires in the 1970s and 1980s, many regulatory jurisdictions such as cities, counties, and states reviewed their building and fire codes and regulations and strengthened the protection requirements to help reduce the loss of life and property. The most prevalent fire safety codes and standards known throughout the USA are the ones developed by the National Fire Protection Association (NFPA). Many of these codes and standards are adopted by regulatory jurisdictions. Similarly, model building codes are developed by private associations for modification and adoption by the regulatory jurisdictions. Prior to 1994, there were three primary model building code organizations: Building Officials and Code Administrators (BOCA), Southern Building Code Congress International (SBCCI), and International Conference of Building Officials (ICBO). Starting in 1994, these three model building code organizations collaborated to develop a single combined organization known as the International Code Council (ICC), which over time replaced their three individual building codes into a single model building code. NFPA has also developed a model building code known as NFPA 5000, *Building Construction and Safety Code*. The requirements in the model building codes as it relates to fire alarm and emergency communication systems (ECSs) typically define the following components:

1. Occupancy classification
2. Location of smoke detection
3. Function of the fire alarm and ECS
4. Operation of the voice/alarm functionality of the system
5. Provision for a fire department communication system
6. Components of the fire command station

7. Power requirements for the system
8. Location of manual pull stations
9. Exit door unlocking requirements

The last two decades of fire alarm system development has overshadowed the fire alarm systems from the previous 100 years of development. Over the years, fire alarm systems have evolved from telegraph systems to signal multiplexing, from the manual ringing of a bell to automatic voice communication systems, from hardwired connections to fiber optics and wireless transmission, from unsupervised smoke detectors to addressable and analog-initiating devices that report their status, from a relay-based architecture fire alarm control units that dubbed "solid state" because of their weight and physical size to today's microprocessor-based control units, and from fire detectors that required huge fires to actuate to smoke detectors that are capable of detecting the fire before you can either smell or see the smoke.

All of the technology developments of the fire alarm systems have influenced and contributed to the development and changes of the fire alarm codes and standards, which are used to detail the performance criteria, and establish the installation requirements, inspection, testing, and maintenance requirements of today's fire alarm systems.

Through the evolution of fire alarm systems, systems were designed and installed to be stand-alone systems which were meant only to detect a fire and provide notification of a fire. Today's system stretches well beyond a stand-alone fire alarm system to a combined and integrated system with the capability: to detect fires from standard conventional means of smoke, thermal, and flame detection to the latest technology using very early smoke detection technology to video detection; to monitor and control security features for a facility; to providing multiple methods of notification of a variety of emergency events using multiple technologies of notification such as voice messaging, visual notification, distributed recipient messaging such as text and email notifications, pop-up on computer screens and message monitors to notify occupants of all types of emergency events such as bomb threats, severe weather, hazardous material incidents, and fire, just to name a few.

It is important to understand the fire protection goals for the system. The fire protection goals of the system will establish the baseline for detection, notification, and operation of the system. The need and design of fire alarm systems for schools are typically driven by the requirements of the building and life safety codes; therefore, the owner's fire protection goal may be as basic as to comply with the *International Building Code (IBC)* or the *International Fire Code* developed by the ICC or the NFPA 101, *Life Safety Code*. When an owner chooses to follow the prescriptive requirements for the code, this typically results in following the minimum requirements of that code as the fire protection goal. Most building codes have been developed to prevent citywide conflagrations and offer minimum occupant protection. In summary, the codes typically specify the minimum requirements to build and occupy a building. Owners or designers may want to consider other fire protection goals for facilities such as life safety, property protection, mission protection, heritage preservation, environmental protection, or multiple methods of notification.

Understanding the local code requirements is often confusing when it comes to the requirements for when a building fire alarm system is required. Typically, local and state jurisdictions adopt building and fire codes. The most prevalent building code adopted is the IBC, which is based on the occupancy classification for a facility that will determine if a fire alarm system is required, and if so, whether that system shall be automatic or manual and if detection is required. Some jurisdictions may also adopt various NFPA codes and standards. A very widely known NFPA code that will also contain requirements for when a fire alarm system is required is the NFPA 101, Life Safety Code.

NFPA 72, National Fire Alarm and Signaling Code, is the industry standard which covers the application, installation, location, performance, inspection, testing, and maintenance of fire alarm systems, supervising station alarm systems, public emergency alarm reporting systems, fire warning equipment and ECSs, and their components. The purpose of NFPA 72 is to define the means of signal initiation, transmission, notification, and annunciation; the levels of performance; and the reliability of the various types of fire alarm systems, supervising station alarm systems, public emergency alarm reporting systems, fire warning equipment, ECSs, and their components. It is important to understand that NFPA 72 does not establish the requirements for when a building is required to be provided with a fire alarm system, but basically establishes the requirements on how to design, install, and test a fire alarm system.

Local codes and NFPA 72 typically require that all equipment used in a fire alarm system be listed by an independent nationally recognized testing agency for the appropriate signaling purpose. As part of the listing and testing process, a sample of each fire alarm system component is tested to confirm its compliance with one or more of the testing laboratory's standards. Furthermore, subsequent follow-up inspections are conducted at the manufacturer's facilities to ensure continued compliance with the appropriate test standard for the respective component. The two most well-known testing laboratories in the USA are Underwriters Laboratories, Inc. (UL) and Factory Mutual Global Technologies (FM). Both UL and FM test fire alarm equipment and components to determine the suitability of the equipment or component for its intended service, and test for compliance with appropriate NFPA codes and standards.

Once the owner and the designer have established the fire protection goals, the fire alarm system type, application, and operation should be integrated with these goals. The type of system installed will vary depending on building occupancy, location, operations conducted in the facility, and the local or state requirements. Typically, the fire protection goals will determine the extent and the type of detection, sequence of operation, level, and method of notification and type of off-premise connection to transmit any alarm, supervisory, and trouble signals.

A fire alarm system, whether it is automatically activated by some type of detection or manually activated, will notify people inside or outside the building that some level of emergency action should be taken to respond to the condition. The system might also be designed to initiate the actuation of an automatic suppression system, such as a preaction or deluge sprinkler system, foam extinguishing system, or a clean agent suppression system.

Although there are basic requirements to all fire alarm systems, specific features of each system should include: primary and secondary power, alarm, supervisory, and trouble signals, supervision of the system and circuitry, and so on—these must be carefully considered by the designer for each fire alarm system.

The initiating devices installed as part of a fire alarm system, such as manual pull stations, smoke detectors, water flow or pressure switch, tamper switches, and so on, are connected to either the initiating device circuit (IDC) or the signaling line circuit (SLC). Generally, addressable or intelligent devices such as smoke detectors, monitor modules, and control modules are connected to the SLC, and the nonintelligent devices such as water flow and tamper switches are connected via the IDC. Notification appliances such as horns, strobes, speakers, bells, and so on, are connected to the notification appliance circuit (NAC).

NFPA 72

NFPA 72 breaks alarm systems down into three separate categories. The first is the "fire alarm system," which consists of a system or portion of a combination system that consists of components and circuits arranged to monitor and annunciate the status of fire alarm or supervisory signal-initiating devices and to initiate the appropriate response to those signals. The second is a "supervising station alarm system," which is a system that monitors and receives the alarm, supervisory, and trouble signals from fire alarm systems and transmits the alarm condition to the municipal communication center. The third category of the alarm system is the "public emergency alarm reporting system." The public emergency alarm reporting system is a system of alarm-initiating devices, transmitting and receiving equipment, and communication infrastructure (other than a public telephone network) used to communicate with the municipal communications center to provide any combination of manual or auxiliary alarm service.

NFPA 72 classifies fire alarm systems into two different classifications, which are based on the type of functions they are expected to perform. The first system is a protected premises fire alarm system, which is where the entire fire alarm system operates within the protected premise, responsive to the operation of manual pull stations, water flow switch of a sprinkler system, or detection of fire by smoke or heat. This system will provide alarm and supervisory signals within a facility and produce notification signals at the facility only. The protected premises fire alarm system may also perform automatic control functions such as closing smoke dampers, releasing fire doors, de-energizing computer equipment, and shutting down heating, ventilating, and air conditioning (HVAC) systems.

The second type of system is a household fire alarm system. A household fire alarm system is a system of devices that uses a fire alarm control unit to produce an alarm signal in the household for the purpose of notifying the occupants of the presence of a fire so that they will evacuate the premises. These systems are installed primarily in residential occupants and are not permitted to be installed in schools.

Supervising station alarm systems are further defined into three different types: (1) central station (service) alarm systems, (2) remote supervising station alarm systems, and (3) proprietary supervising station alarm systems.

The central station alarm system is a system or a group of systems including the protected premises fire alarm system(s) in which the operations of circuits and devices are signaled to, recorded in, and supervised from a listed central station that has competent and experienced operators who, upon receipt of a signal, take such action as required by NFPA 72. Related activities at the protected premises, such as equipment installation, inspection, testing, maintenance, and runner service, are the responsibility of the central station or a listed alarm service local company. Central station service is controlled and operated by a person, firm, or corporation whose business is the furnishing of such contracted services or whose properties are the protected premises.

A remote supervising station is a system including the protected premises fire alarm system(s) in which the operations of circuits and devices are signaled to, recorded in, and supervised from a supervising station that has competent and experienced operators who, upon receipt of a signal, take such action as required by this NFPA 72. Related activities at the protected premises, such as equipment installation, inspection, testing, and maintenance, are the responsibility of the owner.

A proprietary supervising station alarm system is a system or a group of systems including the protected premises fire alarm system(s) in which the operations of circuits and devices are signaled to, recorded in, and supervised from a supervising station under the same ownership as the protected premises that has competent and experienced operators who, upon receipt of a signal, take such action as required by NFPA 72. Related activities at the protected premises, such as equipment installation, inspection, testing, maintenance, and runner service, are the responsibility of the owner. Proprietary supervising station service is controlled and operated by the entity whose properties are the protected premises.

In summary, the primary difference between the three different types of supervising station alarm systems is that a central station alarm system is a listed station, typically run by a for-profit company, where the operation of the system is more regulated and controlled by specific criteria than a remote supervising station or proprietary supervising station. The remote supervising station is also typically run by a for-profit company, but the operation of the system is not as controlled and regulated as that of a listed central station. The proprietary supervising station alarm system is typically under the same control as the entity whose properties are the protected premises. All three types of supervising station alarm systems have the responsibility to receive signals from fire alarm system and transmit the alarm condition to the municipal communication center.

The public emergency alarm reporting system is typically a system operated by a municipality. The most prevalent category of public emergency alarm reporting system is an auxiliary alarm system, which transmits alarm signals to a public or municipal emergency alarm reporting system to the communications center. The circuits of an auxiliary alarm system connect the alarm-initiating devices to a municipal fire alarm system. This connection is made through a transmitter, a master box, or a dedicated telephone line run directly to the municipal connection center switchboard. These types of systems are not as prevalent as they were years ago, but they still do exist in parts of the United States.

A fire alarm system has the capability of producing three different types of signals: alarm, supervisory, and trouble. An alarm signal is a signal indicating an emergency requiring immediate action initiated from automatic or manual detection of an alarm condition from a device such as a manual pull station, water flow alarm, smoke detector, or some other method of detection. A supervisory signal is a signal that results from the detection of a supervisory condition, indicating the need for action. A supervisory signaling device is a device that is not intended to create an emergency need but a supervisory device that is designed to transmit a warning of something that may affect the operation of a fire suppression system, such as an electronic tamper switch on a control valve controlling water to a sprinkler system, low water level in a water storage tank, low-temperature switch in an area monitoring a sprinkler system riser, or other similar device. A trouble signal is an audible or visual signal transmitted to warn of a trouble condition such as an open or short circuit, ground fault on a fire alarm circuit, or even the loss of AC or DC power for a fire alarm system.

Both the IBC and NFPA 101 require a manual fire alarm system to be installed for educational occupancies. The intent of a manual fire alarm system is to provide manual pull stations at the exits of the building to initiate the alarm signal. However, the IBC will require most schools constructed today to be provided with an automatic sprinkler system due to the type of construction used or the size of the building. If the school is fully sprinklered as required by NFPA 13, Standard for the Installation of Sprinkler Systems, manual pull stations are not required at every exit, as permitted by an exception in the IBC. Furthermore, smoke detection throughout the entire school is not required. Typically, smoke detectors are only required by the building or life safety codes above the fire alarm system control panels, at elevator lobbies, shaft and machine rooms (if provided), and in HVAC ductwork as required by NFPA 90A, Standard for the Installation of Air-Conditioning and Ventilating Systems, to shut down the respective HVAC unit to limit smoke from being spread throughout the entire building.

In summary, the amount or number of smoke detectors required in a fully sprinklered school is very limited. Reducing the number of smoke detectors and other detection devices with reduced installation and inspection, testing, and maintenance costs more than the life of the system. It is important to ensure that the design team includes a qualified fire protection engineer to ensure the fire protection and life safety features of the school are being provided as required by the applicable codes and standards.

VOICE SYSTEMS OR ECSs

Voice systems or ECSs, as previously mentioned in this chapter, are generally not required in school buildings by the model building or fire codes. Basic fire alarm systems for schools will typically only activate an alert sound such as a horn, bell, or chime using a Temporal Code-3 pattern, not a voice notification message. However, over the last couple years there have been some changes in the mind-set as to how the building fire alarm system can be used for purposes other than just notifying the occupants and fire department of a fire emergency. The current thought process is to install a system in the schools that can be used for multiple purposes such as background music, public address announcements, and for notification of other emergencies such as severe weather alerts, hazardous material incidents, and terrorist or shooter events, bomb threats, or even for fire drills. Allowing the fire alarm system to be used for these additional purposes or emergency scenarios requires the horns, bells, or chimes to be replaced with a voice system that has speakers to play prerecorded voice messages or to make live voice announcements. The industry may refer to the voice alarm system as a "mass notification system" or an "ECS" when it is used for purposes other than fire emergency notification.

As defined by NFPA 72, the purpose of an emergency voice communication system is to provide for the transmission of information and instructions pertaining to a fire or other emergencies to building occupants and the fire department. The system also allows communications with those persons remaining in the building. An emergency voice communication system can be used to partially evacuate a building in emergency conditions while permitting some building occupants to remain in safe areas.

A voice alarm system or ECS must provide a predetermined message on a selective basis to the area where the problem originated or throughout the entire facility. The alarm must also be designed as to be clearly heard and understood by all hearing-able occupants within all designated areas. The message is intended to tell the occupants what is happening and what they are to do next in response to the emergency event. Each voice message, whether it is a prerecorded message or a live message, should be clear, calm, and informative, and presented so it will motivate people into action.

There are two key components of a voice alarm system that must be achieved: (1) audibility and (2) intelligibility. Audibility is simply the loudness of the alert tone to notify the occupants of the emergency. NFPA 72 requires that an alert tone be played prior to the playing of a prerecorded voice message. The intent of the evacuation alert tone (using a Temporal Code-3 pattern) is to get everyone's attention so that they will somewhat stop talking or making noise so they can hear and understand the voice portion of the message. For public mode of notification, the alert tone is required to be 15 decibels above the ambient background sound pressure level; however, the voice portion of the message is not required to be 15 decibels above the ambient background message. This elevated sound pressure level above the average sound pressure level is defined as the audibility of the system, which is required to be tested for each area of the building.

The intelligibility level is the capability of the message to be comprehended and understood—being "intelligible." NFPA 72 does require that the voice system be tested to confirm that the messages are intelligible. Voice intelligibility should be measured in accordance with the guidelines in Annex A of IEC 60849, *Sound Systems for Emergency Purposes*. It is important that the engineer or designer of the voice system possess skills sufficient to properly design an emergency voice alarm system for the occupancy being protected. Annex D of NFPA 72 offers additional information on this subject.

There currently are two different methods of verifying or testing voice intelligibility of emergency voice alarm systems. The first is subject based, which is when the designer, owner, and authority having jurisdiction listen to the actual prerecorded messages and agree that they can be comprehended and understood. The second method commonly used in the fire protection industry is to test using an intelligibility meter. The intent is to play the STIPA test signal through the system starting at the microphone of the system and utilize an intelligibility meter in each area of the building to confirm that the system can produce an intelligible message. According to the guidance provided in Annex D of NFPA 72, the preferred intelligibility score would be 0.5 using the STI scale.

Installing an emergency voice communication system and allowing the system to be used to play background music, for public announcements, and any daily announcements is encouraged as this will make the school principal or other staff familiar with the system and make them confident to use the system during an emergency event.

In conclusion, fire alarm systems and their use have changed significantly over the last decade or two. The technology of the equipment has been enhanced, which allows the systems to be used for more than just a standard fire alarm system, thus saving costs for the school districts. It is imperative that a qualified fire protection engineer be integrated into the design process of a school to ensure the fire protection and life safety features, including the fire alarm system or the ECS of the school, are compliant with the applicable codes and standards.

APPROACHES TO OPERATIONAL ISSUES, SPECIFIC THREATS, AND SOLUTIONS

3

A LOOK AT SCHOOL SECURITY IN AUSTRALIA

Raymond V. Andersson, RSecP, ICPS, FSyl, AFAIM
International, national, and corporate security professional

INTRODUCTION

Over the past 4 decades, schools and universities in Australia have been the target of arson, vandalism, assault, and other antisocial behaviors that resulted in state governments implementing risk-based strategies to mitigate the ever-present threats to both private and public education schools.

In October 2002, Australia gained first-hand experience of an active shooter incident at a major university in Melbourne, Victoria. Two students died in this incident but the escalation of active shooter incidents generally, in Australia, caused the Australian government to implement wide-ranging gun laws to reduce the number and availability of firearms in Australia. No school shootings have occurred since this incident.

Arson and assaults continued to occur at schools with principals and teachers becoming the targets of parents and students. It was not unusual to read of an arson attack on a school just before the commencement of a new term of schooling. Recent media reports indicate an escalation of assaults on principals and teachers although this has been an ongoing threat for many years with some evidence, in the 1990s, of firearms being kept on school property, for defense.

In recent years, many schools recognized the need for after-hours security and implemented such security for community activities being held on school property after hours. At the local Nakara Primary School in the Northern Territory, Judo lessons are provided by a local club that operates from the school. Activities such as this provided community ownership of the property with after-school activities that also allowed schools to detect and report any antisocial or criminal behavior occurring on their property after teaching hours, while these activities are in progress.

REDUCE OVERALL CRIME

The Australian, State, and Territory governments also recognized the need to adopt risk-based strategies to reduce overall crime that had been escalating in schools around the nation. Many states led the way in operating successful risk management programs that allows the Federal government to be selective in its funding areas. Funding was set aside to support existing controls or implement new controls to protect students and staff at both private and public schools.

The Australian government, through the Attorney-Generals' Department, implemented a Secure Schools Program for schools identified as being at risk of racial, religious, or ethnically motivated violence, property crime, and harassment with funding to cover the costs of installing security systems. Funding under the program typically covered the costs for:

- Digital surveillance systems (closed-circuit television, CCTV);
- Fencing;
- Lighting; and
- Alarm systems.

The program did not cover security measures to deal with:

- Student bullying;
- Harassment;
- Student violence;
- Child protection;
- Opportunistic acts of vandalism; or
- Property crime.

As such, Australia moved toward securing its schools using the security-in-depth principle, utilizing fencing, lighting, CCTV systems, and alarm systems. The Secure Schools Program, funded by the Australian government, has provided funding for many schools to improve security based on their risks. Fencing, lighting, and alarm systems are pretty common now but some have installed CCTV and others have on-site contracted security guards. The gap not covered by the Secure Schools Program was picked up by State and Territory governments.

Some of the strategies adopted by State and Territory government education departments included:

- Site risk reviews of all public schools in their areas of responsibility;
- Adopting School Watch programs, similar to Neighbourhood or Business Watch;
- Employing contracted security guards; and
- Introducing school-based community police.

The introduction of school-based community policing can be tracked as far back as 1984, where a pilot program was introduced at Casuarina High School, one of Darwin's largest schools located in the northern suburbs. In 1997, Victoria introduced the Police/School Involvement Program (PSIP). These programs, although starting on rocky grounds through lack of trust and understanding of what was trying to be achieved, did operate successfully and resulted in a reduction of criminal activity both in the schools and within the community at large. Finite resources and funding constraints have seen many of these initiatives cut back or discontinued.

Despite the current economic environment, school security continues to be an important issue for governments and local schools can now benefit from being able to offer a safe learning environment for children and young adults. An example based on a local primary school with an attached preschool has seen a reduction of itinerants that defecate in areas used by children and leave syringes in sand pits that could potentially infect young children by the simple introduction of fencing and signage, although the risk of assault of staff remains an issue due to the openness of school properties once inside. This risk is a common one and is being addressed by several State governments at present.

Universities remain at risk through their openness and high numbers of national and overseas students concentrated in one area, often having night lectures and returning home late at night through areas that may not meet CPTED principles. Most universities have security guards on site and are quick to respond to incidents, as reported, but many fail to fully protect staff and students as a result of the long-standing culture of universities.

CONCLUSION

Overall, school security in Australia is improving but is consistent with the Australian government's "Protective Security Policy Framework" of putting in place risk-based strategies for individual sites rather than a blanket strategy for all schools. In this way, costs are managed and those schools that require physical security hardening receive the necessary funding. Schools in both Australia and the United States experience similar problems, and we may face them in a similar manner because we do not have a lot of choices. But we must be proactive.

PREVENTION OF CRIME IN AND AROUND HIGH SCHOOLS: LESSONS IN IMPLEMENTATION AND DISSEMINATION*

Paul van Soomeren

CEO, DSP-groep (http://www.dsp-groep.eu/); director of the board, the International CPTED Association and the European Designing Out Crime Association

Sjoerd Boersma

Senior advisor and partner, DSP-groep, and co-owner of IRIS

THE SAFE AND SECURE SCHOOLS (3S) MATRIX: HOW MATURE IS A SAFETY AND SECURITY POLICY?

Based on ideas about implementing quality management,[1] a group of Dutch crime prevention experts[2] have designed a Safe and Secure Schools (3S) maturity matrix (also based on Crosby 1991). The matrix, seen in Table 25.1, presents the five stages that unfold over the course of developing a foundation for an integrated policy for safety and security: denial, awakening, breakthrough, management, and integration.

Our story starts in the Netherlands (17 million inhabitants) in the 1980s. This was during a period (1970-2000) in which the Netherlands experienced a rather extreme rise in a number of crimes like theft, burglary, arson, vandalism, and violent crimes. By that time, Amsterdam (1 million inhabitants)—the capital city with a young and very diverse population—ranked first in the fast rising national crime statistics. In any population, most offenders and victims can be found in the age group of 10-25[3] years; therefore, schools in Amsterdam are obviously at a triple crime risk: the Netherlands ranking high in crime statistics, Amsterdam ranking highest within the Netherlands, and high schools with adolescents aged 12-18 the riskiest. Furthermore, research in the 1990s showed risks at the workplace

---

*This chapter is based on an earlier paper presented by Paul van Soomeren in Brisbane in 2001: http://www.dsp-groep.nl/projecten/p1/4099/.

[1] Demming, W. E. (1982), *Quality. Productivity and Competitive Position*, Institute of Technology, Massachusetts.

[2] Van Hoek, A., de Savornin Lohman, P., van Soomeren, P., and Loef, K. (1994), *Beveiliging en bedrijfsvoering: naar een geïntegreerde aanpak*, DSP, Amsterdam.

[3] Junger-Tas, J., Kruissink, M., and van der Laan, P. H. (1992). *Ontwikkelingen van de jeugdcriminaliteit en de justitiële jeugdbescherming: periode 1980-1990*, WODC, Gouda Quint, The Hague.

Table 25.1 Safety and Security Stages Matrix

Development Stages of a Safety and Security Policy	Attitude of Management	State of the Art of the Policy	Approach
Denial	Act after the fact. Crimes seen in isolation	No policy	Problems unknown. First whistle blowers ridiculed
Awakening	Risks are acknowledged. Management hardly willing to invest in policy. Hardware and a job for police and security	More attention. Main focus technical (target hardening, security surveillance, CCTV)	Problems are dealt with. No long-range policy. No connection inside/outside. "Chain-features" denied, e.g., CCTV and no idea about follow up
Break through	Risks are seen as manageable. Cost benefit ideas emerge	Safety and security officials connect with management. One manager in charge (but is still RE-acting)	Systems approach: what is the problem, what best practices can solve this problem
Management	Active policy is designed with mission statement, registration and analysis, and proper procedures	Safety and security connects to other policies like health and safety, quality management, labor issues, liability and insurance	Attention for weak signals and early warning, root causes and prevention. Process approach, e.g., using scenarios
Integration	Policy is integrated in core business (in processes and culture). Efficient working relations with other stakeholders in a wider area (Let's work together)	Paradoxical: safety and security disappear into other policies like service, quality, heath, environmental policies, etc. Less visible security	Safety and security integrated in business and processes of all stakeholders. Policies are proactive. Target hardening and law enforcement seen as last resort. Multi-agency or partnership approach

to be twice as high as the crime risks in public spaces.[4] The jobs having the most contact with the public have the highest risks: public transportation, schools/education, shops, and hospitals/health care.[5] The workplace risk in these professions is about 4-10 times higher compared to the overall population.

In that era, schools in Amsterdam were thus the top target for crime prevention. But for years not much happened and schools stumbled along without assistance. No one dared to mention problems

---

[4] Van Hoek, A., Huber, J., and Poll, N. (1997). *Agressie en Geweld op de werkplek; Handleiding voor het ontwikkelen van opvangbeleid*, The Hague. Huber, J., Poll, N., van Soomeren, P., Steinmetz, C. H. D. (1996). *Lastige klanten, wat doe je ermee? Een beleidsmatige aanpak van agressie bij publiekscontacten*. The Hague, SDU publishers; Huber, J., Poll, N., van Soomeren, P., Steinmetz, C. H. D. (1996). *Lastige klanten, wat doe je ermee? Een beleidsmatige aanpak van agressie bij publiekscontacten*. The Hague, SDU publishers. Home Office. Research and Statistics Directorate, Young People and Crime Survey, 1992-1993. The Crime Survey for England and Wales (CSEW) (formerly the British Crime Survey) provides an important source of information about levels of crime, public attitudes to crime and other related issues. The CSEW measures the amount of crime in England and Wales by asking people about crimes they have experienced in the last year. This includes crimes not reported to the police, so it is an important alternative to police records.

[5] Flight, S., Abraham, M., and Roorda, W. (2011). *Agressie en geweld tegen werknemers met een publieke taak 2007—2009-2011*, Ministry of Interior/DSP-groep, The Hague/Amsterdam.

of crime, insecurity, and incivilities, afraid that their schools would suffer a market loss because of a wrecked image, along with pupils and staff leaving.

Why did it take that long to start a sophisticated crime prevention initiative for schools? The answer is shown in the matrix in Table 25.1. It takes a while to adjust to higher crime levels and build a sound foundation for a mature and integrated safety and security policy. Schools are no different in that respect and, in facing higher crime trends, the schools also went through the stages of denial, awakening, breakthrough, management, and integration.

DENIAL

Seeing the general crime trends in the Netherlands, it is difficult to explain why not only schools in Amsterdam but also police, neighborhood residents, health and safety officials, and public transportation officials defined crime and insecurity as a problem they had to deal with by themselves for so long. Until the beginning of the 1990s, the development stage in schools was still mostly the denial mode. At best, the problems with crime and insecurity were defined as vandalism problems: youngsters purposefully demolishing public objects, breaking a few windows, and playing a bit too rowdily. An approach to these vandalism problems had already been developed more than a decade before, and schools could participate in the approach if they wished to do so.[6] This antivandalism policy had more or less faded away by the end of the 1980s due to changes in personnel and thus the antivandalism policy simply evaporated.

AWAKENING

Of course, the shift from denial to awakening was helped by factual information about the crime and insecurity situation in the Netherlands, in Amsterdam, and in the schools.[7] However, most of this knowledge was already publicly available for years, but it lay dormant. The awakening for schools in Amsterdam was actively helped by a push from the health and safety officials from the city of Amsterdam who simply followed new regulations issued by the National Ministry of Social Affairs and Employment. These regulations—which were part of the Health and Safety Act since 1995—forced employers to take precautionary measures against aggression, violence, and sexual intimidation in the workplace. Two groups of officials from the city of Amsterdam now realized they were more or less pursuing the same cause:

- On the one side, the health and safety officials and
- On the other side, a newly appointed, but very experienced, project coordinator for school security.

Health and safety officials looked only at the staff (teachers, management, administrators, technical staff/facility management in schools). The project coordinator for school security was mainly driven

---

[6] Van Dijk, Van Soomeren & Walop (1984). *Vandalisme in Amsterdam* (in: Claude Lévy-Leboyer: *Vandalism (behaviour and motivations)*), Amsterdam-New York-Oxford.

[7] SBR/Stichting Bouwresearch (1990; revised edition 1995), *Beveiliging van gebouwen deel 6: scholen*, SBR, Rotterdam. Mooij, T. (1994). *Leerlinggeweld in het Voortgezet Onderwijs, Sociale binding van scholieren*, ITS, Nijmegen. Mooij, T. (1997). *Safe(r) at school*. Summarising report. Paper presented to EU expert conference in Utrecht February 1997, ITS, Nijmegen.

by his or her task to help implement a new citywide policy aimed at youth (in general) and safety in Amsterdam. Within this broader policy, there was also substantial funding available for a big school project. The officials of the city of Amsterdam (health/safety as well as school security officials) asked a group of private and public experts to help formulate a policy. This public-private partnership—a rather unique construction—joined under the name Amsterdam Partnership for Safety and Security on Schools. The first task of this partnership was to start diagnostic research in all high schools: schools with pupils in the age range of 12-18 years, where on average each school has a population of between 1000 and 2000 students.

BREAKTHROUGH: RESEARCH SHOWING THE RISKS, VICTIMS, OFFENDERS, AND INCIDENTS

The diagnostic research[8] started as a pilot for a group of four schools and was then held in the eastern region of Amsterdam (1997), then the western region was added (1998), and later on (1998/1999) the southern school region of Amsterdam was added. This step-by-step approach reflects the necessary efforts to gain the participation of the schools as well as the methodological difficulties in combining separate research traditions. In fact, this research established for the first time a structural liaison between schools within one region concerning crime and insecurity issues. Another unique feature of this research was that it succeeded in combining several types of diagnostic research:

- A general questionnaire for staff and personnel following the standard model of a risk assessment questionnaire on health and safety (as obliged by the Health and Safety Act mentioned earlier).
- A victim survey/ questionnaire for pupils and staff using the model for standard Crime Victims Survey.[9]
- A self-report questionnaire asking pupils to indicate what incidents they committed or witnessed in and around their school; the standard Dutch national youth and crime self-report study was used as a basis here.[10]

Integrating these different types of research, each having its own traditions and background, proved to be a difficult job which only succeeded because the research was a combined effort of health and safety researchers in Amsterdam and researchers specialized in victim and self-report crime research (DSP). What was born here was the idea of an integrated survey/monitor that included a victim survey as well as a self-report survey, for both pupils and staff. The survey we developed during this period (or monitor as we called it later on) became part of a complete web-based tool to monitor school safety called Incident Registration in School (IRIS) and is used by schools to register incidents, do surveys among pupils and staff, and include factual reviews of crimes and incivilities (e.g., arson, a broken window, graffiti) by using an app. All this information can be shown on a uniform dashboard in each

---

[8] Van Dijk, E. (1999). *Veiligheid op school; samenvatting*, ASVOS, Amsterdam. Van Dijk, E., and Frielink, S. (1998). *Veiligheid op scholen in Amsterdam-Oost/Amsterdam-West*, Gemeente Amsterdam.

[9] Van Dijk, J. J. M., and Steinmetz, C. H. D. (1979). *De WODC slachtoffer enquêtes 1974-1979*, Staatsuitgeverij, The Hague. ICVS (International Crime Victims survey): e.g., Mayhew and Van Dijk 1997 and Van Kesteren et al. 2000. Note the ICVS was modelled after the Dutch victim surveys and the British Crime Victim Survey mentioned in Note 4.

[10] Junger-Tas, J., Kruissink, M., and van der Laan, P. H. (1992). *Ontwikkelingen van de jeugdcriminaliteit en de justitiële jeugdbescherming: periode 1980-1990*, WODC, Gouda Quint, The Hague.

school; but since all IRIS input is anonymously stored in one national database, easy benchmarking with other schools is also possible.

Victimization (staff and pupils), incidents, and seriousness of offenses/offenders

The number of incidents reported in the survey (shown in Table 25.2) astonished everyone; not only the number of incidents reported by victims (staff and pupils) but also the number of incidents reported by the offending pupils themselves. In addition, the fact that about 40% of all incidents were considered serious incidents convinced people that action had to be taken. The research showed that schools only had knowledge of about 15% of all incidents. For the police, this figure was about 1%. Pupils themselves knew about far more incidents compared to the school and the police, and of course pupils talk about these incidents with one another.

The research also showed that young pupils committed more crimes than older pupils. This result is similar to the result of research done in primary schools in Amsterdam (pupils aged 4-12 years). According to that research, children start committing incidents/crimes at the age of 10.[11] Boys report they commit more such incidents than girls, and boys are also more often a victim of such incidents. The research also showed some important regional differences. From the perspective of crime victimization studies, self-report research, and risk assessment studies, these results were not extremely surprising: On a global scale, the Netherlands ranks high on the crime charts, Amsterdam ranks high within that country, and schools (youth/workplace contacts) are a risky part of society.

Table 25.2   Number of Incidents (Staff/Pupils) per Year as Reported by Victims and Self-reported by Offending Pupils[12]

Total: 39 Schools	
Period: 1997-1999	
Pupils	
Number of pupils	19,236
Number of incidents from victim survey	155,000
Number of incidents self-reported	244,000
Number of self-reported incidents considered serious	94,000
% of self-reported incidents known to school	15%
% of self-reported incidents known to police	1%
Staff	
Number of staff	2212
Number of incidents from victim survey	13,000

Response rate for staff was 50-70%, and for pupils was 80-90%. Incidents included aggression/violence, burglary, sexual intimidation, arson, vandalism/graffiti/demolishing objects, theft, and nuisance (bullying, conflicts). Seriousness ranking: see Steinmetz (2001).[13]
Note: the first pilot research in four schools (3400 pupils/470 staff) is excluded from the table because results are difficult to compare.

---

[11]Van Barlingen, M., van Overbeeke, R., and van't Hoff, C. (1997). *Veilig op de basisschool?*, Gemeente Amsterdam Dienst SEC, Amsterdam.
[12]Van Dijk, E., and Frielink, S. (1998). *Veiligheid op scholen in Amsterdam-Oost/Amsterdam-West*, Gemeente Amsterdam. Van Dijk, E. (1999). *Veiligheid op school; samenvatting*, ASVOS, Amsterdam.
[13]Steinmetz, C. H. D. (2001), VIOS gegevens secondair geanalyseerd (intern verslag t.b.v. strategisch overleg), SAO, Amsterdam.

However, the schools reacted in a surprised or shocked manner and were angry sometimes. Evidently, this thorough research brought most schools to the development stage of Breakthrough as mentioned in the 3S maturity matrix presented above. Schools—as well as other institutions like local authorities, police, and so forth—started to ask themselves questions like "How come there are so many and such serious incidents?" "What can be done about this?" and "Why shouldn't we work together to combat crime and insecurity?"[14]

There was one more important outcome of the research. Everyone realized that structural registration and research was important to monitor the development of safety and security in schools. Hence, the research was also the starting point of a project to register incidents, not only for high schools but also for primary schools and professional education institutes in Amsterdam. Registration of incidents by schools themselves was an essential component. To be able to compare results and analyze these data, they were stored in a CD-ROM that made it possible to register incidents in a uniform way. The result was the start of the tool IRIS. The CD-ROM was distributed to all schools in Amsterdam by a researcher who traveled to all schools every few months to collect the data. This registration tool became an instant success; later on it became web based and was used in more and more schools in the Netherlands.

START OF THE MANAGEMENT STAGE: SIX TYPES OF FOCUS GROUPS

Focus groups were created, consisting mainly of staff and pupils from the schools. However, the CPTED (Crime Prevention Through Environmental Design) group also included police, public transport authorities, civil servants, local authorities, and maintenance officials. The aim of the focus groups was for schools to interpret together the research results for their region and formulate counter and preventive measures in six fields:

1. School building, surroundings, neighborhood, and travel from/to school (this focus group mainly looked into CPTED issues);
2. Rules and enforcement/sanctions;
3. Victim support and follow-up care;
4. Mediation, complaints policies, coaching, and school counselors;
5. School climate and training of staff and pupils to discuss and handle crime and insecurity;
6. Policy plans, implementation, and registration/monitor systems.

Each focus group had to come forward with measures, ideas, schemes, and initiatives and then rank all those ideas in a priority scheme. As an example, we will concentrate on the work done by two of these focus groups: the one on CPTED and the one on registration/monitor systems.

CPTED focus group

The research summarized above had already shown the importance of looking at the routes from and to school and the school neighborhood and surroundings. Not only were the routes from and to school and the school neighborhood perceived as more unsafe and insecure than the school premises and the

---

[14]See also Schneider, T. (1998). *Crime Prevention Through Environmental Design, School CPTED Basics Presented to the 3rd International CPTED Conference*, Washington, DC. Cleveland, G. (2001). *School Safety as an Educational Construct: Tips for school administrators on how to avoid the "policing model" trap.*

school building itself by the pupils but also the real crime or incident risk was high. The perception of crime and insecurity problems outside the school were sadly proven true by an incident that happened around this time: Several schools in Amsterdam-West are located next to a line of the light rail public transport system. There were frequent rows and fights between pupils at the roads to the station and on the platform. One day, two girls were fighting on the platform and one of them pushed the other onto the rail, where she was killed by the approaching train.

This case sadly showed several things: a strict division between inside school and outside school is not a very helpful distinction for incidents because problems and conflicts often start inside and explode once outside or the other way around. This case also showed the difficult intermingling of problems and solutions and the number of participants involved. For instance, possible solutions were to prevent fights, take quick action when fights are seen or reported (the station was equipped with closed-circuit television, CCTV, but no one monitored the images), change school hours and thus prevent students of different schools from clashing into each other while leaving school, have more tram carriage capacity available on peak hours, crowd control, and educating pupils about risks and about quick intervention tactics.

Within each regional CPTED focus group, the schools learned a lot from the practices and experiences of each other. Schools, together with officials from police, public transport, local authorities, and city management, were able to formulate a set of new and comprehensive measures in the fields of public transport, neighborhood maintenance, fire prevention and evacuation, and multiagency cooperation. Some of these measures were so simple that they could be implemented instantaneously while other plans—such as architecture and urban planning—needed more time. Also, a new way of analyzing problems emerged: mixed groups of stakeholders (pupils, teachers, police, staff, etc.) simply walked in and around the school premises to make an inventory of problems they perceived. This was later elaborated upon in a structured method for risk assessment: a review. This so-called review emerged where individuals or groups walking around—in sun and rain, light and darkness—made notes and took photographs, resulting in prestructured risk/solution assessment reports. Years later (2009), this prestructured method for risk assessment was integrated with IRIS. This review—nowadays everyone uses the IRIS review app (see Figure 25.1)—enables schools to register incidents (e.g., a broken window), mark and photograph hot spots, and assess security risks.

Another thing the CPTED focus groups found out while identifying measures already taken was that most schools were already very active in the field of combating crime and insecurity. However, most security measures are not really incorporated into sophisticated policy plans. There is no connection between the research outcomes and analysis of the problem and the goals/plans and the measures. There is much action, but often the wrong action. For instance, the biggest problem for pupils is the unsafe and insecure situation in the school neighborhood and the routes from and to school, but schools had hardly implemented any measures aimed at this problem and did not invest in cooperation with those who might be able to change this situation. There was also a profound lack of systematic evaluation of measures already implemented. In short, there is a lot of action but it is questionable how effective and efficient this action is.

Registration and monitoring

The same problem could be seen by the registration policies; schools did put effort into the registration of incidents, but it was done in a rather clumsy way (e.g., by the registration of incidents in the personal files of pupils). This way there is never a systematic and statistical sound overview available because

FIGURE 25.1

IRIS app.

the registration is completely personalized; there is no central place to compile the information. From the beginning of the 1990s, it was clear that not much was known about the actual crime situation and/ or the risks in a school as long as there was no (uniformity in) registration. In one of the focus groups, the layout of a sound system for IRIS was developed step by step. Altogether, this process took about 10 years. This digital tool was distributed on a CD-ROM to all schools in Amsterdam and from there it was copied by schools nationwide. The first real investigation into incidents in Amsterdam was started by a researcher on a bicycle who visited all schools and tried to get the data that were registered on a stand-alone computer somewhere in a school. There was a uniformity in registering incidents, but it was hard to gather the information.

The CD-ROM spread through the Netherlands, and schools in other cities (Rotterdam and Haarlem) started to use it as well. By this point, schools wanted to access the tool on the Internet and thus have easier accessibility and better and easier benchmarking possibilities, though in the beginning privacy issues scared some schools. IRIS developed into a web-based tool in 2004. First, a school must know basic facts about what the problems with crime and incivilities are (what, where, when, who), but an even more important next step is to know what to do to tackle and prevent these problems. Hence, a standardized method on how to organize school safety, one for which a school could get an official national certificate, had to be developed. It was based on the plan-do-check-act (PDCA) control cycle, where schools decide for themselves what their goals are and how they are going to reach these goals. This PDCA (or adjust) cycle is an iterative four-step management method used in business for the control and continuous improvement of processes and products. It is also known as the Deming circle/cycle/wheel and it forms the basis for a lot of international standards for quality management (e.g., ISO 9000 series) and crime prevention (e.g., the European standards of the CEN 14383 series).[15] The standardized method for safe and secure schools was developed with the Dutch Ministries of Interior and Justice.

This standardized method[16] starts with a step in which a school has to do a thorough analysis of the crime and safety situation, preferably not only in and around the school but also in the wider neighborhood. As we have seen above, this was not that easy a task. In Amsterdam only, 15 years ago, we had to do long and difficult victim surveys that lead to a breakthrough for action to tackle and prevent crime. But nowadays, this difficult and costly research is no longer needed. Every incident that a schools feeds into the registration tool IRIS—and the info from school surveys/monitors and factual reviews as well—is stored (anonymously) in a central database (see Figure 25.2). Hence, every school using the IRIS tool can not only research and analyze its own crime and safety situation but can also compare and benchmark their situation with other schools (e.g., of the same type). An interesting side effect of using this crime and safety registration/survey/review tool was that the terminology of the problems with crime and incivilities (for example) were standardized (the "what is the problem" question), but also the indications of places (where, hotspots), time, and types of offenders and victims was more standardized. The IRIS tool was used for a while as a stand-alone software package, but later on it was completely integrated in the regular administrative school software which is sold by the main administrative software companies in the Netherlands. The same incident can now be seen in the personal file of a student and it can be used to make a complete safety analysis. Nowadays, the IRIS system is used in 30% of all the Dutch high schools, 20% of the primary schools, and 20% of the professional education sites.

---

[15]ISO = International Standardisation Organization. CEN is the European Committee for Standardization; an association that brings together the National Standardization Bodies of 33 European countries.

[16]http://www.hetccv.nl/instrumenten/Veilig+rond+en+in+school/index?filter=Stappenplan. CCV is the Dutch Centre for Crime prevention and Safety which is governed by ministries, municipalities, police and insurers.

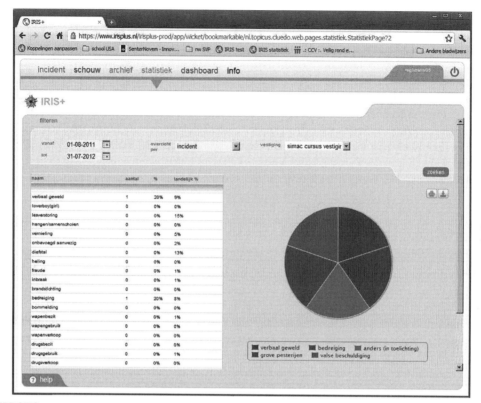

FIGURE 25.2

IRIS database.

CONCLUSION

Thinking back to the scheme which introduced the Safety and Security Stages matrix (3S), we have seen the Amsterdam School Safety and Security initiative slowly reach the stage of management: an active safety and security policy had emerged between the end of the 1990s and 2005. By then, everyone was convinced that an integrated multiagency approach was really necessary. There were safety and security coordinators appointed within each school. A real policy was formulated not only within the school but also for the different school regions and Amsterdam as a whole. CPTED was an integrated and important part of this policy. It took all participants about 5 years to come from the stage of denying crime and insecurity problems in and around schools to the stage of a more integrated approach.

Unfortunately, in Amsterdam, this whole machinery still proved to be considerably weak. In 2009, the city of Amsterdam decided to stop funding this policy, so schools had to take care of their own security and safety, including the exchanges between schools as well as between schools and the local authorities. Schools were assumed to have reached the final stage in the security matrix by that time. Within a few years, it showed that schools were not willing to pay for the integrative machinery by themselves. Obviously, the last stage in the maturity matrix—integration—had not yet been completely implemented in Amsterdam. This may come as no surprise since the term *multiagency approach* is easily tossed around, but the implementation of a sophisticated multiagency approach is not light a task[17] and it showed to be a heavy burden in the Amsterdam school safety and security policy too. From then on, it was mostly once again each school working on its own. With no integration (stage 5), the machine was stuck in stage 4 (management). However, a lot was learned by then. There was knowledge about crime prevention and CPTED[18] and most schools had a better and more realistic focus on safety and security. Full integration of the safety and security policies in all schools in a city of 1 million inhabitants was obviously a bridge too far. Amsterdam and the high schools in Amsterdam settled for the management stage.

What did blossom most of all was the digital registration, review, and the survey tool IRIS. This tool started out in Amsterdam, but was used all over the Netherlands within a couple of years and not just in high schools but also in all types of schools in the country. Essential in a 3S Safe & Secure School policy is a program that includes social safety, environmental safety, and organization around safety. School management needs to develop safety policies based on facts. To feed a school—from management down to every classroom—with information on safety and security, factual information and data have to be collected and processed. IRIS proved to be an easy solution for this. In the end, the system was collectively used through the full integration in the administrative school software, enabling an evidence— or at least fact—based school safety approach to tackle and prevent crime in an individual school using the information of other schools to benchmark and compare. Hence, while most schools nowadays are in the management stage of the 3S maturity matrix, the crime registration and analyses has reached full integration.

[17]Pressman, J. L., and Wildavsky, A. (1984). *Implementation*, University of California Press, London. Hope, T., and Murphy, D. J. J. (1983). *Problems of Implementing Crime Prevention: The Experience of a Demonstration Project*, The Howard Journal, Volume XXII 1938, pp. 38–50.
[18]Van Soomeren, P., and Woldendorp, T. (1996). Secured by design in the Netherlands, *Security Journal 7*, pp. 185-195, Elsevier Science, Ireland.

OPERATIONAL ISSUES, SPECIFIC THREATS, AND SOLUTIONS

26

Lawrence J. Fennelly, CPO, CSS, HLS-III
Security expert witness and consultant, Litigation Consultants Inc.
Marianna A. Perry, M.S., CPP
Training and development manager for Securitas Security Services USA, Inc.

The issues and solutions concerning school security are changing and expanding almost daily, it seems. To help keep up with the avalanche of information, we have compiled a list of 47 items and resources of which you should be aware. Some may be new to you (A.L.I.C.E. training or WATCH D.O.G.S), while others may be more familiar (combatting vandalism and graffiti). For each, we have tried to provide points to consider and information on how to access needed resources.

ACTIVE SHOOTER

The Quick Response (QR) code in Figure 26.1 links to a paper entitled, "Active Shooter: Behavior Conditions and Situation," by Samuel Mayhugh of the U.S. Department of Homeland Security.[1] A smartphone scanning app is required to read it (see Chapter 27 for more detailed information about the use of QR codes). Mayhugh's paper contains a wealth of useful information on active shooters and recommendations for risk mitigation.

A.L.I.C.E. (ALERT-LOCKDOWN-INFORM-COUNTER-EVACUATE) TRAINING

A.L.I.C.E. training is considered a proactive response to school violence, as opposed to the more passive actions, such as hiding or teachers barricading themselves and their students in classrooms. A.L.I.C.E. training has become a part of the emergency crisis response plans at many schools. According to the A.L.I.C.E. Training Institute in Ohio, "ALICE training exists so that schools and the employees have the necessary information to keep our children safe in the event that an active shooter threatens one of the places we are supposed to feel most safe, outside of our own homes."[2]

---

[1] Samuel Mayhugh, "Active Shooters: Behavior, Conditions, and Situations," September 27, 2011, Active Shooter Awareness Roundtable, Washington, D.C., http://fieldcommand.org/wp-content/uploads/2013/06/Active-Shooters-Behavior-Conditions-and-Situations.pdf.

[2] www.alicetraining.com (accessed Sept. 2013).

FIGURE 26.1

Scan this QR code to access the active shooter paper.

The A and L in A.L.I.C.E. training refers to the standard concepts of *alert* and *lockdown*. *Inform* refers to someone being inside the school building who is able to monitor the location and actions of an armed gunman in the building and communicate that information to others. A.L.I.C.E. training is not much different from what is a standard practice for most schools, but there is much controversy over the *counter* portion of the training for the K-12 environment. We need to consider if the best approach in this situation is to have K-12 students attack an armed gunman in their school and whether or not this is a reasonable response. When asked, the majority of security professionals do not think it is the appropriate response for this age group. With the proper training, it may have some merit in the college or university setting. Most schools have *evacuation* plans, so this is not a new concept in school security.

There is not a simple solution to the issue of effective school security. The most logical response is to be proactive by using a layered approach to security: policies and procedures, physical security, electronic components, training and awareness for the faculty, staff, and students.

BACKGROUND INVESTIGATIONS AND BACKGROUND CHECKS

Preemployment screening or background investigations are an essential step to maintaining a safe and secure workplace. In order to reduce the potential for internal theft, fraud, and other disruptive incidents from occurring in the school environment, either by long-term employees or new hires, background information can provide the data necessary for prudent hiring or retention decisions. It is estimated that up to 40% of job applicants are not truthful on their job applications and/or resumes.

Depending on the expected role of the employee, a school should pursue a background investigation commensurate with the level of trust, confidence, and job impact on the school. A tiered system based upon specific concerns, degree of involvement with students, and access to proprietary data is recommended. Such a program will provide the desired information necessary and at the same time, control costs.

The background investigation should include any or all of the categories listed below, depending on the level of sensitivity or concern.

- *State and local criminal records*: Check for seven years at all previous addresses.
- *Criminal records/federal district courts*: Specifically deals with federal offenses.
- *Civil court records at local, state, and federal levels*: Specifically deals with finances, real property, tax records, bankruptcy, and Uniform Commercial Code (UCC) filings.
- *Credit history*: Strict compliance with Fair Credit Reporting Act.

There is an ongoing discussion among security professionals, school district personnel, and school principals as to how often background investigations (criminal records searches) should be conducted on employees. It is standard practice in the industry to conduct preemployment investigations, but what about the employee who works for the same school for years or even decades and their background is never rechecked? Many times, an individual who works for a school will be involved in criminal activity that goes undetected—especially if the school is located in close proximity to the border of a neighboring state or if the employee travels frequently. A prolonged timespan between searches of criminal records poses a risk to students, faculty, and staff. We believe it is prudent for schools to conduct annual, nationwide criminal records searches and be certain to include all employees, including custodians, maintenance staff, and those who work in the cafeteria or kitchen. Consider it due diligence because the safety of your faculty, staff, and students is of the utmost importance.

We have all heard horror stories about criminal record searches on long-time and much-loved school faculty and staff members whose records had not been checked since before they were hired. Recently, the city of Boston, MA, conducted full background checks on all employees within the school system. Fifteen employees were fired because of their criminal records.

If your child or loved one was put in danger or at risk because a school failed to conduct annual background investigations, would a reasonable person believe that the school had a "duty of care" to conduct annual background investigations, especially on someone who works with children? We believe so. A security assessment of your campus will point out areas of security vulnerability, but it is important to be certain that you don't have a threat within your own school buildings.

BACKGROUND CHECKS OF EMPLOYEES

The following actual cases show the importance of background checks before hiring employees.

Case No. 1. At a local bank, in the division that handled stocks and bonds, a young woman was in the lobby who was applying for a position in this division. I was initially very impressed with her—well dressed and very professional. After her fingerprints were checked, it was discovered that she had been arrested in St. Thomas, BVI, for passport forgery.

Case No. 2. A young woman about 22-25 years of age was going through our background check process. The report came back that she had been arrested for assault and battery with a dangerous weapon. The weapon was a Tonka truck and the complainant was her husband. He apparently had come home late one night and she picked up the toy and hit him with it. The police were called. She was arrested and he went to the hospital where he received 12 stitches in his head.

Case No. 3. We did drug testing and a variance of 0-15 was considered an acceptable range to allow for prescription medication the individual may be taking. There was one woman, approximately 35 years of age, who was tested. When the results of her tests came back, she had scored a 335—an all-time record for the company.

Case No. 4. This happened several times at one company in particular. When we handed out a form for new employees to fill out, we would tell them that all of their information was going to be loaded into a computer in order to make their employee identification badge and that they would also be fingerprinted. This process only took about 8 minutes to complete. At that point, there were many instances when the individual said, "I have changed my mind. I don't think I want to take this job."

If a typical background check can reveal information such as that identified in the above cases, cost should not be a deciding factor as to whether or not they are conducted. You have a need to know as well as a duty to find out criminal background information on your employees.

Today, routine drug screening and fingerprints that are submitted to the FBI for comparison are standard procedures. Background checks and drug testing are pre-hiring processes as well as ongoing processes. A drug testing program should be implemented that includes preemployment testing, for-cause testing, and random and postaccident drug testing. A 10-panel drug screen is standard for most school districts.

Background investigations that are conducted on school employees should not be any different than those conducted on employees in corporate America. There is no exception in this area for schools. Utilize several different methods for obtaining information on prospective employees, even if they are well known in your community. Consider performing a Google search on the individual and check out their Facebook page as well as other social media sites—not just before you hire them, but every year.

INFORMATIONAL WEBSITES FOR BACKGROUND SCREENING

www.instantpeoplecheck.com
www.criminalcheck.com
www.yourownprivateeye.com
www.accuratecredit.com
www.web.public-records-now.com

BULLET-RESISTANT DOORS, WINDOWS, AND WHITEBOARDS (SEE SECTION "GLASS AND WINDOWS" FOR ADDITIONAL INFORMATION ON THIS TOPIC)

Today, because of recent shootings, companies are selling bullet-resistant doors, windows, and even classroom whiteboards that meet U.L. levels 1-8, ASTM tests, and other certifications. Should you want to have doors to block an explosion, protect personnel, or just stand up to heavy wear and tear, there is hardware, doors, and windows out there for you.

Physical barriers are used to control, impede, or deny access and to direct the flow of personnel through designated portals. Barrier system effectiveness is measured against specific standards and performances testing: specifically, to reduce the number of entry and exit paths, facilitate effective use of protective force personnel, delay the adversary so the threat can be assessed, and protect personnel from hostile action and channel adversaries into preplanned neutralization zones.[3]

---

[3]Implementing Physical Protection Systems—A Practical Guide, second edition, David G. Patterson CPP, PSP, ASIS, 2013.

MINIMAL GLASS[4]

Large window and vision panels, while visually attractive, are easily defeated. Minimizing glass presents a more secure image and makes forced entry more difficult. General guidelines for the use of glass in the main and rear entrance are as follows:

- Full windows should be a minimum of 72 inches off the ground.
- Narrow windows/vision panels below 72 inches should be a maximum 12 ft wide.
- Install security window film to reinforce glass at the main entrance.

BULLYING

Bullying is an upsetting topic because of the cruelty and harassment suffered by the victims. The injustice to the victims just doesn't seem to stop. Entire books are written on this topic, but here we will address it just briefly.

It is easy to say that zero-tolerance programs must include bullying, but for parents who are trying to stop the injustices their child is experiencing, this can be very difficult. It's time to stop the bullying and for schools to take control of this issue.

Who is doing the bullying? Teenage boys and girls, teachers, bus drivers, coaches, and school staff are the perpetrators. The effects of bullying on a victim can be devastating. Suicide, crying, depression, weight loss, bedwetting, stress, drug and alcohol abuse, headaches, stomach aches, frequent absences from school because the victim feels ill, and stuttering are just some of the negative side effects a victim of bullying may experience.

CHEMICAL LABS

Access to chemical labs must be reliable and you must have absolutely 100% key or card access control. If you don't have this, you must rekey or put the door on an access control system.

Chemicals must be properly labeled and kept in a secured cabinet that is properly labeled. All chemicals must be inventoried. Hazardous materials and explosive material should be removed from the school property. Refer to NFPA standards for specific guidelines.

COMMUNITY POLICING AND SCHOOLS: COMPONENTS AND BENEFITS

Partnerships, problem-solving, organizational change, and presenting—that's community policing in a nutshell, but more importantly, it's a partnership between law enforcement, emergency medical responders, the fire department, and other local, state, and federal agencies.

---

[4]Brad Spicer, ASIS School and Safety Council Newsletter, July 2013.

COMMUNITY POLICING COMPONENTS

- Community partnership recognizes the value of bringing people back into the public safety process.
- Problem-solving identifies concerns that community members feel are most threatening to their safety and well-being.
- Change recognizes that a police department will have to change its organization to forge partnerships for problem-solving.

A FOCUS ON PREVENTION

In community policing, officers still maintain law and order, but they move beyond just catching the bad guys to examining specific conditions, including problems of disorder and neglect, that breed both minor and serious offenses. People talk about their concerns, ranging from burglaries to speeding cars, with community police officers who are familiar faces in their neighborhoods.

Many programs that support community policing are old news to crime prevention specialists— Neighborhood Watch, School Watch, Business Watch, citizen academies, graffiti cleanups, neighborhood education centers, after-school programs for children and teens, school resource officers, citizen patrols, and so on.

BUILDING TRUST

Community policing cannot work without trust. Residents who trust law enforcement can provide valuable information that can lead to the prevention as well as the solution of crimes. Mutual trust leads to advocacy for police activities and productive partnerships that find solutions to community problems. A police officer who listens to the community respects the residents' instincts and concerns. On the other hand, residents need to learn how the police department works and what it can and cannot do. Then they need to work together.

NOT A QUICK FIX

Community policing strategies have evolved over the past 25 years, based on work by scholars and police research organizations. It became the focus of policing in the 1990s, but community policing is not a quick fix. Getting the public to cooperate with the police can be difficult, especially in the neighborhoods with a record of antagonistic relationships between residents and law enforcement. Similar antagonistic relationships may exist between schools, community organizations, and law enforcement.

The police must win the support of the public, through regular meetings with residents and by delivering on commitments they make to solve problems. Community policing requires a long-term commitment to work with community members and schools to forge lasting partnerships.

BENEFITS OF COMMUNITY POLICING

- Using the community's talents and resources effectively helps extend severely strained police resources.
- Citizens gain a voice in defining and prioritizing their law enforcement needs.

- Satisfaction with police services increases.
- Officers who develop creative solutions to community problems and find new roles also enjoy increased job satisfaction.
- Crime has gradually decreased since the early 2000s. Police executives, government officials, and researchers credit community policing initiatives as a contributing factor in the decline.

COMPUTER LABS, MUSIC ROOMS, THE LIBRARY, AND THE GYMNASIUM

These areas must have 100% key control or card access control and be monitored by video surveillance. Inventory should include model numbers, serial numbers, and manufacturer information on every unit or piece of equipment. For high-value items, you may also want to have photographs on file. Consider an asset management system with inventory tags or an operation identification system to track inventory. An electronic article surveillance system may be utilized to prevent items from being removed from the area unless the tag on the item is deactivated.

At a school where we recently had conducted an assessment, the gym, which was a part of the school, had double-doors that faced a very nice neighborhood. The lock on the door had been destroyed by the residents of the neighborhood who would use the gym for friendly games of basketball. School personnel knew the gym was being used after hours and that members of the community were gaining access to the gym because of the broken lock on the doors. They were aware of the activity and basically assumed the risk of the events that were taking place in the gym. Control access and use of your property and buildings to reduce incidents of injury or crime as well as fear of crime. This will improve the quality of life for your school and the surrounding neighborhood and may also help control liability issues.

Ask yourself the following question, "What is the right and proper thing to do for the school?"

Don't wait for an incident to occur or for something to be stolen before you implement good security practices. Access control, video surveillance, and good inventory practices are all proven deterrents to unauthorized use and crime.

CLERY ACT COMPLIANCE—K-12

We live in an ever-changing world where our work behavior and job descriptions are governed by laws, standards, guidelines, and regulations.

In the article "School Security: Clery Act Compliance" in *Security Technology Executive*, July 2013,[5] the word "compliance" stands out for me (Fennelly). Why? *Because change comes from standards, guidelines, regulations, and acts of compliance.* Alison Kiss, the author of the article, is the executive director of the Clery Center for Security on Campus. Having worked for over 35 years on a campus police department, I am very familiar with requirements of reporting, publishing, and distribution of annual security reports.

---

[5]http://www.securityinfowatch.com/article/11004334/avoid-these-four-common-mistakes-in-reporting-campus-crime-and-security-policies.

Kiss states that, "Clery compliance is not the sole responsibility of campus police, public safety officers or the security department; however, often a single administrator or campus security department is charged with the responsibility of Cleary compliance. This is a near impossible task for one person and should be approached from a team perspective."[6]

Colleges and universities are now compelled to report crime statistics for three preceding calendar years, but some schools report for a longer period of time. The Clery Act requires that sex offenses, gun incidents, and alcohol-related issues also be reported.

K-12, get ready! We believe that K-12 facilities will soon be required to report all crime data, similar to what colleges and universities are currently doing. The only secret to complying with the Clery Act is to simply tell the truth and don't try to hide the facts. "Since K-12 institutions are not bound by the Clery Act, criminal statistics are less accurate for those facilities and other sources have to be relied upon," according to Frank J. Davies, CHS-IV (see Chapter 11).

CYBER BULLYING

Cyber bullying, by definition, is: stalking, sending threatening messages, altering images, and then distributing them with the intent to harass or intimidate.

Believe it or not, the problem is bigger and more prevalent than you may think. Why? Simply put, almost every child or young person today has a cell phone and access to a computer or an electronic device. All social media sites, such as Facebook and Twitter as well as communication through e-mail, webcams and chat rooms are available to those who wish to bully. It is in these venues that aggressive, intentional acts of cruelty are carried out by individuals or by a group of individuals against a person who cannot easily defend himself or herself.[7]

To help combat bullying behavior, one high school in California implemented a solution by monitoring all social media accounts for specific key words or phrases that could possibly be linked to bullying behavior. This practice could easily be put into place at schools throughout the country.

Here is some practical advice for parents, if you suspect your child is being bullied:

- Document everything.
- Be a good listener and be alert.
- Send letters to the superintendent of schools and copy the school principal, your child's teachers, the local newspaper, and your attorney. Confront everyone! Demand confidentiality in your letters. Copy everyone you can think of up and down the ladder.
- Make sure your child's teachers are trained in dealing with this problem.
- Enroll your child in martial arts training for his/her confidence and self-defense.
- Make sure your school has a zero-tolerance policy for bullying.
- Talk to your child about bullying.
- Understand that many times, bullying behavior may escalate into violence.
- Call other parents and organize them.

---

[6]http://www.securityinfowatch.com/article/11004334/avoid-these-four-common-mistakes-in-reporting-campus-crime-and-security-policies.
[7]The Bully Action Guide by Edward F. Dragan, Palgrave Macmillan Publishers, 2010.

- Obtain legal advice and file a civil lawsuit
- Contact the media.
- Have your attorney attend PTA meetings with you to get the school's attention.
- Know your rights.
- Let everyone know (including the bullies) that bullying behavior will not be tolerated.
- Call the police immediately. On page 187 in the book, *Bullying*, it states:

> Contact the police for safety issues. Call the police and notify school officials any time your child's safety is at stake.[8]

We need to be protecting our children far more effectively than we are currently!

SUMMARY TRENDS

A news story in August of 2013 announced that a several million dollar lawsuit had been filed against a school district. The mother of a student claimed that her daughter had been bullied for over 2 years and even though the school officials knew about the bullying, they did nothing to stop it. The school district will probably be tied up in the lawsuit for at least 2 years and will be the subject of numerous negative media reports before finally settling the case. Schools need to be proactive by getting in front of the issue. Document every complaint and document exactly what action was taken by the school.

Informational Websites for Bullying.

www.angriesout.com
www.bullystoppers.com
www.cyberbullying.ca
www.kidscope.org.uk/kisdcope
www.litigationconsultants.com
www.McGruff.org
www.mentahelp.net
www.safenetwork.org
www.stopbullying.gov
www.help4kids@freespirit.com

CELL PHONE SAFETY

Schools should encourage families to have a signed cell phone agreement with their child or young adult that outlines basic safety and security rules that must be followed if they are going to have a cell phone. We as parents and/or guardians must remember that children and young adults model our behavior, so we have to be sure that we are setting a good example for them.

Some of the topics that should be included in the cell phone agreement that the child or young adult will sign with the parent or guardian include the following:

- I will keep the cell phone in good condition and fully charged.
- I will stay within the contract of the cell phone provider plan regarding minutes and texts.

---

[8]Bully by Lee Hirsh, Cynthis Lowen, & Dina Santorelli, Weinstein Books, 2012 p. 187.

- I will answer the phone when a parent or guardian calls or texts, other than when in class.
- I will follow school rules for cell phone use.
- With my parent or guardian, we will establish an appropriate cell phone schedule to include time for homework, sleep, and meal time.
- I will contact a parent/guardian if someone sends a threatening or inappropriate message.
- With my parent or guardian, we will establish a code word that I can say or text if I am involved in a potentially dangerous situation.
- I will not send messages that could hurt, embarrass, or bully someone.
- I will not take or send inappropriate photos of myself or forward inappropriate photos of others.
- I understand that anything that I text or a photo that I send on my cell phone is not confidential.
- I will not text while driving (for those young adults of driving age).
- I understand that my cell phone can be taken away if I do not abide by this agreement.

GEO-TAGGING FEATURES

Due to geo-tagging software that is building into cell phones with digital cameras, there is a potential risk anytime a photo is taken with a cell phone and it is posted or transmitted electronically. Geo-tagging may reveal the exact location where the photo was taken and expose the child or young adult to a dangerous situation if someone is trying to locate them. This has been a concern of the US Military as well as law enforcement officials. Contact your cell phone carrier or manufacturer for specific directions to disable the geo-tagging feature of your phone.

SOCIAL MEDIA SAFETY

Parents and guardians should discuss social media safety and security with their child or young adult and establish ground rules for use. It is also a good idea to have a signed agreement that outlines the rules that must be followed to stay safe. The agreement that outlines the basic ground rules for social media safety and security should include the following:

- I will not give out any confidential information, such as my full name, address, date of birth, or phone number without my parent's or guardian's permission.
- My passwords are private and can only be shared with my parents or guardian.
- I understand that everything that I read, hear, or see online may not be factual.
- If I feel uncomfortable or pressured by any online post or inappropriate material, I will talk to my parent, guardian, or another trusted adult.
- I will not humiliate or upset anyone by sharing embarrassing photos or videos online.
- I will not post inappropriate photos or videos of myself online.
- I understand that any pictures or videos that I post online or anything that I write online can be saved and shared with others without my knowledge.
- I will not spread rumors or gossip online and I will defend others when it is done.
- I understand that there are scams online and I will not reveal confidential information.
- I have read and I understand the privacy policies of the social media sites that I use.

CYBER CRIME SECURITY

In a recent study conducted by Securitas Security Services, USA, Inc., it was reported that cyber security is the number one concern among Fortune 1000 companies.[9] How does this relate to schools? Recently, a senior in a local high school was able to access the main computer at his school at the end of the school year and deleted all of the grades for the entire senior class. Stealing or altering electronic information is easier than you may think.

Consider implementing the following safeguards:

1. Strong firewalls to prevent hacking.
2. Antivirus software.
3. Instruct all faculty and staff to not open or download unknown files.
4. Develop safeguards for data loss and cyber threats.
5. Select strong passwords and usernames.

You have an obligation to prevent identity theft and other crimes by protecting and preventing access to your systems. Reduce the threats and the risks!

DRIVING SAFETY ON AND AROUND SCHOOL PROPERTY

The American Automobile Association (AAA) offers the following recommendations for motorists to help keep children safe:

- *Slow down.* Obey school zone speed limits. Speed limits in school zones are reduced for a reason. A pedestrian struck by a vehicle traveling at 25 mph is nearly two-thirds less likely to be killed compared to a pedestrian struck by a vehicle traveling just 10 mph faster.
- *Stop for the school bus.* When meeting or overtaking a school bus in either direction—or a school bus receiving or discharging children on a road, in a parking area, or on school property—a driver must stop and not proceed until the bus resumes movement or the school bus operator signals you to proceed. www.drivinglaws.aaa.com/laws/school-buses
- *Come to a complete stop.* Research shows that more than one-third of drivers roll through stop signs in school zones or neighborhoods. Always come to a complete stop, checking carefully for children on sidewalks and in crosswalks before proceeding.
- *Eliminate distractions.* Research shows that taking your eyes off the road for just 2 seconds doubles your chances of crashing. And children can be quick, crossing the road unexpectedly or emerging suddenly between two parked cars. Reduce risk by not texting, using your cell phone, or eating while driving, for example.
- *Watch for bicycles.* Children on bikes are often inexperienced, unsteady, and unpredictable. Slow down and allow at least 3 ft of passing distance between your vehicle and a bicyclist. If your child rides a bicycle to school, require that he or she wear a properly fitted bicycle helmet on every ride. Find videos, expert advice, and safety tips at ShareTheRoad.AAA.com.

---

[9]Securitas Security Services USA, Inc. (Walker, Don; Glovka, Lynne; Greenawalt, Bernard), *"Top Security Threats and Management Issues Facing Corporate America: 2012 Survey of Fortune 1000 Companies,"* (Parsippany, NJ: 2013).

- *Talk to your teen.* No matter how good a student or how much you trust your teen, they are still an inexperienced driver. Car crashes are the leading cause of death for teens in the United States, and more than one in four fatal crashes involving teen drivers occur during the after-school hours of 3 p.m. to 7 p.m. Consider the *AAA Onboard Teen Safe Driver Program.* AAA Onboard (www.aaa.com/onboard) utilizes an in-vehicle device and web portal to help parents identify coaching opportunities and stay connected with their teen driver.[10]

Traffic enforcement issues around school property will require the assistance of local law enforcement to focus efforts in problem areas and increase community awareness of school safety issues. Law enforcement agencies recognize that traffic safety, especially in the areas of schools is a major concern of the public. There is a relationship between school safety and local crime prevention efforts. Public awareness of traffic laws about marked crosswalks and speed limits in school areas can be increased by law enforcement.

Some of the possible traffic safety issues problems where enforcement is part of the solution include the following:

- Speeding in school zone
- Illegal passing of school bus
- Not yielding to pedestrians in a crosswalk
- Parking violations—bus zone, crosswalks, residential driveways, time zones
- Risks to pedestrians and bicyclists during drop-off and pick-up times
- Lack of safety patrol/crossing guard operations
- Unsafe pedestrian and bicycle practices
- Other traffic law violations in school zone

SCHOOL TRAFFIC SAFETY RESOURCES

National Safe Routes to School (SRTS) Program www.hsrc.unc.edu/websites/index.cfm

The National Center for Safe Routes to School www.saferoutesinfo.org/

US Dept. of Transportation, Federal Highway Administration, Safe Routes to School http://safety.fhwa.dot.gov/saferoutes/srtsguidance.htm

National Highway Traffic Safety Administration, Safe Routes to School http://www.nhtsa.dot.gov/people/injury/pedbimot/bike/Safe-Routes-002/index.html

Walk to School http://www.walktoschool-usa.org/

The Pedestrian and Bicycle Information Center http://www.pedbikeinfo.org/

Institute for Transportation Research and Education at North Carolina State University http://www.itre.ncsu.edu/stg

Texas Transportation Institute, Safety at School Guideline http://tti.tamu.edu

FEAR OF CRIME

Schools should be safe havens for our children to learn and grow. Children should not be afraid that they will become the victim of a crime while on school property or on the way to or from school.

---

[10]"School's Open: Drive Carefully," The AAA Exchange, accessed March 4, 2014, http://exchange.aaa.com/safety/child-safety/schools-open-drive-carefully/.

In our society, fear of crime is more prevalent than actual victimization rates. There are Gallup Polls that attempt to measure fear of crime and many times fear is based on perception or media reports. In one such poll, conducted in October of 2013, "25% of U.S. parents said they 'frequently' worry about their child being harmed at school."[11] Children may hear their parents or other adults talk about crime or hear reports of violent and property crime in their area on the local news and become fearful.

For adults, fear of crime may confine people to their homes and have an economic impact on the community. It is a similar situation in schools. If a child is afraid at school, it may affect their quality of life. If a child is afraid to eat lunch in the cafeteria, use the restroom at school, or is afraid to ride the school bus, it may cause them to withdraw and lead to emotional as well as physical problems. If children are afraid, it may affect their willingness to get involved in extracurricular or after-school activities and negatively affect their overall school experience.

Children should be taught to use common sense and good judgment to keep themselves safe and we as parents should be involved at our child's school to know what measures have been implemented to ensure their safety. Get involved! Be a part of the parent, teacher, and student organizations. Ask about security and safety at your child's school. Observe safety and security procedures at the school. Organize other parents and petition the school to help change security procedures that you feel are outdated or ineffective. As school administrators, keep yourself up-to-date on what other schools in your area are doing and implement safety and security policies and procedures to keep children safe while they are at school.

FIRE ALARMS AND BUILDING EVACUATION

Why are teachers also fire wardens? The answer is simple. When the bell goes off, the teachers line up their students in an orderly fashion and march them outside to a designated location. After conducting a head count, they report back to the school office that the class has left the building and that all students are accounted for. It is important that fire drills are conducted at various times throughout the day (and night, if your school is residential) to ensure that all teachers, students, and dorm monitors are aware of notification and evacuation procedures.

Ensure that all students—visually impaired, hearing impaired, physically disabled, and so on can safely evacuate the building and that any special equipment and/or assistance is provided as necessary.

During your next fire drill, arrange for the local fire department to be present and consider this a training exercise. The total evacuation of the building should be timed. The fire department can confirm whether or not you have an efficient evacuation system that is 100% effective. The secret is to have your service company onsite the week before to confirm that all fire alarm units are operational. This is done by actually tripping each individual alarm unit for 5-10 seconds.

A bullhorn will be needed to give the all clear, so that teachers can bring the students back inside the building. You need to practice, practice, and practice. Your peers will tell you that after their incident, they were glad they conducted monthly drills. Another piece of advice is to invite the local police and fire officials to conduct a walk-through of your buildings so they are familiar with your campus.

---

[11]Jeffrey Jones, "Harm to Child at School a Top Crime Concern for U.S. Parents," Gallup, October 23, 2013, http://www.gallup.com/poll/165554/harm-child-school-top-crime-concern-parents.aspx.

SUMMARY

1. Train teachers how to be fire wardens and how to evacuate the building.
2. Have your service company conduct a 100% check of your fire alarms before your drill.
3. Purchase a bullhorn if you do not have one.
4. Mix up the days and times in which you conduct your drills.
5. Discuss details of your drill with fire and police departments so everyone is on the same page.
6. Establish a command post area with local officials.

FIRES AND FIRE EXTINGUISHERS[12]

The NFPA classifies fires into four types. The type of fire is determined by the materials that are being burned, or in other words, the fuel type.

There are basically four ways to put out a fire:

1. Cool the burning material.
2. Exclude oxygen.
3. Remove the fuel.
4. Break the chemical reaction.

It is important to use the appropriate fire extinguisher for the type of fire that is burning.

Fire and fire extinguishers are classified as follows:

Class A. Class A fires consist of ordinary combustibles such as wood, paper, trash, or anything else that leaves an ash. Water works best to extinguish a Class A fire.

Class B. Class B fires are fueled by flammable or combustible liquids, which include oil, gasoline, and other similar materials. Smothering effects that deplete the oxygen supply work best to extinguish Class B fires.

Class C. Class C fires are energized electrical fires. Always de-energize the circuit then use a non-conductive extinguishing agent, such as carbon dioxide.

Class D. Class D fires are combustible metal fires. Magnesium and titanium are the most common types of metal fires. Once a metal ignites, do not use water in an attempt to extinguish it. Use a dry powder extinguishing agent. Dry powder agents work by smothering the fire and absorbing the heat.

Class K. Class K fires are fires that involve cooking oils, grease, or animal fat and can be extinguished using Purple K, the typical agent found in kitchen extinguishers.

An easy way to remember what type of fire extinguisher to use is:

- Class A fires leave **ASH**.
- Class B fires **BOIL**.
- Class C fires have **CURRENT**.
- Class D fires have **DENSE** material
- Class K fires occur in the **KITCHEN**.

---

[12]Inge Sebyan Black, "Stages of Fire," in *Effective Physical Security*, 4th ed., ed. Lawrence J. Fennelly (Boston: Elsevier, 2013), 277–78.

GAY, LESBIAN, AND TRANSGENDER ISSUES

Item 1. Recently, I asked a teacher what she would do if a male student came up to her and said, "I'm transgender and I don't feel comfortable using the boy's/men's restroom." She replied that she would give him a key to the staff bathroom or tell him he could use the nurse's bathroom. I was surprised by the reply in that I was glad to hear a positive response to the question.

Item 2. The harassment or bullying of gay students in any way could be a federal Civil Rights issue. If you say no to their demands or handle a bullying or harassment situation poorly, you may create problems with gay rights advocates and have federal investigators knocking on your door.

Item 3. Sports issues may be another sensitive situation if not addressed properly. Establish school policies and procedures that will provide you with the tools you need and to address such issues and handle them on a case-by-case basis. Check with your legal department on these and all issues of a sensitive nature that could possibly be a future legal issue for the school and school district.

GLASS AND WINDOWS[13]

The purposes of windows, aside from aesthetics, are to let in sunlight, allow visibility, and to provide ventilation. When you research the types of windows and glass available, you start to see terms like *weather-ability, durability, thermal performance, triple-insulating glass, thermal barriers,* and *solar windows.* Every day another building is going "green," such as by diffusing light that enters a building, which cuts down on cooling costs, and the technology goes on and on from there.

"Healthy" buildings using current and innovative technology are contributing to healthier people, through the use of proper cleaning chemicals and green cleaning. All of this creates a better environment and reduced energy costs.

TYPES OF GLASS

There are five main types of glass: laminated, sheet, tempered, bullet-resistant, and float:

Laminated glass. This is a type of safety glass that contains polyvinyl butyral (PYB) or a similar substance and therefore holds together when shattered. It comes in high-performance laminated glass for structurally efficient glazing.

Sheet glass. Sheet glass is the least expensive and most vulnerable to breakage, with a thickness of typically 3-4 mm.

Tempered glass. Tempered glass is treated to resist breakage and is three to five times stronger than sheet glass, because it is 10 mm tempered.

Bullet-resistant glass. This glass is constructed using a strong, transparent material such as polycarbonate thermoplastic or by using layers of laminated glass. The polycarbonate layer is often sandwiched between layers of regular glass, and since the glass is harder than the plastic, the bullet is

[13]Lawrence J. Fennelly, "Glass and Windows," in *Effective Physical Security*, 4th ed., ed. Lawrence J. Fennelly (Boston: Elsevier, 2013), 329–33.

flattened and prevents penetration. It can be designed for both bullet and blast resistance. It will let in light and keep out trouble.

Float glass/Annealed glass. This glass has the quality of plate glass combined with the lower production cost associated with sheet glass manufacturing, and is virtually distortion and defect free.

GLASS AND SECURITY

A police department might recommend to a company that for tighter security, a glass wall and counter need to be added to create a barrier between the general public and the receptionist. Additionally, a glass door is also installed that works off an access control system. If a visitor needs access to the building they would remotely be granted access or escorted by personnel. Some people might not like this inconvenience, but it is the trade-off for security.

The following are factors to be considered for the selection of the type and size of a window:

- Energy efficiency and quality of unit
- Amount of sunlight, ventilation, and visibility
- Material and desired finish
    - Wood
    - Metal, aluminum, stainless steel
    - Finish color and "green" products

Window hardware should be durable, functional, and locking. Consider the following:

- Type of glazing available for effectiveness of weather stripping and wind pressure, explosion blasts, and fire
- The size and shape to prevent access, and the cost to replace if vandalized
- The use of grilles or bars on the inside or outside

In addition, the following are other considerations to keep in mind:

- Determine whether to use tempered glass, laminated glass, wired glass, bullet-resistant glass, and plastic glazing (e.g., polycarbonate or acrylic).
- Consider visibility requirements.
- Consider the thickness required. By altering the thickness and composition, such as by adding layers of glass or polycarbonate, security glass laminates can be customized to meet your requirements for specific risks/threats.
- The solution to security problems are to identify risk factors through an assessment, use laminated glass with a thicker vinyl interior layer, and use compression operating window frames, awnings, and casements.
- Float glass can be broken with an average rock, but toughened glass will shatter when it breaks.
- A crowbar can break or destroy standard window frames.
- Standard laminated glass (6.38 mm thick) can be broken with several blows from a hammer.[14]
- Consider energy savings.

---

[14]Stegbor, Security data sheet, V1. Available at www.stegbor.com, 2011.

- Hardware, such as glass, door hinges, locks, sliding glass door systems, and clamp supports are available online or at any hardware store.
- Sliding glass doors should be installed so as to prevent the lifting and removal of the glass door from the frame from the exterior of the building.
    - Each sliding panel should have a secondary locking or securing device in addition to the original lock built into the panel. The secondary device should consist of:
        - Charlie bar-type device, secondary locking device
        - Track lock, wooden, or metal dowel
        - Inside removable pins or locks securing the panel to the frame
- Fixed panel glass door (nonsliding) should be installed so that the securing hardware cannot be removed or circumvented from the exterior of the building.
- All "glass" used in exterior sliding doors and fixed glass panels should be made of laminated safety glass or polycarbonate sheeting. Plexiglas or single-strength glass will not qualify.
- Doors should open on the inside track, not the outside track

The following are factors to consider when selecting the type and size of windows:

1. Requirements for light, ventilation, and view
2. Material and desired finish—wood, metal, aluminum, steel, stainless steel
3. Window hardware—durability, function
4. Type of glazing
5. Effectiveness of weather stripping
6. Appearance, unit size, and proportion
7. Method of opening (hinge or slider), choice of line of hinges
8. Security lock fittings
9. Accessible louver windows
10. Ground floor—recommend lower windows, large fixed glazing, and high windows, small openings
11. Size and shape to prevent access
12. Size because of cost due to vandalism
13. Use of bars or grilles on inside
14. Glass:
    a. Double glazing deterrent
    b. Types of glass:
        (i) Acrylic glass, also known as Plexiglas or polycarbonate
        (ii) Tempered glass and laminated glass
        (iii) Wired glass and bullet-resistant glass
        (iv) Mirrors and transparent mirrors
        (v) Electrically conductive glass
        (vi) Rough or patterned glass
        (vii) Vision requirements
        (viii) Thickness
        (ix) Secured fixing to frame
        (x) Laminated barrier glass—uses
        (xi) Use of plastic against vandalism

(xii) Fixed, obscure glazing

(xiii) Shutters, grilles, and louvers for sun control and visual barriers as well as security barriers

Window Ironmongery

- Security window locks built-in during manufacture
- Security window locks fitted after manufacture
- Transom window locks
- Locking casement stays
- Remote-controlled flexible locks

Double-Hung Wood

1. All locking devices to be secured with ¾-inch full-threaded screws.
2. All window latches must have a key lock or a manual (non-spring-loaded or flip-type) window latch. When a non-key-locked latch is used, a secondary securing device must be installed. Such secondary securing devices may consist of
   a. Each window drilled with holes at two intersecting points of inner and outer windows and appropriate-sized dowels inserted in the holes. Dowels should be cut to provide minimum grasp from inside the window.
   b. A metal sash security hardware device of an approved type may be installed in lieu of doweling.
   Note: Doweling is less costly and of a higher security value than more expensive hardware.
3. Follow the balanced design principle. The glass falls first approach; that is, the walls are stronger than the anchors, the anchors are stronger than the frame, and the frame is stronger than the glazing.

Windows require protection when they:

- Are less than 18 ft from ground level
- Are less than 14 ft from trees
- Have openings larger than 96 sq. inches

BULLET-RESISTANT MATERIALS, BULLET-RESISTANT GLAZING FOR A SECURE SCHOOL

Some companies offer a full line of bullet-resistant glass in acrylic, polycarbonate, and glass-clad poly-carbonate. These products are available at UL protection levels 1-5, providing protection against guns ranging from a 9 mm to a 12 gauge. These bullet-resistant products are typically used in banks, credit unions, gas stations, and convenience stores, but are appropriate for any school that wants a secure environment.

In addition to providing bullet-resistant products to glaziers and mill shops, companies may provide custom milling and installation of secure barrier systems. Typical materials used in construction or sold directly include:

- Interior/exterior transaction windows
- Bulletproof doors

- Ballistic counters
- Package passers
- Bullet-resistant barriers and framing
- Bullet-resistant transparencies and fiberglass

Bullet-Resistant Fiberglass Wall Panels. These are used to provide bullet-resistant protection to the walls of offices, conference rooms, lobbies, reception area counters, and safe rooms. This bullet-resistant fiberglass can be installed by the manufacturer or even by a general contractor. Once installed, this product will never be seen but will provide high-quality ballistic protection and peace of mind for years and years to come.

Bullet-Resistant Doors. Along with protection of walls and lobbies, there is a wide variety of bullet-resistant doors to meet different needs. For example, solid executive-style veneered doors to match existing doors can be installed, but with bullet-resistant protection. Again, this is invisible bullet-resistant protection; therefore, nobody will know It is there. In addition, there are also full-vision clear doors, half-vision clear doors, plastic laminate no-vision doors, and bullet-resistant steel doors. All of these doors are pre-hung, so any contractor can install them within minutes.

Bullet-Resistant Windows. Bullet-resistant windows can be custom-built for the needs of each individual school. School windows can be replaced with bullet-resistant windows ranging from levels 1-5, or existing windows can be left in place and a second bullet-resistant window can be added behind the existing window in such a way that it will be virtually invisible to the general public.

Bullet-Resistant Lobby or Reception Area.

- Bullet-resistant window systems
- Package exchange units
- Bullet-resistant reception door with electric strike for access control
- Bullet-resistant fiberglass for reception counter die wall

Window Film. Window film is not completely bullet-resistant and there is *no* film product out there that is. Window film can be resistant to small arms and shotguns; however, some window film products have a bomb-blast-proof film product.

Window film comes in four categories:

1. *Security or safety film.* The benefits are that an outer pane of glass may break but the inner pane will stay intact. It is used to protect schools from the damages of flying glass due to earthquakes, windstorms, attacks, vandalism, theft, and accidents.
2. *Decorative film.* This makes glass surfaces clear and visible, enhances safety in public spaces, and allows you to customize your space with a school name or logo.
3. *Anti-graffiti window film.* This is a protective film that helps prevent scribbling or other defacing of the surface. The film is easy to peel off and replace, eliminating graffiti and the cost to replace glass.
4. *Solar film.* This has many benefits, such as it reflects and absorbs heat and light and it increases energy efficiency, reduces HVAC cost, protects furniture and carpets, and provides greater temperature stability.

Informational Websites for Glass and Windows.
International Window Film Association, www.iwfa.com
Extreme Window Solutions, www.extremewindowsolutions.com

Ace Security Laminates, www.acelaminate.com
Total Security, www.securityfilm.biz/index.htm
Pacific Bullet Proof, www.pacificbulletproof.com

GLOBAL HARMONIZATION SYSTEMS (MSDS AND HazCom)

There are hazardous chemicals that are used in many schools, especially in science labs and those chemicals used by custodians for maintenance and cleaning. The purpose of hazard communications (HazCom) is to provide everyone with information regarding chemicals, their hazards, and how to protect yourself and others. The Globally Harmonized System (GHS) is a set of universal recommendations for hazard communication developed by the United Nations. The primary benefit of GHS is to increase the quality and consistency of information that is provided about chemicals. Under GHS, there is a new hazard classification system, standardized labeling, and a new safety data sheet requirement. Material Safety Data Sheets (MSDSs) will now be referred to as Safety Data Sheets or SDS. In order to minimize the chemical hazards in your school, it is important to evaluate them. Chemical manufacturers perform most of these evaluations for us and establish hazard designations. The hazard information for a chemical can be found on the safety data sheet as well as on the label. Under GHS, the method of classification has been standardized to include health and environmental hazards, physical hazards, and the ability for the chemical to mix with another substance.

The following dates may be relevant to your school:

December 1, 2013. Employers must train their employees on the new label elements and safety data sheet format.

June 1, 2015. Employers must comply with all of the modified provisions of the final rule.

December 1, 2015. Chemical distributors will no longer be able to ship products labeled under the old system.

June 1, 2016. All employers will be required to have all alternative workplace labeling and HazCom programs in full compliance as well as provide additional training for newly identified health hazards. For more information on GHS, visit: www.osha.gov

GUNS VERSUS NO GUNS IN SCHOOLS

During an educational session at the 2013 ASIS International Annual Seminar in Chicago, a panel of security experts had approximately 80 security professionals respond to the following: "Please raise your hand if you are in favor of having guns in schools."

The response was that 50% of the attendees raised their hand.

Currently, about 20 states allow firearms in schools with few restrictions. At the same panel, the audience was asked if teachers should be armed. Again, the response was 50-50.

I (Fennelly) asked Peter Hassenfuss, a friend and former teacher, the same question. Mr. Hassenfuss is also a former police officer and trained in the use of firearms. He stated, "This is a very hard question." He had previously stated that in the school where he taught, he and two other male teachers who had classrooms on the same floor would be willing to carry a firearm for security in the school. He also said, "I feel the other teachers would feel *uncomfortable*." He stated that he could not say if any of the female teachers would be willing to carry a firearm. Mr. Hassenfuss said that if it became mandatory for teachers to be armed, he felt that some would refuse. His final comment was, "I think your 50-50 response is a typical response to this ongoing controversial question."

People today are looking for answers. Unfortunately, we do not have all of the answers. The following quote was taken from the book, *Thinking about Crime* by James Q. Wilson:

> A substantial body of research, such as that by Franklin Zimring confirms that the availability of a gun influences the outcomes of angry encounters.[15]

IDENTITY THEFT

This topic is included because children have social security numbers that in many cases may be associated with their school records. This increases the likelihood that a student may become the victim of identity theft. It is important that all student records that contain social security numbers or other personal identifying information be kept secure. Access to these records should be restricted. Ideally, records should be secured in locked cabinets in a locked room, protected by an alarm or intrusion detection system and/or video surveillance. It is important to train staff and faculty that student records are not be left on desks overnight or in unsecured areas during the school day.

> [In 2011,] the annual cost of identity theft [was] $37 billion dollars....identity theft schemes made up only 9.8% of all cybercrime in 2010.[16]

WHAT SHOULD YOU DO IF YOU OR YOUR CHILD IS THE VICTIM OF IDENTITY THEFT?[17]

Step 1: Chase down any problem account. Contact the credit card companies, banks, or any other creditors to close the accounts that you know have been tampered with or opened fraudulently.

Step 2: Contact the credit bureaus. Contact the fraud department of any one of the three major credit bureaus to place a fraud alert on your credit file. The fraud alert requires that creditors contact you before opening any new accounts or making any changes to your existing accounts. When you place a fraud alert on your credit file, all three credit bureaus are required by law to automatically send a credit report free of charge to you. This "one-call" fraud alert will remain on your credit file for at least 90 days.

Step 3: Contact the fraud department of each of your creditors. Make sure that each of your creditors is aware that an identity thief may have your account information. Ask each of your creditors to place a fraud alert on your account.

---

[15]James Q. Wilson, *Thinking about Crime,* Vintage Books, 1985 Revised Edition.

[16]Gordon M. Snow, Assistant Director, Cyber Division, Federal Bureau of Investigation, Statement before the Senate Judiciary Committee, Subcommittee on Crime Terrorism, Washington, D.C., April 12, 2011.

[17]This section on what to do if you or your child is the victim of identity theft is adapted from "Identity Theft: Don't Let It Happen to You!" a paper released by the Cape & Islands District Attorney's Office, Barnstable, MA.

Step 4: Promptly make a report with your local police department. File a police report with your local police department, keep a copy for yourself, and give a copy to your creditors and the credit bureaus.

Suggested precautions to take to avoid becoming a victim:

- Do not give out personal information—such as social security number, mother's maiden name— to anyone unless you have initiated the contact and know who you are dealing with.
- Do not respond to phone, e-mail, or mail solicitations from businesses attempting to confirm your personal information in exchange for an offer of something that seems too good to be true.
- Destroy or shred credit applications or any documents with personal information before you throw them away.
- Review your monthly statements and report any unauthorized charges.
- Order yearly credit reports for you and your child and check your credit history for fraudulent activity.

Contact one of the three national credit reporting agencies to report problems.

EQUIFAX: 800-270-3435 OR 800-525-6285
TRANSUNION: 800-680-7289
EXPERIAN: 888-397-3742

LATCH-KEY KIDS

The term latch-key kids refers to students that go home to an empty house after school and stay home alone until a parent or caregiver gets off from work.

According to the U.S. Census Bureau, one-third of all school-age children in the United States are, for some part of the week, latch-key kids. The total number of children between 5 and 13 years of age who spend time home alone is between five and seven million. The Census Bureau also states that 15% of children are home before school, 76% after school, and 9% at night. Because of these statistics, it is important that parents and schools together teach all children in their school about basic safety and security. This may be a topic parent, teacher, and student groups work on together with local law enforcement to provide education and advice.

Many security professionals are promoting the use of home video surveillance as well as GPS to monitor or track their child until the parent arrives home.

LIABILITY

Schools are ripe for lawsuits. This statement is based on recent events as well as inadequate levels of security that we have seen.

For example, at a recent consulting job I (Fennelly) performed, a school had a newly employed janitor/building manager. He was told to cut back the bushes and trees around the school to be in compliance with CPTED principles. He trimmed the trees and bushes and did a great job. However, the school groundskeeper later filed a complaint because the janitor completed the job he (the groundskeeper) was supposed to have done. The complaint was rejected because it was discovered that the groundskeeper had not been doing his job of controlling the overgrowth of the vegetation.

Case No. 1. Consider the following scenario: A female teacher was attacked and raped on school property. The next day, photos were taken of every bush, tree branch, and walkway in the area of the attack. Add to the facts of the case that many lights in the area were inoperable (either burned out or damaged) for 6 months prior to the attack and that four work-order requests had been initiated to have the lights repaired or the bulbs replaced, but the work was never done. Further investigation revealed that this had been the third assault in the same area. The teacher's attorney had a documented history of prior and similar acts as well as a pattern of neglect. The issues with this case are as follows: failure to trim trees and bushes to meet CPTED recommendations; failure to maintain lights by replacing or repairing inoperable fixtures; failure to properly supervise and monitor the work of the school maintenance employee and/or electrician; failure to maintain a proper and safe environment for students, faculty, staff, and visitors. Since the assault was the third such similar crime on the property, it could be determined to be a foreseeable act. A case of this type could go on for several years with the end result being the city or town writing a check to end the negative publicity. This case sounds simple, but a civil lawsuit is serious. How do you measure the effectiveness of security at the school? Do you want this type of incident on the six o'clock news every night? Certainly not, so manage your property and liability issues properly.

Case No. 2. A 12-year-old girl was bullied for over a year. Fifteen girls kept telling her to die and encouraged her to kill herself. When the twelve-year-old finally reached her limit, she committed suicide, and left the following note, "I can't take the bullying and harassment anymore." The student's parents had tried talking to the parents of the bullies and it did not work. The parents tried talking to the teacher and it did not work. The parents requested that the teacher help them have their child moved to another class and the response was no. The parents talked to the principal and were sent back to the teacher. The parents went back to the teacher again. More negative responses. In the meantime, the child had been taken to the doctor for black and blue marks and a sprained arm. The parents' only course of action was to contact an attorney and the police and then go to the media. It was at this point that the student killed herself. The parents had exhausted their options. The school failed to protect a student in its care and had also failed to provide the proper standard of care in protecting students.

Authorities considered filing criminal charges against all fifteen girls who bullied the young girl. The police were quoted as saying she was "terrorized on social media." The young girl's father filed a complaint with the school district. Two of the fifteen bullies, aged twelve and fourteen, were charged with felony aggravated stalking. "People deserve to live a healthy, normal life," the sheriff who worked this case told Robin Roberts on *Good Morning America*. "We will prosecute anyone we can prove has bullied or stalked someone." [18]

Everything about this case was on the 6 o'clock news every night until well after the funeral services for the student. Why? Because, allegedly, the school did nothing—it gave the student's parents the run-around and then tried to make less of the situation by ignoring it.

---

[18]Jerriann Sullivan, "Sheriff in Rebecca Sedwick Suicide: Cut Cyberbulling Cord," *Orlando Sentinel*, October 16, 2013, http://articles.orlandosentinel.com/2013-10-16/news/os-rebecca-sedwick-grady-judd-today-show-20131016_1_judd-rebecca-ann-sedwick-social-media-sites.

Did the school have a duty to take action and to protect this student?

If we assume, after notice was given, the school did nothing, then the school failed in their duty to take corrective action. The school also failed to take reasonable action as it pertains to the incident.

Liability in the early stages is not complicated. Numerous times, security professionals will tell school administrators:

1. Conduct a threat assessment.
2. Establish policies and procedures.
3. Train the teachers and staff.
4. Train the bus drivers.
5. Implement best practices.

Now, let's assume your school has done none of the above steps. Also, assume that you have a student commit suicide after her mother told you six times that her daughter was being bullied.

Now, ask yourself the following questions:

1. Did you have a duty to protect this child after you were notified of the problem?
2. Did you provide a reasonable degree of care?

Your failure to do so would be the proximate cause of her death.

MANAGE YOUR RISK AND YOUR LIABILITY![19]

What is the liability of schools when students are harmed?

Failure to Adhere to Law or Policy. In some instances, liability may be premised on failure to adhere to current local, state, and federal school safety laws and regulations on school district safety policy. School officials should do the following:

1. Ensure compliance with all current applicable local, state, and federal statutes addressing safety and harassment issues.
2. Ensure that school districts' safety and harassment policies are fully implemented.
3. Ensure compliance with the school's safety and harassment policy.
4. Evaluate any existing school campus access policy to determine its adequacy and ensure that it is being followed.
5. Train school employees on these issues.

Failure to Use Reasonable Care in Selecting Personnel. In some instances, liability may be premised on failing to use reasonable care in screening, hiring, training, supervising, and retaining personnel who are regularly on site and who commit acts of violence.

School officials should do the following:

1. Implement appropriate screening and hiring standards to minimize the likelihood of hiring personnel with propensities toward violence, consistent with applicable law.
2. Ensure proper training of teachers and school staff in the recognition of warning signs for violent behavior on steps to take to minimize violence, and on appropriate responses if violence occurs.

---

[19]Section adapted from *Guide for Preventing & Responding to School Violence*, Bureau of Justice Assistance, 2007, p. 29, Grant 2007-DD-BX-K112.

3. Seek the advice of an attorney before implementing any policy on the search or seizure of students' property.
4. While a warrant may not be required, school officials must justify any search or seizure based on the following:

   a. Reasonable suspicion that the law or a school rule has been violated.
   b. Information, facts, or circumstances that would lead a reasonable person to conclude that evidence of a crime or rule violation would be found in the search.
   c. The relationship between the extensiveness of the search and the evidence being sought.
   d. The relationship between the severity of the threat and the degree of intrusiveness in conducting the search.
   e. The presence of any special legal considerations, such as whether the student did not have a reasonable expectation of privacy; the objects seized fell within the plain view of an official who had a right to be at that location; the person who seized the object was not affiliated with, or directed to do so by, the government; or the student voluntarily consented to the search.

5. Take into consideration the legal liability related to any type of nonconsensual search of students or students' property, including but not limited to the following:
   - Locker searches
   - Vehicle searches
   - Use of metal detectors
   - Use of drug- or weapon-sniffing dogs
   - Drug testing
   - Body searches
   - Use of cameras
   - Police-assisted searches
   - Searches of abandoned articles
   - Book bag, purse, and backpack searches
   - Searches of outer clothing
   - Strip searches

LIGHTING

1. Increase street lighting as well as lighting around the area of the school.
2. Lighting may reduce crime by improving visibility. This deters potential offenders by increasing the risk that they will be recognized or interrupted in the course of their activities.[20]
3. Determine what works to reduce crime—video surveillance, lighting, and active police patrol.
4. In the Home Office Research Study (251),[21] several cities reported that "improved street lighting was most clearly effective in reducing crime…"

---

[20]David P. Farrington and Brandon C. Welsh, Home Office Research Study 251: Effects of Improved Street Lighting on Crime: A Systematic Review, Home Office Research, Development and Statistics Directorate, August 2002.
[21]Ibid.

Why improve lighting? To create a psychological deterrent to intrusion and criminal activity and to enable detection once a breach of security has occurred.[22]

Recommended illumination levels in foot candles:

- Outer Perimeter 0.15 fc
- Vehicular Entrance 1.0 fc
- Pedestrian Entrance 2.0 fc
- Entrance that is inactive 0.1 fc
- Sidewalks 1 fc
- Parking Lot 3 fc

TURNING OFF ALL LIGHTS

There was a time when it was popular to turn off all of the lights around a school. This was called the "black-out" method. The entire school campus was in total darkness. The thought process was that if a school was in total darkness, it would be easy to spot criminals on the property because they would be unable to commit crimes in total darkness and would have to bring lights. The police would then respond to the lights. Unfortunately, unless the criminals provided their own lights, the police could not see anything that happened on the property. Neighbors could not see anything but could hear the sound of breaking of glass. When schools started using video surveillance, the lights had to be turned back on and crime was deterred because the lighting increased the likelihood that someone would see and identify the intruders. There is documented research indicating that lighting is effective in reducing crime.

MENTALLY ILL AND CHALLENGED (ACTIVE SHOOTERS)

Having attended classes about active shooters over the years, it appears that most aggressors have had major traumas in their lives such as mental breakdowns, PTSD, or some sort of disruption in his or her life. Active shooters are sometimes victims themselves and are looking for solutions to their problems. Regardless, we believe to a degree the shooter should be held responsible for their actions. He or she usually prepares well for the attack by securing a weapon and ammunition. The shooter will conduct a security assessment of the site and plan the attack. The specific time and place are selected and at this point, the shooter is in control. Because of this planning, all of the elements for a surprise attack are in place. Like a game of chess, the shooter will move in and execute the attack when ready. At this point, the school (and later, law enforcement) is forced to react and respond.

The majority of active shooters are confident individuals, but they are looking for a soft target that will require the least amount of effort. The shooter will move around to target specific individuals, shoot as many victims as possible, or simply shoot victims indiscriminately. For this reason, school personnel are advised to lock classroom or office doors and stay out of sight. In most instances, a locked door will cause the shooter to move on.

---

[22]David G. Patterson, *PSP Study Guide*, 2nd ed., (Alexandria, VA: ASIS International, 2007)

So what is the answer? Schools must have administrative support for effective security policies and procedures as well as adequate physical and electronic security measures.

When you have an attack at your school, you are in crisis mode. Your emergency procedures are implemented immediately. All of the training that you have conducted and the drills that you have practiced are put to the test. When there is an individual with a gun in the building, you *must* do what is necessary to prevent injuries and save lives.

METAL DETECTORS

If your school has a history of weapons being brought to school, metal detectors may be your answer. If there is a high fear of crime in your school, metal detectors may be the solution for a weapons-free environment.

In addition to a metal detector, the school lobby design should include adequate lighting and several angles of video surveillance to capture full view of the area. Additionally, there should be a well-trained staff and policies and procedures.

Simply put, a metal detector is an electromagnetic field, with lines passing through a metallic object. Generating eddy currents on a metal detector distorts the normal electronic magnet field. This is how weapons are detected.

Metal detectors are frequently used to:

- Increase security at schools.
- Increase security at transportation terminals.
- Increase security at courts, jails, and prisons.
- Protect presidents and world leaders.
- Protect spectators at sports and cultural events.

At a local school, a surprise inspection was conducted and knives, brass knuckles, mace, and two guns were discovered. Any person passing through a metal detector that trips the machine needs to be inspected further, generally with a handheld unit. It is the operator's responsibility to make certain that every alarm be investigated.

Keep in mind that no metal detector can ever be expected to function at 100% efficiency, 100% of the time. Proper training of personnel operating the metal detector is crucial.

Metal detectors have these characteristics:

- They are a deterrent.
- They work.
- They are durable.
- They are portable and rugged.
- They can detect weapons.
- They are adjustable.
- No touching is required.
- Cost is reasonable, about $3,200.

Metal detectors are a deterrent and can detect metal (specifically weapons, usually guns or knives) and they will, in most cases find every weapon. It is important to note that you may not discover a device that is carefully or cleverly concealed.

NONINSTRUCTIONAL AREAS
THE CAFETERIA AND THE KITCHEN

Cafeterias and kitchens aren't just for preparing and eating food. Many times these are the most unsecure areas of the school campus. Exterior doors are left open, dumpsters are located just outside the door, and trash is taken out the door throughout the day. Doors in this area are frequently used for entry and as an exit for school personnel not assigned to the kitchen, windows are often left open and/or unlocked, and kitchen and cafeteria staff are many times not included in safety and security training programs.

LOADING DOCKS/RECEIVING AREA

Schools must control access to the loading dock area and must have a system in place to not only restrict, but identify individuals gaining access to the loading dock area. All loading dock doors should be alarmed and annunciated to the security control center. Written emergency procedures should be in place with instructions for shipping and receiving goods. Appropriate security procedures, including a panic or duress alarm that is monitored by security personnel or video surveillance, should be utilized.

Chemicals in this area must be properly stored. Tanks must be secured with either chain or heavy-duty rope. All loading docks equipped with remote door release systems must also be equipped with two-way radios and video surveillance, to identify individuals prior to allowing them access into the loading dock area or the school building interior.

PARKING LOTS

All school parking lots must have signage posted indicating property boundaries and that access is restricted to authorized persons only. In addition, parking lots should be equipped with the following:

- Video surveillance systems to display and document activity.
- Emergency communications systems (mass notification).
- Lighting to illuminate the parking lot area and support video surveillance systems.

All systems must be monitored by appropriate school personnel—building security, school staff, security control centers, and so on. Additionally, there should be random security patrols of all parking lots.

PHYSICAL SECURITY

You need physical security devices to make your schools safe. If you disagree, then why do you lock the doors and windows to your school at night?

In this section, we're going to discuss the many types of physical security devices that are available and why you need them. We'll then discuss approximate costs. A logical way to approach physical security is to develop a 10-year acquisition and implementation plan.

KEYS AND ACCESS CONTROL BADGES

Key Control Question—How often do I need to rekey?

- At least every 5 years.
- When you have lost control of your keys.
- When someone has left and he/she has not returned the keys.

- Exterior door key control should be very restricted.
- Consider a system where the key cylinders can be removed and a new key core can be installed, so rekeying can be done quickly with a new core.

ACCESS CONTROL BADGE READER

We recommend card access control over mechanical locks and keys. Why? If you hand out 50 keys, how many will you get back at the end of the year? How many keys have been duplicated? With electronic access control, you can immediately delete the badge to remove access and regain control of your security. Electronic access control for 10 locations costs approximately $70,000.

DOORS

All doors and hardware must be heavy-duty. Hinge pins must be nonremovable. If glass is on the door, it must be break and bullet resistant.

BOLLARDS

Bollards can be made of reinforced concrete or steel. Bollards can be decorative as well as effective. Many bollards also contain landscape or walkway lighting. The cost of 15 installed bollards is approximately $30,000.

WINDOWS

- All windows should have locks.
- Ground-level windows must be secured with a grille to prevent entry.
- Windows also should have shades or blinds.

INTERCOMS

There are several different types of intercom systems depending upon the application and environmental conditions in your area. Consider those that are weatherproof and sealed to prevent access from rain and snow.

LIGHTING

There are several points concerning lighting:

- Use cost-effective lighting. Consider and explore LED lights. (See chapter on lighting that discusses many aspects of lighting and the various types of lights as well as recommended lighting levels.)
- Consider an even distribution of light around your buildings and property.
- Lights should not be on in the daytime. If they are, something is wrong such as a broken ballast or a timer needs adjustment. Don't waste energy.
- Every light on the school property should be checked monthly both at night as well as during the day.
- If an area is used heavily at night or for special events, consider additional, designated lighting that is on timers for additional illumination.
- If video surveillance is used around the perimeter of the building or property, consider the level of lighting needed for those specific areas.

VIDEO SURVEILLANCE

- Digital and IP cameras should utilize motion and analytics, and recordings need to be kept for 90 days. The cost for about 15 digital video surveillance systems is approximately $37,500.
- Assume four youths break into a school. The alarm will notify a central station and the cameras will be recording the break-in. When the police respond, the youths are apprehended and their parents contacted. This is the working scenario that you want in place in your school.
- Now assume four youths break into the school but you don't have an alarm system, video surveillance, exterior lighting, or police response. They vandalize the school by breaking windows, break into a trophy case, the principal's office, classrooms, etc. Consider your repair costs in this situation.
- A video surveillance system is a deterrent.

INTRUSION ALARM SYSTEMS (ALARM SYSTEMS)

- Control access to the school by using an intrusion detection system or an alarm system.
- Intrusion detection systems are the most expensive vandalism control measure a school can use.
- An intrusion detection system can detect vandals, but they cannot apprehend them. It can merely signal the alarm-system monitor, which may be miles away.
- Intrusion detection system can be an effective deterrent and should be considered as part of any comprehensive plan to control vandalism.
- If intrusion detection systems are integrated with video surveillance, the likelihood of identifying and apprehending intruders is greatly increased.

POLICIES, PROCEDURES, GUIDELINES, AND STANDARDS

We as security professionals have said many times over the last few years that times have changed and we must also change to meet the new challenges. Polices may remain the same over a period of time, but procedures tend to change more often to meet these changes. Compare school safety and security procedures from 10 years ago to what is considered a best practice today. The primary cause for these security changes are because of the many active shooter events across the country.

What factors cause change?

- Standards
- Guidelines
- Regulations
- Auditors
- Best Practices
- Crises

STANDARDS

In 2009, ASIS International developed a standard entitled, *Organizational Resilience: Security, Preparedness, and Continuity Management Systems—Requirements with Guidance for Use* (ASIS SPC.1-2009).

GUIDELINES

In 2009, ASIS International developed ASIS GDL FPSM-2009, the *Facilities Physical Security Measures Guideline*, which covers many topics that we put in this book: doors, windows, locks, site hardening, access control, layers of security, physical barriers, CPTED, lighting, alarms, video surveillance, and security personnel.

The purpose of guidelines such as this is to introduce you to these topics, and gain the insight of the authors, based on their education, training, and experience. The guidelines include documents for emergencies, drills for evacuation, and lockdowns. All guidelines are subject to update and change.

REGULATIONS

The NFPA, OSHA, and your individual local and state laws contain information that you must follow to be in compliance with all applicable regulations.

AUDITORS

Conduct risk assessments as a working review of your security processes and programs. If you have not implemented best practices or if your security program is not up to standard for schools, the auditor, or assessor will make recommendations to bring your processes and programs into compliance.

BEST PRACTICES

Best practices are based on the most current data available from leading security professionals about what policies, procedures, and techniques have been successful in a similar environment or industry.

A CRISIS

The Merriam-Webster Dictionary defines a crisis as an unstable or crucial time or state of affairs in which a decisive change is impending, *especially* one with the distinct possibility of a highly undesirable outcome.[23] Can you guarantee that there will never be major crisis at your school? Are you prepared if it does happen?

RESTROOMS AND LOCKER ROOMS

Video surveillance cannot be conducted in areas of the school where there is a reasonable expectation of privacy. This includes restrooms in the school and locker rooms in the physical education or gymnasium area. To ensure the safety of students, faculty, and staff, consider installing panic buttons or duress alarms in these areas.

RISK AND PROTECTIVE FACTOR ASSESSMENTS

Goal and Purpose of the Assessment. For an assessment to be successful, a key goal is to develop a profile of risk factors, protective factors, and problem behaviors in the community. The assessment report

---

[23]*Merriam-Webster Online,* s.v. "crisis," accessed March 11, 2014, http://www.merriam-webster.com/dictionary/crisis.

is designed to provide a profile that can be shared with the community partners. The ultimate goal is to develop and implement a community action plan as a result of the assessment.

Even though data may be collected on crime and violence in a community using statistics from law enforcement, many times it will be the first time the community has collected data based on the risk and protective factors that predict violence and other problem behaviors in a structured, scientifically valid way. The data collection processes must be monitored to ensure they are valid and accurately represent the area based on community and school assessments and surveys.

These assessments or surveys provide detailed information about specific risk andprotective factors. This will help community members make truly informed decisions thatwill appropriately correspond to the specific needs of their neighborhoods.

Risk Factors in Schools and Communities—In Priority Order.

1. Early and persistent problem behavior
2. Family management problems/family conflict
3. Friends engaging in problem behavior/weak social ties
4. Lack of commitment to school
5. Exposure to violence
6. Gang involvement
7. Availability of drugs/drug use
8. Academic failure beginning in late elementary school
9. Family history of problem behavior
10. Low neighborhood attachment

SCHOOL BUS DRIVERS

Very little is written about school bus drivers or the training that they receive. We can honestly say we know several school bus drivers and all of them are honorable and hardworking individuals. They know the names of the children that ride their bus and genuinely care about them and their safety. Many of them will ask a child if they are okay if the child seems upset. We overheard the following exchange between a school bus driver and a student. "Abby, where is your sister, Emma?" "Mr. Bill, she is home sick today." They notice when something is wrong with a child and look out for their safety.

School bus drivers have proven to be valuable sources of information for law enforcement and school administrators. Additionally, they can provide support for school programs and safety issues and give important feedback on results of the programs.

SCHOOL BUS DRIVER TRAINING

Below is a partial list of common scenarios for school bus drivers, provided by the National Highway Traffic Safety Administration:

1. Smoke is coming from the front engine of the bus.
2. The bus is stuck on a railroad track.
3. The bus has broken down on a major highway. Where is the best assembly point?
4. The bus has broken down on a major highway with limited sight distance, just past a blind curve.

5. The bus has skidded off the road in icy weather and is lying on its side.
6. The bus has been hit and is leaking fuel.
7. A car has run into the rear of the bus and is partially under the bus.

Additional information on training for school bus drivers can be obtained from the school insurance company or your local law enforcement agency.

CAUSE OF VANDALISM

The causes of vandalism remain obscure. Though research addressing the "why" of vandalism is growing, it has yet to yield clear-cut answers. Among the motivating factors often cited are anger, frustration, hostility, bitterness, alienation, futility, inequality, restricted opportunity, emotional pain, failure, prejudice, revenge, and the need for attention. Although much of the research is convincing, the fact remains that many vandals do not appear to be among the most angry, frustrated, hostile, alienated, or needy youth. Only a small fraction of the youngsters who fall into that category actually commit acts of vandalism. So, while most experts agree that vandalism is not totally senseless, they do not claim to fully understand its causes. In fact, vandalism is often not understood by vandals themselves. Many vandals report that they do not know why they did it. Many others, according to case reports, offer the unsolicited observation that destruction is fun. Still others express satisfaction and exhilaration.

Few consider themselves criminals. For the time being, we can conclude only that motives for vandalism are diverse. But the whys notwithstanding, the vandal profile suggests that our task is, in large part, to anticipate and redirect the impulses of young teenagers. Schools are by no means the helpless victims of early adolescence. Many school factors, most of which are amenable to change, influence the amount of vandalism that schools experience.

The following characteristics are typical of schools that suffer high property damage or loss:

- Vandalism is higher when there is poor communication between the faculty and the administration (such as when the principal fails to define policy or makes policy decisions unilaterally).
- Hostility and authoritarian attitudes on the part of teachers toward students often result in students "taking it out" on the school. Limited contact between teachers and students reduces student involvement with the school and increases the likelihood of vandalism.
- Schools characterized by intense competition for leadership positions suffer greater property damage and loss.
- The chances for vandalism increase when the students do not value their teachers' opinions of them.
- Schools at which students strive to get good grades experience more vandalism.
- Parents of students in high-damage schools express less favorable attitudes toward their schools than do other parents.
- The school is a convenient target for vandalism when it is close to students' homes.
- Damage is greater in larger schools where there is more property to destroy. This correlation between school size and vandalism prevails regardless of whether the school is located in an urban, suburban, or rural setting.
- Fewer offenses occur when rules are well understood by students and are consistently and firmly enforced by teachers and administrators.

VANDALISM PREVENTION[24]

If the special problems of early adolescence, often intensified by social or personal pressure, interact with school conditions to produce vandalism, then preventive measures must address the nature of both the child and the school. Furthermore, prevention must include both physical and human responses. At present, most vandalism-prevention or -reduction programs rely on physical security—bigger and better electronic alarm systems, patrol guards, dogs, tamper-proof locks, and window grilles. These techniques help, but they address only 20 percent of the problem—those incidents involving breakage. These incidents usually occur when school is not in session and in the absence of witnesses. The techniques have little effect on the day-to-day trashing of the school or on the disruptive acts aimed at the school's routine (bomb threats, the setting of fires, and false fire alarms) that are committed during school hours. The most sophisticated physical and electronic barriers are not sufficient to keep vandals from what they consider an attractive target. In fact, it has been argued that alarms and armed police officers, besides lowering student and staff morale, often themselves become a challenge, inviting rather than deterring vandals. Vandalism prevention requires not a narrow or piecemeal approach, but a varied and comprehensive effort that includes both physical and human components geared to the school's specific problems. Furthermore, an effective long-term program must involve partnerships with the community, parents, neighbors, police, and civic groups as well as students, teachers, and school administrators.

SCHOOLS ARE AN EASY TARGET

Schools are an easy target for vandals. Most are public, secular, and often unoccupied. Most will remain public and secular, but they need not remain unoccupied, unprotected, or unobserved. The following are techniques that have made some schools less vulnerable to vandals. These are especially effective against problems occurring during nonschool hours.

Occupy the School. Employ a custodial force around the clock. In most schools, the entire custodial force works at one time, leaving the school at night. As an alternative, custodians can be assigned staggered shifts so that the school is always occupied. Twenty-four-hour custodians are particularly appropriate in schools suffering sporadic property damage that demand more than a roving patrol but less than permanent security officer or police officer.

Invite police to use the school buildings at night. Police can be issued keys to the schools in their patrol areas so that they can use school offices to write their reports. This places a police officer in the school when it might otherwise be unoccupied, and it places a police car in front of the school.

Bring the community into the school. The school is an excellent place for recreational programs; health clinics; adult-education classes; counseling centers; community gatherings; plays; and Boy Scout, Girl Scout, and Parent-Teacher Organization (PTO) meetings. The presence of people in the school building not only reduces the opportunity for vandalism but also stimulates community and student interest in the school.

Watch the School. Use school neighbors as eyes and ears. Ask nearby homeowners to watch the school and report suspicious activities. Emphasize careful observation and rapid reporting, but discourage direct involvement in any situation observed. Such programs work best if they are organized but

---

[24]Ibid.

based on informal involvement, if they are accompanied by overall involvement of parents and community with the school, and if they offer some sort of prestige to participants.

PATROL

Employ Roving Patrols. A uniformed patrol used instead of or in conjunction with an alarm system can deter vandalism. The individuals who patrol should establish rapport with neighborhood youths and open communication with community leaders. They should also vary their patrol patterns. Consider parking a local police car in the school lot, but be sure to move it around.

Hire student patrols during the summer and on weekends. The school district or community can provide its youth with part-time or summer employment and, at the same time, curb vandalism by paying students to patrol the school grounds during weekends, holidays, and summer vacations. These students should be paid an adequate wage and considered an integral part of the school's security force.

INTRUSION ALARMS

Control access to the school by using an alarm system. Alarms are the most expensive vandalism control measure a school can use. While they can detect vandals, they cannot apprehend them; they can merely signal the alarm system monitor, which may be miles away.

They can, however, be an efficient deterrent and should be considered as part of any comprehensive plan to control vandalism. If alarm systems are linked with video surveillance systems, the chances of apprehending intruders are greatly increased.

Design the school with vandalism prevention in mind. The following designs for preventing vandalism can be implemented for schools:

- Limit ground-to-roof access.
- Eliminate low, overhanging roofs.
- Avoid unnecessary exterior fixtures.
- Plant trees that cannot be climbed near buildings, but the first branch must be 8 ft from the ground as a CPTED recommendation.
- Consider "raising" as much of the school building as possible, from ground level.
- Build the school at some distance from residential areas. While it should be located near the homes of most of those it serves, it will suffer less property damage if there is a buffer zone between it and surrounding residential areas.
- Design the school with plenty of defensible space so that the normal flow of school traffic allows continuing, casual surveillance of the premises.
- Use vandal-resistant surfaces. Use harder surfaces in damage-prone areas. For walls, use epoxy paint or glazed tiles that are easily and inexpensively replaced or repaired; use small wall panels and keep replacement panels in stock; and place permanent signs, building names, and decorative hardware at a level that cannot be reached from the ground. Replacing damaged areas immediately shows a sense of pride in the appearance and helps to eliminate copycat acts of vandalism. Plan windows carefully. Avoid windows that are vulnerably placed. Use small panes of glass to simplify replacement; use thick, tempered glass, thick acrylic, or Plexiglas® for windows in heavily traveled or hangout areas. Avoid useless windows.

- Plan entries with multiple uses in mind. Install flexible internal gates to block off specific areas or corridors when necessary. Provide separate exterior entries for community and student use. Inside the building, create areas for informal gatherings near entrances and exits by installing soft-drink machines and benches.
- Locate or relocate the playground's access roads to provide better surveillance by roving patrols.
- Consider outdoor lighting. Opinions on this issue are divided. Many schools report a decline in vandalism after installing hardened exterior night lighting. Others report that elimination of all night lighting reduces vandalism, presumably because young adolescents are afraid of the dark.

If lighting is used, it should be directed away from windows to keep vandals from seeing the process of destruction or its outcome.

GRAFFITI[25]

Graffiti artists will usually select light, smooth surfaces rather than dark, rough surfaces. Therefore, school officials can channel graffiti onto one or two walls designed to withstand such treatment. Students or maintenance staff can paint most walls at regular, but not too frequent, intervals. One wall can be officially designated a "legitimate" graffiti wall, although this approach removes some of the challenge inherent in informal graffiti. It is recommended that all graffiti be removed within 24 hours of being discovered.

SCHOOL LOCKDOWNS

According to a recent *Security Technology Executive* article, to implement a lockdown in case of a hostile intruder, basic procedures should include:

- Locking all doors.
- Closing all windows and window treatments.
- Remaining low to the ground and away from windows and doors.
- Turning off lights.
- Moving out of hallways and open spaces if it is safe to do so.
- Returning indoors, if it is safe to do so.
- Remaining calm.
- Awaiting the all-clear signal before releasing anyone from the room.[26]

Summary:

- Establish evacuation routes based on prior drills.
- Establish transportation needs, if necessary.
- Be aware of the location of medical kits and make sure the nurse has a two-way radio or cell phone.
- Practice total evacuation after the all clear with school buses lined up and ready.
- Bus drivers must be trained in your procedures.
- A crisis team needs to evaluate every incident and make recommendations for improvement.

---

[25]Ibid.
[26]April Dalton-Noblitt, "School Lockdowns," *Security Technology Executive*, July/August 2013, page 59, http://securitytechnologyexecutive.epubxp.com/i/143243/58.

SCHOOL PARTNERSHIPS

As with all partnership programs, you must start off with specific strategic goals and a set of priorities by which to manage and govern the partnership. There also have to be provisions in place to track progress and implement changes. Each partner in the program has to understand what they will gain by participating in the partnership and how they "fit in" to the overall success.

Consider holding meetings with law enforcement, students, faculty, school support personnel (i.e., SRO security staff, cafeteria workers, janitors, bus drivers), and parents. Be sure to include all individuals with a vested interest in the school and who support the mission of the school. Each of these groups may bring different skills and information to the partnership. The goal is for each member of the group to work with other groups and members in the program to achieve stated goals. This support team or partnership program is vital to the health of your school. They will assist with day-to-day issues as well as emergency situations.

SCHOOL SECURITY OFFICERS[27]

In a school, they may be called hallway assistants, administrative support, SROs, security officers, or any number of terms used in local traditions. When many of us were in school in the 80s and 90s there was no such thing as school security. Disturbances and fights were handled by the vice principal, a history teacher, and the football coach. Likely two of them were combat veterans of World War II and the third had been in Vietnam. It was a rare situation that this team could not manage. For this discussion, we will simply use "security" or "security officer."

THE SECURITY OFFICER

A professional security officer is a highly trained, highly skilled security officer who is capable in all aspects of the job. The professional likely has a college degree, and might be working toward an advanced degree. He or she builds relationships with students, staff, parents, and the community. The professional can jump in and break up a fight when needed, but is more likely to prevent the fight in the first place. The professional plays a crucial role on the school's crisis team and understands the Incident Command System.

SROs

Sworn security officers come in two forms: the SRO who works for the local police or sheriff's department and is assigned to the school, and the school police officer who works for the school board or district. Both are typically armed with a pistol and less-than-lethal weapons, and attend a police academy for training. The SRO reports to the chief or sheriff of the municipality. Without a clear memorandum of understanding and constant communication between the chief and superintendent and the SRO and principal, issues may develop. The school police officer reports to the superintendent or the school board. While this makes the chain of command clearer, caution must be exercised so that allegations do not arise that schools are covering up criminal offenses by using their own police.

In today's litigious society, schools should have some sort of security operation. These specifics will be determined by law and regulations, and the type or style will come from the school or district culture and expectations. In any event, officers should be trained, regulated, and managed. There must be accountability, and communication with administration, students, and parents is paramount.

---

[27]This section was contributed by Donald R. Green, CPP, CEMA.

SCHOOL UNIFORMS

Many of us wore a school uniform to school, particularly if you attended a parochial or private school as a child. Some schools today have implemented either a dress code or school uniform for students. Many administrators have found it sets the tone of the school and changes the overall climate within the school. A sense of pride in one's appearance is developed as well as improvement in the educational environment. In order to be effective, school uniform policies and dress codes must be enforced. It is important that school administrators utilize the benefit of their partnership with law enforcement to ensure that school uniforms and dress codes do not display local gang dress or colors.

SCHOOL WATCH PROGRAMS

A School Watch Program is similar to a Neighborhood Watch or Business Watch Program. The students, parents, faculty, and staff of the school become the "eyes and ears" of law enforcement to help prevent criminal activity from occurring on or near school property. It is essentially a crime prevention group within the school that works with law enforcement. This will help the school establish or reclaim informal control of their school by the observation, visibility, and increased interaction between the school and law enforcement. The national program, If You See Something, Say Something, was based on the premises of Watch Programs.

SECURITY—HOW MUCH IS ENOUGH?

There are levels of security that range from none to maximum. To determine what level of security you need in your school, first look at your assets you want to protect. The assets of any school are the people (students, faculty, staff, visitors, etc.), property (the building and contents), the reputation of the school, information and records, and the continued activities that are held on the campus.

The following are comments and concerns often voiced about school security:

- Is it reasonable to have a minimal amount of security in a high-crime neighborhood?
- What price do you place on a parent's peace of mind that their child will be in a safe environment at school?
- Security has to be in the school budget, with short-term and long-term goals, the same as any other item for the school.
- Are we going too far with cameras, badges, lights, and access control? Not in the opinion of security experts. It has become a necessity in our society.
- Do we need armed officers in our schools? There are two parts to this answer. There are actual crimes in schools as well as the fear of crime in schools that must be addressed. Secondly, school security officer must be trained and qualified, using criteria similar to law enforcement officers. Firearms and equipment must be considered. There is not a simple answer. A process must be followed to make this determination. What are your goals by having an armed officer at the school and what are your actual risk factors?
- Consider your liability. What would happen if there was an incident at your school that could have been prevented if the proper level of security had been in place? Could this cause the school to have adverse publicity as well as a judgment against the school or school district for inadequate security?

- Are there mental health concerns for children in those schools that utilize armed security officers or implement high levels of security? What about a child's mental health if there is a crisis at your school? This can be discussed with your child's pediatrician by explaining the symptoms your child is experiencing. Seek his or her advice and then determine if you need to take additional action. Consider the help of mental health professionals in your community. Mental health issues should be considered a part of your post-incident plan.

TEN STEPS TO IMPROVE SECURITY

1. Conduct a threat assessment annually.
2. Follow the principles of CPTED.
3. Implement access control and visitor control in the lobby and develop a security policies and procedures.
4. Utilize natural surveillance.
5. Design your campus using territorial reinforcement.
6. Use target hardening techniques, such as bullet-resistant windows.
7. Ask school boards to increase security budgets for your school.
8. Develop video feed and intercom systems with radio communication.
9. Install more cameras and at more strategic locations to ensure adequate video surveillance coverage.
10. For better control, reduce the number of exterior doors that are used for entry.

SITUATIONAL CRIME PREVENTION USING CPTED CONCEPTS[28]

Dr. C. Ray Jeffrey said "the CPTED concept is the proper design and effective use of the building environment that can lead to a reduction in the fear of crime and the incidence of crime and to an improvement in the quality of life."

A. Crime prevention approaches, like CPTED, are also known as situational crime prevention to remove crime from a specific area.
B. Crime and the fear of crime can be reduced using design methods.
C. The Situational Crime Reduction in Partnership Theory is also known as SCRPT.

WHAT IS THE CPTED CONCEPT USING CPTED APPLICATIONS?

Reduce opportunities for crime and fear of crime by making schools and open areas more easily observable, and by increasing activity in the neighborhood.

- Provide ways in which neighborhood residents, business people, and police can work together more effectively to reduce opportunities and incentives for crime.
- Increase neighborhood identity, investor confidence, and social cohesion.

---

[28]Timothy D. Crowe and Lawrence J. Fennelly, *Crime Prevention Through Environmental Design*, 3rd ed. (Boston: Elsevier, 2013).

- Provide public information programs that help schools, businesses, and residents protect themselves from crime.
- Make the area more accessible by improving transportation services.
- Improve the effectiveness and efficiency of governmental operations.
- Encourage citizens to report crimes. The steps taken to achieve these objectives include:
    - Outdoor lighting, sidewalk, and landscaping improvements.
    - Neighborhood Watch, Business Watch, and School Watch Programs.
    - Neighborhood cleanups.
- A campaign to discourage people from carrying a lot of cash.
- A major improvement and expansion of public transportation.
- Improved cost-effective lighting.
- Public transportation hubs that are purpose built.

These improvements have enhanced the quality of life and provided an atmosphere of improvement in your community. The application of CPTED to school design has been promoted in a number of locations through the country successfully.

THE SITUATIONAL APPROACH

Several years ago, a college dormitory was experiencing a large number of thefts. Cash and small items were being stolen from unlocked rooms. We addressed this two ways. First, we took one of our police cars that was going to be traded in and parked it in front of the building. Campus law enforcement was responsible for moving the car up and down the roadway so it appeared to be an active vehicle. Second, we conducted an educational program to get students to lock their dorm rooms. Crime stopped and fear of crime was reduced from the site. Whenever possible, consider a positive action versus a negative solution.

STUDENT LOCKERS

Most schools have student lockers in the hallways or classrooms. At the beginning of the school year, students need to be advised that the lockers are the property of the school and are subject to random searches. The student's book bag, if stored in the locker, may also be subject to a search as well. Coordinate locker searches with local law enforcement officials and consider asking them if the department's drug-sniffing dog can be utilized to ensure that your school is a drug-free environment.

TAILGATING (THROUGH ACCESS CONTROL)

Tailgating is when a person enters a building behind a person who has used their credentials to enter the building. The person who tailgated may or may not have legitimate access to the building. Tailgating is how Michael Brandon Hill allegedly gained access to a school in Georgia in August of 2013.[29] Two staff members were held hostage for a short period of time and several shots were fired before Hill finally surrendered to the police. Incidents such as this should be discussed during your training program.

---

[29]Bill Barrow and Kate Brumback, "Michael Brandon Hill Charged McNair Elementary School Shooting Suspect," *Huffington Post*, August 20, 2013, http://www.huffingtonpost.com/2013/08/20/michael-brandon-hill-mcnair-elementary-school-shooting-_n_3787676.html.

TRAINING

> The only thing worse than training your employees and having them leave, is not training them and having them stay.
>
> **Henry Ford**

In the past 25 years, how training programs are delivered has changed tremendously. Years ago, police officers and security officers were trained using VHS recorders and an easel flipchart. Many times, training sessions were recorded by the instructor teaching the class. The training tape was used until a new one was made. Sound primitive? Yes, but it was still effective. The tape and notes documented the presentation.

KEY ELEMENTS FOR A SUCCESSFUL PROGRAM

1. Subject matter—you must know the subject matter and be prepared to defend your presentation. Be prepared to answer questions.
2. Passion—tell them something new and of interest. Tell them stories of successes and failures. Quote facts. Provide handouts.
3. Enthusiasm goes a long way with passion. You have to bring excitement to your presentation and not address the audience in a deadpan or monotonous tone. If your enthusiasm and passion is high, your audience will not be bored. The majority of trainers use PowerPoint presentations.
4. Style—via practice, help develop a style. We've seen people start by telling a joke; it loosens up the audience. If you try it, you better be good or you will bomb. Speaking of bombs, we all do it. Years ago, Larry Fennelly was scheduled to lecture for an hour. He was introduced and walked up to the front of the room and opened his briefcase. His notes for the lecture were not there! Everyone in attendance clapped as Larry was introduced and he said that he died a very slow death on that very spot.
5. PowerPoint presentations are a great tool. You have your notes next to the computer and your main points are on the screen. You should know the material. After all, you prepared the presentation. For smoother presentations, rehearse your speech, making sure that all of the material on the subject has been covered.

   Consider the following:

   - "Two (or three) points I wish to make in conclusion," and state your points.
   - "To summarize, ladies and gentlemen…"
6. Personal touch—make eye contact with the class, even those at the back of the class. Make sure you are speaking at their level. If you tell old stories, make sure they are relative to the topic.
7. Your audience—show respect to them. They are there to learn from you. Be patient. They will feel your passion for the topic. They will assess this by how you answer their questions.

   If while at a training program, you learn at least one great thing, it was worthwhile. Three important points for conducting training and presentations:

1. Be a passionate and enthusiastic speaker.
2. Conduct a smooth presentation.
3. Have fun doing it. Teach the attendees something new *and* different!

There are many security professionals who offer quality training programs that are designed specifically for the school environment.

Glen Kitteringham, CPP, said something interesting at a recent security conference that we had never heard anyone say before. "There is good training and bad training. Good training is rare. Most consultants provide training. Many in fact do not have any formal training in conducting training."

So much is written about training for school faculty and staff on a variety of issues. Make sure that the training you conduct (or contract with someone else to conduct) is quality training.

VANDALISM AND GRAFFITI[30]

Today's vandals often attack their own territory. School vandalism—the illegal and deliberate destruction of school property—is committed by students themselves. So many windows are broken in many large districts that the funds spent annually on replacing broken windows could easily pay for a new school.

Vandals destroy about $3 million worth of school bus seats annually and they commit enough arson to account for 40% of all vandalism costs. School vandalism outranks all other assaults on private and public property. At the end of the 2012 school year, the average cost of damages from vandalism was estimated at $163,031 per school district. That figure could have paid the salaries of eight reading specialists or could have financed a school breakfast program for 100 children for 1 year. A typical school's chances of being vandalized in a month are greater than one in four, and the average cost of each act of vandalism is $180. Yet, these figures do not include the hidden costs of school vandalism—increased expenses for fencing, intrusion and fire detectors, special lighting, emergency communications equipment, and vandal-resistant windows. Every dollar spent to replace a window or to install an alarm is a dollar that cannot be spent on education.

School vandalism can also have enormous social cost. The impact of a $2.99 can of spray paint used to cover a wall with racial epithets far exceeds the monetary cost of removing the paint. An abusive word scrawled across a hallway can destroy student morale, disrupt intergroup relations, undermine the authority of an administration, or even close the school. Incidents with high social costs damage the educational process as much as those with high monetary costs.

Today's vandal is not a hardened, war-scarred veteran. Instead of grizzled whiskers, he often sports peach fuzz on his face. He is literally the boy next door. In fact, the typical school vandal differs quite dramatically from the typical juvenile delinquent.

It is significant that vandals fall into a well-defined and relatively narrow age group.

They are usually early adolescent males who are highly subject to group pressures and transitory impulses. It is not at all unusual for adolescents to act out whatever is controlling them at the moment—rage, boredom, pent-up energy, or the sheer joy of "wreck reaction." While there are conditions that may predispose or provoke a youth toward vandalism, the problem seems to be almost human nature. Few among us have never written on a sidewalk or scrawled initials on a school desk. Vandalism cuts across all strata of society, all geographic regions, and all racial lines.

---

[30]This section is adapted from the US Army Physical Security Field Manual, FM-3-19.30, updated 2013, p. B.39 to B.43. This is an updated version of the material. Also adapted from *Crime Prevention Through Environmental Design* (Elsevier, 2013).

VIDEO SURVEILLANCE SYSTEMS—SIX SECRETS

1. Video surveillance systems are a security tool used to assess or document activities.
2. They may be a deterrent in the minds of individuals who see the camera when they are about to commit a crime.
3. School administrators have told us that when something happens in their school, they review the camera footage to determine who was involved in the incident.
4. To obtain the best resolution, position cameras 30 ft from the ground.
5. More secrets about video surveillance:

   a. Define the purpose of each camera.
   b. Document the areas of coverage.
   c. Choose the proper lenses for the area.
   d. Hardwire the system.
   e. Choose proper storage requirements.

6. With the use of video surveillance, schools can actually witness an event, document exactly what happened, contact the police for assistance, if necessary, contact the parents, and then decide on the appropriate action to take.

WATCH D.O.G.S

What is WATCH D.O.G.S? It stands for Dads of Great Students and it is comprised of volunteers who give their time to be role models and to help the educational programs in our schools. The D.O.G.S. spend time with the students in K-12 and may even eat lunch with them. One participant said that it gives him time to be with his own kids. But it's not just dads that walk the halls of schools; it's also uncles, grandfathers, and cousins. The WATCH D.O.G.S. have become an extra set of eyes and ears, sort of an unofficial Neighborhood Watch Group. Some dads are at school when the children arrive and others are there when the children leave for home.

Visit www.fathers.com for more information. WATCH D.O.G.S. is located in 46 states.

WEBSITES WITH ADDITIONAL INFORMATION FOR SCHOOL SAFETY AND SECURITY
CONTROL SOFTWARE FOR SCHOOLS/PARENTS/GUARDIANS

- www.internetsafety.com
- www.onlinefamily.norton.com
- www.bsecure.com
- www.netnanny.com
- www.spectorsoft.com/home-solutions.html
- www.opendns.com
- www.Wellresearchedreviews.com

CELL PHONE SAFETY REVIEWS

- www.cell-phone-monitoring-software-review.toptenreviews.com/

CYBERBULLYING

- www.stopcyberbullying.org
- www.digitalkidsinitiative.com/files/2012/01/Cyberbully_handout.pdf
- www.cyberbullying.us

GAMING SYSTEMS

- www.support.xbox.com
- www.support.us.playstation.com
- www.nintendo.com

KEY LOGGER SOFTWARE AND SPYWARE

- www.Webwatcherkids.com
- www.Iambigbrother.com
- TrueCare: www.truecare.com (works with Facebook, Google+, Twitter, Instagram, and YouTube)
- www.socialshield.com (Social network monitoring and alerts)
- www.funamo.com
- www.mobicip.com
- www.k9webprotection.com

SECURITY

- www.asisonline.org/education/activeShooter.xml
- www.training.fema.gov/EMIWeb/IS/IS100SCA.asp
- www.2.ed.gov/about/offices/liswt/oese/oshs/rems-k-12-guide.pdf
- www.gallagherpost.com_post/

SEX OFFENDERS

- www.familywatchdog.us
- www.nsopr.gov

SOCIAL MEDIA HELPFUL SITES

- www.netlingo.com
- www.urbandictionary.com
- www.commonsensemedia.org
- www.tomsguide.com/us/Parental-Controls

- www.connectsafely.org
- www.snapchat.com/static_files/parents.pdf
- Instagram Parent Guide by www.ConnectSafely.org:www.connectsafely.org/wp-content/uploads/instagram_guide.pdf
- www.connectsafely.org/wp-content/uploads/snapchat_guide.pdf

TERRORISM AND VIOLENCE

- http://www.dhs.gov/xlibrary/assets/active_shooter_booklet.pdf
- www.youtube.com/watch?v=FQDnDzOWLLE
- www.pbs.org/programs/path-to-violence/
- www.oktotalk.org
- www.ncpc.org/topics
- www.familywatchdog.us
- www.stopbullying.gov
- www.gallagherpost.com/gallagher_post/
- www.pbs.org/programs/path-to-violence/
- www.youtube.com/watch?v=FQDnDzOWLLE
- www.asisonline.org/education/activeShooter.xml
- www.training.fema.gov/EMIWeb/IS/IS100SCA.asp
- www.2.ed.gov/about/offices/liswt/oese/oshs/rems-k-12-guide.pdf

WORKING WITH ARCHITECTS

The first building project that Larry Fennelly worked on at Harvard University involved working with an architect to determine the appropriate door hardware that would be installed in a new building on campus and what type of lighting would be utilized to ensure the proper level of illumination behind the building. A risk assessment is what helped Larry determine the answer about the door hardware and the lighting. Be very specific about the type of alarm equipment and access control features you want or need. Find out what equipment will work best for your particular application and fight to get what is necessary to secure the building. You will find that is less expensive in the long run to build security features into the construction of a building rather than to retrofit them after the building is complete.

To complete the building project at Harvard University, Larry had to design a set of security standards because none existed at that time. The standards were approved by the chief of police and when the architect would argue in favor of a particular feature, Larry would simply state, "I'm sorry that equipment does not meet our standards," and the proper equipment would be installed. Don't allow junk to be installed in your building. Today, however, there are standards and recommendations in place to help you with building design projects.

ZERO TOLERANCE VERSUS GUIDELINES FOR CRIMINAL BEHAVIOR

While industry professionals as well as federal officials have recently steered away from "zero tolerance" policies for a variety of reasons, we strongly urge school administrators to establish well-promulgated policies and disciplinary guidelines that include potential consequences of infractions and further outline the adjudication process to be followed when infractions are reported. Understanding that there is no "one size fits all solution" moving away from "zero tolerance" allows for each infraction to be evaluated based on the totality of circumstances and merits of the evidence presented.

These policies, procedures and processes should not only be well promulgated to staff and students, but also to parents and guardians. Having an informed parental community and educating others why certain policies and/or consequences exist not only demonstrates transparency, but also provides a forum to receive constructive feedback and gives constituents a sense of ownership in the process. This can increase the likelihood of community support, accountability and compliance.

One way schools often foster such an environment of safety and compliance is by providing staff, students, parents and others with the ability to report infractions or concerning behavior to school administrators anonymously. Incident reporting and surveys can be very effective tools to allay what we often hear are fears or concerns of retribution, making things worse or "tattling." There are many ways to facilitate feedback dedicated telephone contact numbers, websites, e-mail or "text" messaging, mobile phone apps, etc. School administrators should review and investigate each complaint as outlined by OCR Dear Colleague Letters and internal policy, and seek the advice of legal counsel when necessary.

At a minimum, schools should establish policies that prohibit, limit or determine unacceptable behaviors and consequences of the following:

- Weapons Possession/Use
- Drug Possession/Use
- Alcohol/Tobacco Possession/Use
- Bullying/Harassment
- Hazing
- Cyber bullying/Harassment/Stalking
- Sexual Assault/Misconduct/Harassment
- Bias Crimes
- Use of cell phone and personal computing devices
- Social Media Standards
- Any Criminal Acts

It is critical that school administrators understand that even though we stress the value of policies and administrative guidelines as essential, they alone do not address the multi-faceted and often unique disciplinary challenges facing our schools and administrators. They are, in fact, critical ingredients of a larger recipe for developing a culture or awareness, civility and compliance in our schools.

100 THINGS YOU NEED TO KNOW ABOUT SCHOOL SECURITY

27

Rick Draper

Principal advisor, managing director, Amtac Professional Services Pty. Ltd.

INTRODUCTION

The community expects that our schools will be safe and protective environments within which our children can learn, play, and enjoy experiences that set a sound foundation for their lives ahead. But outside observers rarely give consideration to the wide range of security-related risks that need to be managed to achieve those outcomes. Many aspects of effective school security seem like common sense when they are presented; however, to misquote a somewhat self-evident observation from early this century, "We don't know what we don't know." The following "100 Things" are intended to prompt thought about a diverse range of security risk management considerations–some of which you may know and others you may be considering for the first time.

Each topic is deliberately kept to a brief introduction to the subject and readers are encouraged to pursue further reading in areas of interest. A number of the topics include a QR code (QR stands for Quick Response) that can be scanned with a smart phone to access further information on the subject. Free QR code scanning applications can be downloaded for all types of smart phone (e.g., "QRafter" for iPhone http://keremerkan.net/downloads/ or "Scan" for Android and Windows devices https://scan.me/download). Alternatively, you can access the same content on your desktop computer by visiting the QR2id.com Website and entering the serial number that appears in the caption under the QR code.

1. HELP IS AVAILABLE

School security cannot be managed in isolation and no principal can be expected to have the range of expertise and expanse of knowledge necessary to address the many aspects of security and emergency management. Don't try to reinvent the proverbial wheel. Use other schools and agencies as resources; draw on reputable material available online, such as from www.edpubs.gov or www.ncpc.org; and invest in professional specialist advice from independent consultants (see Figure 27.1).

2. SECURITY MEANS DIFFERENT THINGS TO DIFFERENT PEOPLE

The term *security* is often interpreted in different ways. In the context of schools, security implies a stable, relatively predictable environment in which staff and students may pursue teaching and

FIGURE 27.1

Scan the QR2id code to access links and resources, or visit QR2id.com and enter serial#:
PMNB-R9BT-NPPD.

learning without disruption or harm, and without fear of disturbance or injury.[1] In essence, managing school security requires the implementation of a range of strategies to manage risks to five key areas:

1. People (staff, students, visitors, contractors, etc.)
2. Information and Data Protection (records, examinations, etc.)
3. Property (teaching resources, cash, equipment, etc.)
4. Activities (teaching and learning, extracurricular, fund raising, etc.)
5. Reputation (goodwill of staff, parents, community, etc.)

3. THERE ARE TWO ESSENTIAL QUESTIONS IN SECURITY MANAGEMENT

There are two fundamental questions that must be asked in determining the most appropriate strategies to reduce the security-related risks to the school and its population:

- What are we trying to protect? (the asset/resource)
- From whom are we trying to protect it? (the threat source)

Determining the appropriateness of security strategies to reduce or eliminate the risk depends on the answers to the first two questions, and two more:

- What are the objectives of the threat source? (e.g., steal for personal gain, escape undetected, attract media attention, for "entertainment," satisfy malice or revenge, etc.)
- How might they set about achieving their objectives? (e.g., break into the library and steal the large-screen TV)

---

[1] Adapted from Fischer, Halibozek and Green, *Introduction to Security*, eighth edition, (2008): p. 31.

FIGURE 27.2

Scan the QR2id code to obtain a copy of the ISO Standard, or visit QR2id.com and enter serial#: UBEK-HWFR-ZAKX.

4. THERE IS A SCIENCE TO UNDERSTANDING AND MANAGING RISK

Security-related risks always comprise two elements; without either there is no risk:

(a) the likelihood the nominated risk event (or threat) will occur (e.g., theft of a data projector)

(b) the level of harm or consequences within a specific context (e.g., the seriousness of injury to staff, the amount of financial harm to the school, the level of damage to the school's reputation, etc.)

The International Standards Organization (ISO) publishes standards that clearly define structured processes that should be used to understand risks, including security-related risks. Following the processes outlined in ISO 31010 and ISO 31000 provides a defensible and scientifically robust basis for risk management decisions. Using these standards effectively doesn't have to be complex; it simply requires a structured and consistent approach (see Figure 27.2).

5. THERE ARE MANY DIMENSIONS TO CONSEQUENCES

The consequences of any particular risk event are always contextually based and multi-dimensional in character. For example, the consequences to a public school and its associated Department/Board in relation to theft of property are different—the school suffers the inconvenience of the loss of the item, but the Department/Board may need to meet the actual cost of the replacement. The nature of the harm suffered as a result of a risk event is dependent upon the nature of the event, but might include personal consequences (physical and/or psychological injury), direct and indirect financial loss, damage to reputation/goodwill, human resource impacts (e.g., attracting and retaining good staff), and potentially legal consequences associated with regulatory breaches or civil action.

6. THERE ARE TWO SIDES TO SECURITY VULNERABILITIES

Vulnerabilities are those things that increase the likelihood that a risk will be realized, and/or increase the consequences should it be realized. For example, the lock on the external door to the art room may be faulty, making it easier for someone to break in and vandalize the room. Similarly, the absence of a policy with respect to staff challenging trespassers may lead to staff being at risk of assault or the school at risk of litigation for negligence.

7. PLANNING IS ESSENTIAL TO EFFECTIVE SECURITY RISK MANAGEMENT

Schools cannot always control all of the security-related threats to which they may be exposed, but effective security planning is essential to reducing the likelihood of many foreseeable events, as well as reducing the consequences should a threat be realized. Start strategically and then drill down to the detail on critical issues first—a single piece of paper with the outline of a strategic plan may help avoid the most serious of consequences. Wherever possible, integrate security into operational plans, rather than having it as a separate consideration.

8. THERE ARE KEY CONSIDERATIONS IN EVERY SCHOOL SECURITY MANAGEMENT PLAN

The range of security-related risks and strategies applicable to mitigating them will vary significantly, but there are several key considerations in every school. The underlying test that should be applied to every security strategy includes three basic questions: is it philosophically compatible with the school and the community it serves; is the strategy operationally appropriate and workable; and is the strategy fiscally responsible in the context of the risks being addressed? It is goes almost without saying that it also essential that the strategy be lawful. For example, locking a nominated fire exit path with a chain and padlock would not be legal in most jurisdictions. Some of the key strategies that might be considered include:

- Security site assessments
- Mass notification and communication strategies
- Perimeter security and surveillance
- Access control with campus lockdown
- Visitor management
- Physical security information management (PSIM) for entire districts
- Alarm monitoring of duress buttons

Other strategies that may be considered commonly within higher risk contexts include:

- Intercom/door release for identification of visitors
- Wireless duress pendants
- Driver's license scanning and predator database verification for visitors
- Video monitoring and recording systems
- High-resolution IP digital video cameras
- Metal detectors
- Timed locking hardware
- Emergency call stations
- Visitor and access control auditing (via database)

9. WRITTEN SECURITY POLICIES ARE IMPORTANT, AND PROVIDE A SOLID FOUNDATION TO DEFENDING LITIGATION

Policies not only document the school's position and requirements in relation to routine and extraordinary matters but also serve to guide important decision making. Developing and implementing effective security policies is a progressive process and starts with the first policy statement. Don't wait until you have a comprehensive manual; every policy you complete puts you in a better position to effectively manage security-related risks, as well as consequential risks such as civil litigation. Keep the policy statements short and develop separate procedures applicable to the relevant stakeholders. For example, a general "security philosophy" policy statement might read:

Sample School is concerned about the safety and welfare of our staff, students, volunteers, visitors, and contractors, as well as the protection and preservation of property, equipment, information, and the reputation of our school. It is *Sample School's* policy that all staff, students and their families, contractors, and visitors will be made aware of all security-related responsibilities and obligations relating to their school-related activities (on and off campus), and will discharge those responsibilities and obligations to the best of their abilities.

10. SECURITY PROCEDURES ARE ROLE DEPENDENT

It is self-evident that the tasks to be performed by staff in an active shooter situation will be different from those of students. But even within the staff group, responsibilities will vary and it is important that clearly documented procedures be developed for all stakeholders who may be impacted by a given situation. Procedures facilitate the implementation of policy, so the policy statement (and those of related policies) should be the guiding reference for each procedure.

11. RELATED PROCEDURES SHOULD BE COMPILED INTO INSTRUCTION OR RULES

Whether it is staff, students, contractors, or parents, stakeholders often have limited time and are subject to competing priorities. For any given task or event, there may be a number of security-related procedures and it may be useful to consolidate the key points into a set of instructions or rules, which are sometimes referred to as standing orders or standard operating procedures (SOPs). These instructions should also be reviewed whenever procedures are updated to ensure that they remain current.

12. YOUR SCHOOL WILL HAVE SOME POLICY AND PROCEDURE DIFFERENCES FROM OTHER SCHOOLS

No matter how similar schools may seem, there will necessarily be differences in procedures, if not policies, related to specific security-related incidents and emergencies. However, there are certainly some areas that need to be addressed by all schools. These include:

- Bomb threats (see Figure 27.3)
- Fires
- Utility failures
- Severe weather
- Weapons

FIGURE 27.3

Scan the QR2id code to access a bomb threat resource, or visit QR2id.com and enter serial#: SNMV-T4TE-VLH2.

- Active shooter
- Assault
- Workplace violence
- Bullying
- Hostage situations
- Radiological and chemical incidents

13. SECURITY STRATEGIES NEED TO BE ABLE TO BE ESCALATED AND DEESCALATED IN A CONSISTENT MANNER

The nature of security strategies appropriate for a school will be dependent upon a wide range of variables, but specifically the nature of the threats to which the school is exposed. For example, if there have been a series of thefts of property some additional security patrols may be implemented. But when is it appropriate to reduce them again? By having a hierarchy of security levels and standard procedures/actions applicable for different types of threat, decision making becomes much easier and defensible. A typical set of security levels might carry the following descriptors:

- Routine Security
- Enhanced Security
- Security Alert
- Incident Response
- Post-Incident Security

The levels and terms should be relevant for the school and incorporated into procedures and contracts as applicable.

14. NOT EVERYONE NEEDS TO KNOW EVERYTHING ABOUT YOUR SECURITY

Security plans, policies, and procedures are essential, but they detail requirements for many potentially serious situations. As such, they should be subject to qualified distribution. The term "need-to-know" should be applied with care and consideration. Certainly, putting all the school's security policies and procedures on the Internet for anyone to access represents a serious vulnerability and must be avoided.

15. POLICIES AND PROCEDURES SHOULD BE REVIEWED REGULARLY AND AFTER EVENTS

All security policies and procedures should be subject to regular review and updated to ensure that they remain current with operational, regulatory, and societal changes (e.g., every 2 years). Whenever a serious event occurs that requires security procedures to be followed, those procedures, the overarching policy, and all related policies and procedures, should all be subject to review, and updated as may be appropriate, to better meet security risk management objectives. All security-related policies should be reviewed whenever there is a change in senior management to ensure that they remain consistent with executive requirements for given situations.

16. IT'S OK TO MAKE ASSUMPTIONS AS LONG AS THEY ARE DOCUMENTED AND TESTED

Most security management strategies are based to some extent on assumptions. This only becomes a problem if the assumptions subsequently are proven to have been flawed and were not adequately tested before being accepted. Where assumptions are involved in security risk management in schools, it is important to explore whether the assumptions are valid under the range of conditions likely to be encountered and that these details are recorded. For example, a routine communication strategy may rely on email and two assumptions involved with this are that the recipients have timely access to their email and that there is network connectivity to send and receive the message.

17. REGULAR DRILLS ARE IMPORTANT, BUT DESKTOP EXERCISES CAN BE AN INVALUABLE INSIGHT FOR DIFFICULT-TO-REHEARSE SCENARIOS

Schools regularly practice fire evacuations and lockdown drills, and necessarily these need to be based on fairly predictable scenarios. However, events can and do occur at the most difficult times or under less-than-ideal circumstances. While it might not be possible to do a physical drill that incorporates difficult conditions, it is important to have considered them, and engaging with other agencies and stakeholders to undertake desktop exercises can reveal important issues. Take, for example, an actual situation at a school where an active shooter caused a lockdown just at the end of class for the day. Police had roads blocked, with some parents at the school and others unable to reach the school. Some classes had been released and some were still in their rooms. How would your school handle this situation?

18. THE COMPOSITION OF OFF-CAMPUS EMERGENCY KITS SHOULD BE REVIEWED REGULARLY AND KITS UPDATED

It is important for a range of resources to be accessible by staff and emergency services personnel, should they not be able to be accessed on school property due to an incident. It is important that the kits be reviewed and updated regularly to ensure they remain current. Seek advice from your local emergency services and law-enforcement agencies about your situation, but an off-campus emergency kit might include:

- Crisis response team roster and contact information
- Emergency staff contact card
- Map of the school and floor plans, including locations of utilities, shut-off valves, and hazardous materials
- Aerial photos of the campus
- Maps of the surrounding neighborhood
- Emergency plans
- Designated command posts and staging areas
- Evacuation and reunification site details
- Keys and access control cards/tokens
- Operating procedures for key equipment and systems, such as sprinklers and alarms
- Broadcast notification strategy, including username and password, if applicable
- Transportation routes and contacts
- Student/teacher rosters and emergency data
- Roster of special needs students, including details of those with specific disabilities requiring consideration
- Yearbooks and student photos
- Checklists and forms

19. THE LOCATIONS OF OFF-CAMPUS EMERGENCY KITS MUST BE KNOWN BY, OR ACCESSIBLE TO, EMERGENCY SERVICES PERSONNEL AND THE SCHOOL MANAGEMENT TEAM

Given the nature of the contents and need for timely access, the locations for off-campus emergency kits must be carefully chosen. It may be appropriate to have kits at different locations that may be more easily accessed after hours or during school hours. Having alternative locations that are known by emergency services personnel and the school management team is an important strategy in preparing for an emergency.

20. SECURITY AWARENESS HAS TWO DIMENSIONS

Security awareness is the process through which stakeholders are made conscious of, and accept, their roles and responsibilities related to the management of security-related risks at the school. These two dimensions are equally important, in that it is relatively easy to tell someone that they have a role or responsibility, but getting them to accept and act on that information is a separate matter. It is crucial that as part of security awareness consideration is given to the skills and resources that may be required to discharge the assigned responsibilities. Like effective marking campaigns, a robust security awareness strategy will not only communicate the message to the target audience but also facilitate the outcomes and actions required.

21. YOU DON'T KNOW WHAT YOU DON'T KNOW

It is vital to security management planning and security awareness in general that you develop strategies to consult with and seek input from staff, students, parents, and other stakeholders regarding their perceptions and experiences in relation to school security issues. Similarly, members of the same stakeholder group may need to be informed about things that might seem routine and trivial to those skilled in school security matters, but which may be outside the normal sphere of consideration for others.

22. TERMINOLOGY IS IMPORTANT

Certain terms have special meaning in a security context, and a particular term may not be interpreted with the intended meaning by someone not routinely exposed to security risk management. It is important to use consistent terminology across the school and ideally between schools in the same region. Technical terms should be avoided and plain language adopted with concise simple explanations of meaning within the contexts in which the term might be expected to be used (see Figure 27.4).

23. TRAINING GOES HAND IN HAND WITH IMPLEMENTING POLICIES AND AWARENESS

Whenever we ask someone to perform a task related to the management of security-related risks, we need to be confident that they are competent to do so. It is vitally important that schools provide the skills, knowledge, and resources to all those who need them to implement security-related policies. While the content will obviously be different, this is as applicable to students as it is to staff. When someone receives training, as opposed to static information, they are engaged with the subject matter and have the opportunity to better understand what is required of them in a given context.

FIGURE 27.4

Scan the QR2id code for a glossary of security terms, or visit QR2id.com and enter serial#: CNAQ-L79T-RZLT.

24. TRAINING REQUIREMENTS FOR ADMINISTRATION, TEACHING, AND MAINTENANCE STAFF WILL VARY

Depending upon their roles in different scenarios, it will be necessary to provide specific training to different groups of staff. However, consideration should be given to ensure that all staff and selected volunteers are trained in key areas such as:

- Basic first aid and CPR/AED
- General school security issues and responses
- Fire drills and building evacuations
- Handling bomb threats
- Shelter-in-place (including active shooter and toxic spill initiations)
- Discipline and code of conduct processes
- Counter aggression and violence de-escalation techniques

25. INCIDENT REPORTING, RECORDING AND ANALYSIS ARE DIFFERENT THINGS

Irrespective of regulatory requirements to do so, it is important that schools have simple and accessible means of receiving reports about security-related matters, as well as recording and analyzing information associated with the subject of the report. The initial reporting process should provide sufficient information to support any immediate action or response that may be required. These reports should then be recorded in a manner that allows the information to be recalled, reviewed, updated, and analyzed in the future. Any action taken, procedural changes or other matters arising from the report should also be recorded.

26. REPORTING AND RECORDING OF EVEN MINOR MATTERS OF NOTE CAN BE IMPORTANT

Often, schools will receive reports about what appear to be minor matters and then don't record them. Similarly, reporting of minor issues may not been seen as necessary by staff, students, or contractors because they feel that no action is required or would be taken. However, minor matters of note can be symptomatic of more serious issues and having historic and trend data can support more proactive risk management decisions. The process of reporting minor matters does not need to be as expansive as more serious incidents or observations, and should be as simple as possible to encourage reporting.

27. PROVIDING FEEDBACK TO THOSE WHO REPORT INCIDENTS AND OBSERVATIONS LETS THEM KNOW THAT WHAT THEY DID WAS WORTHWHILE

It can be a difficult task to get people to report security-related incidents and observations, so when someone takes the trouble to make a report it is important to reinforce the value of their contribution. It doesn't take much effort to provide follow-up feedback, which in many cases can be automated (e.g., incident is entered into a database and automatically sends an acknowledgment email). A phone call, even if it is to advise that nothing came of the report but to again express appreciation, can be a powerful motivator and even prompt the person to discuss security reporting with others.

28. SCHOOLS HAVE LEGAL AND REGULATORY REPORTING OBLIGATIONS

As part of security and safety management planning, all schools should have a clear understanding of all legal and regulatory obligations. Maintain a list of the legislation, regulations, and agencies responsible and develop checklists to ensure that compliance requirements are being met.

29. REWARDING INDIVIDUAL CONTRIBUTIONS TO SECURITY AND SAFETY NOT ONLY ACKNOWLEDGES THAT PERSON, BUT ALSO REINFORCES SECURITY AWARENESS ACROSS THE SCHOOL COMMUNITY

Students, staff and members of the community like to be acknowledged and it is so easy to do. In some circumstances it might even seem a little trite, but imagine the broader value to a student receiving a certificate of recognition for a contribution to security or safety. Would they include it on their resume? Would a prospective employer take notice of such a certificate? Of course the answer is yes on both counts. Experience has shown that security and safety contributions can be made "cool" in even the most difficult of environments.

30. IT IS AS IMPORTANT TO DOCUMENT AWARENESS COMMUNICATIONS, TRAINING, AND DRILLS, AS IT IS TO DO SO FOR SECURITY-RELATED INCIDENTS

It is a sad reality that serious and tragic incidents can and do happen in schools. Following such incidents it is not unusual for a school to face litigation, and the foundation of any defense will be documentation. Apart from the human resource management benefits of doing so, all security awareness communications and training provided to any stakeholder should be documented in a simple and consistent manner. This does not need to be complex, but should provide sufficient detail to interpret at a later date, who was responsible, what was done, who participated, and what (if any) follow-up action was taken.

31. PROVIDING STAFF AND BUS DRIVERS WITH SPECIFIC TRAINING ON HANDLING AND DEFUSING AGGRESSIVE BEHAVIOR CAN HAVE FOLLOW-UP BENEFITS FOR THE SCHOOL

It should never be assumed that common sense is all you need to defuse bad behavior. There is a science to handling aggressive behavior and potentially volatile situations. Those likely to encounter aggression directed to themselves or those in their care need to be given the training and resources to deal with those situations. Not only does the school benefit directly from the mitigation of related risks, but there can be many follow-up benefits for the reputation of the school.

32. AS DIFFICULT AS IT IS, SCHOOLS MUST BE CONSCIOUS OF AND EFFECTIVELY MANAGE ISSUES RELATING TO CHILD CUSTODY, DOMESTIC VIOLENCE, AND COURT ORDERS

Issues such as whether a parent can make decisions about their children's school activities have access to records, collect the child from school, or have access to the child during school hours are not always as straightforward as they might initially seem. They can be made even more complex if a parent impacted by a court order is also a teacher or member of staff. It is important to develop very clear strategies for receiving, storing, and communicating to those that need to know information about child custody, domestic violence, and court orders. Such information is highly sensitive and subject to rapid change, making management even more challenging. Equally important are the policies and procedures to be followed in the event of incident.

33. ZERO IS AN EASY NUMBER TO REMEMBER AS FAR AS TOLERANCE IS CONCERNED

In retail security it is not uncommon to have a budget for losses through theft, and as one retail security manager put it, "if you set a budget of 3% you will achieve it every time." Zero tolerance is a simple and realistic approach to many school security issues, but this does not mean that responses to incidents are not graduated, or that there are never any excuses or exigent circumstances that should be taken into account when managing events. Per the ASIS School Safety and Security Council, the term Zero Tolerance has been replaced by "Guidelines for Criminal Behavior" (see Chapter 26).

34. EMERGENCY SERVICES PERSONNEL WILL LIKELY APPRECIATE THE OPPORTUNITY TO TRAIN AT YOUR SCHOOL

Ideally, the first time that emergency services personnel set foot on your campus will not be during a serious incident. With due consideration to avoid creating concern for students or disruption to normal activities, engaging with emergency services agencies to use the campus for training has many benefits. Evidently the most obvious is that if emergency services personnel are familiar with the campus, this knowledge can save valuable time when time is a precious commodity. One school has taken to supporting the canine unit of their local police and erected signs stating that police dogs train on the campus after hours; this clearly has a deterrent value for anyone considering breaking into the school.

35. EMERGENCY SERVICES ACCESS SHOULD BE ARRANGED IN ADVANCE

In the event of an emergency out-of-school hours, emergency services personnel need to be able to access affected areas of the school in a timely manner. Ultimately if they need to, first responders will force entry, but it is a much better strategy for everyone concerned to have provided keys or access cards in advance of any incident. Special consideration should be given to perimeter access and areas where hazardous substances may be stored.

36. EMERGENCY CONTACT LISTS FOR SCHOOL PERSONNEL NEED TO BE MAINTAINED

In the event of an emergency after hours, getting in touch with the right people is not always as simple as it should be; staff go on vacation, roles change, and distribution of details to all that need to know is not always done in the most timely manner. Apart from ensuring that there is well-documented policy and procedures relating to maintaining the school's emergency contacts, consideration may be given to using technology that simplifies the process of contacting the right staff. Some services offer the ability for contact details to be conveniently managed and simultaneous email and/or SMS text messages to be sent to on-call school personnel (see Figure 27.5).

FIGURE 27.5

Scan the QR2id code to see an example, or visit QR2id.com and enter serial#: TB6T-2AMV-KPY9.

37. SCHOOLS SHOULD ACTIVELY LOOK FOR OPPORTUNITIES TO INVOLVE STUDENTS IN SAFETY AND SECURITY MANAGEMENT

Security and safety risks must always be considered in the range of contexts within which they may arise, and it is therefore vital that student input be sought in planning for at least some of these risk events. Some schools have even introduced crime prevention into the curriculum and leveraged the power of experiential learning to benefit both the students and their learning environments (see Figure 27.6).

FIGURE 27.6

Scan the QR2id code to access FEMA's emergency preparedness "Be a Hero" curriculum resources, or visit QR2id.com and enter serial#: XM3A-XC9F-2NLQ.

38. FINGERPRINTS AND PHOTOGRAPHS CAN BE FUN

While offenders don't necessarily appreciate the process or the outcomes, it can be a lot of fun and have very real benefits as an exercise for elementary school children. Consider having law enforcement personnel come to the school to speak to the children about protective behaviors, and then work with the children to create a take-home artwork that incorporates the child's fingerprints and photo. By using digital photos and scanned prints (and subject to privacy considerations in individual jurisdictions) the school could also retain a copy, should it ever be needed.

39. THERE ARE IMPORTANT ROLES FOR LAW ENFORCEMENT PERSONNEL IN SCHOOLS

While the options and availability will vary across jurisdictions, there are many benefits to engaging sworn members of local law enforcement as part of the school. Creating positions such as a police school precinct officer or SRO supports direct involvement by law-enforcement personnel.

40. DEFENSE-IN-DEPTH IS NOT LIMITED TO PHYSICAL LAYERS OF PROTECTION

Defense-in-depth or security-in-depth is a concept familiar to most security professionals, where security strategies are organized in layers and protection of any asset is not reliant on any one strategy. Typically this will be discussed in terms of physical strategies, such as fencing, fabric of the building, doors, interior spaces, and so on. However, it is important to remember that the security-in-depth concept can, and should, be applied more broadly. In considering staff, bus drivers, and contractors as possible sources of threat, a security-in-depth approach might include pre-employment screening, policies and procedures, codes of conduct, supervision, and screening reviews.

41. PRE-EMPLOYMENT SCREENING DOESN'T LAST FOREVER

While there are differences among jurisdictions, it is not uncommon for all staff, contractors, and even volunteers to be subject to criminal history screening before employment. However, it is equally as important to maintain routine updates of the standing of those who have been screened (see Figure 27.7).

FIGURE 27.7

Scan the QR2id code for information about personnel screening, or visit QR2id.com and enter serial#: NGBT-UTW4-ENLU.

42. THERE IS ALWAYS A NEED FOR INDUCTION TRAINING AND ONGOING PROFESSIONAL DEVELOPMENT

Just because someone is qualified in a specific discipline doesn't mean that they understand how to apply their knowledge and skills in the context of your school. Whether it is an SRO, external security contractor, or newly appointed emergency management coordinator, they all need to be supported in developing localized understanding and improving their capabilities to support their skills. When it comes to safety and security management, the return on the investment in professional development may never actually be seen, because it is a "great day at the office" when nothing happens.

43. KNOWING YOUR NEIGHBORS AND ACTIVELY ENGAGING WITH THEM HELPS REDUCE POSSIBLE POINTS OF FRICTION AND POTENTIALLY BUILDS OWNERSHIP AND CARE FOR THE SCHOOL

Those who live close to schools or on pedestrian routes taken by students can have varying perceptions about the school and its population. It is important to engage with the wider community and look for opportunities to work cooperatively for mutually beneficial outcomes, and in particular to develop a sense of engagement in the life of the school.

44. THE MEDIA CAN BE A VALUABLE RESOURCE AS WELL AS A POTENTIALLY DANGEROUS SOURCE OF THREAT

In emergencies and following major security incidents, there may be media interest in your school. The media can be of assistance in gaining public assistance, but they can also do significant damage to the reputation of the school if handled poorly. It is important for every school to develop media policies and procedures, and wherever possible limit contact through only one person. Media release templates for a variety of situations can be prepared in advance without the pressures present during incidents and then simply updated with relevant content prior to release.

45. LEARN FROM THE EXPERIENCES OF OTHERS WITH THE MEDIA

In preparing media policies and procedures, identify the media outlets likely to cover stories related to security and safety at your school. Review media reports about security-related incidents in your area and try to understand what came across well and what was potentially an issue for the subject of the story. Talk to media advisors and other schools about their experiences and consider any lessons to be learned.

46. AN EMERGENCY BOX CAN BE HIGHLY VALUABLE AS A CLASSROOM PROJECT

There is enormous value in having a box with emergency resources in classrooms. By actively involving the classes and their teachers in preparing or updating these boxes, there is not only the direct benefit of ensuring the resources are available should they be needed, but there is an opportunity as well for students to understand their own roles and responsibilities in an emergency situation. Students might, for example, have direct input into the types of games and activity resources to be included.

47. IN PREPARING EMERGENCY PLANS AND RESOURCES, IT IS IMPORTANT TO CONSIDER STAFF, STUDENTS, AND VISITORS WITH SPECIAL NEEDS

Schools routinely serving students with special needs are obviously conscious of issues related to access and communication. However, there are people who may be within the school at any given time who may have special needs should an incident occur. Schools should take care to note, and be prepared to assist, students, visitors, and staff who may have special needs at any given time. One approach is to incorporate applicable questions as part of issuing visitor and contractor passes, and this can also operate as part of the security awareness strategy.

48. HAVING A DEDICATED PHONE FOR EMERGENCY SERVICES COMMUNICATION CAN SAVE TIME AND FRUSTRATION DURING AN INCIDENT

In any emergency at a school, concerned parents will be seeking information and it is important that at least one phone line be available for outbound and inbound communication with emergency services agencies. Consideration should also be given to a dedicated cell phone that may be issued to an applicable staff member during an emergency.

49. THERE ARE INTERNATIONAL STANDARDS THAT CAN BE FOLLOWED FOR ADVICE ON CRISIS MANAGEMENT TEAMS AND INCIDENT COMMAND SYSTEMS

In the USA the FEMA Incident Command System (ICS) is a standardized, on-scene, all-hazards incident management approach that:

- Allows for the integration of facilities, equipment, personnel, procedures, and communications operating within a common organizational structure.
- Enables a coordinated response among various jurisdictions and functional agencies, both public and private.
- Establishes common processes for planning and managing resources. (see Figure 27.8)

FIGURE 27.8

Scan the QR2id code to access the FEMA Incident Control Guidelines, or visit QR2id.com and enter serial#: WBTJ-DEAC-K6D6.

50. MORE THAN ONE FAMILY REUNIFICATION SITE MAY BE NEEDED

Emergencies, by their very nature, include factors that are unpredictable but foreseeable and it is for this reason that alternatives need to be built into crisis and security planning. Schools should consider working with other schools and community groups to support each other with establishing reunification sites. It will be important in an emergency to be able to quickly and clearly communicate details of the location (or locations) to parents and other stakeholders, so the use of codes to describe these locations should be avoided.

51. INFORMATION EVENTS AT EVACUATION AND REUNIFICATION CENTERS CAN BE VALUABLE OPPORTUNITIES TO ENGAGE WITH THE SCHOOL COMMUNITY

Consideration should be given to showing stakeholders the locations that will be used for major evacuations and reunification. Incorporating these locations into related awareness and training programs can provide another layer of interest, as well as have practical value to orient families, staff, and even the media with specific areas that they may need to know in an emergency.

52. THERE ARE TEN STAGES TO ACUTE TRAUMATIC STRESS MANAGEMENT[2]

The goal is to stimulate adaptive coping mechanisms and stabilize more severe reactions among students. The ATSM stages are:

1. Assess for danger/safety for self and others
2. Consider the mechanism for injury
3. Evaluate the level of responsiveness
4. Address medical needs
5. Observe and identify
6. Connect with the individual
7. Ground the individual
8. Provide support
9. Normalize the response
10. Prepare for the future

53. NO TWO SCHOOLS ARE IDENTICAL, SO LOCAL PLANNING IS CRITICAL TO SUCCESSFULLY MITIGATING RISKS

The second edition of the *Guide for Preventing and Responding to School Violence*[3] presents different strategies and approaches for members of school communities to consider when creating safer learning environments. No two schools are exactly alike, so it is impossible to establish one plan that will work well in all schools (see Figure 27.9).

---

[2]U.S. Department of Education, *Practical Information on Crisis Planning*, p. 6-47, http://www2.ed.gov/admins/lead/safety/crisisplanning.html.
[3]U.S. Department of Justice, *Guide for Preventing and Responding to School Violence*, (2012).

FIGURE 27.9

Scan the QR2id code to access the IACP/BJA Guide for Preventing and Responding to School Violence, or visit QR2id.com and enter serial#: 6BFM-LZDN-9X9K.

54. IT IS VITAL TO HAVE CONSIDERED A RANGE OF INTERNAL COMMUNICATION OPTIONS FOR USE DURING EMERGENCIES, AND THAT EVERYONE WHO NEEDS TO KNOW UNDERSTANDS HOW AND WHY CERTAIN OPTIONS WILL BE USED

There are no guarantees that public infrastructure-based communications will be available (or suitable) to use in emergencies; the term emergency covers such a wide range of situations. Cell phones are prolific and may be a good first choice for instant SMS text messaging in some circumstances. However, schools should consider alternative strategies, such as Wi-Fi-based instant messaging to smart phones using the school's own infrastructure. Coded public address announcements and alert tones, radios, in-class intercoms and telephones, indicator lights, and other visual cues all have their place in emergency communications.

55. SCHOOL COMMUNITIES COMPRISE TALENTED INDIVIDUALS WITH A HOST OF SKILLS AND EXPERTISE

Staff, parents, and neighbors all have lives and activities outside their standard interactions with the school. They can be an exceptionally rich resource to draw upon in the development of plans and implementation of risk management strategies. It is unlikely that they will know what is needed or even that they have something they can contribute. Consider building a resource list through simple surveys, but be careful not to scare them away.

56. SOCIAL MEDIA CAN SERIOUSLY IMPAIR OR FACILITATE OUTCOMES DURING AN INCIDENT

With so many of the school community now connected through social media, this means of communication must be actively considered by schools in the development of security policies and

FIGURE 27.10

Scan the QR2id code for an article about social media issues in schools, or visit QR2id.com and enter serial#: 6N6G-AMJY-MQHP.

procedures. It is important for schools to actively monitor social media and respond to misinformation that can, in some situations, cause intense fear and potentially lead to accident or injury. Similarly, fears can be allayed early in incidents by using social media as part of a wider communication strategy. However, it is important that all communication is consistent and that those posting information through social media are aware of the accessibility and openness of this form of communication (see Figure 27.10).

57. COMPROMISED SOCIAL MEDIA ACCOUNTS CAN CAUSE MAJOR DISRUPTION

Schools should be aware that social media accounts can be hacked, resulting in anything from mischievous "Tweets" to dissemination of potentially harmful or disruptive misinformation. For example, the Associated Press Twitter account was hacked in April 2013, with the offender sending out a Tweet that there had been an "attack on the White House." Schools should take steps to prepare for a social-media-related security incident; understand how they will identify and confirm an incident; what they will do to contain and eradicate the threat; and importantly, what steps will be necessary to recover and restore normal use of social media.

58. PRIVACY MARKINGS AND CAVEATS ON DOCUMENTS FACILITATE COMPLIANCE WITH INFORMATION SECURITY REQUIREMENTS

Schools handle a variety of information that has different levels of sensitivity; however, the use of standard privacy markings and caveats to guide handling of that information is less common. In order to facilitate compliance and avoid accidental compromise of information, schools should adopt the practice of always assigning privacy markings to documents, and having clearly defined procedures for storing and transporting documents of differing classifications.

59. FOLLOWING CPTED GUIDELINES CAN CONTRIBUTE TO THE PREVENTION OF CRIMINAL ACTIVITY ON SCHOOL CAMPUSES

Crime prevention through environmental design (CPTED) is a term that was coined in the early 1970s by Professor C. Ray Jeffrey, a criminologist from Florida State University. CPTED is a multidisciplinary approach to reducing crime through the effective design and use of space. In a school setting, the priority for CPTED is to support behavioral objectives within a given context, while at the same time limiting support for undesired behaviors, including crime.

Some CPTED-related considerations may include:

- Effective use of signage and natural access control to manage the flow of pedestrians
- Maintaining grounds to improve natural surveillance and perceptions of ownership/territorial reinforcement
- Managing the use of spaces to ensure that time or distance is used to separate potentially conflicting user groups (see Figure 27.11).

60. LOOSE BRICKS, ROCKS, AND CONSTRUCTION WASTE CAN CAUSE HARM TO PEOPLE AND PROPERTY

A loose brick might seem like a basic maintenance issue and not really a high-priority issue to repair, but apart from the aesthetics these items can be used as convenient weapons in spontaneous violence. Similarly, waste from construction is often not secured because the perception is that there is nothing of value (it is waste), but it frequently contains materials that can be used to facilitate vandalism, break into the school, or be used as a weapon.

FIGURE 27.11

Scan the QR2id code for a copy of the Florida Safe Schools Design Guidelines, or visit QR2id.com and enter serial#: RBJT-7WFJ-NRM4.

61. USING ROCKS CAN SERVE PRACTICAL PURPOSES IN LANDSCAPING, BUT CARE NEEDS TO BE TAKEN THAT THEY DON'T BECOME WEAPONS OR TOOLS OF THEFT AND VANDALISM

Apart from providing an aesthetic element, rocks are frequently used in landscaping as ground-covers to support drainage and inhibit erosion; subject to size and positioning, they may also be used as a textural element to support natural access control on a campus, or simply as an attractive visual feature in landscape design. However, it is easy to see that having loose hand-sized rocks near the parking lot potentially increases the opportunity for them to be used as tools to gain entry to the vehicles or as weapons. Similarly, smaller stones can cause damage or serious injury, and need to be carefully considered. It is possible to use rocks and stones in landscaping with due consideration to these issues. For example, size selection, orientation, and companion strategies such as gabion (wire) cages and anchoring can be used to excellent effect to mitigate the risks that might otherwise arise from using rocks and stones in landscaping (see Figure 27.12).

62. LOCATION IDENTIFICATION CAN SAVE VALUABLE TIME AND IMPROVE INCIDENT ANALYSIS

The designs of school campuses vary significantly around the world, to a large extent influenced by weather conditions and cultural factors. For example, schools in Queensland, Australia comprise large open campuses with many separate buildings in what might appear to be a haphazard layout, whereas schools in Massachusetts tend to be compact "alphabet" configurations in "U-, O-, or H-shaped" buildings. Whatever the design, it is important to be able to describe areas and specific locations using consistent identifiers. The installation of prominent door numbers, corridor, and area signage, which is reflected on site plans and drawings, can be extremely valuable to emergency services personnel responding to an incident, and in more accurately recording the location of incidents such as theft.

FIGURE 27.12

Scan the QR2id code for guide on managing vandalism, or visit QR2id.com and enter serial#: DC4G-FJTX-G8J8.

63. NUMBERING AND LABELING CAR PARKING BAYS CAN REDUCE CONFUSION AND IMPROVE REPORTING

Having designated parking bays for specific purposes or identifiable zones, along with labeling each bay with a unique identifier, serves the purpose of reducing anonymity and making it far easier to accurately report observations, issues, and incidents. For example, if reports of theft of personal property from cars in a parking lot can be identified as being more prevalent in a specific bay, this information enables a more precise analysis of the factors that might be contributing to that location being targeted.

64. LIGHTS DON'T PREVENT CRIME, BUT THEY MAY REDUCE THE OPPORTUNITY FOR SOME TYPES OF CRIME

In order for lighting to be an effective deterrent, the offender needs to perceive that illumination will increase the risk of being identified, caught, and punished for the crime being considered. Lighting is obviously a key factor in the operation of the CPTED principle of natural surveillance, but if there are no opportunities for natural surveillance and the area of the school is not used for night activity, it is important to consider whether or not the lighting itself may actually support criminal or undesired activity. Some alternatives to continuous after-hours illumination might include motion-activated lighting and infrared lighting to support CCTV.

65. THE TYPE OF LIGHT CHOSEN FOR AN APPLICATION CAN HAVE UNINTENDED CONSEQUENCES

There is a wide variety of lamps used in school lighting, with energy efficiency, lamp replacement cost, and luminous efficacy being major considerations. One of the most cost-effective lighting sources in terms of running cost is low-pressure sodium (LPS). However, its monochromic yellow light has such poor color rendering that unless there are other sources of light in the space, complexions, clothing and vehicle colors are impossible to determine, enhancing anonymity for offenders. The hazardous nature of sodium also means that extreme care needs to be taken when it is time for disposal (see Figure 27.13).

66. SCHEDULED MAINTENANCE ON LIGHTS SAVES MONEY AND REDUCES RISKS

All types of lamps have performance characteristics that include a standard life cycle. Many lights have a point in that life cycle where their performance starts to degrade, before eventually failing. Understanding these life cycles and scheduling routine replacement of lamps at the optimum time before the light actually fails is the most cost-effective approach. If the objective of lighting is to illuminate a given space, it makes no sense at all to wait until all the lamps in a given area have failed before bringing in the electrician to replace them, or wasting money by replacing them one at a time as they fail. (NB: Lumen output does not degrade with age for incandescent, LPS, or LED lights, but they all have standard life expectancy.)

FIGURE 27.13

Scan the QR2id code to read more about low pressure sodium lighting, or visit QR2id.com and enter serial#: RBF9-NYLR-X4J6.

67. HORTICULTURAL MAINTENANCE IS IMPORTANT FOR NATURAL SURVEILLANCE, AS WELL AS PERCEPTIONS OF SAFETY

Inherent within the CPTED concept of natural surveillance is visual permeability through landscaping and planting. There can be a considerable difference between winter and summer foliage and it is important to maintain vegetation with a general rule that shrubs should be spaced or trimmed to no higher than 3′ (900 mm) to prevent them from being used for concealment. Similarly, tree branches should generally be no lower than 8′ (2400 mm), so that visual access is not impeded.

68. CHALLENGING UNKNOWN PERSONS ON CAMPUS REQUIRES AN ABILITY TO KNOW WHO BELONGS

It is all well and good to require visitors and contractors to wear temporary ID passes, but it is a flawed strategy if all anyone has to do to blend in is remove the badge. It is important to develop a comprehensive approach to identification and challenging unknown persons, including safety and reporting protocols.

69. SIGNAGE HELPS REDUCE CONFUSION AND SPOT POTENTIAL INTRUDERS

Schools should ensure that signage is located at transition and decision points around campus, with clear directions to the administration offices and spaces used for after-hours activities. Whenever there is scope for confusion, this can be exploited by offenders to create crime opportunities and also to develop excuses for being in unauthorized locations.

70. SIGNAGE CAN BE REINFORCED WITH TRAIL MARKERS

It is important that from their point of arrival visitors are oriented as to where to go and what is expected of them. An extremely simple and effective strategy is to use colored lines of footprints on the pavement leading from arrival zones to the visitor entrance. This not only helps the visitor, but also makes it easier to spot potential intruders who stray off the trail.

71. ELECTRONIC ACCESS CONTROL DOESN'T ALWAYS EQUAL IMPROVED SECURITY

On the surface it may seem that adding electronic access control to a door will increase security. However, care needs to be taken in the selection of electric locking hardware and routing of cables or the addition of the technology may actually introduce vulnerabilities. Seek expert independent advice and ask questions about how the new access control solution could be defeated.

72. THERE IS A DIFFERENCE BETWEEN ACCESS CONTROL AND ACCESS PROHIBITION

Fences can range from little more than a symbolic definition of a border through to hardened structures designed to physically prevent access under most foreseeable circumstances. When you are defining requirements for access at any point around the perimeter of the school, the question needs to be asked as to whether it is access "control" or "prohibition" that is required, and under what circumstances. Apart from cost, there will be philosophical and operational considerations to take into account. As with most aspects of security risk management, defining and understanding objectives are key to informing sound decision making.

73. THE LED (INDICATOR LIGHT) ON A MOVEMENT DETECTOR CAN BE USED BY AN OFFENDER TO ESTABLISH VULNERABILITIES

The "walk test" indicator on intruder alarm detectors should be disabled after the optimum detection pattern has been established and checked. Some schools have seen lines actually drawn on the floor, indicating where it is safe to walk without triggering the detector.

74. TESTING INTRUDER ALARM SYSTEMS SHOULD INCLUDE VERIFICATION THAT THE CORRECT ZONES ARE BEING DISPLAYED

Regular intruder alarm maintenance is important and this should include testing all the detectors, but not just that the LED goes on and off as you walk across the classroom. The alarms should be set and the alarm tested all the way back to the monitoring room, ensuring that the location reported by the alarm system matches the actual location on site. It is not uncommon for a detector to appear to be working, but the alarm signal not even reaching the panel due to a wiring change or fault. Similarly, changes in room designation and expansion of alarm systems can lead to alarm lists getting out of date, which can potentially lead to the alarm response being sent to the wrong location.

75. THERE ARE THREE BROAD OBJECTIVES FOR CCTV CAMERAS, AND IT IS IMPORTANT TO KNOW WHAT IT IS YOU WANT

International standards for CCTV define the objectives for cameras, in increasing order of detail, as:

1. Detection (of a person or activity)
2. Recognition (of a person or activity)
3. Identification (of a person).

While ultra-high-resolution CCTV cameras can satisfy multiple objectives, the majority cannot deliver what you see on television crime shows. Understand what you need the camera to do and then get reliable professional advice on camera, lens, housing, and recording selection.

76. VIDEO FROM SCHOOL CCTV CAMERAS MAY BE ABLE TO BE ACCESSED OR EVEN COMPROMISED BY OFFENDERS

Networked CCTV systems and Internet protocol (IP) cameras provide the possibility that staff can view areas of the school remotely to check on any number of security and operational matters. In an attempt to instill confidence and openness, some schools even promote use of remote viewing of cameras by parents. However, the security around IP cameras is often very poorly managed, with default usernames and passwords often left in place. When using networked CCTV systems, it is important for schools to consider the security of the system itself and ensure that policies, procedures, and technical strategies are developed and implemented to address potential vulnerabilities.

77. THE TIME AND DATE ON CCTV SYSTEMS SHOULD BE CHECKED

An often-missed element of CCTV maintenance is checking and adjusting the time and date on systems. While it might seem like a minor issue, it can be misleading for an investigation and can make a big difference if the footage needs to be used in evidence. A good practice to adopt when exporting or saving video is to check the current time and date against a known good source and note any anomalies, just in case an offset needs to be applied. A better practice is to regularly check, and adjust if necessary, the time and date for the system to accurately reflect the correct time. It is also important to consider daylight savings adjustments, where applicable, and to log for later reference any changes made to system time and date.

78. DOCUMENTED SPECIFICATIONS, OR AT LEAST WELL-DEFINED BRIEFS, SHOULD BE PREPARED FOR ANY WORKS INVOLVING SECURITY-RELATED SYSTEMS

All too frequently schools describe works to be done and are left disappointed when the outcomes are not as they expected. The costs of developing comprehensive documentation to support works related to security are routinely offset by the savings in management of the contractors and prospects of having to apply change-orders/contract variations.

79. ANY WORK ON SECURITY-RELATED SYSTEMS SHOULD BE COMMISSIONED BY A MEMBER OF STAFF OR SUITABLY QUALIFIED CONSULTANT

Like almost any trade, unfortunately some security integrators and contractors fail to deliver on what may have been contractually required of them. It is important that someone with knowledge of the works check to ensure that they have been completed to the standard required, and document and communicate any defects that may be found. While consultants add cost, their specialist knowledge and familiarity with systems often mean that traps and pitfalls are avoided, and that the school gets the optimal return on its investment.

80. ALL ROUTINE AND BREAKDOWN MAINTENANCE ON SECURITY-RELATED SYSTEMS SHOULD BE LOGGED

Apart from warranty and contract management requirements, logging maintenance can be invaluable in defending litigation that may arise from the failure of a security-related system. The historic logs and records provide a defensible basis for decisions and support analysis against metrics from other systems.

81. IT IS NECESSARY TO CLEARLY DEFINE REQUIREMENTS FOR SECURITY PATROLS AND ALARM RESPONSE

It might be assumed that security contractors know what they are doing and don't need the school telling them what they should do in any given circumstances. However, the actions of security officers undertaking patrols or responding to alarms should be totally in line with the school's philosophical position and operational requirements. The actions or inactions of security personal can lead to a range of consequential risks for the school and, as such, it is vital that the school clearly define the requirements to be incorporated into procedures and standing orders for security staff.

82. CORE FACTORS RELATING TO CONTRACT COMPLIANCE ARE NOT KEY PERFORMANCE INDICATORS

In monitoring contractual obligations for security, all too often schools confuse key performance indicators (KPI) with what are really basic contract compliance factors. The number of times officers have staffed a particular post that forms part of the contract is not a KPI, but the level of absenteeism and staff turnover could be used as KPIs.

83. HAVING CLEARLY DEFINED OBJECTIVES FOR SECURITY-RELATED SYSTEMS CAN SAVE MONEY AND AVOID DISAPPOINTMENT

Richard P. Grassie, CPP, noted that all security-related systems deliver on one or more of the following broad objectives[4]:

- *Prevent* something from happening.
- *Control* something that is happening, or is about to happen.

---

[4]PRISM training resources.

- *Detect* something that is happening.
- *Intervene* in something that is happening or has happened.

These strategic objectives for security-related systems can then be overlaid with more specific objectives. For example, is the objective for a given CCTV camera to detect someone in an area, or identify an intruder? The latter requires a great deal of image detail with the focus being to gain a clear image of the person's face, whereas the use of a camera to detect movement in an area requires a suitable field of view to generate situational awareness. Two very different objectives that may require separate cameras if both objectives are to be delivered, or a high-end megapixel camera may be able to deliver on both requirements.

84. EXIT INTERVIEWS SHOULD BE CONDUCTED WITH STAFF AND LONGER-TERM CONTRACTORS LEAVING THE SCHOOL

A structured exit interview process is important to ensure that staff and contractors have an opportunity to provide relevant feedback and also for the school to reinforce confidentiality policies. A basic checklist can ensure that all applicable topics are covered, and keys, identification cards, access cards, and other security-related items are recovered. The last element of the checklist should nominate disabling any system access credentials previously used by the person, as well as changing safe combinations or common codes that the person may have used during their time at the school.

85. PROPERTY MARKING AND ASSET MANAGEMENT IS A GOOD INVESTMENT, IF YOU CHOOSE THE RIGHT STRATEGIES

There is a range of options when it comes to directly protecting school property from loss or theft. Probably the most common is simple property marking, where the school's name is engraved on the asset. The research about the deterrent value of indelible property marking is very clear, in that if an offender wants to sell the item, having to obscure the details of the rightful owner and the potential of being caught with identifiable property makes these assets far less attractive to steal. Schools have to balance the time and cost of property marking with the likelihood of loss and costs should it occur. With valuable assets being much more portable, indelible property marking techniques can also serve as an important lost property recovery tool, as well as being transferrable if the asset is sold (see Figure 27.14).

86. RADIO-FREQUENCY IDENTIFICATION CAN ENHANCE ASSET MANAGEMENT

Electronic article surveillance systems are most commonly used in school libraries as a security strategy, with it being a logical step to move to individual radio-frequency identification (RFID) tags to further leverage what is effectively the same technology. RFID for asset management effectively comes in three categories:

- Passive tags with mobile readers
- Passive tags with fixed readers
- Active tags with fixed readers

The major advantage of RFID over conventional barcode asset management systems is the speed of reading the tag. The characteristics of the material on which the tag is applied, difficulty in marking small

FIGURE 27.14

Scan the QR2id code to see an example, or visit QR2id.com and enter serial#: VVL4-C3SN-2EK3.

items, and potential confusion created by reading assets on the other side of a wall are all considerations. Notwithstanding these issues, RFID can provide significant benefits for schools in managing their assets, provided that it is understood that one size does not fit all and a combination of technologies may be required.

87. COVERT ASSET IDENTIFICATION HAS A PLACE, BUT DOES HAVE LIMITATIONS

Covert asset identification strategies are to some extent similar to CCTV recording in that they provide evidence after the fact to support investigations and prosecutions. If an offender perceives that the advertised presence of the technology increases the likelihood of being caught and adversely impacted by punishment they may act as a deterrent, but this is highly context sensitive and nowhere nearly as effective as overt and indelible property marking. However, the size and characteristics of some assets are not suited for property marking techniques, making these covert strategies an important consideration. However, it needs to be recognized that a range of property marked with the same batch of these materials will be permanently identifiable as belonging to the same registered owner, which may be a consideration should they need to be sold or repurposed in the future.

88. THE MOST COMMONLY EXPLOITED VULNERABILITY IN SCHOOLS IS POOR KEY CONTROL

Locks and keys are a central element in any physical security program, but all too often poor key control leads to unauthorized access. There are many technological solutions available to assist with managing key issue and return, but the most important strategy is effective policy and procedures around the issue and timely recovery of keys.

89. ELECTROMAGNETIC LOCKS NEED TO BE MAINTAINED

While electromagnetic locks have no internal moving parts, the security they provide is directly related to the bonding force between the armature (the metal plate on the door) and the electromagnet (the larger component on the door frame). Because the materials involved are ferrous, oxidation on the surface reduces holding force and needs to be removed. The surfaces of the electromagnet and armature also need to be checked for the presence of tape and the like, which can be placed there to deliberately reduce the strength of the magnetic force and facilitate unauthorized entry. The armature should also be 'floating' to allow it to align with the face of the electromagnet; if it is rigidly mounted on the door, it is likely that misalignment will also reduce the holding force.

90. RAPID REMOVAL OF GRAFFITI REDUCES THE LIKELIHOOD OF BEING RETARGETED

Research shows that while it can initially be costly and require perseverance, in the long term the removal of graffiti within 24 hours is the key to lowering the frequency of a space being retargeted. The science behind the concept can be attributed to a mix of crime prevention theories, including situational crime prevention, CPTED territorial reinforcement, and to a lesser extent an extrapolation of the broken windows theory.

91. ORIENTING ADMINISTRATION WORK POSITIONS CAN ENHANCE NATURAL SURVEILLANCE

It is somewhat self-evident that people seated at desks facing walls are limited in what they may observe. Orienting work spaces to provide opportunities to see people moving or loitering in key areas of the school can greatly enhance responsiveness to potentially problematic situations, as well as delivering improved operational outcomes.

92. CONVEX MIRRORS IN HALLWAYS AND STAIRWELLS HAVE MULTIPLE BENEFITS

Convex mirrors installed in hallways or stairwells provide a number of safety and security benefits, provided that they are installed correctly and lighting conditions are taken into account. The primary purpose of the convex mirror is to provide a way of seeing around corners, which can assist those approaching the corner to detect and avoid potential conflict with others moving in the opposite direction. They can also provide the opportunity to enhance general surveillance and the increase the perception of natural surveillance, impacting on a potential offender's perception of the risk of detection and opportunity for concealment.

93. MANAGING BUS LOADING AND UNLOADING ENHANCES SAFETY AND REDUCES PROVOCATIONS

Having teaching staff assigned to the bus loading and unloading zone pay particular attention to maintaining order not only enhances safety around large vehicles but also reduces frustration and potential provocations that can lead to violence. Dispersing groups of students after arrival before allowing a new group to unload reduces the opportunity for conflict.

94. HAVING DESIGNATED BUS QUEUING AREAS IN GENERAL PROXIMITY OF THE LOADING/UNLOADING ZONE ENHANCES EFFICIENCY AND SAFETY

It may be necessary to consider changing the allocation of roadways and parking areas to achieve optimum efficiency and safety. It is worth taking advice from transport planners to see what options you may have available at your school.

95. TEACHERS SUPERVISING STUDENT COLLECTION ZONES NEED TO BE AWARE OF SPECIAL NEEDS STUDENTS AND STUDENTS WITH ADVERSE FAMILY SITUATIONS

Schools need to ensure that staff allocated to supervising the collection of students by parents are fully informed and aware of any issues likely to increase the risk of harm to students or the staff themselves. While privacy is a clear consideration, staff must be aware of the potential for conflict arising from custody disputes and domestic violence.

96. COURTS HAVE HELD THAT SCHOOLS HAVE A RESPONSIBILITY TO ACT ON OFF-CAMPUS THREATS

Just because a threat is not made on school property or as part of an off-campus supervised activity does not mean that schools are powerless to act. One case in the State of Nevada held that threatening instant messages sent by a student represented a "real risk of significant disruption to school activities and interfered with the rights of other students," and the school was right to act in disciplining the student, without needing to wait for an actual event to take place[5] (see Figure 27.15).

97. THIRD-PARTY USE OF SCHOOL FACILITIES CAN REDUCE CRIME OPPORTUNITIES

There is a wide range of activities that can be supported within school facilities, which in and of themselves, reduce crime opportunity. Martial arts clubs, police youth programs, and community groups all need spaces to meet and can deliver a win-win outcome by using school facilities.

98. SCHEDULING THIRD-PARTY ACTIVITIES IN DIFFERENT AREAS OF THE SCHOOL CAN INCREASE CRIME OPPORTUNITIES

Dependent upon the layout and design of the school, the scheduling of third-party activities can create conflict between user groups or increase the range of excuses for people being in unauthorized/

FIGURE 27.15

Scan the QR2id code to see the full ruling, or visit QR2id.com and enter serial#: MPAS-B9UE-VNGY.

[5]WYNAR v. DOUGLAS COUNTY SCHOOL DISTRICT. 11–17127.

unintended locations within the school. Care should be taken to separate potentially conflicting groups by time or distance and to schedule spaces that have easier and more direct access for those attending.

99. SECURITY STRATEGIES NEED TO BE REVIEWED WHENEVER THERE IS A HIGHER CONCENTRATION OF ATTRACTIVE ASSETS

Schools frequently take delivery of assets during term break in order to prepare them for use. It is important to recognize that security strategies that may have been adequate to manage the risk/effort/reward ratios for prospective offenders with the previous asset mix may no longer be effective. Situational Crime Prevention theory and Rational Choice Perspective teach us that for a greater reward, offenders are prepared to go to more effort and accept higher levels of risk of being caught. Prior to taking delivery of new assets, consider where they will be stored, how knowledge of the presence of the assets will be minimized (e.g., don't put all the new boxes out the front of the school for recycling), and what additional security may be needed until individual security strategies such as indelible property marking are applied.

100. THERE CAN BE OPPORTUNITIES TO INTEGRATE RISK MANAGEMENT STRATEGIES INTO THE CURRICULUM

The traditional responses to security-related risks will always have a role to play, but schools should consider innovative approaches that link with the curriculum. For example, a school in Australia that was having trouble with people from an adjacent residential area trespassing through the school grounds and causing vandalism sought to block their path by upgrading the fencing. This approach failed, even after several attempts and the costs of both the vandalism and repairs to fencing were escalating.

Looking at the topography and factors that supported the path of travel, the school developed a plan that incorporated students in a number of different areas of the curriculum to build a wetland area inside

FIGURE 27.16

Scan the QR2id code for more information about applying CPTED concepts, or visit QR2id.com and enter serial#: HMM2-LECY-HMK3.

the fence boundary at the primary point of entry. The school recognized that just building a wet area to disrupt the path would not be enough, and they needed to support the required behavior of walking around the school perimeter.

The adjacent parkland provided an opportunity to build a pathway to connect the road with the existing informal track used by the trespassers, so the first stage of the plan involved making a better way to get from Point A to Point B. Once this was in place, the construction of the key elements of the wetland area to make it unsuitable for pedestrian access was done in 1 day. The result was an outstanding success and an excellent example of CPTED and situational crime prevention principles working together to support desired behaviors, while inhibiting undesired behaviors (see Figure 27.16).

ASIS INTERNATIONAL'S LIST OF SCHOOL SECURITY WEBSITES ASSOCIATIONS, ORGANIZATIONS, PUBLICATIONS[1]

WEBSITES

ABC'S OF SCHOOL SAFETY, AMERICAN ASSOCIATION OF SCHOOL ADMINISTRATORS

This document outlines some elements of school safety organized under three categories: awareness, balance, and control. Also includes a list of School Safety Resources.

http://www.aasa.org/content.aspx?id=7354&terms=abc%27s+of+school+safety

IN THE SPOTLIGHT, SCHOOL SAFETY, THE NATIONAL CRIMINAL JUSTICE REFERENCE SERVICE

In the Spotlight highlights topics of current interest. Each topic includes the latest information and statistics, online Federal and State legislation and testimony, a list of available publications, examples of state and local programs and initiatives available online, a sample of training and technical assistance opportunities available through nationally recognized agencies and associations, links to Federal funding opportunities, and examples of nationally recognized agencies and organizations that provide services or information.

http://www.ncjrs.gov/spotlight/school_safety/summary.html

KEEP SCHOOLS SAFE, SCHOOL SAFETY AND SECURITY CENTER

School safety, security, and violence prevention resource.

http://www.keepschoolssafe.org/

LESSONS LEARNED, SCHOOL EMERGENCY PLANNING, U.S. DEPARTMENT OF HOMELAND SECURITY

Site registration required Original research will be continually highlighted on this page along with after-action reports, documents, templates, sample plans, related links, recent news, upcoming

---

[1]This appendix is reprinted with permission from ASIS International.

conferences, and more. LLIS.gov has assembled these resources to help emergency planners, responders, and administrators work together to develop and maintain comprehensive school emergency plans.

https://www.llis.dhs.gov/DynamicPage.cfm?pageTitle=SchoolEmergencyPlanning_external

NATIONAL SCHOOL SAFETY CENTER

The National School Safety Center (NSSC) serves as an advocate for safe, secure, and peaceful schools worldwide and as a catalyst for the prevention of school crime and violence. NSSC provides school communities and their school safety partners with quality information, resources, consultation, and training services. The NSSC identifies and promotes strategies, promising practices and programs that support safe schools for all students as part of the total academic mission.

http://www.schoolsafety.us/home

SAFE AND DRUG-FREE SCHOOLS, U.S. DEPARTMENT OF EDUCATION

A list of resources on school violence prevention, a guide and brochure that provides schools and communities with basic guidelines and useful ideas on how to develop emergency response and crisis management plans; a report on preventing school attacks based on examination of 37 incidents, suggestions for developing a threat assessment team in a school or district, steps to take when a threat or other information of concern comes to light, when to involve law enforcement personnel, and emergency planning information to help school leaders plan for any emergency, including natural disasters, violent incidents, and terrorist acts.

http://www.ed.gov/admins/lead/safety/edpicks.jhtml?src=ln

SCHOOL VIOLENCE, CENTERS FOR DISEASE CONTROL AND PREVENTION

Resources on school violence, including risk factors and prevention resources.

http://www.cdc.gov/ViolencePrevention/youthviolence/schoolviolence/index.html

SCHOOL SAFETY, NATIONAL INSTITUTE OF JUSTICE'S (NIJ'S) OFFICE OF SCIENCE AND TECHNOLOGY, THE NATIONAL LAW ENFORCEMENT AND CORRECTIONS TECHNOLOGY CENTER (NLECTC), JUSTICE TECHNOLOGY INFORMATION NETWORK (JUSTNET)

Provides publications, news articles, presentations, and more relating to school safety.

http://www.justnet.org/Pages/Topic.aspx?topic=196

OFFICE OF COMMUNITY ORIENTED POLICING SERVICES (COPS), U.S. DEPARTMENT OF JUSTICE

As a component of the Justice Department, the mission of the COPS Office is to advance community policing as an effective strategy in communities' efforts to improve public safety. Includes links to guides and reports on school safety.

http://www.cops.usdoj.gov/default.asp?Item=140

SCHOOL VIOLENCE FACT SHEETS, CENTER FOR THE STUDY AND PREVENTION OF VIOLENCE, UNIVERSITY OF COLORADO AT BOULDER

Includes fact sheets on violence in American schools, preventing firearm violence in and around schools, reducing violence in schools, safe school planning, as well as other resources.

http://www.colorado.edu/cspv/infohouse/publications.html

ASSOCIATIONS AND ORGANIZATIONS

INTERNATIONAL ASSOCIATION OF CAMPUS LAW ENFORCEMENT ADMINISTRATORS (IACLEA)

An association that advances public safety for educational institutions by providing educational resources, advocacy, and professional development services.

http://www.iaclea.org/

NATIONAL ALLIANCE FOR SAFE SCHOOLS (NASS)

A not-for-profit corporation whose purpose is to provide technical assistance, staff training, school safety assessments, safe school plans, and emergency response training to individual school and school district personnel.

http://www.safeschools.org/

NATIONAL ASSOCIATION OF SCHOOL RESOURCE OFFICERS (NASRO)

A not-for-profit organization made up of school-based law enforcement officers and school administrators. Serves as the largest training organization for school-based police and district personnel in the nation. Includes an online library of sample contract and forms and for members only. Publishes the Journal of School Safety for members.

http://www.nasro.org

NATIONAL ASSOCIATION OF SCHOOL SAFETY AND LAW ENFORCEMENT OFFICERS (NASSLEO)

NASSLEO membership is comprised of educators, law enforcement and security officers, as well as other professionals that share the common goal of protecting our students, staff, and physical assets.

http://www.nassleo.org/

SECURITY ON CAMPUS, INC.

A nonprofit organization provides a wealth of information on campus security issues to everyone from prospective students to campus law enforcement administrators.

http://securityoncampus.org/

PUBLICATIONS

ADAMS, JEFFREY A.; SINAI, JOSHUA, PROTECTING SCHOOLS AND UNIVERSITIES FROM TERRORISM: A GUIDE FOR ADMINISTRATORS AND TEACHERS, ASIS INTERNATIONAL, ALEXANDRIA, 2003

It is the objective of this guide to provide administrators and teachers with the security framework and necessary checklists to ensure that their facilities and students are properly protected against a terrorist attack, whether biological, chemical, radiological, or, in the absolute worst-case scenario, nuclear. This guide also addresses more conventional tactics used by terrorists, such as detonating explosives and indiscriminately shooting students. University administrators and teachers need to become aware of such potential threats and adopt the necessary preventative measures to ensure that their campuses and students are properly protected. Preparation for defending against a terrorist attack can help prevent one. Additionally, should an actual incident occur, this book provides information that will help to effectively manage the crisis and consequence phases of an attack. Available for sale from the ASIS bookstore at http://www.abdi-secure-ecommerce.com/asis.

BOVE, VINCENT, LISTEN TO THEIR CRIES: CALLING THE NATION TO RENEWAL FROM COLUMBINE TO VIRGINIA TECH, VINCENT BOVE PUBLISHING, 2008

Book review in July 2009 issue of *Security Management*.

DEADLY LESSONS: UNDERSTANDING LETHAL SCHOOL VIOLENCE: CASE STUDIES OF SCHOOL VIOLENCE COMMITTEE, NATIONAL ACADEMY PRESS, WASHINGTON, D.C., 2002

This book is the outcome of the National Research Council's effort to glean lessons from six case studies of lethal student violence. These are powerful stories of parents and teachers and troubled youths, presenting the tragic complexity of the young shooter's social and personal circumstances in detail. For each case study, events are related leading up to the violence, along with quotes from personal interviews about the incident, and explorations of the impact on the community.

DINKES, RACHEL, INDICATORS OF SCHOOL CRIME AND SAFETY: 2011, DEPT OF JUSTICE, NATIONAL CENTER FOR EDUCATION STATISTICS, 2012

This report covers topics such as victimization, fights, bullying, classroom disorder, weapons, student perceptions of school safety, teacher injury, and availability and student use of drugs and alcohol. Indicators of crime and safety are compared across different population subgroups and over time.
    http://bjs.ojp.usdoj.gov/index.cfm?ty=pbdetail&iid=2295

FEDERAL BUREAU OF INVESTIGATION, CRIME IN SCHOOLS AND COLLEGES: A STUDY OF OFFENDERS AND ARRESTEES REPORTED VIA NATIONAL INCIDENT-BASED REPORTING SYSTEM DATA, FEDERAL BUREAU OF INVESTIGATION, WASHINGTON, D.C., 2007

This study particularly analyzes data submitted to the FBI's Uniform Crime Reporting (UCR) Program by law enforcement agencies and examines specific characteristics of offenders and arrestees who participated in criminal incidents at schools and colleges from 2000 through 2004.
    http://www.fbi.gov/ucr/schoolviolence/2007/schoolviolence.pdf

FEDERAL BUREAU OF INVESTIGATION, RESOURCES ON SCHOOL VIOLENCE, FBI, WASHINGTON, D.C., 2012

http://www.fbi.gov/stats-services/school-violence

THE FINAL REPORT AND FINDINGS OF THE SAFE SCHOOL INITIATIVE: IMPLICATIONS FOR THE PREVENTION OF SCHOOL ATTACKS IN THE UNITED STATES, SECRET SERVICE; U.S. DEPT. OF EDUCATION, WASHINGTON, D.C., 2002

This final report details how the Department of Education and U.S. Secret Service studied school-based attacks and what was found. These findings suggest that some future attacks may be preventable, if those responsible for safety in schools know what questions to ask, and where to uncover information that may help with efforts to intervene before a school attack can occur. Report based on examination of 37 incidents of targeted school shootings and school attacks.

http://www.secretservice.gov/ntac/ssi_final_report.pdf

FOX, JAMES ALAN AND HARVEY BURSTEIN, VIOLENCE AND SECURITY ON CAMPUS: FROM PRESCHOOL THROUGH COLLEGE, ABC-CLIO/PRAEGER, SANTA BARBARA, CA, 2010

Book review in May 2011 issue of *Security Management*.

FURLONG, MICHAEL; MORRISON, GALE, ISSUES IN SCHOOL VIOLENCE RESEARCH, HAWORTH PRESS, BINGHAMTON, 2004

Contents: Introduction; Methodological and measurement issue in school violence research; Warning signs of problems in schools; Using office referral records in school violence research; Identification of bullies and victims; Data quality in student risk behavior surveys and administrator training; An examination of the reliability, data screening procedures, and extreme response patterns for the youth risk behavior surveillance survey; Structural equation modeling of school violence data; Beyond guns, drugs and gangs: the structure of student perceptions of school safety.

GUIDE FOR PREVENTING AND RESPONDING TO SCHOOL VIOLENCE, 2ND ED., INTERNATIONAL ASSOCIATION OF CHIEFS OF POLICE, ALEXANDRIA, 2009

This updated guide addresses both prevention and intervention from a systemic view, clarifying roles of the school, the community, families, and law enforcement and the justice system, and how these groups can work together effectively to respond to the problem.

http://www.theiacp.org/LinkClick.aspx?fileticket=MwvD03yXrnE%3d&tabid=378

GUIDE FOR PREVENTING AND RESPONDING TO SCHOOL VIOLENCE, INTERNATIONAL ASSOCIATION OF CHIEFS OF POLICE, ALEXANDRIA, 1999

The purpose of this document is to present different strategies and approaches for members of school communities to consider when creating safe learning environments. Most of the interventions presented in this document have the potential to yield benefits beyond just reducing hazards associated with school shootings. It will assist in auditing schools' existing policies, procedures, and plans; help public safety and other crisis response agencies assess their school safety plans, and provide guidance to members of the school community.

http://www.theiacp.org/Portals/0/pdfs/Publications/schoolviolence2.pdf

JOURNAL OF SCHOOL VIOLENCE

Published quarterly. The Journal of School Violence is a peer-reviewed journal devoted to publishing the latest information on this difficult issue.

KELLAM, SHEPPARD, PREVENTING SCHOOL VIOLENCE: PLENARY PAPERS OF THE 1999 CONFERENCE ON CRIMINAL JUSTICE RESEARCH AND EVALUATION— ENHANCING POLICY AND PRACTICE THROUGH RESEARCH, VOLUME 2, NATIONAL INSTITUTE OF JUSTICE, WASHINGTON, D.C., 2000.

This resource can be found at https://www.ncjrs.gov/pdffiles1/nij/180972.pdf

PREVENTING SCHOOL VIOLENCE: PLENARY PAPERS OF THE 1999 CONFERENCE ON CRIMINAL JUSTICE RESEARCH AND EVALUATION—ENHANCING POLICY AND PRACTICE THROUGH RESEARCH, VOLUME 2

This resource contains the following three papers:
* Community and institutional partnerships for school violence prevention
* Research-based prevention of school violence and youth antisocial behavior: a developmental and educational perspective
* Controlling violence: what schools are doing; The Federal Government responds to school violence.

KIDD, DONALD H, THE PREVALENCE OF SCHOOL-RELATED VIOLENCE: AN OVERVIEW OF STATISTICAL AND PERCEPTUAL DATA, UNIVERSITY OF ARKANSAS, 2002

The focus of this overview was an examination of recent qualitative and quantitative research to determine how school-related violence was both measured and perceived among various social groups. The primary purpose of this overview is to enhance understanding of school-related violence among educators, students, parents, law enforcement officials, local government, community service organizations, and community leaders.

http://www.arsafeschools.com/Files/Prevalence.pdf

MCCANN, JOSEPH T, THREATS IN SCHOOLS: A PRACTICAL GUIDE FOR MANAGING VIOLENCE, HAWORTH PRESS, BINGHAMTON, NY, 2002

The focus of this book is on students who make or pose a threat in school settings.

NICOLETTI, JOHN; SPENCER-THOMAS, SALLY, VIOLENCE GOES TO COLLEGE: THE AUTHORITATIVE GUIDE TO PREVENTION AND INTERVENTION

A solution-oriented resource for preventing the growing problem of violence on college campuses. Written by a police psychologist, a health psychologist, and a residence life director, the authors combine their expertise to create a how-to prevention resource that gives real answers to real issues, including sexual assault, hazing, hate crimes, rioting, workplace violence, and more. (Published by Charles C. Thomas, Ltd., Springfield, Illinois.)

O'TOOLE, MARY ELLEN, THE SCHOOL SHOOTER: A THREAT ASSESSMENT PERSPECTIVE, FBI ACADEMY, QUANTICO, VA, 1999

This report combines the research of the National Center for the Analysis of Violent Crime (NCAVC) into 18 school shootings that began in 1998 and a 1999 symposium by NCAVC on school shootings and threat assessment for teachers and administrators from those 18 schools along with law enforcement, academic and professional groups. The result is this analysis of the school shooter phenomenon. The report analyzes the different possible scenarios and differing threat levels, and gives profiles of people who become school shooters. Gives proposals that can be taken in a school to strengthen its threat response program.

http://www.fbi.gov/publications/school/school2.pdf

POLLOCK, WILLIAM S, PRIOR KNOWLEDGE OF POTENTIAL SCHOOL-BASED VIOLENCE: INFORMATION STUDENTS LEARN MAY PREVENT A TARGETED ATTACK, DESIGN COUNCIL, WASHINGTON, D.C., 2008

In the wake of several high-profile shootings at schools in the United States, most notably the shootings that occurred at Columbine High School on April 20, 1999, the United States Secret Service (Secret Service) and the United States Department of Education embarked on a collaborative endeavor to study incidents of planned violence in our nation's schools. Initiated in 1999, the study, termed the Safe School Initiative, examined several issues, most notably whether past school-based attacks were planned, and what could be done to prevent future attacks.

http://www.ustreas.gov/usss/ntac/bystander_study.pdf

SAFE SCHOOLS FACILITIES PLANNER, PUBLIC SCHOOLS OF NORTH CAROLINA, STATE BOARD OF EDUCATION, RALEIGH, 1998

Experience has shown a direct relationship between the design and use of school facilities and the occurrence of unacceptable and criminal behaviors. Crime prevention through environmental design (CPTED) principles underlie the concept that proper design and effective use of the physical environment can reduce both the incidence and the fear of crime. A safer environment can, in turn, create a psychological advantage for positive behavior and for learning. Unacceptable behavior, campus crime, and violence can be significantly reduced through the application and interaction of the following seven key components of CPTED.

http://www.schoolclearinghouse.org/pubs/safesch.pdf

SAFE SCHOOL INITIATIVE: AN INTERIM REPORT ON THE PREVENTION OF TARGETED VIOLENCE IN SCHOOLS, NATIONAL THREAT ASSESSMENT CENTER, WASHINGTON, D.C., 2000

Interim results of a study by the National Threat Assessment Center of the U.S. Secret Service on school shootings. Includes statistics and analysis on the behavior and thinking of young people who commit targeted acts of violence in our nation's schools. This information is designed to help law enforcement professionals to prevent targeted school violence.

THREAT ASSESSMENT IN SCHOOLS: A GUIDE TO MANAGING THREATENING SITUATIONS AND TO CREATING SAFE SCHOOL CLIMATES, U.S. SECRET SERVICE; U.S. DEPT. OF EDUCATION, 2002

This work sets a process for identifying, assessing, and managing students who may pose a threat of targeted violence in schools. It is intended for use by school personnel, law enforcement officials, and others with protective responsibilities in our schools. It includes suggestions for developing a threat assessment team within a school or school district, steps to take when a threat or other information of concern comes to light, consideration about when to involve law enforcement personnel, issues of information sharing, and ideas for creating safe school climates.

   http://www.ed.gov/admins/lead/safety/threatassessmentguide.pdf

UCHIDA, CRAIG D. SCHOOL-BASED PARTNERSHIPS: A PROBLEM-SOLVING STRATEGY, DEPT. OF JUSTICE (U.S.), WASHINGTON, D.C., 1999

The Office of Community Oriented Policing Services (COPS) funded the School-Based Partnerships (SBP) grant program for the purpose of partnering law enforcement agencies with schools to address crime and disorder problems in the around middle and high schools. This document was funded to conduct an assessment of the SBP grant program. The information in this document was gathered from the findings of this assessment grantee testimonies, progress reports, and COPS staff reports. This report focuses on three SBP sites and their use of the SARA problem-solving process to address specific issues in their schools.

   http://www.cops.usdoj.gov/files/RIC/CDROMs/SchoolSafety/Related_Resources/SchoolBasedPartnerships.pdf

VIOLLIS, PAUL, ET AL., JANE'S WORKPLACE SECURITY HANDBOOK, JANE'S INFORMATION GROUP, ALEXANDRIA, 2002

This practical handbook provides detailed checklists and procedures to aid the planning for, response to, and recovery from wide-range of security threats from violence in the workplace to a terrorist attack. Designed to be used as a training tool, a guide to implementing security plans, or for distribution to employees. Available for sale from the ASIS bookstore at http://www.abdi-secure-ecommerce.com/asis.

WHALEY, JAMIE, PREVENTING SCHOOL VIOLENCE: RESOURCE GUIDE TO SAFE SCHOOLS, ASPEN PUBLISHERS, INC., GAITHERSBURG, 2001

Issues ranging from the recognition of warning signs for preventing violence to developing crisis management steps for managing those incidents that cannot be prevented are included in this manual. Contents focus on school safety strategies in the form of policies and procedures, planning, prevention, intervention, security, crisis management, community partnerships, legal issues, and related resources.

WHEELER, EUGENE D, VIOLENCE IN OUR SCHOOLS, HOSPITALS AND PUBLIC PLACES: A PREVENTION AND MANAGEMENT GUIDE, PATHFINDER PUBLISHING OF CALIFORNIA, VENTURA, CA, 1994

This book provides information for the public and a guide for schools, colleges, hospitals, libraries, courts, and government organizations to develop plans to prevent violence and manage the possible aftermath.

WHITAKER, LEIGHTON C, CAMPUS VIOLENCE: KINDS, CAUSES, AND CURES, HAWORTH PRESS, NEW YORK, NY, 1993

Contents: (1) Conceptualizing campus violence: definitions, underlying factors, and effects; (2) Administrative perspectives on disruptive student conduct; (3) Violence is golden: commercially motivated training in impulsive cognitive style and mindless violence; (4) Violence, alcohol, other drugs, and the college student; (5) The role of the mental health consultant in dealing with disruptive college students; (6) Keeping their antennas up: violence and the urban college student; (7) Race relations and poly-cultural sensitivity training on college campuses; (8) Violence against lesbian and gay male college students; (9) Violence and the male gender role; (10) The topography of violence in college men: frequency and comorbidity of sexual and physical aggression; (11) College men and sexual violation: counseling process and programming considerations; (12) Psychological challenges and responses to a campus tragedy: the Iowa experience; (13) Homicide in the university residence halls: one counseling center's response; (14) Cures for campus violence, if we want them.

WONG, MARLEEN AND JAMES KELLY AND RONALD D. STEPHENS, JANE'S SCHOOL SAFETY HANDBOOK, JANE'S INFORMATION GROUP, ALEXANDRIA, 2001

A comprehensive and practical tool to assist teachers, school administrators, and other agencies prepare for, respond to, and recover from security incidents in schools. Tailored to meet the needs of the U.S. education system, the handbook includes security checklists, threat assessment, crisis response, and post-incident recovery procedures. The types of problems that might arise, the characteristics of violent youth, the effects of psychological trauma on different age groups, and intervention are just some of the topics addressed. Procedural guidelines are offered in the case of suspicious packages, in a school lockdown situation, and for biological or chemical attacks. There are suggestions for sample letters to send to parents in the event of a violent incident on or near school property. Case studies and checklist are included. Available for sale from the ASIS bookstore at http://www.abdi-secure-ecommerce.com/asis.

ADDITIONAL RESOURCES

ASIS International	www.asisonline.org
American Board for Certification in Homeland Security (ABCHS)	www.abchs.com
"CDC now considers bullying a public health problem," June 23, 2013, *The Examiner*	www.examiner.com/article/ cdc-now-considers-bullying-a-public-health-problem
Center for the Prevention of School Violence	www.ncdjjdp.org/cpsv
Centers for Disease Control and Prevention (CDC), "Suicide Prevention: Youth Suicide" programs and resources	www.cdc.gov/ViolencePrevention/suicide/youth_suicide.html
Centers for Disease Control and Prevention (CDC), "Connectedness as a Strategic Direction for the Prevention of Suicidal Behavior"	www.cdc.gov/violenceprevention/pdf/Suicide_Strategic_Directio_-One-Pager-a.pdf
Construction Specifications Institute	www.csi.net
Consultant Registry	www.ConsultantRegistry.Org
InfraGard	www.infragard.org
International Association of Campus Law Enforcement Administrators	www.iaclea.org
National Association of School Resource Officers	www.nasro.org
National Fire Protection Association (NFPA)	www.nfpa.org
U.S. Department of Education (DOE)	www.ed.gov
U.S. Department of Education, National Center for Education Statistics	www.nces.ed.gov
U.S. Department of Education, Office of Safe and Healthy Schools	www.ed.gov/emergencyplan
U.S. Department of Education, REMS Technical Assistance Center	www.rems.ed.gov
U.S. Department of Homeland Security (DHS)	www.dhs.gov
U.S. Federal Emergency Management Agency (FEMA)	www.fema.gov
The Campus Safety and Security Data Analysis Cutting Tool, U.S. Department of Education, Office of Post Secondary Education	www.ope.ed.gov/security
"Wisc., Va., Ark., Pa., N.J., N.H., Conn. Schools Announce Security Upgrades," *Campus Safety*, September 4, 2013	http://www.campussafetymagazine.com/Channel/ School-Safety/News/2013/09/05/Wisc-Va-Ark-Pa-N-J-N-H-Conn-Schools-Announces-Security-Upgrades.aspx

Index

Edwards Brothers Malloy
Ann Arbor MI. USA
January 30, 2015